03/28/02

READING RAPE

Reading Rape

THE RHETORIC OF SEXUAL VIOLENCE
IN AMERICAN LITERATURE AND CULTURE,
1790–1990

Sabine Sielke

PRINCETON UNIVERSITY PRESS

PRINCETON AND OXFORD

Library of Congress Cataloging-in-Publication Data

Sielke, Sabine, 1959–
Reading rape : the rhetoric of sexual violence in American literature
and culture, 1790–1990 / Sabine Sielke.
p. cm.
Includes bibliographical references (p.) and index.
ISBN 0-691-00500-1 (alk. paper)—ISBN 0-691-00501-X (pbk. : alk.
paper)
1. American fiction—History and criticism. 2. Rape in literature.
3. Feminism and literature—United States—History. 4. Women and
literature—United States—History. 5. Rape—United States—History.
6. Rape victims in literature. 7. Sex crimes in literature. 8. Violence
in literature. I. Title.
PS374.R35 S54 2002
813.009′355—dc21   2001036274

This book has been composed in Minion

Printed on acid-free paper. ∞

www.pup.princeton.edu

Printed in the United States of America

1   3   5   7   9   10   8   6   4   2

1   3   5   7   9   10   8   6   4   2
(Pbk.)

Contents

—◦◦◦—

Acknowledgments

⁓•∿∿•⁓

"**W**HY RAPE?" was the question that friends, colleagues, and interested strangers posed to me repeatedly while I was working on this book. My answer was simple and nonsensational: I first got into the subject thanks to my colleagues Hans Joas and Wolfgang Knöbl, who invited me to contribute to a lecture series and publication titled *Gewalt in den USA* (Violence in the U.S.A.). Having agreed to participate with a piece on violence against women as a subject of both feminist theory and literary practice, I was surprised to learn that in the context of American feminist criticism after 1970 violence against women seemed to figure almost exclusively as rape. "Why rape?" thus became the question that moved my own inquiry.

For generous financial, professional, and personal support I do owe many individuals and institutions. The John F. Kennedy-Institut für Nordamerikastudien at the Freie Universität Berlin has continued to be my academic backbone (and more). My debt to all the people who make this institution what it is has increased steadily. The Förderkommission Frauenforschung of the Berlin Senate and the Freie Universität Berlin have sponsored my research at Harvard University in its initial phase. An American Studies Fellowship granted by the American Council of Learned Societies (ACLS) and a Fellowship from the W.E.B. Du Bois Institute for Afro-American Research at Harvard University allowed me to spend the academic year 1994–95 as part of a most inspiring group of scholars in Cambridge, Massachusetts. I thank the Du Bois fellows for many illuminating discussions, and Henry Louis Gates for his relentless intellectual and personal generosity. The Du Bois Fellowship also granted me the privilege of engaging a research assistant, and I was privileged indeed when Mary Ebbott found me and took on that task with such clairvoyance and verve. Without her excellent, independent, and illuminatingly intelligent work I would not have produced the book as it is. Between the fall of 1996 and spring 1998 as well as in winter 1998 the Deutsche Forschungsgemeinschaft generously supported my work—the final research at Harvard University and the completion of both the manuscript and the degree it was part of, the German *Habilitation.* This support was invaluable.

Heinz Ickstadt has continued to keep the faith in my work, and my gratitude to him comes straight from the heart. If it were not for him, I would not be doing what I indeed love to do: to teach and to write. Cristanne Miller has once again been a first-rate counselor in more than scholarly matters, and so have Sacvan Bercovitch and Werner Sollors. Many colleagues and friends have been right there when intelligent commentary or openhearted consolation was needed; they themselves know best how much that meant. I want particularly to thank Susanne Rohr and Dorothea Westphal as well as Christoph Irmscher, who shared a great part of the way, the experience, and the laughs. Ulfried Reichardt and I have kept comparing notes over the years, and I have cherished this exchange as both reassuring and inspiring. Ute Bartetzko, Eva Boesenberg, Gabriele Dietze, Maria Moss, Susanne Rohr, Cornelia Voigtländer, and Dorothea Westphal were perfect proofreaders and soothers when time was scarce—ready to engage even way past midnight. My gratitude also belongs to Deborah Malmud and Thomas LeBien, editors at Princeton University Press, and to Lauren Lepow for excellent copyediting work and Maura Roessner for much appreciated assistance. The bottom line of my thankfulness is reserved once again for Edgar Muschketat, my treasure (and meanwhile my spouse too), who has been part of all this even when we were apart.

I gratefully acknowledge permission to reproduce artwork by Kara Walker, courtesy Brent Sikkema, New York City.

All translations from the German are my own.

READING RAPE

—◦◦◦—

What We Talk about When We Talk about Rape

*R*EADING RAPE is an exploration of representations of rape, of what I have come to call the *rhetoric of rape*, not an analysis of rape as a social fact. Since I do hold, though, that we experience the real by way of its various representations, I want to begin by calling back to mind a prominent case of "real rape."[1] On April 20, 1989, a twenty-nine-year-old white female jogger—an investment banker, as it turned out, at Salomon Brothers in downtown Manhattan—was found in Central Park, near 102d Street, her clothes torn, her skull crushed, her left eyeball pushed back through its socket, the characteristic surface wrinkles of her brain flattened, her blood reduced by 75 percent, her vagina filled with dirt and twigs: the victim of a beating and gang rape of utmost brutality by six black and Hispanic teenagers. Crucial in this context is not the incident itself. There were thousands of rapes reported that year, some of which lacked nothing in brutality, including one, a week later, "involving the near decapitation of a black woman in Fort Tryon Park" (Didion 255).[2] What's more: the sociology of real rape is not my trade. Instead, what is significant for me about the Central Park case is the prominence to which it advanced and the discourse it generated, a rhetoric aptly exemplified by news headlines such as "The Jogger and the Wolf Pack" or "Central Park Horror" (qtd. in Didion 255).

"[C]rimes are universally understood to be news," Joan Didion writes in "Sentimental Journeys," her brilliant reading of the case, "to the extent that they offer, however erroneously, a story, a lesson, a high concept" (255–56). The story offered by the Jogger Rape Case is an old and well-established one: rape, we are assured, is an encounter of total strangers in public parks. Accordingly, media coverage did not center upon the (gender) issues involved in the sexual violation but, as Didion emphasizes, interpreted the case as a conflict between two parties clearly distinguished by race, ethnicity, and class: on the one hand, whites, affluent enough to keep the city's realities at a safe distance, to whom the violation of the young urban professional signified the loss of sacrosanct territory; on the other, African Americans who considered the treatment of the violators as yet another lynching campaign, a kind of rape. The discursive scene of the crime thus draws upon a whole cultural register generated in the course of late-nineteenth-century interracial conflicts and national identity formation. Specifically, it invokes what W. J. Cash in the early 1940s labeled the "Southern rape complex,"[3] according to which the presumed sexual violation of white beauty by black beast figured the "rape" of the South during Reconstruction and legitimized retaliation through lynch violence. At the same time, this complex inflicted a fear of rape that, like the threat of lynching, kept a subordinate group—women just in the process of fighting for suffrage—subjugated (Hall, *Revolt* 153). Cited and recontextualized one century later, this register's rhetoric frames present conflicts by past interpretations and reinforces "solutions" such as segregation. More than that: since the metonymic drift of the paradigm of rape and lynching, as I will show, has dominated the discourse on sexual violation at and of the borders of race, class, and ethnicity, the "objects" of such violations are left behind in the debris of displacement.

What I mean to suggest by this introductory excursus is that talk about rape does not necessarily denote rape, just as talk about love hardly ever hits its target.[4] Instead, transposed into discourse, rape turns into a rhetorical device, an insistent figure for other social, political, and economic concerns and conflicts. Fictions of rape belong with the allegorical master narratives Fredric Jameson considers "a persistent dimension of literary and cultural texts precisely because they reflect a fundamental dimension about our collective thinking and our collective fantasies about history and reality" (*Political Unconscious* 34). Accordingly, it does not suffice to capitalize on rape, as Leslie Fiedler does, as "an image of true archetypal resonance" ("Pop" 91) or to characterize the "symbolic" dimension of (female) rape fantasies, as does Molly Haskell, as "archetypal rather than individual" ("Rape Fantasy" 92), thereby dehistoricizing rape. Instead, I want to insist that talk about rape has its history, its ideology, and its dominant narratives—narratives that, as I argue, are nationally specific, even if they rely on widely established textual predecessors (such as myths) and patterns (such as the "othering" of sexual violence).

In the United States—as anywhere else—these narratives are inextricably intertwined with constructions of sexuality and gender. In fact, as I show in chapter 1, the very discourses that establish gender differences as differences in sexuality also construct female sexuality as victimization. At the same time American rape narratives are overdetermined by a distinct history of racial conflict and a discourse on race that itself tends to overdetermine issues of class.[5] The "southern obsession with rape," for that matter, "touched a responsive chord in the nation at large," as Jacqueline Dowd Hall writes, "rooted" as it was "in the deepest of American communal preoccupations: the conflict between 'civilization' and 'savagery,' historically acted out in the destruction of the Indians and the subjugation of African slaves" (*Revolt* 147). Therefore just as sexuality is not, as Michel Foucault has argued, a stubborn drive but a dense transfer point for relations of power, narratives of sexual violence ponder not an alien and uncontrollable part of human nature but the power dynamics of a particular culture.

As a consequence, rape narratives relate to real rape incidents in highly mediated ways only. They are first and foremost interpretations, readings of rape that, as they seem to make sense of socially deviant behavior, oftentimes limit our understanding of sexual violence while producing norms of sexuality in the process. As they have evolved in historically specific contexts, these narratives moreover interrelate with, produce, and subsequently reproduce a cultural symbology that employs sexual deviance for the formation of cultural identities—identities that, figured by way of the sexual, do have a particular resilience. In this way, sexual violence, bodies in pain, and the "unmaking" of worlds, as Elaine Scarry has it, have participated in the making of a world that tends to care little about violated bodies.

Analyzing paradigmatic representations and functions of rape in both canonical and lesser-known American literary texts from the late eighteenth to the late twentieth century, I trace a history of the rhetoric of rape. Consequently, at stake throughout *Reading Rape* is not the question of how literature "respond[s]" to or "record[s]" "a particular historical issue," this being the question that drives Sandra Gunning's study *Race, Rape, and Lynching*, for instance (16). Such an approach may "correspond" to the declared function of realist literature yet falters when faced with modernist texts that refigure rape as an inherent systemic violence of cultural sign systems. More significant, though, literature does not *express* its historical conditions; it rather transforms, as Louis Althusser has it, a "determinate given raw material into a determinate product" (qtd. in Storey 111). The determinate given raw material of rape narratives, though, is not necessarily rape. Therefore I attempt to make visible the contexts *within* the texts and to show how our very sense of any historical issue is inseparable from its various cultural representations, representations that are themselves driven by cultural anxieties and desires. My aim is to decipher the ways and the contexts in which American culture talks about rape, what cultural work that rhetoric has been able to achieve over the last two centuries, why some of its lines have come to be dominant, "inescapable" even,[6] and why rape has gained so much prominence as a figure of power relations in the second half of the twentieth century. Since texts mean just as much by what they leave unsaid as by what they say, by what is absent as by what is present, those texts that explicitly employ rape in turn raise questions about their silences, their absent centers, about what they chose to obscure.

Obviously, my subject was generated by feminist criticism that, during the last three decades, has deployed the term "rape." At the same time my perspective diverges from and takes issue with feminist antirape discourse, which, as I show, is itself a product of the history I delineate. Feminism of the Dworkin/ MacKinnon kind has not only identified all heterosexuality as rape and turned rape into "*the* master metaphor, for defining the violation of woman by patriarchy" (Warren Warner 13). So-called radical feminism also labels the United States a "rape culture"[7] and thus misleadingly suggests that rape occurs more frequently in a culture that talks about rape excessively than in one that denies its existence. To my mind, though, the term "rape culture" says more about the prominent status of rape as a central trope within the American cultural imaginary than about the state of real rape. What is more, in its attempt to break the silence on sexual violence, the (feminist) deployment of rape has nurtured its own silences that are as meaningful as the silences with which dominant culture has veiled sexual violence.

In addition, unlike contemporary rape narratives, which are highly self-reflexive, feminist antirape discourse remains quite unconcerned about how it is itself inflected by established representations of rape, about how much its conceptions of sexuality and sexual violence result from and further reinforce and nourish dominant fictions. Convinced that the erasure of evil images leads to a decrease of evil acts, radical feminism displays both a debatable notion of signification and a lack of self-knowledge. By appropriating what I describe as the antebellum precursors to a rhetoric of rape, recent rape-crisis discourse[8] has revitalized nineteenth-century notions of female sexuality and gender. In this way the anti-rape movement, as Katie Roiphe puts it, has moved to "the front lines of sexual regulation" (*Morning After* 171), bemoaning a crisis that "is not a rape crisis, but a crisis in sexual identity" (27).

Instead of reproducing a rhetoric of victimization, my own agenda is thus to recontextualize and challenge readings of rape, paying close attention to the relation between rape and representation, to an economy wherein "*rape and its meaning*," as Eve Kosofsky Sedgwick trenchantly puts it, "*circulate in precisely opposite directions*" (*Between Men* 10). In contrast to rape-crisis discourse—which, for the sake of its political agenda, realigns explicit, (porno)graphic representations of rape with acts of real rape—theorists of narrative and visual poetics acknowledge that rape in many ways resists representation. Mieke Bal, for instance, insists that rape

> cannot be visualized not only because "decent" culture would not tolerate such representations of the "act" but because rape makes the victim invisible. It does that literally first—the perpetrator "covers" her—and then figuratively—the rape destroys her self-image, her subjectivity, which is temporarily narcotized, definitely changed and often destroyed. Finally, rape cannot be visualized because the experience is, physically, as well as psychologically, *inner*. Rape takes place inside. In this sense, rape is by definition imagined; it can exist only as experience and as memory, as *image* translated into signs, never adequately "objectifiable." ("Reading" 142)[9]

Presuming with Bal that central aspects of rape—such as physical pain and psychic violation—escape representation, yet that rape can be communicated as text only, I argue that the central paradigm of a rhetoric of rape is not simply one of rape and silencing, as feminist criticism suggests, insinuating that this silence can be broken, that we can and should read the violence back into the texts. Since silences themselves generate speech, the central paradigm is rather that of rape, silence, and refiguration. If our readings focus on refigurations of rape as well as on rape as refiguration, we acknowledge that texts do not simply reflect but rather stage and dramatize the historical contradictions by which they are overdetermined. At best, readings of rape therefore reveal not merely the latent text in what is manifest, explicit, and thus produce a text's self-knowledge; they will also evolve a new knowledge pertaining to the ideological necessities of a text's silences and deletions.[10]

Refiguration works by way of displacement and substitution. In metonymy such substitution is based on relation, association, or contiguity that forms syntactical connections along horizontal, temporal lines and has therefore been associated with realism. Metaphor, by contrast, substitutes on the basis of resemblance or analogy, and creates semantic, spatial links along a paradigmatic, vertical line, often suggesting (poetic) truth-value. Owing to these asymmetrical, hierarchical, complementary rather than exclusory rhetorical processes at work (Barbara Johnson, *World* 155), readings of rape cannot be reduced to the study of a motif. Nor would it suffice to recover "the unspeakable aspects of the experience of rape" (Bal, "Reading" 137) by foregrounding the "violence of representation" (Armstrong and Tennenhouse), and thus reinstalling on the level of rhetoric the violence choked by the story line. Such practice could be applied to any text; it evolves systemic violence yet tends to ignore the particular cultural functions and the historically specific meanings texts assign to sexuality and sexual violence. Reading rape figuratively, as a rhetoric, I follow the symbolic traces of violation instead, exploring its business within the structure of particular literary texts and larger cultural narratives as well as within the construction of individual and communal identities.

Such correspondences between aesthetics and politics can be probed because literary texts and the formation of cultural identities involve similar processes of refiguration. Like metaphors, identities are structured against difference (of race, class, gender, ethnicity, and age, for instance) and "directed toward the gradual overcoming of difference by identity" (Lloyd 257). Yet even if identity subordinates difference to the demands of likeness, "[t]o see the like," Paul Ricoeur argues, "is to see the same in spite of, and through, the different." The "logical structure of likeness" is consequently characterized by a "tension between sameness and difference" (qtd. in Lloyd 256), and constructions of identity require both the assignment and the subordination of difference. The rhetoric of rape is one of many discourses by which such differences are being ascribed, victims and violators othered, set off, while the subject who assigns difference remains unmarked and unlimited in his or her possibilities.[11]

The structural likeness of processes of identity formation and refiguration makes the analysis of literary texts particularly productive in this context. Literary texts translate pain into art, transform the unspeakable into figures of speech whose structure and function both disfigure and bespeak their cultural work. They tell stories and translate tales of violation into nationally specific cultural symbologies and conclusive narratives. As such, they both form and interfere with the cultural imaginary. Like news about crimes, they may even offer a lesson, some high concept. Why, however, should literary discourse be the privileged medium for an analysis of the rhetoric of sexual violence—apart from the fact that literary criticism *is* my trade? Literature is central here not so much because, unlike the discourses of the social and natural sciences, it has allowed marginal voices to enter into the conversation on gender, race, and sexuality at an earlier time. Literature may have accommodated "other" perspectives, but their otherness has nonetheless been channeled and limited by the institutional frames in which they appeared. Likewise we no longer share the (formalist) faith in the powers of fiction and its particular aesthetics to represent and level conflicting cultural forces, or assume that literary texts are generically more "telling" than other discourses and thus manage to subvert and crumble cultural hegemonies. In fact, antebellum American literature, for instance, was subjected to generic constraints that tended to reduce rather than expand its thematic range, if compared with other cultural discourse of the time.

I do hold, however, that the analysis of literary texts is particularly revealing for a study focused on the rhetoric of rape, because, on the one hand, (some) literary texts conclusively narrativize and, by way of dispelling contradictions, manage to "naturalize" sexual violence into seemingly consensual views on gender, sexuality, and the world at large. In this way, I hold that—taking my clue from Althusser again—literary (rape) narratives both give answers to the questions they pose and produce "deformed" answers to the historical questions they steer away from. Reading rape thus also involves deciphering "the 'symptoms' of a problem struggling to be posed" (Storey 113), such as the problem of sexuality and race, for instance. At the same time, fictional texts, and modernist and post-modernist texts[12] in particular, by way of an insistent intertextuality foreground the historicity of their (rape) rhetoric and thus the constraints as well as the possibilities of the meanings they assign to sexual violence. Echoing and playing upon their literary forerunners, they refigure, re-present, repoliticize, and thus reinterpret previous literary interrogations of rape and sexual violence, and in this way inscribe themselves into a tradition of readings of rape, a tradition they simultaneously remember and interfere with. At the same time we have to acknowledge that the questions we bring to our inquiries into literary texts—such as issues of rape and representation— are motivated, mediated, and framed by our present concerns about identity and difference. Accordingly, the texts, their textuality, temporality, and tradition tell us as much about themselves as about the ways in which we project our selves.

Taking off from the proliferating discourse on rape in contemporary American culture,[13] *Reading Rape* thus attempts to describe *how American culture talks about sexual violence* and, more important, *how it has learned to do so* in the course of the last two centuries. My argument follows the American rhetoric of rape through four distinct phases of literary history, stretching from its antebellum precursors (the novel of seduction and the slave narrative) across its postbellum "realist" versions (including realist and naturalist fiction as well as racist romances and their African American "counternarratives") to modernist inquiries into rape and representation and their post-modernist refigurations. These phases can be separated, as I argue, by paradigm changes that, effected by political, economic, and cultural transformations, have also affected the function of fiction. I consequently use the terms of established literary history not to reaffirm its trajectory. Assembling rather diverse texts under rubrics such as "realist" or "modernist," I acknowledge, on the one hand, what Ernst Bloch called the synchronicity of the nonsynchronic. On the other, I want to keep in mind that literary texts have at different times used different strategies to legitimize themselves.

As part of an ongoing transformation of the American symbolic system, the rhetoric of rape therefore allows us to reassess the changing function of fictional texts within this cultural development. Most important, though, my analyses of the literary aesthetics and politics of rape underline that the meanings culture assigns to sexual violence evolve from an interplay between constructions of cultural parameters of identity and difference (such as gender, race, and class) and their specific forms of representation. As a consequence, this interplay has generated ideas about gender, race, and class that keep monitoring our perception and interpretation of real rape. Throughout, *Reading Rape* in turn stages dialogues between fiction and its repercussions in radical feminism aimed at putting crucial feminist positions into perspective.

In part guided by the rhetorical drive of contemporary feminist antirape discourse, my readings begin, in chapter 1 ("Seduced and Enslaved: Sexual Violence in Antebellum Literature and Contemporary Feminist Discourse"), at the end of the enlightened eighteenth century. I chose the turn of the nineteenth century as my point of departure because it is a time of paradigmatic changes, changes effected by and themselves effecting new conceptions of race, sexuality, gender, and genre. The reason for addressing the novel of seduction and the slave narrative first is consequently not that this is where American literature begins; rather, this is where American literature begins to take on particular functions. With the emergence of the novel and (African American) autobiography, literary texts cease to be primarily a means of religious edification and self-inspection and come to mediate a cultural imaginary of a different kind.

According to Winfried Fluck such an imaginary is generally a set of meanings that a culture thrives to articulate. The fund of images, affects, and desires generated in the process in turn stimulates the individual imagination anew, thus driving a process of cultural symbology that continuously challenges our sense of reality. The narrative strategies of the early American novel, in particular, created comprehensive, conclusive, and effective illusions tied to constructions of individual and national identity. In this emergent cultural imaginary change was projected by way of the human body, which became a "figure for an entire repertoire of human and social arrangements" (Spillers, "Mama's Baby" 456). While the late-eighteenth- to mid-nineteenth-century textual precursors turned the (vulnerable) female body into a focal point of meaning production, late-nineteenth-century cultural discourse directed its attention toward the previously indistinct male body. The black body, in particular, became a crucial figure in processes of remasculinization and (national) identity formation during the transition of the American nation from Victorianism to modernism, processes that generated what I consider the dominant, overdetermining line within the American rhetoric of rape.

The very blanks and blind spots of antebellum fiction, pertaining particularly to the (black) male body and (white) female sexuality, thus prepared the ground for a "realist" literary discourse that established (black-on-white) rape and the specter of the rapist "other" as central tropes of cultural transformation. In chapter 2, "The Rise of the (Black) Rapist and the Reconstruction of Difference; or, 'Realist' Rape," I trace this discourse in turn-of-the-century realist, naturalist, and sentimental narratives that echo, epitomize, or respond to the (racist and racializing) diction prevalent at a time when rape, as Frederick Douglass emphasized, turned into a national affair. Reading Thomas Nelson Page and Thomas Dixon in dialogue with Frank Norris, Frances E. W. Harper, Sutton E. Griggs, Upton Sinclair, Edith Wharton, and William Vaughn Moody, I show that this dominant rhetoric of rape is in fact the product of highly conflictual and stylistically varied discourses that conflate matters of race, class, and nationhood with issues of gender and sexuality.[14]

Partly owing to the overdetermining racial fracture of American culture and society, all the texts I discuss in chapter 3 employ the figure of the racialized "rapist" other and project sexual aggression and aggressive sexuality as interracial or interethnic encounters between different classes. Discriminating violator and victim on the basis of race, class, and ethnicity as well as gender, the "realist" rhetoric of rape thus constitutes a discourse of difference. Dramatizing crucial social, cultural, regional, and national conflicts, this discourse evolved fictions or "myths" about gender, race, and sexuality that have subsequently achieved truth-value and that keep informing feminist perspectives on sexual violence as well. At the same time the "rapist" rhetoric of turn-of-the-century literary texts exposes the anxieties informing processes of identity formation in a time of transition. Most particularly, the "realist" rhetoric of rape monitors reconstructions of gender and sexuality, the threat of which materializes in figures pertaining to the "crisis of homo/heterosexual definition"[15] (as in Norris's *McTeague* [1899] and Dixon's *The*

Clansman [1905]) and to redefinitions of the gender divide (as in Page's *Red Rock* [1898], Wharton's *The House of Mirth* [1905], and Moody's *A Sabine Woman* [1906]).

The third chapter, entitled "Rape and the Artifice of Representation: Four Modernist Modes," shifts focus. Modernism translates the figure of rape from primarily cultural into predominantly textual categories, capitalizing on the very artifice of fictional representation that realism means to obscure. In the process modernist fiction diffuses the established meanings of rape to a certain degree and reveals their ideological subtexts without themselves subscribing to particular ideologies. Instead, their textual strategies ranging from ellipsis to mimicry target sexual violence from within its discursive modes. As modernist texts acknowledge rape as a figure and form of representation rather than an event, they also hint that the insights of narrative theory and visual poetics I started out from are themselves insights generated by modernism.

Owing to modernism's preoccupation with perception and process rather than history and cultural consensus, texts such as Djuna Barnes's *Ryder* (1928), William Faulkner's *Sanctuary* (1931), Richard Wright's *Native Son* (1940), and Ann Petry's *The Street* (1946) no longer project rape as a figure of "othering," difference, and social boundaries. Instead, they turn sexual violence into a trope of transgression and border crossing that recognizes the disturbing proximity of figures and phenomena that "realist" rape narratives so obsessively separated—or segregated—from each other. This does not mean that differences dissolve. Rather, modernism questions realism's claims to authority and authenticity. Modernist rape narratives either playfully expose and mime their rhetorical tradition (as Barnes does), or (as does Faulkner) reassess the "realist" rape rhetoric by capitalizing on the representation of rape and blurring the borderlines that realism had managed to implement. As both texts insistently conflate rape and incest, they also dramatize the uncanny subtexts of that rhetoric. Owing to a difference in subject position that impacts on aesthetics, African American modernist fiction at the same time represents rape in its own ways. Wright's protagonist Bigger, so I argue, reenacts the racist/"rapist" projection and rebirths himself in an abortive act of modernist mimicry. Petry's first novel, by contrast, which daringly explores intraracial sexual violence, occupies an in-between position leaning toward post-modernist literary modes. As she challenges the modernist aestheticization of the sexual(ly violated) black female body and exposes the significance of the visual, the cinematic "real" for the late-twentieth-century American cultural imaginary, Petry evolves a black female subject in transition.

In the second half of the twentieth century, American fiction has subsequently retransformed modernist notions of rape and representation into cultural categories. As it projects the aesthetics of rape onto the level of content and theme, post-modernist writing tends to repoliticize and oftentimes literalize the trope of rape, in this way renegotiating the constructions of identity and difference effected so "successfully" at the turn of the last century. At the same time—and this is crucial to the argument of my final chapter, "Voicing Sexual Violence, Repoliticizing Rape: Post-Modernist Narratives of Sexuality and Power"—post-modern fictions have retained modernist insights into textuality and the processes of meaning formation. In fact all post-modernist refigurations of rape, no matter whether they aspire to verisimilitude or radicalize modernist modes, display and play upon an awareness of their own essentially rhetorical character.

Post-modernist fiction thus only seems to be "about" sexual violence. More often than not, it is preoccupied with the cultural effects of the established rhetoric of rape, with the ways in which the rhetoric of sexual violence informs and structures our perspectives on real rape, and with how "rape myths" and rape as a social fact have become inseparably intertwined. These cultural effects frequently affect subjectivity: novels as incomparable as Chester Himes's *A Case of Rape* (1963) and Lois Gould's *A Sea Change* (1977), for instance, expose the impact of commonplace readings of rape on their protagonists' sense of self. In this way, post-modernist texts dramatize the privileged relation of rape narratives to what Sedgwick calls "our most prized constructs of individual identity, truth, and knowledge" (*Epistemology* 3). They not only insist that, like the discourse of sexuality, the rhetoric of sexual violence has become "a very real historical formation" (Foucault 157). Post-modern fiction also recognizes that now that rape can be spoken, its cultural significance and function are being equivocated and displaced in turn. And while old silences may have been broken, new ones have taken shape in their stead. Rape and its meaning therefore keep circulating in opposite directions. It is no longer the representation of rape that gets displaced and diffused, though, but its signifying power. The ongoing significance of the literary predecessors to which post-modernist rape narratives attest at the same time underlines that, just as rape can exist as experience and memory only, the literary rhetoric of rape evolves in part as the memory of its own history of representation.

This brings me back to the case of real rape I started off with, and to one particular reading it has produced, Didion's "Sentimental Journeys." For just as the lynching-campaign interpretation produced by the African American "community" wrongly suggests that no rape has taken place, Didion's own words (which I have appropriated in my introductory paragraph) re-present the jogger rape case as a kind of lynching. As Didion appropriates images and narratives of decapitation and castration replete with "skull[s] ... crushed" and "eyeball[s] pushed back through [their] socket[s]" (254), her rhetoric acknowledges that some cultural narratives have indeed become inescapable. She moreover hints that the displacement of rape by lynching bespeaks male anxieties and fears of disempowerment more than it manifests male power.

Most significant, though, Didion's depiction attests to the fact that the rhetoric of rape conduces not to rape but to readings, interpretations, a cultural literacy concerning matters of rape. These readings in turn determine the signifying power of real rape. Accordingly, instead of either censoring or celebrating representations of sexual(ly violent) acts, as some feminist critics urge, I propose that challenging our ways of reading rape may be most productive.

Seduced and Enslaved: Sexual Violence in Antebellum American Literature and Contemporary Feminist Discourse

S EXUAL VIOLENCE has always been a central issue of feminist debate, whether more implicitly, as in the writing and speeches of nineteenth-century reform movement activists, or explicitly, as in today's rape-crisis discourse. Both early and contemporary feminist thought has related the viola-tion of women's bodies to the denial of women's personhood or subject posi-tion, though it is exactly in regard to subject position that nineteenth- and twentieth-century women differ. Downplaying woman's sexuality to upgrade her claims to citizenship and subjectivity, nineteenth-century reformers still had to argue that the political, economic, cultural, and physical oppression of women was a wrong because women—"even" black women—were not only rational but also morally superior beings. Rape as a dominant contemporary feminist issue, by contrast, emerged in the 1970s because "control over one's body and sexuality became a major area for concern and activism" (Smith, "Split Affinities" 274). And control is a key term here if we take it in a Fou-cauldian sense. For curiously enough, the 1970s desire to liberate from sexual oppression a supposedly other, subversive female sexuality has led the rape-crisis discourse of the 1980s to reassert the gender differences that the nine-teenth century had so firmly inscribed. In the context of black feminist criti-cism, by contrast, discussions of sexual violence tend to focus on the historical difference of African American women's experience, on interracial rape, and on the survivor narratives delineated in African American women's history and literary tradition. Like the dominant antirape rhetoric, African American feminism thus draws upon nineteenth-century discourses.

By redirecting their attention to the past, both perspectives attest to a conti-nuity between early-nineteenth- and late-twentieth-century views of sexuality and sexual violence—that is, to a history of the rhetoric of rape. By grounding this history in antebellum American literary texts, I will, in the following pages, first suggest why contemporary feminism talks about rape the ways it does, and, second, explore what the current revival of the victimized woman holds in store for female subjectivity and sexual politics. Such historization under-scores that the debates around sexual violence have always channeled (female) sexuality. More than that: in reducing rape to matters of either gender or race, feminist criticism has also tended to limit our perspectives on the subject. Let me first, however, look more closely at recent feminist discussions around rape.

"Rape Crisis" or "Crisis in Sexual Identity"? The Feminist Rhetoric of Rape

Central to the feminist debates on sexual violence has been and still is the question of whether rape is to be considered a crime of violence or one based in sexuality. Separating rape as an expression of violence from intercourse as a sexual act, Susan Brownmiller, among others, objected to the predominant notion that rape is a natural expression of male sexual desire and an act of sex and lust. Redefining rape as a crime of violence and power, Brownmiller in turn limited rape to contexts of riots, wars, and revolutions, setting it apart from daily life.[1] Objecting to a separation of sexuality and power, Catharine MacKinnon, by contrast, has insisted on the convergence of sexuality, or, to be exact, of male sexuality and violence. For her, as for Andrea Dworkin, "acceptable sex, in the legal perspective, can entail a lot of force" (*Feminist Theory* 173), and, in fact, the use of force or, as she puts it, "penile invasion of the vagina," is pivotal to male sexuality (172).[2] "Rape," so MacKinnon insists, "is not less sexual for being violent. To the extent that coercion has become integral to male sexuality, rape may even be sexual to the degree that, and because, it is violent" (173).[3]

The dominant rape-crisis discourse of Dworkin and MacKinnon has been opposed by proponents of so-called sex-positive feminism, a label that covers feminist authors, artists, and activists with rather diverse backgrounds, interests, and agendas. They all resist, however, the sense of sexuality and gender promoted by antirape discourse and hold that the censorship (and self-censorship) ensuing from antipornography activism and legislation, which identifies representation and agency, eventually endangers sexual expression, art, and free speech in general.[4] More direct attacks against rape-crisis discourse have been launched by a group of young writers, including Roiphe, who take issue with the "victim mentality" of the date rape debates[5] and with a "new Victorianism" (Denfield) that appropriates nineteenth-century notions of female purity in order to control male sexual behavior and in this way manipulates women's sexuality and subject position in very familiar ways.

Unlike sex-positive feminism, whose cultural practices—including writing, art, pornography, and performance—are geared to reconstruct desire, these "postfeminist" critics offer little more than their discontent with the dominant drive of the discussion around sexuality and sexual violence. In this way, just like the right-wingers who support MacKinnon's antipornography campaigns, they have unintentionally assisted in moving MacKinnon and Dworkin from the margins to the center stage of feminist discourse. Polarizing the discussions around sexuality and sexual violence, Roiphe's own rhetoric thus cannot be separated from that of her opponents. While we need to acknowledge the distinct cultural work achieved by MacKinnon's legal defense of women violated in the pornography industry, Dworkin's analysis of heterosexual intercourse as an "institution," Roiphe's intervention into the date rape debate, and Annie Sprinkle's "post porn modernist" performance art, we also need to keep in mind that all this work affects the cultural significance of sexual violence and sexuality. More specifically, I argue, rape-crisis discourse and "postfeminist" crusades against the "new Victorians" share the same history and operate with the same rhetoric—a rhetoric whose confessional mode means to reveal the truth about sexuality and sexual violence while necessarily displacing some of the issues at stake.

Let me take as an example Roiphe's book *The Morning After: Sex, Fear, and Feminism on Campus*, which, despite its limited scope, I have found suggestive. Roiphe to my mind rightfully argues that "[t]he movement against date rape is a symptom of a more general anxiety about sex" (26), that "the crisis is not a rape crisis, but a crisis in sexual identity" (27), and therefore of identity itself, which has come to depend so much on bodies and sexual preferences. I agree with the author when she reads the rape epidemic on campuses as more "a way of interpreting, a way of seeing, than a physical phenomenon," more about a "change in sexual politics than a change in sexual behavior" (53). Roiphe's argument is hampered, however, by theoretical inconsistency. Her criticism of rape-crisis discourse, her objection to MacKinnon's notion of pornography as act (versus speech), and her insistence on the literariness of literary texts only seem to reflect poststructuralist insights into matters of representation. While Roiphe reads the rapes recovered in speak-out rituals as "fictions in the service of political truth" (40), she herself conjures up fictions of "free love" and "liberation and libido" (15, 12). Likewise, Roiphe appropriately calls the confessional mode of "Take Back the Night" marches on Ivy League university campuses "a construction of the articulate" (34). Yet as Barbara Johnson observed in her response to Roiphe's talk at Harvard University,[6] Roiphe similarly empowers herself by claiming the position of the powerless, one who—silenced for so long by feminist dogma—finally dares to speak her mind. Moreover, Roiphe's deployment of concepts such as confession, repression, and liberation attests to her familiarity with Foucault without making her argument Foucauldian. Thus while Roiphe correctly situates feminists on "the front lines of sexual regulation" (171), it does not occur to her that she herself may be part of that regulation; that the alternative is not between repression and liberation, but between a rhetoric of repression and a rhetoric of liberation that—owing to shared silences and articulations—necessarily cooperate in the construction and control of sexuality.

Like her opponents, Roiphe "regulates" by what she says as well as by what she prefers to leave out. Even though the subtitle of the first paperback edition of her book, as Johnson pointed out, eliminates the qualifier "on campus," thereby appealing to a larger audience, this deletion cannot conceal that Roiphe's perspective hardly ever peeps beyond the campuses of privileged universities and blatantly omits issues of race and class. While during her talk Roiphe repeatedly insisted that such matters were none of her primary concerns, her very defensiveness foregrounds how much race and class are at stake here. Focusing upon date rape debates at universities that, according to Roiphe, are not really about rape after all, the author necessarily reinforces the belief that real rape happens in other places and to other kinds of women.[7] In this way, her attack on rape-crisis discourse engages the very dynamics that has structured the rhetoric of rape ever since it emerged in eighteenth-century American criminal rape narratives:[8] a dynamics that displaces and overdetermines rape by the categories of class, ethnicity, and, first of all, race.

Taking a closer look at antebellum American literary texts, we can illuminate parts of the world that this dynamics has helped to construct. More particularly I want to show how much the dominant feminist rhetoric of rape, as well as the crusade against the New Victorianism, rely upon nineteenth-century perspectives on gender and race relations, how much they are indebted to the history of a rhetoric of rape whose narratives we cannot escape. One of these narratives is the reconstruction of gender and race relations at the end of the eighteenth and during the first half of the nineteenth century that cast female sexuality as victimization while projecting sexual violence into (inter)racial and class-inflected contexts. By victimizing women nineteenth-century style, contemporary rape-crisis discourse calls upon these narratives and reinstigates—even if "only" figuratively—the limitations they set on female sexuality and subjectivity. In addition, the particular use that feminist criticism makes of both the image of the delicate true woman and the sexually violated female slave bespeaks the common, yet reductive, view of Victorian morality and a misguided sense of what sexual violence meant to late-eighteenth- and nineteenth-century women whose legal, economic, and political disposition bears little resemblance to ours. Rereading these texts and their specific concerns, displacements, and silences allows us to put both the revival of Victorian ideals of womanhood and the identification of the rape-crisis feminists as "New Victorians" into a historical perspective.

"GUILTY PASSIONS" AND "FOUL WORDS": THE POWERS OF SEDUCTION AND THE RACIALIZATION OF SEXUAL VIOLENCE

The enlightened late eighteenth century not only saw the rise of two genres central to American literary history, the novel and the slave narrative.[9] It witnessed paradigmatic changes in the conceptions of sexuality, gender, and the body as well. As sexuality ceased to be conceived as a by-product of procreation and instead became an end in itself,[10] it threatened the patriarchal family and increased social anxieties concerning sexual relations. The "deployment of sex-uality" (Foucault)[11] displaced the "one-sex model" by the "two-sex model"[12] and, in the course of the nineteenth century, effected the categorization of di-verse sexualities and the medicalization of supposedly deviant sexual practices, all of which were racialized in the process. The sexuality of blacks, and of black women in particular, transformed into the very icon of deviant sexuality.[13] Such racialized constructions of sexuality have always been overdetermined, Evelyn Brooks Higginbotham underlines, by an additional amount of institutionalized violence, "rhetorical and real, against black women and men" (102–3). In the course of history the supposedly deviant black sexuality justified "everything," Marcia Ann Gillespie points out, "from rape to castration, to murder, to court-ordered sterilization, and most recently, forced contraception" (80).

Early novels and slave narratives both partly produced and challenged these racialized conceptions of sexuality and sexual violence. Their entanglement in the formation of sexuality, gender, and race shows most clearly in the centrality of the female body, which by the eighteenth century had emerged "as the locus for the inscription of meanings" (20) and was most fully dramatized in the nineteenth-century novel. According to Peter Brooks, the novel evolves along with the concept of privacy as a mark of personhood and physical integrity, which itself, in Enlightenment thinking, is "consubstantial with the idea of [the body's] violation" (37). This implies that in the context of American cul-ture the modern notion of personhood or subjectivity, which applied to nei-ther women nor blacks, partly depends upon the subjection of female and black bodies.

Both the novel of seduction and the slave narrative interrogate such subjec-tion yet, owing to their utterly different cultural functions, do so in rather different ways. Adapting the seduction motif[14] to dramatize the consequences of premarital sexuality as a fatal "fall," Susanna Rowson's best-seller *Charlotte Temple* (1791) and Hannah Foster's *The Coquette* (1797), for instance, engage in the construction of polarized gender differences that cast female sexuality as victimization and violation. In Harriet Ann Jacobs's *Incidents in the Life of a Slave Girl* (1861), by contrast, (the threat of) sexual violence and the hero-ine's trials to regain control over her enslaved body and self serve both an abolitionist agenda and an identity politics built upon the survival of the vic-tim. Whereas Rowson produces a rhetoric of containment and victimization, Jacobs engages in a rhetoric of emancipation that partly circumvents black women's victimization by both black and white abolitionists while channeling sexuality in its own way.[15] What emerges from this (re)birth is a sense of per-sonhood coterminous with sexual violation, which eventually gives rise to no-tions of black women's supposed invulnerability, "an ability," as Michael Awk-ward underlines, "not to conquer oppression but to negotiate it successfully" ("Representing Rape" 109). Elizabeth Keckley's *Behind the Scenes. Or, Thirty*

Years a Slave, and Four Years in the White House (1868), in turn, presents a narrator who admits having been a victim of sexual violence while also attempting to literally veil her confessions. Keckley's text thus exemplifies the "cult of secrecy" and "culture of dissemblance" that, according to Darlene Clark Hine, form black women's central strategy of coping and protecting "the sanity of inner aspects of their lives" (294).

Since none of the aforementioned novels and slave narratives talk about sexual violence explicitly, the first question is: how does it figure? In *Charlotte Temple* and *The Coquette*, as well as in *Incidents in the Life of a Slave Girl*, the invasion of the heroine's privacy, directed at her private parts, is metaphorized as the penetration of her mind by rituals of persuasive rhetoric more powerful than physical attraction. "In affairs of love," Rowson's narrator advises, "a young heart is never more in danger than when attempted by a handsome young soldier. . . . but if she listens to him with pleasure, 'tis all over with her, and from that moment she has neither eyes nor ears for another object" (25). And since Charlotte does indeed take pleasure in listening, what she meant to be a final interview turns out to be her fall:

> "Now," said Montraville, taking Charlotte in his arms, "you are mine for ever."
>
> "No," said she, withdrawing from his embrace, "I am come to take an everlasting farewel."
>
> It would be useless to repeat the conversation that here ensued, suffice it to say, that Montraville used every argument that had formerly been successful, Charlotte's resolution began to waver, and he drew her almost imperceptibly toward the chaise.
>
> "I cannot go," said she: "cease, dear Montraville, to persuade. I must not: religion, duty, forbid."
>
> "Cruel Charlotte," said he, "if you disappoint my ardent hopes, by all that is sacred, this hand shall put a period to my existence. I cannot—will not live without you."
>
> "Alas! my torn heart!" said Charlotte, "how shall I act?"
>
> "Let me direct you," said Montraville, lifting her into the chaise.
>
> "Oh! my dear forsaken parents!" cried Charlotte.
>
> The chaise drove off. She shrieked, and fainted into the arms of her betrayer.
> (47–48)

Overpowered by the villain's sweet talk, the heroine swoons and is ravished from her mother country, England, "seduced from [her father's] protection" (25). And even if Rowson's novel reenacts the "robbery" of African Americans by slave-traders and renders a tale of captivity, "seduced" remains the right word here. By convention any equivocation or acquiescent gesture on woman's part signals seduction; "unequivocal resistance" alone marks rape (Rooney 1273).

In Rowson's text, verbal coercion promises pleasure while quibbling over the consequences, thus turning Charlotte into the "hapless victim of imprudence and evil counsellors" (59) like Montraville, La Rue, and Belcour. In Jacobs's narrative, by contrast, coercion comes by way of slaveholder Flint's "foul words," words that invade Linda Brent's innocent mind, making her "prematurely knowing, concerning the evil ways of the world" without ever being revealed to the reader (54). Both texts' emphasis on rhetoric, though, attests to the dominance of the seduction motif as a figure of (hetero)sexual encounters. Rendering sexual assault as a conquest of the mind through speech, through forceful rhetoric—as opposed to physical force—both Rowson and Jacobs at the same time underline that rape is "a crime on the level of mental states" (Ferguson, "Rape" 91), a crime "against the will," an act that is violent because it overrides ambivalence or nonconsent.

The issue of consent generates questions of subject position. As Charlotte is prevented, through unconsciousness, from signaling either consent or nonconsent, the novel manifests her lack of personhood. Accordingly, we are never told how long in fact she remains unconscious. And while it is unlikely that this state outlasts the "tempestuous" sexual encounter (Rowson 115), there is no need for precision. The ensuing pregnancy itself signals lost virginity and grants consent after the fact, for conception itself was considered, by legal commentary, as consent.[16] Just like legally fixed ages of consent and intent, this perspective circumvents the difficult task of determining nonconsent—a concept that, as Ferguson points out, has always been central to the definition of rape. The seduction novel thus not only highlights how biology came to figure destiny (Newman xxi). It also identifies premarital sexuality with (economic) danger and (social) death while at the same time equivocating the violence that the sexual act may (or may not) entail.

Having failed and fallen, "brought from all her connections, and robbed of innocence" (Rowson 67), Charlotte is ruined; her sexual slip effects her social decline, her economic, physical, and psychic deterioration. When she identifies herself as a "poor sailor, tost on a tempestuous ocean" (82), she actually recalls the moment of loss that occurred during the passage from England to America, in a space beyond national borders and social conventions. That "vast expanse of sea"—which, as Montraville deemed, was to divide the lovers (37)—bears sexual gratification (for Montraville) and self-division and shipwreck (for Charlotte).[17] First silenced by having the letters to her parents destroyed (57–58), Charlotte eventually loses both speech and writing (80, 83) to an increasingly insistent body language that is further enhanced by the invisibility of male bodies and sexual acts throughout the text. Signifying pain, "soul murder" (Painter), and a suicidal disposition,[18] this sign language remains semantically indefinite and delivers a double-voiced message: its emphasis on the physical, on the one hand, rewrites seduction as rape while, on the other, conveying "the idea," as Bal puts it, "that the victim is responsible for her own destruction" ("Reading" 142), that it is not the violator's coercion but the victim's nonconsent that constitutes rape.

The novel retains this ambivalence because whether Charlotte did or did not consent, in the overall scheme of things, does not affect the outcome of her foreign affair. Instead, the figurative displacement of the sexual act underlines that both sexuality and sexual violence meant something significantly different to the late-eighteenth-century reader from what it means to us. Once it was acknowledged a crime,[19] rape was still considered not a violation of women's personhood (which throughout most of women's history has not been acknowledged) but a damage to male property, a kind of robbery, and thus primarily a threat to the established socioeconomic order and a class issue.[20] Accordingly, while sexual assault first ranked as a physical violation— and continued to do so among the lower classes[21]—the late eighteenth century reinterpreted rape as a theft of (a poor) woman's only capital: her chastity.

In the conventional seduction narrative such loss of virtue and honor, whether enforced or not, leads one way only: downhill. Thus Rowson's heroine dies, because—conventionally, ideally—a woman's life meant either marriage or celibacy, not "the thorny paths of vice" (70). Charlotte's social displacement is signified by her being first situated, like a concubine, in her own house outside New York—an arrangement that Flint proposes to Brent as a rise in status—and later ejected out onto city streets. Marriage remains the only possible cover-up of the mishap—"the only gem," as Charlotte has it, "that could render me respectable in the eye of the world" (84). Likewise rape could be made right. In accordance with Saxon law, Ferguson points out, the raped virgin could retroactively consent to her rape and extricate her attacker from his death sentence by agreeing to marry him. As marriage thus "recasts rape," it becomes "a misunderstanding corrected, or rape rightly understood" ("Rape" 92). Charlotte, however, asserts her deep morality by refusing Belcour's marriage proposal. Her deterioration and death furthermore dismiss the value of female independence and underline that an "innocent child" like Charlotte belongs within the domain of paternal protection and patriarchal power. Therefore Charlotte considers her own child, as Ann Douglas points out, not a "fruit of guilty passion" but an "offspring of disobedience" (XXX). Insisting on woman's need of proper male guidance, the seduction narrative channels both female sexuality and patterns of manhood.

Charlotte Temple both nostalgically longs for and, in its portrayal of a forgiving father, dismantles paternal authority and thus dramatizes its political allegory, which concerns both the secularization of religion[22] and the development of the early republic. In the political context, Marybeth Hamilton Arnold writes with reference to Linda Kerber's work, "female passion, trickery, and extravagance" were equated "with the corruption ever threatening civic virtue." Outside of the protected space of the family, women "formed a potent threat to the young republic's stability" (51–52). In Rowson's novel, though, that stability rests on shaky grounds and double standards. Unlike their female counterparts, rakes such as Rowson's Montraville and Foster's Sanford as well as Harrington, the would-be seducer of William Hill Brown's "The Power of Sympathy" (1789), take their sexual liberties and still obey filial duty as they consider marriage, in accordance with paternal attitudes and patriarchal traditions, a matter of finances, status, and heritage, not of romantic love and sexual passion. Foster's "coquette" Eliza Wharton, by contrast, whose need for gaiety and amusement corresponds to her desire to postpone marriage, to a reluctance to give herself up to a singular man and tiresome domestic responsibilities, gambles away her capital.

Neither Montraville nor Sanford intends to marry his "coquette." "The heedless Fair," we are informed, "who stoops to guilty joys, / A man may pity— but he must despise" (Rowson 63). Montraville retrospectively describes his "regard" for Charlotte as "but the momentary passion of desire" (88). Sanford, by contrast, keeps desiring Eliza Wharton while neglecting his wife. Keeping to social conventions and family tradition, the seducer nonetheless ruptures kinship ties at the same time. "It was seduced her, Belcour," Montraville admits. "Had it not been for me, she had still been virtuous and happy in the affection and protection of her family" (92–93). Female desire in turn finds no space, either without or within matrimony.

Like early feminist texts published in such journals as *The Friend of Virtue*, Rowson's and Foster's novels thus take issue with a culture that demands sexual purity of women, but not of men; a culture that disregards circumstances and blames the victim for her violation, assuming her to be of "easy nature" (93) and prone to prostitute herself. Suggesting that Charlotte "go to the barracks and work for a morsel of bread" (113), Charlotte's landlady associates her with female camp followers who ministered to the needs of soldiers congregating in cities (D'Emilio and Freedman 50). Underscoring women's limited opportunities to support themselves[23] and dramatizing Charlotte's fall as a decline in class status, this scene foreshadows late-nineteenth-century realist fiction. At the same time, it acknowledges that women's "oldest profession" is condoned by the institutions it serves. Since Montraville himself is a military officer, his assault on Charlotte corresponds to the illegal, yet tolerated, exploitation of women.

Like Foster's epistolary novel, whose heroine is much less a victim than a subject of her fate, Rowson's "Tale of Truth" is conceived as a lesson "[f]or the perusal of the young and thoughtless of the fair sex" (Douglas XLIX) whom the climate of Enlightenment and revolution has given wrong ideas about their place in life. The new liberties and the decline of parental control of marriage, the seduction narrative insists, make women increasingly vulnerable. No longer could it be assumed that pregnancy results in marriage (D'Emilio and Freedman 52). The rise of premarital pregnancies that attested to this shift in sexual economy triggered the fetishization of virginity as capital. It also increased the awareness that sexual favors could be traded for capital. Accordingly, Rowson's text addresses lower-middle-class women first and foremost, projecting the risks involved in gambling away their only commodity of exchange value. Dramatizing premarital female sexuality as irreversible defeat, the power of seduction, so Jenny Newman puts it, "brings not pleasure but knowledge" (x) geared to channel female desire into the—supposedly safe—realm of matrimony, where sexual intercourse, consensual or not, is a legitimate act and "duty." Teaching deferred sexual gratification, the novel of seduction at the same time testifies to men's sexual dependence on women and to an empowerment of women that comes at the cost of female pleasure.

Significantly enough, Montraville learns his lesson, too. In fact, he eventually suffers physical pains that compare to Charlotte's own. "Tortured almost to madness" by the "shocking account" of Charlotte's fate (128), Montraville finally deems himself her "murderer" (129). The "disorder," "dangerous illness and obstinate delirium" he experiences vanish under his wife's tenderness. Till the end of his life, however, he remains "subject to severe fits of melancholy" (130), a state of depression that afflicts Charlotte's family as well (58). As his body and mind thus echo Charlotte's own deterioration, which itself figures the violence she was subjected to, Montraville is emasculated, feminized. According to Jan Lewis, *Charlotte Temple* thus anticipates a topos recurring in many nineteenth-century novels: the seduction of a man by a woman's virtue (701). The lesson thus is to both sexes. Or as Pat Califia puts it in "Slipping": "The Victorian solution [to the dangers of sexuality] was to preach a single standard of chastity for men and women" (87).

Compared to *Charlotte Temple*, Jacobs's narrative comes out a success story. Having fought off Flint's repeated advances, Brent aspires to make her confessions a triumph. Since the construction of privacy partly depends on its invasion, this "chance" to resist such invasion endows the heroine with the privacy and personhood that the enslaved were generally denied. At the same time, I myself resist readings that celebrate black women's act of telling their pain-ridden story as a claim to subjectivity.[24] First of all, after calculated romance and seven years of hiding, Brent's "rebirth" comes at a high price. Ironically referencing *Jane Eyre* and Victorian ideals of domesticity, it locates liberty in conventional female spheres. Moreover, reading Jacobs's narrative, one gets the sense that even if Brent's experiences were finally empowering, the very telling of them was immensely painful.

I thus agree with Karen Sanchez-Eppler, who claims that acts of sexual violence are displaced onto the act of narration. I object to her conclusion, though, that "for Jacobs the act of writing often seems to recapitulate the sexual violations at stake in the scenes she narrates" (10–11); that by "the act of voicing her sexual experiences," Brent "realizes the abuses of which she speaks" (96); and that "Linda finds that the act of telling her sexual story subtly reenacts that story" (100).[25] To my mind, the sense of pain emerging from the text results from an awareness that the actual pain cannot be told: first, because the original "text" resists representation; second, because the slave system does not recognize the rape of the enslaved; and third, because rape had its own particular significance in the contexts of abolitionist arguments. Any confession of sexual violation necessarily elided that violation; thus confession became a self-defeating act. This is why "[i]t pains [Brent] to tell [the reader] of it" (53). The subject emerging in the act of telling is clearly racialized; her sexuality is a public, in fact a national affair wherein sidelines of passion dissolve for the sake of political correctness.[26]

Owing to the double function of their texts as abolitionist propaganda and media of self-authentication,[27] writers such as Jacobs and Keckley faced the problem of how to confess black women's sexual violation while at the same time convincing a mainly white audience of their deeply moral character. The difficulty was to avoid reinforcing, by their well-intended confessions, the projections they meant to undo. Struggling against the image of the black seductress,[28] African American women take issue with their exclusion from the spheres of virtuous Victorian womanhood and refuse to take responsibility for their own sexual violation.[29] Preoccupied with matters of morality, their texts at the same time validate the charges leveled against them. In fact, the narratives reenact the very process that habitually served to prove the crime, a process through which the crime is displaced by additional information supposed to make the charge plausible. Whereas the Puritans did not assume a victim to be lying about an offense as serious as rape (Lindemann 72), discussions of the "good" or "evil fame," the "sexual history" of a woman bringing charges, meanwhile impacted on her credibility.[30]

In Jacobs's case things are even more complex. First of all, her narrative is constrained by generic conventions. The seduction motif—the dominant fictional frame for rendering matters of sexuality and sexual violence—on the one hand undermines Jacobs's agenda. On the other, many of the liberties it takes were deemed immoral and thus eliminated from the mid-nineteenth-century sentimental and domestic novel.[31] Second, owing to their dual status of property and person, slaves were criminally liable, and black males have always been more likely than their white counterparts to be prosecuted for rape.[32] The rape of slave women, however, by white or black men, legally did not exist.[33] Gender difference among African Americans thus emerges, as Saidiya Hartman points out, in relation to negligible (sexual) violation (554). Since the enslaved were incapable of giving consent or exercising will, the rape of slave women was considered adultery, sexual intercourse between white men and enslaved women "an unspoken but normative condition" (543), "a legitimate use of property" (544), and the only form of miscegenation that was not prohibited.[34] And finally, as black women were deemed hyper-sexualized and promiscuous, their sexual violation seemed "a contradiction in terms" (Smith, "Split Affinities" 275).

Somewhat paradoxically, rape becomes legible only in the discourse of seduction, which equivocates violence and, endowing the weak with strength, suggests social harmony. As it mimes the seduction tale, Jacobs's narrative highlights the very mechanisms of such equivocations that keep the violence behind a "veil of enchanted relations" (Pierre Bourdieu, qtd. in Hartman 545). At the same time, as it integrates the seduction tale, the slave narrative helps to segregate sexual violation and reduce it to interracial relations. And yet neither in terms of the law nor according to Brent's tale is Flint a rapist or sexual assaulter. Instead, Brent establishes her personhood by insisting that Flint never touched her. In fact, as Nell Irvin Painter points out, Jacobs was able to extensively comment on the sexual harassment of slave women only because her account concerns not sexual violence but "inappropriate sexualization" (135). Foregrounding that Brent is untimely robbed of her childhood, the narration appeals particularly to middle-class audiences, who are preoccupied with the sexual life of children and committed "to protecting children from premature sexual experience." Campaigns against childhood sexuality were launched in Europe and North America from 1700 to the end of the First World War and were based on the belief, Elizabeth Wilson explains, "that adequate development required the deferral of sexual experience until adulthood" (42). Jacobs's text is so controversial partly because it questions the common assumption that crimes such as incest or rape are perpetrated by racial, ethical, or social others incapable of controlling their physical impulses, and instead insists that such crimes thrive within middle- or upper-class families and threaten social inferiors considered part of the "extended family." The damage, Jacobs's narrative implies, is to civilized life as such.

Yet while Brent's is not a case of rape, in the eyes of her contemporaries she remains guilty of premarital, illicit sexuality, of miscegenation and sin. She achieves control over her body only by giving it, if not voluntarily, then with "deliberate calculation" (54) to someone other than Flint. The assertion of her will that dissociates her from sexual domination thus corresponds to a criminal act, criminalizes her. At the same time, it manifests the power of the powerless, the supposed equality inherent in the institution of slavery (Hartman 546–47). Challenging Flint's authority, this move utilizes the common hypocritical morality as well as male rivalry (which never gets played out in the text). By having Brent's lover, Sands, "triumph over" Flint (55), Brent appropriates Flint's very pretense of protectiveness and deploys it against his own interests. In some sense, Sands therefore holds a position like that of Belcour. Unlike the latter, though, he cannot make a wrong thing right; in the public eye, he achieves quite the opposite. Yet while Jacobs's narrative thus subverts the traditional seduction (and victimization) plot, it still figures Brent's decision to live with Sands as her yielding to temptation or, as Jacobs puts it, to "kind" eloquence (54). As she claims that repeated sexual harassment forced her heroine to act, thereby reaffirming Brent's innocence and dispelling thoughts of prostitution, Jacobs urges the reader to hold the evils of slavery, not herself, responsible for this loss of virtue. And yet her narrative makes it all too evident that in the context of slavery the threat of sexual violation "surfaces obliquely and only as the captive confesses her guilt" (Hartman 541).

Thus even if Jacobs does not elaborate on this matter, her rhetoric still reinforces the racialization of sexuality. As she legitimizes Brent's relation to Sands, she deploys the same silences that characterize Brent's confessions of Flint's sexual threat: highly apologetic about their offensive content, she in fact never reveals that content. Yet it is these silences that put sexual violence to work within abolitionism. Within the frame of her editor's introductory note, Jacobs must have deemed it appropriate to go through the motions of disclosure and still keep her subject veiled. "I am well aware," Lydia Maria Child wrote,

> that many will accuse me of indecorum for presenting these pages to the public; for the experiences of this intelligent and much-injured woman belong to a class which some call delicate, and others indelicate. This peculiar phase of Slavery has generally been kept veiled; but the public ought to be made acquainted with its monstrous features, and I willingly take the responsibility of presenting them with the veil withdrawn. I do this for the sake of my sisters in bondage, who are suffering wrongs so foul, that our ears are too delicate to listen to them. (Jacobs 3–4)

Categorizing the sexual exploitation of slave women as a delicate matter, Child pays as much heed to her audience as to the person subjected to the abuse. Proper narration is as crucial here as the pains inflicted by "monstrous" acts. As a result, Jacobs's narrative attempts both to protect and to penetrate the sensibilities of her audience. In this way, the narrator appears a violator indeed, reinforcing the common notion that white women living among sexually available (because enslaved) black women are the actual victims of slavery.[35] Rather than realizing the abuses of which it speaks, Brent's account is pained by the (mis)readings she knows her narrative will provoke. Anticipating the excruciating judgments of her audience, the narrative evolves not a strong, independent sense of self but a self strongly aware of her dependence on others.[36]

Let me demonstrate this point by looking at a crucial scene. In the chapter entitled "The Jealous Mistress," Brent confesses Flint's threats to his wife. She is confronted with the disbelief of Mrs. Flint, who subsequently attempts to elicit the truth by bending over Brent's bed at night and whispering in her ear, "as though it was her husband who was speaking" (34). Unlike Sanchez-Eppler, who reads this scene as a depiction of rape that "displaces the role of rapist from husband to wife" (97), I propose that not rape but seduction and racialized sexuality are at issue here. Reinterpreting Brent's confession as a tale of seduction, Mrs. Flint apparently does not question her husband's involvement with Brent yet casts the latter as the complicit, driving force of the liaison, as the agent of her husband's downfall. Since Mrs. Flint's words are unlikely to be the same as his (all of which remain unrecorded), her act does not so much rehearse Flint's harassment as it stages that behavior as a case of adultery enforced by the slave's deviousness.[37]

This kind of seduction tale recasts the nature of power: it is no longer the oppressor's domination but a manipulation by the dominated. The slave becomes the master not only of her own subjection[38] but of the subjection of all women, black *and* white, including the apparently complicit mistress. The very intimacy of the bedroom scene hints that "female slaves and female slaveholders," as Painter acutely observes, "were in the same sexual marketplace and . . . in this competition, free women circulated at a discount due to the ready availability of women who could be forced to obey" (136). The "seduction scene" thus reveals a knowledge disavowed throughout the narrative and most insistently by Brent's own idealization of Victorian womanhood.[39]

Since her confessions transform the victim Brent into a violator, she feels forced to maintain silence concerning her chosen sexual identity as well. In order to make her relation with Sands morally digestible to the reader, the narrator presents it both as a last resort, taken after her "love dream" to marry a free black man was shattered, and as a means of attaining personal integrity. "It seems less degrading to give oneself," she explains, "than to submit to compulsion. There is something akin to freedom in having a lover who has no control over you, except that which he gains by kindness and attachment" (55). Yet while Brent's desire for the African American man gets highly romanticized, the quality of her affair with Sands is merely hinted at. Both men remain similarly absent, invisible, silent.

Jacobs pictures her decision to accept Sands's offer as "a plunge into the abyss" (53) and "a headlong plunge" at that (55); she thus associates with it deliberation ("headlong"), force, and sexual pleasure, as well as a sense of a fall ("plunge"), transgressing the racial border into uncharted territory ("abyss"). While these figures illuminate the various angles from which Brent's move can be viewed, they are systematically followed by the pleadings and apologies on the part of the narrator that focus in on the dominant racializing perspective. "Confessing" to her daughter, Ellen, the circumstances of her involvement with Sands, Brent admits that her "early sufferings in slavery" "nearly . . . had crushed" her and drove her "into a great sin" (188). Projecting her deliberate decision as a fall from grace, the trope of "sin" exposes the seduced while covering up the seducer. Accordingly, the daughter's interjection ("Oh, don't, mother! Please don't tell me any more" [188]) masks her father and causes the mother to choke on her sexual history (189). This tendency itself has turned into a tradition: up to this very day African American literary texts privilege the pain of struggle, trauma, and survival over the pleasures of desire and sexuality.

Unlike Jacobs's *Incidents*, Keckley's *Behind the Scenes* relates an instance of rape and performs a paradigmatic displacement in the process. The second chapter of the book, entitled "Girlhood and Its Sorrows," reduces a history of sexual assault to these remarks: "I was regarded as fair-looking for my race, and for four years a white man—I spare the world his name—had base designs upon me. I do not care to dwell upon this subject, for it is one fraught with pain. Suffice it to say, that he persecuted me for four years, and I—I—became a mother" (39). The awkward repetition of the "I" transports multiple meanings: it renders the ambivalence accompanying the confession, the "duplication" in pregnancy, and the split of the person affected by sexual violation. As a kind of stuttering it also underscores that American culture lacks an appropriate term for sexual violence against the enslaved. As the phrase "I do not care to dwell" echoes an almost identical formulation elsewhere, in the language that concludes a detailed description of stripping and brutally violent whipping, the passage also suggests that physical torture dislocates, in fact anticipates, the sexual violation. As the narration of both sexual violence and physical torture employs the same device of silence, rape and rope become curiously linked to one another.

In addition, this rhetorical analogy between rape and torture highlights that "rape has historically been easiest to prove when it is most nearly identical with battery and mayhem" (Ferguson, "Rape" 90). Figuring as torture, rape becomes in part legible, even if in translation only. Like the pregnancy that turns Charlotte's body into a signifier, the wounds that torture imprints on the slave body are part of a modern semiotics of the body. Hardened and "healed" into scars, such wounds, inflicted by "the keen lash that cuts deep into . . . flesh" (Keckley 34), turn into traces of violation that—signifying lack of privacy as well as the economic value of the enslaved—mark racial difference.[40] At the same time, the analogy of rape and whipping "neutralizes" the particular "wrongs, and sufferings, and mortifications" of the female slave (Jacobs 77) while recognizing the slave as a "pained body or a body in need of punishment" (Hartman 552).

Interestingly enough, both Olaudah Equiano and Douglass in turn dramatize the cruelties of slavery by focusing, as Henry Louis Gates puts it, on "a few vivid scenes of sadism and sexual abuse practiced by white masters and mistresses against black women" (*Classic Slave Narratives* xv). Such scenes thus mark the distinct function physical violence serves in the construction of an African American gender identity. Unlike Jacobs's self-conception, which builds upon a maternal lineage of moral strength, that of Douglass depends upon his mother's physical endurance. Likewise his heroic Madison Washington experiences the shooting of his wife as an agony that triggers his rebellion. Thus unlike Keckley, whose narrator endures her physical pains "like a statue" (34), yet seemingly en passant, Douglass "situated the image of the victimized—often 'whipped'—female body at the emotional center of his critique of slavery," and, as Jenny Franchot points out, "acquired his virile autonomy somewhat at her expense" (141, 143). As a consequence black male subjectivity came to depend to a certain degree on (black) women's violation and victimization by a system that registered, as Hartman puts it, "black *and* female difference . . . by virtue of the extremity of power operating on captive bodies" (544). And this gender difference is further reinforced when—in Jean Toomer's *Cane*, Claude McKay's "The Harlem Dancer," and Wright's *Native Son*, for instance—the invocation of black women's suffering constitutes black male subjectivity.

Significantly enough, Keckley deploys the same silence she uses to align rape with torture in order to frame references to her (black) husband, a man she remembers as "trouble," "a burden instead of a helpmate" (63). "With the simple explanation that I lived with him eight years," she pleads, "let charity draw around him the mantle of silence" (50). Unwilling "to share his degradation," she calls him a "[p]oor man" who "had his faults, but over these faults death has drawn a veil. My husband is now sleeping in his grave, and in the silent grave I would bury all unpleasant memories of him" (64). This particular silence on the part of black women authors insinuates that the "rough 'equality' of powerlessness" slavery imposed upon African Americans (Foner, *Reconstruction* 87) coexisted with a substantial amount of gender trouble.[41] Owing to their political agenda, such trouble finds little reflection in early African American autobiography and fiction. To my knowledge, Petry is the first black female author who makes intraracial domestic and sexual violence a prominent issue in her work and takes issue with the racialized construction of sexuality and gender, established to a substantial degree by antebellum literary texts. These texts cast both white and black femininity in terms of property relations and physical violation. The crucial racial difference is that only black womanhood seems immune to such violation: her injuries become negligible, and her rape finds no retribution. Black femaleness, so Hartman puts it, is engendered "as a condition of unredressed injury" (556).

THE DEPLOYMENT OF SEXUAL VIOLENCE AND THE "CULT OF SECRECY": HISTORICIZING THE FEMINIST RHETORIC OF RAPE

The rhetoric of rape I have so far described has been both reinforced and reconfigured in the meantime, and in the following chapters I will delineate in what ways. Why, we may wonder, have current feminist debates around rape and sexual violence revitalized some of the discourse as well as the silences kept in late-eighteenth- and nineteenth-century literary texts? And to what effect?

Late-eighteenth-century seduction novels reconstructed women's economic, legal, and political powerlessness as social difference and figured this difference in biological or bodily tropes. The reinforcement of such social difference by part of contemporary feminist discourse in turn tends to reinstall a sense of woman's biological destiny and her powerlessness in the face of the law. In her "Reflections on Sex Equality under Law" (1991), for instance,

MacKinnon convincingly argues that even though women have meanwhile achieved legal equality with men, this transformation of women's difference into sameness could not eradicate their "lived sex inequality" because it did not address and thus perpetuated women's social inequality (376). It is this subordinate social status, MacKinnon insists, and not woman's biological disposition, that makes her prone to sexual violation. The fact that "[m]en can be raped" but women are "the overwhelming numbers . . . in the rape victim population," she argues, "expresses inequality, not biology" ("Sex Equality" 383).

While MacKinnon's legal analysis—which is oftentimes ignored in quick dismissals of her work—persuasively shows how the "legal sex equality theory" continues to discriminate against women, especially with regard to matters of sexuality and reproduction,[42] some of her sweeping claims generated along the way have damaged the argument as a whole. MacKinnon's sense that all "intercourse under conditions of unequal power" (370) amounts to the simple facts that "[m]en . . . harass and rape women," and "[w]omen are raped and coerced into sex" ("Sex Equality" 383, 387) not only makes female sexuality a utopian project. To argue, as MacKinnon and Dworkin do, that in a "heterosexist society" consent for women is simply impossible[43] may be theoretically consistent. At the same time such claims disenfranchise and infantilize woman and relocate her in the space she occupied in antebellum literature, a space characterized by unconsciousness, silence, lack of knowledge and subject position. Insisting that "[t]o be rapable, a position that is social not biological, defines what a woman is" (MacKinnon, *Feminist Theory* 178)—or that "[t]o be a means to the end of the sexual pleasure of one more powerful is, empirically, a degraded status and *the female position*" ("Sex Equality" 379, my emphasis)—MacKinnon means to de-essentialize female difference. Practically, rhetorically, she reinforces women's reification. Arguing that "[s]exual violation symbolizes and actualizes women's subordinate social status to men" (379), MacKinnon acknowledges using sexual violence as a metaphor. As she reduces women's social inequality to sexual vulnerability, she also aligns her argument with the moral message of the eighteenth-century seduction tale. Moreover, by personifying sexuality—"[i]n traditional gender roles," she states, "male sexuality embodies the role of aggressor, female sexuality the role of victim" (380)—MacKinnon dissociates sexuality from its agents and social contexts. Overdetermined by race and class, these contexts usually do not separate social inequalities into male dominance and female subordination as neatly as MacKinnon's rhetoric does.[44]

As they foreground aspects of sexual violence that parts of feminism prefer to ignore, early American novels at times touch upon a sense of female subjectivity that seems more consistent with contemporary women's lives. As the seduction narrative identifies rape as a crime on the level of mental states, it forces us to rethink easy alliances of heterosexual intercourse and rape and to refocus on the psychology of consent and nonconsent. For not unlike early

rape law, which meant to solve interpretative dilemmas by replacing the psychic dimension of rape by the "intense formality" of ages of consent and intention (Ferguson, "Rape" 93), rape-crisis discourse abolishes ambiguity by redrawing rigid gender divisions. Whereas the literary texts raise but do not
care to answer the question of consent, instead focusing on the net result of
supposedly biological imbalances, MacKinnon makes consent irrelevant by
redefining all sexuality as sexual violence. Critics of antirape rhetoric, by contrast, suggest that instances of emotional brutality may be more disturbing
than actual physical sexual violence (Gaitskill 267) and rape possibly "less
disturbing than any number of consensual sexual experiences" (Taubin 173).
While such propositions may seem to be yet another denial of rape that affirms
the perspective of Dworkin and MacKinnon, they also insist that women who
have experienced both sexual intercourse and rape are able to differentiate
between the two. Just like late-eighteenth-century literary texts, they under-
score that such distinctions are not a matter of physical mechanics but depend
upon women's own sense of subjectivity and sexuality.

The attempts on the part of some feminists "to legislate ambivalence out
of sex" (Gaitskill 263), by contrast, have revitalized the more traditional
lines of these narratives. As fallen women, subsequently labeled "unwed
mothers," continue to draw national attention, the dominant take on the issue
rings familiar bells. "We must tell our children," Bill Clinton recommended,
"not to have children until they are married and prepared to be good parents."[45] *Boston Globe* (feminist) columnist Ellen Goodman even suggested
the application of statutory rape laws to fight the sexual abuse that to her
mind has caused the rise in teenage pregnancies, thus enhancing a position
shared by MacKinnon.[46] At this point in American history, it is still more
appealing to criminalize adolescent sexuality than to wonder whether the
seeming problem (premarital pregnancies) and its supposed solutions (marriage or legal action) relate to a historically consistent denial of women's
subject position and sexuality.

We have to acknowledge antirape discourse as the historically necessary response to the various forms of violence against women that have been ignored
or accepted by society for so long. However, as Biddy Martin puts it, "the
stress on victimization suffers strategic and theoretical limitations insofar as
it reproduces, at least implicitly, the notion of women's passivity and suggests
the presence of an essential and as yet undiscovered female eroticism. It is an
emphasis which does not get beyond the discursive limitations and manipula-
tions of the object of its attacks" (280). Tending to reduce sexuality to the
violation of women by men, contemporary American feminist discourse on
sexuality and sexual violence—and this goes for Roiphe as well as for MacKinnon[47]—has little to say about female pleasure; even less maybe than the early
American novel, which recognizes woman's desire for gaiety, entertainment,
and distraction, for flirtation, pleasure, and—yes, indeed: sex.

At the same time, both the antirape movement and its opponents have given leeway to male sexuality. If male sexual aggression is seen as a natural given, as both MacKinnon and Camille Paglia see it,[48] why be surprised if men themselves think that is what American manhood is all about? Punishing the villainous rake as severely as his hapless victim and reforming him in a process of guilt-ridden survival and suffering, the novel of seduction, by contrast, reminds us that sexually aggressive masculinity is in fact a more recent invention. Just as women had to be instructed into Victorian notions of femininity, the recon-struction of masculinity as economic, political, *and* physical dominance did not come naturally. Intent on controlling male sexuality, the feminist turn to nineteenth-century views is itself an effect of the postbellum drift of remascu-linization that shifted the rhetoric of sexual violence from female to male body. While in this process masculinity was associated with (sexual) passion and ag-gression, sexual violence (against white women) was simultaneously being pro-jected, in literary texts and in contexts of racial conflict, on black men.

This continuous displacement of sexual violence gave ample reason for Afri-can American feminism to retain the veil that Keckley's narrative carefully draws over intraracial gender conflicts. As a consequence black feminism has remained marginal to the dominant antirape movement, whose (explicit or implicit) critique of (black) machismo appeared to reinforce the so-called myth of the black rapist. Instead, African American women historians and feminist critics relentlessly frame the debate of rape within the history and legacy of slavery, emphasizing the violation of both women and men. While there is no denying the impact of slavery and its legacy for American culture, in the context of current debates on sexual violence this repeated emphasis on historical heritage is as ahistorical as the revival of victimized womanhood.

Voices that break the self-imposed "cult of secrecy" sound most clearly in nonacademic African American contexts whose interest is (sexual) politics rather than political and "sexual correctness." Gillespie, for instance, in her article "In the Matter of Rape," published in *Essence* in 1992, bluntly claims that

> within our community, that particular four-letter word only seems to draw our outrage when the penis being wielded like a sword is white and the victim Black, or vice versa. Then rape becomes a race issue, conjuring up ugly stories of women raped on slave ships and in cotton fields, plantation houses and slave cabins. They stir memories of the evil days of Jim Crow and night riders and robe-wearing Ku Kluxers, of innocent men accused, imprisoned, castrated, lynched, and women abducted, of no justice.

Yet while Gillespie, emphasizing that "[i]nterracial rape is the exception, not the rule" (60),[49] wants African Americans to become "incensed about the cold facts about rape in our community," she undermines her argument by "con-juring up" a supposedly unified black community. This term, however, does not denote a homogeneity among African Americans or the intactness of black families but reflects the history of racial segregation and its imperatives (McDowell 85), which has discouraged the discussion of intraracial gender and class conflicts. This tendency persists even in a context that, like Gillespie's text, calls for such distinctions.

While the return to a nineteenth-century inventory of the feminine allows current feminist discourse to refocus on, while also "rearresting," the female body, contemporary literary texts reengage that body in their own ways. Whereas radical feminism deplores the distortion of both male and female sexuality as an effect of hierarchical power relations and aims at legal changes, contemporary literary texts explore the complexities of these relations (for which rape may be a trope), as well as the power of an established rhetoric of rape. Highly ironic at times, they thus challenge the very rhetoric that informs feminism, foregrounding how discourses of sexuality and sexual violence are inextricably entangled and how American culture frequently addresses matters of sexuality by way of sexual violence. While black feminists tend to veil intraracial sexual violence, rape-crisis discourse continues to identify male subjectivity with sexual aggression, and "postfeminism" invokes the occasional "decent guy," contemporary literary texts—so I show in chapter 4—interrogate masculinity.

To be sure: I do not mean to suggest that analyses of American manhood will simply undo the common iconography that is constantly being reinforced on a larger cultural and political scale. They do make us more aware, though, of how we are produced by as well as reproduce such imagery, thus enabling us to challenge the commonplace and counterbalance what critics of rape-crisis discourse polemically call an "iron-fisted denial of complexity and ambiguity" (Gaitskill 264). For just as the seduction metaphor tends to reduce a range of consensual and nonconsensual sexual acts—including illicit intercourse, sexual harassment, and rape—to one single narrative, dominant rape-crisis discourse lumps together under the label of rape a series of acts such as consensual heterosexual intercourse, consensual sexual violence, and acquaintance and stranger rape, as well as verbal coercion and representations of sexual violence[50]—acts that need to be clearly differentiated lest actual violence be trivialized.

This deployment of rape as a master trope of (female) violation by patriarchy, I would like to suggest, has been triggered in part by the constructions of race, gender, and sexuality effected at the turn of the twentieth century and still operating now. To a considerable degree it has also been encouraged by modernist discourse and its own deployment of the figure of rape, which at the same time challenges the relation of rape and representation in hitherto unknown ways. Before I address these modernist paradigms in chapter 3, I trace the evolution of the dominant "realist" rhetoric of rape from a series of novels—realist, naturalist, and sentimental fiction, as well as racist romances—

that employ the figure of the (black) rapist and a "rapist" rhetoric, both of which function distinctly in each. As the focus within the rhetoric of rape shifts from the female to the male body, the "veil" or "mantle of silence" that authors such as Jacobs and Keckley drew over the subject of black masculinity is violently torn, the blanks they left gaping filled with wild images of bestial dark male creatures with uncontrollable sexual desires. Such images, of course, did not come out of the blue. They mark a particular moment in the history of gender, race, and nation, a moment that generated the dominant line within the American rhetoric of rape, informing American readings of rape to this very day.

—〰—

The Rise of the (Black) Rapist and the Reconstruction of Difference; or, "Realist" Rape

THOMAS NELSON PAGE's 1898 novel *Red Rock: A Chronicle of Reconstruction* calls its sexual violator Doctor Moses and casts him—a "trick doctor" and savage leader of freed blacks—as a satanic seducer, "bowing and halting with that peculiar limp" and reminiscent "of a species of worm" (254). Obviously Page's portrayal defines racial difference in terms of physique, which figures ambiguously as both phallic masculinity and powerlessness. Transforming Uncle Tom into a violent sex offender, American turn-of-the-century culture thus retains an oppositional logic and reduces blackness to what Robyn Wiegman appropriately calls "extreme corporeality" ("Anatomy" 455).[1] Significantly enough, this logic still governs images of black masculinity. It clearly shows, for instance, in the current prominence of the gangsta rapper and the black diva, two polar, and yet, as Andrew Ross argues, dialectically linked theatrical postures. These postures can be traced back to their "originals," which emerged from late-nineteenth-century political, economic, and social constraints and transformations.

The (re)construction of blackness was generated, as I argue, by various—literary as well as legal—cultural practices that reinterpreted postbellum American history and eventually canceled out Reconstruction politics. These cultural practices undid black emancipation so "successfully" because they translated Southern struggles over political and economic supremacy into emotionally charged narratives of sexuality and gender. More specifically, since (re)constructions of blackness work predominantly through a racialization of sexuality, they directly engage in remasculinization[2] and constructions of sexuality that figure distinctly in realist and naturalist texts, in racist romances as well as in African American literary counterdiscourse. Since the turn-of-the-century crisis of masculinity is also a crisis of national identity, the conflict of a nation that felt robbed of its virility, the rise of the black rapist is inextricably intertwined with processes of national identity formation and the anxieties that inform them.

The so-called myth of the black rapist—the image of the oversexed and bestial African American man—is by no means exclusively a postbellum phenomenon.[3] In the 1840s, for instance, proponents of slavery insisted "that the

descendants of Ham had overdeveloped sexual organs and were the original
Sodomites of the Old Testament" (Fredrickson 276), thereby also acknowledging the homophobic and homoerotic dynamic that informs projections of racialized sexuality. At the time, though, such views of black masculinity were
still tempered by abolitionist rhetoric as well as a preoccupation with the female body. The rise to prominence of that "moral monster," as Douglass cynically has it, "ferociously invading the sacred rights of woman and endangering
the home of the whites" (495), according to Genovese, became an obsession
only after emancipation. It marks a significant change in the American rhetoric
on body and sexuality and a moment in American cultural history that generated notions of difference still current today. It is this rhetoric and the complex
cultural processes it negotiates that center my readings here.

While scientific racism was highly effective in engendering the figure of the
oversexualized (black) beast, literary texts mediate the complexities involved
in the struggles around hierarchies of race, class, gender, sexuality, and nation
that converge in this figure. Fiction couches political, economic, and gender
conflicts in conclusive narratives and wraps racism and xenophobia in the garb
of historical romance and realism. Significantly enough, naturalist novels like
Frank Norris's *McTeague* (1899) and Upton Sinclair's *The Jungle* (1906), realist
texts such as Edith Wharton's *The House of Mirth* (1905) and William Vaughn
Moody's *A Sabine Woman* (1906), as well as racist revisions of Reconstruction,
such as Page's *Red Rock* and Thomas Dixon's *The Clansman* (1905), neatly
cooperate in this project. As they resituate crucial conflicts within the American imaginary, thereby transforming it, they also expose the complex cultural
work achieved by projections of demonized masculinity and racialized sexuality—projections contested wholeheartedly, yet to little avail, by African American authors such as Frances E. W. Harper and Sutton E. Griggs. Relying on
figural mediation, they furthermore dramatize the cultural anxieties that inhabit these projections and establish what became a dominant line within
the American rhetoric of rape. The continuing effectiveness of that rhetoric,
confirmed by feminism itself, illustrates "that the metaphors that still govern
our beliefs about gender at the end of the twentieth century were born at the
turn of the nineteenth" (Rotundo 294).

Deeply engaged in the (re)construction of racial difference, this rhetoric
builds upon its antebellum precursors and itself becomes the frame of reference for modernist and post-modernist (re-)presentations of sexual violence.
Working mainly through realist and naturalist texts, its "success" results from
the cultural functions these fictions serve within the shift from Victorianism
to modernism, a shift that involved fundamental symbolic as well as economic
and political transformations.[4] Whereas the novel of seduction, the domestic
novel, and the slave narrative, focused as they are on the transition of family
structures, offer inside perspectives on economic and epistemological changes
and provide models for human agency, postbellum fiction aims at making

experience and understanding consensual. Interrogating aspects of human experience that were previously taboo, including sexual aggression, realist (and
naturalist) literary practices negotiate an altered social reality in order to reestablish cultural coherence. Far from being "the masculine discourse par excel-
lence," Fluck argues, "a discourse . . . of the battle-field and the boxing-ring"
("Masculinization" 73), "the school of hard knocks, in short . . . the Mike
Tyson of literary history" (74), realism instead evolves "ongoing processes of
communication and interaction" (73–74), "a rhetorical strategy designed to
support a cultural claim for authenticity and authority" (71).[5]

Curiously enough, by evoking infamous Mike Tyson in this context, Fluck
retains the bias against realism he means to do away with and circumscribes
the common (modernist) critique of realism's supposed lack of technique, its
reduction of style (which is Tyson's very trademark). At the same time Tyson
brings to mind the infamous other of this era's literature, the figure of the
sexual violator looming large in turn-of-the-century texts as diverse as Norris's
McTeague, Dixon's *Clansman*, and Wharton's *House of Mirth*. Why, however,
the centrality of the figure of the black rapist, the dark villain? And what is his
office in texts by Wharton or Moody? The following readings evolve the black
rapist as a complex figure of manifold and long-lasting cultural effects.
Throughout, this figure marks class difference and is juxtaposed to images of
femininity that reinforce Victorian ideals. As a consequence, realist and naturalist texts have reduced both (female) sexuality and (male) sexual violence to
the representation of particular bodies (like that of the adulteress, the prostitute, the rapist), to marginal races, alien ethnicities, and "inferior" classes.
Accordingly, just as the new "scandalous" understanding of female sexuality
is frequently couched—as in the work of Kate Chopin, for instance—in the
context of an "other" ethnicity, sexual violence and aggressive sexuality remain
limited to the realms of the working class and ethnic or racial minorities.[6]

"BLACK CLAWS INTO SOFT WHITE THROAT" AND OTHER BESTIALITIES: RAPIST RHETORIC, RIVALRY, AND HOMOSOCIAL DESIRE IN THOMAS NELSON PAGE'S *RED ROCK*, THOMAS DIXON'S *THE CLANSMAN*, AND FRANK NORRIS'S *MCTEAGUE*

In the course of Reconstruction, black men turned from chattel to citizenry,
achieved cultural visibility, (limited) political presence, and economic power,
as well as some social equality, which manifested itself, for instance, in the
exchange of white women across the color line. In fact, as the ultimate manifes-
tation of equality, miscegenation or amalgamation became the central taboo.
Novels such as Page's *Red Rock* that make use of miscegenation to defend racial
discrimination are consequently key texts: there the sexual violator's main ambition is to prove that he is "jest as good as any white man" by "marry[ing] a
white 'ooman and meck white folks wait on me" (291). The fear that the

emancipation of African American men provoked thus results less from racial difference, Wiegman argues, than from gender equality ("Anatomy" 450). This equality is quite different from the "sexual likeness" of black and white men that Montesquieu proposed in 1750 and which underlay the black male body as an object of representation in early abolitionist writings (Saillant 405, 409–10). In antebellum America, this emphasis on physical likeness asserted racial difference as gender difference. The postbellum recognition of black and white men's gender sameness, by contrast, proposes an identity beyond corporeality and based on political and economic equality (notwithstanding the fact that such equality did not become social reality).

In order to preserve Anglo-Saxon supremacy, as Walter Benn Michaels argues, Reconstruction and its aftermath transformed the economic hierarchies of antebellum slaveholding America into the racial difference of segregationist postbellum society ("Souls"). In this way, the distance between black and white was both retained and naturalized, just as the late eighteenth and early nineteenth centuries had naturalized gender polarities. In postbellum American culture, these processes of naturalization overlap, and gender difference is further overdetermined by race and ethnicity. Though involving white and black female and male bodies, the central trigger of these processes is the black male body, which ceased to function as a (feminized) other in a sentimentalized homoeroticized male *communitas* (Saillant 403). Late-nineteenth-century racism instead reasserts racial difference by insisting upon black male sexual difference. This (re)feminization of the black body is dramatized by a complex plotting of rape and lynching that excludes the alleged rapist from the community—in Page's, Dixon's, and Griggs's narratives he is forced to leave town—and culminates in actual or symbolic castration.[7]

The effectiveness of the claim that an increasing number of white women were sexually assaulted by black men—a claim that has repeatedly been proven false[8]—affirms the crucial cultural function of rape rhetoric and its reiteration through fiction. In African American literature the paradigm of rape and lynching generated a tradition that—from the mid–nineteenth century on—has tended to mark the black male as the main target of racial subjection. Postbellum racist fiction, by contrast, geared to assert racial difference as sexual difference in order to disavow gender likeness, reproduces the tension between likeness and difference that underlies the logical structure of identity formation and lays bare its mechanisms. Displacing the postrevolutionary "dialectic between the view of the black man as an alien and the view of the black man as a sentimental friend" (Saillant 407) by the paradoxical image of the emasculated black sexual violator, this process exposes the homoerotic tensions infusing racial conflicts and engenders a sense of black masculinity that signifies both racial *and* sexual otherness.

The novels of Page and Dixon project this double difference in order to prove Reconstruction to be history gone wrong. Resting on the theory of racial retrogression, which assumes blacks to have relapsed further into primitivism after the controlling force of slavery was abolished,[9] they scapegoat African Americans for all political and economic tensions of the time. The "reign of terror," as Dixon calls the alleged "negro rule" during Reconstruction, is dominated by corruption, overboard taxation, and theft—misdemeanors that supposedly reflect black man's uncivilized and criminal nature and culminate in his supposedly irrepressible lust for white women. Accordingly, rape finds its first "realist" representations in racist novels, where it drives a complex cultural narrative.

Clearly juxtaposing black rapist and white bodyguard, fragile white woman and promiscuous black wretch, rape narratives fulfill multiple functions. They translate an economic crisis into sexual and gendered terms, redefine rape as "an attack on the integrity of the race,"[10] and create a means to contain the entire black community both psychologically and physically (Wiegman, "Anatomy" 456). As they assert the superiority of the Anglo-Saxon male, discourage white women's increasing "outgoingness," and reinforce gender conventions, they simultaneously serve remasculinization. Insofar as they involve lynching and other figures of castration, rape narratives also bespeak the subtexts of this process. The increasing use of castration as a means to mutilate African American men realigns the supposedly hypermasculine black body, as Wiegman points out, with "those still disenfranchised" (446), "literalizes his affinity to the feminine" (448). In this way, lynching and its cultural representation function both as a "disciplinary practice for racial control"[11] and as a "sexual encounter" (446) that evokes and disavows homoerotic desire.

The projected affinity between black male and white female bodies in turn remasculinizes the white male. At the same time, the reduction of blackness to extreme corporeality, to the literal, helps to recast white womanhood in spiritual and figural terms. Throughout *Red Rock*, for instance, Southern women embody the sacred element of the antebellum South. Likewise Dixon pictures his rape victim, Marion Lenoir—"the one human being that everybody had agreed to love" (254)—as an icon of common morality and social consensus. Where white women symbolize the South, their alleged violation mutilates the Southern body politic and signifies the "rape" of the South during Reconstruction.[12] Projecting Marion's ravishment as "a single tigerspring," as "black claws" sinking into a "soft white throat" (304), Dixon's rape scenario discloses this symbolic significance. In fact, it literalizes the author's metaphor for the postbellum South, which likens the conditions under "Negro rule" to "[t]he sight of the Black Hand on [Southern people's] throats" (276). The figure of the white woman thus displaces the complex relations between black and white men (Wiegman, "Anatomy" 462); her sacrifice "on the altar of outraged civilization" (Dixon 325) legitimizes retaliatory attacks. In this way rape triggers political change: the rise of the KKK, the destruction of

"Negro rule," and the reinforcement of Anglo-Saxon supremacy and true womanhood.

The chapter preceding the scene of Marion's rape both foreshadows and frames the assault, juxtaposing depictions of the victim's innocent beauty—her "exquisite figure had developed into the full tropic splendour of Southern girlhood" (284)—with images of "black violence" and instances of "Negro rule," such as overboard taxation (288). Sexual assault is thus quite literally cast as a robbery whose very nature legitimizes violent retaliation in a way tax legislation does not. As "four black brutes" forcibly enter the Lenoir home, Dixon at the same time plays upon his literary antecedents, including Shakespeare's *The Rape of Lucrece*,[13] the captivity narrative, and the Western.

> The door flew open with a crash, and four black brutes leaped into the room, Gus in the lead, with a revolver in his hand, his yellow teeth grinning through his thick lips.
>
> "Scream, now, an' I blow yer brains out," he growled.
>
> Blanched with horror, the mother sprang before Marion with a shivering cry:
> "What do you want?"
>
> "Not you," said Gus, closing the blinds and handing a rope to another brute. "Tie de ole one ter de bedpost."
>
> The mother screamed. A blow from a black fist in her mouth, and the rope was tied.
>
> With the strength of despair she tore at the cords, half rising to her feet, while with mortal anguish she gasped:
>
> "For God's sake, spare my baby! Do as you will with me, and kill me—do not touch her!"
>
> Again the huge fist swept her to the floor.
>
> Marion staggered against the wall, her face white, her delicate lips trembling with the chill of a fear colder than death.
>
> "We have no money—the deed has not been delivered," she pleaded, a sudden glimmer of hope flashing in her blue eyes.
>
> Gus stepped closer, with an ugly leer, his flat nose dilated, his sinister bead-eyes wide apart gleaming ape-like, as he laughed:
>
> "We ain't atter money!"
>
> The girl uttered a cry, long, tremulous, heart-rending, piteous.
>
> A single tiger-spring, and the black claws of the beast sank into the soft white throat and she was still. (303–4)

The primitivism of the black aggressor clashes with the preceding depictions of the chivalry of Marion's (white) admirer Ben Cameron and of delicate white womanhood. Just as the physical violation takes shape in tropes—the "crash" of the door, the "single tiger-spring," the women's "shivering" cries and screams[14] (echoed, during the capture of the rapist, by the clansmen's "single tremulous call like the cry of an owl" [316]), and the victim's unconsciousness—the victims obscure its traces by symbolic acts. Rape itself figures as defilement whose only "catharsis," keeping Marion's "name . . . sweet and clean" (305), is suicide. The notion that the violated body, a contaminated region, can be severed from the chaste mind and soul is integral, as Stephanie Jed points out, to Western thought (13). Just as Lucretia's rape was triggered by a chastity contest, Marion's innocence makes her particularly desirable. Likewise, as Lucretia kills herself to prove that chastity is more important to her than life itself, the Lenoirs take their own lives. And just as the legend of Lucretia's rape "mark[s] Rome's transition from [the tyranny of] monarchy to a republican form of government" (Jed 2), Dixon's paradigm of rape and suicide serves to legitimize the overturn of "Negro rule" by Anglo-Saxon supremacy.

And yet, of course, the text clearly marks its historical difference. No kinsman—or clansman, for that matter—tries to convince Marion that her violated body is inhabited by a chaste mind. Instead, "[t]he thought of life" becomes "torture," "the light of day a burning shame," making death appear "sweet," the "grave . . . soft and cool" (306). The figures of "torture" and "burning" mark the metonymic drive from female victimization to white men's retaliation and link rape with lynching. As the novel obscures the sexual violation and elaborates on the suicide instead, it affirms the common notion that rape is worse than death, yet also makes the victim at least partly responsible for her fate. By privileging the women's housecleaning activities and self-destruction over the sexual assault, the text metonymically displaces and metaphorically condenses the violation. Rape, Dixon suggests, both leads to and equals suicide. Read as both metaphor and metonymy, the paradigm of rape and suicide thus reaffirms the idea that rape is perpetrated by the victim. Eliminating the victim from its narrative, the novel moreover circumnavigates other consequences of rape, spares us the humiliations of psychic suffering and social death.[15]

At the same time Dixon's text doubles the severity of the crime by having it affect both mother and daughter. Accordingly, the Lenoirs take concerted action. In fact, they are portrayed as one entity prior to the assault and appear identical throughout the rape scene: when the mother is hit, the daughter staggers and echoes her mother's cry. Jumping off the cliff "hand in hand," they mirror each other's smiles (308). The mother dies dressing her daughter's wound, "her head resting on her fair round neck as though she had kissed her and fallen asleep" (311). As the women face death, a new "régime" dawns mistily in images of baptism and rebirth; the forces of fecundity, femininity, and divinity merge and generate the vague vision of a bright future, which justifies the clansmen's "hunt for the animal" (309). If read as synechdoche, rape becomes the figure "for the entire story: the rape and its consequence" (Bal, "Reading" 143), which includes the victims' complicity in their own violation, the fate of the rapist, and this promising perspective. Accordingly, the mother's very posture ("her head resting . . .") curiously puts her in the rapist's position. After all, it was she who heard the intruders approach, "leaping to her feet" (303), thus anticipating both the rapist's "single tiger-spring" and the clansmen's later leap at Gus, which in turn echoes the rape and reveals its homoerotic subtext. This explains why it is the mother's eye/I that reflects the sexual aggressor. Given the Lenoir women's figurative identity, this union of victim and violator reaffirms the dominant ideology of rape: the notion that the victim is responsible for her own violation.

This ideology underwrites Dixon's rape narrative as well as the conventions of true (Southern) womanhood this narrative reconfirms. In fact, the novels of Page and Dixon employ the threat of black assault to teach emancipated women an old lesson and thereby redistribute public space. Marion is raped right after the Lenoirs turned down Ben Cameron's offer to be their body-guard. Accordingly, during the capture of Gus, Reverend McAlpin complains that while "the heathen walks his native heath unharmed and unafraid, in this fair Christian Southland, our sisters, wives, and daughters dare not stroll at twilight through the streets. . . . The terror of the twilight deepens with the darkness, and the stoutest heart grows sick with fear for the red message the morning bringeth" (319). On their way to the cliff, the Lenoirs themselves recall walking through the woods "with reverent feet and without fear" (306). Meanwhile, as a contemporaneous editorial in the Atlanta *Constitution* put it, "women and girls . . . live in practically a state of seige," "afraid to venture to a neighbor's or a school house lest some black beast shall leap from the bushes and give them over to a fate worse than death" (qtd. in Hoffman 232). Re-conceiving public space as dangerous territory, Southern discourse reinscribes the limits Victorianism set on women's mobility,[16] even if it pleads for their physical freedom and implicit political participation, legitimizing lynchings under a pretense of female emancipation: "As the world is to be made safe for democracy, so ought the South be made free for white women" (Collins 65). The scandal is, according to Dixon, that Southern women are not safe even in their own homes (300).

In *Red Rock*, by comparison, lustful Doctor Moses scares no Southern maiden but the Northern abolitionist Ruth Welch—signpost of the Recon-structionist "world turned upside down" (O'Brien 155) where blacks rule over whites, women act like men, and miscegenation thrives. Proving "philanthro-pists" wrong, critics of Reconstruction right, this choice serves the political allegory well. Page presents no rape, though, but a close encounter between Ruth and Moses, dramatized as a rape attempt that allows Steve Allen—cham-pion of the dethroned antebellum aristocracy, leader of the local KKK, and knight in shining armor—to come to Ruth's rescue. Riding out unaccompa-nied, self-reliant Ruth had repeatedly "declined, with much coolness" Allen's "request to be allowed to escort her" (249). Paying no heed to his warnings and outraged that he "issue[d] orders to her" (253), she eventually finds herself caught on a dead-end with and Moses right behind her.

> The blood deserted Ruth's face. He [Moses] had always made her flesh creep, as if he had been a reptile. She had often found him on the side of the road as she passed along, or had turned and seen him come out of the woods behind her, but she had never been so close to him before when alone. And now to find herself face to face with him in that lonely place made her heart almost stop. After regarding her for a moment silently, the negro began to move slowly forward, bowing and halting with that peculiar limp which always reminded Ruth of a species of worm. She would have fled; but she saw in an instant that there was no way of escape. The bushes on either side were like a wall. The same idea must have passed through the man's mind. A curious smirk was on his evil face.
> "My Mistis," he said, with a grin that showed his yellow teeth and horrid gums.
> "The path seems to end here," said Ruth, with an effort commanding her voice.
> "Yes, my Mistis; but I will show you de way. Old Moses will show you de way. He-he-he." His voice had a singular feline quality in it. It made Ruth's blood run cold. (254)

In this version of Beauty and the Beast, Moses's bestiality remains inconsistent. Casting him as satanic seducer, the episode recontextualizes the Fall and foregrounds the bias against "disobedient" women and the Christian ideology that informs Southern history—the belief that "the apelike Negro was the actual 'tempter of Eve'" (Fredrickson 277). Depicted as wormlike cripple, Moses appears powerless and impotent, though—an impression reinforced by his pitiful performance during the skirmish that ensues. Blocking Ruth's way, Moses grabs hold of her bridle and drops it on her command before catching it again. Symbolically significant throughout the scene of "assault" and rescue, this bridle figures both Ruth's "unbridled" temper and her intact virginity. Giving "a snarl of rage," Moses "sprang at her like a wild beast; but her horse whirled and slung him from his feet." As he misses her yet tears her skirt, the text hints at the threat of a torn hymen (Page 254–55).

Throughout this scene Moses appears both brutish and cowardly: he is easily outwitted by Ruth's riding skills and "plunge[s] into the bushes" upon Allen's approach (255). Ruth's politics, in turn, is proven erroneous at one stroke. Sexually harassed by Moses, she physically experiences what it means to be "conquered," and thus cannot help but sympathize with the South. And while putting a single-minded woman in her place, the text gives Allen ample occasion to display chivalry and courage. His foresight legitimizes lynch justice and revitalizes patterns of paternalism. The white woman thus serves, so Wiegman writes, as a pivotal figure for shaping the mythology of both the black rapist and the white protector of civilization and property rights ("Anatomy" 461). At the same time, the rhetoric of rape wrests from women even their meager function as moral guardians. Accordingly, Ruth, who previously held her head "as high as Captain Allen's" (348), is significantly humbled. After the event, "it never occurred to her to oppose him" (360). Their marriage seals her conversion to the Southern cause, domesticates her personal and political ambitions, and symbolizes the reconciliation of North and South in the face of a common enemy.

The Clansman similarly figures the reunion of North and South by the trope of matrimony. Turning enemies into brothers, the (racist) historical romance thus not only monitors social integration and narrative closure. Like the historical novel it complements the history of individual characters with that of the nation and employs the patterns of courtship and marriage as a national metaphor (Fluck, "Masculinization" 73). More precisely, though, Dixon realigns, as Michaels argues, Northerners and Southerners on the basis of their white souls, thereby transcending political barriers, redefining racial difference, and serving segregation much more effectively than could scientific proof of racial inferiority. Making whiteness a spiritual matter helps to exclude even those (groups of immigrants) whose skins are white, yet whose souls are supposedly stained.[17] Harper, by contrast, proposes the identity of black and white souls: "When we have learned to treat men according to the complexion of their souls and not the color of their skins," her protagonist Iola Leroy claims, "we will have given our best contribution towards the solution of the negro problem" (212).

Dixon's white-soul symbology centers largely upon the white female body. The depiction of soiled Marion, for instance, privileges the immortal beauty of her soul over her body's fleeting charm. Though her clothes are torn to "shreds," her "blue eyes" still "shin[e] with a strange light" (305), displaying her soul's full radiance even after the "mystic light of maidenhood" has faded (307). This particular power of Southern womanhood can dispense with beautiful garments and thrives even in extremity (301–2). Accordingly, rape resembles a civil war raging upon women's bodies. Reconstruction, Dixon claims in his preface, was "the darkest hour of the life of the South . . . her wounded people . . . helpless amid rags and ashes under the beak and talon of the Vulture," when "suddenly from the mists of the mountains appeared a white cloud the size of a man's hand" (2). The dress that displaces Marion's "torn clothes"—"spotless white" and worn the very "night Ben Cameron kissed her and called her a heroine" (305)—corresponds to that white cloud, which itself figures the dawning of the KKK organized by Cameron.

The complex relations and power struggles between black and white men that got displaced onto the white female body come more clearly to the fore when we approach the racist historical romance by way of the naturalist novel. For significantly enough, the paradigm of the black rapist finds its counterpart in *McTeague*, which figures its protagonist's sexual awakening as the rise of his "brute," "other" self, emerging when his future wife Trina lies "absolutely without defense," anesthetized, "unconscious and helpless and very pretty" in his dentist chair (27). This parallelism between racist romance and naturalist novel reflects a certain, albeit limited, kinship in politics and aesthetics. Dixon's projections of black bestiality interrelate with Norris's portrayal of the masculine primitive, which reassesses physical power and lower-class life as parameters of true manhood and thus partly reverses the moral dichotomies that legitimate social hierarchies.[18] The likeness of Norris's and Dixon's beasts closely associates the masculine primitive with the savagery racist discourse deemed to be resulting from racial retrogression. Both authors draw upon the naturalist topos of the *bête humaine*, the image of xenophobic fears of cultural decline, and project their primitives as born criminal degenerates.[19] McTeague's abuse of alcohol, for instance, is considered a hereditary trait, "[t]he evil of an entire race flow[ing] in his veins" (29). Thus even though *McTeague* and *The Clansman* engage distinct politics, their portrayals of primitive masculinity similarly reinforce their agendas. This effect is enhanced by generic conventions both Norris and Dixon employ. Just like popular naturalism,[20] the racist romance fuses reality effects with moral analyses by articulating dominant ideologies. And just as Norris allies naturalism and romance, Dixon partakes in the renaissance of romance as a literature of liberated desires and masculine self-realization. The consistent recurrence of the masculine primitive—as, for instance, in feminist conceptions of male sexuality from Charlotte Perkins Gilman to Dworkin—attests to how strongly these narratives have taken hold of the cultural imaginary.

In McTeague we meet a man whose "mind was as his body, heavy, slow to act," a man "immensely strong, stupid, docile, obedient," rather than "vicious" (7), yet with "that intuitive suspicion of all things feminine—the perverse dislike of an overgrown boy" (22). Personified by Trina, "the feminine element," this "strange and alluring" power (25) bound to create "discord" (46), "entered his little world" and "tardily awakened" a "male, virile desire," "strong and brutal," "resistless, untrained, a thing not to be held in leash an instant" (25). Trina thus triggers McTeague's brutality, and he becomes a victim of circumstances. His "evil instincts" (27), "the sudden panther leap of the animal, lips drawn, fangs aflash, hideous, monstrous," as well as "the footprint of the monster" he fears to engrave on Trina's forehead (28), are all familiar to readers acquainted with racist texts. Projecting the brute as one-half of a whole being involved in a struggle fundamental to human existence, Norris stages the conflict between hero and beast as the struggle between two dimensions of manhood, between human and animal, white and black. And like Dixon, Norris thus locates sexual threat in the image of the outsider, the foreigner, the lower social caste.

Presenting McTeague's "crisis," the fight between animal and "better self" as "the old battle, old as the world" (28), Norris's text at the same time insinuates that (Dixon's) racialized other is not so other after all; that what is outside, alien, is also somehow internal, intimate, so that dominant culture polices the line between the two as vigilantly as it does just because it has always already been transgressed.[21] In fact, turn-of-the century novels draw the very lines that modernist texts prove untenable. By ascribing sexual aggression to others, they evoke and disavow aggressive sexuality as an element of remasculinized manhood while dressing it up in the garb of racial, ethnic, and class difference. Yet it is not simply that, as Paul Hoch argues, the hypersexualized black stud is "an unconscious projection of those aspects of [the racist's] own sexuality which society has made taboo" (54), "an *externalization* of a beast within who is, in another sense, an *internalization* of the repression without." Hoch's assumption that the actual castrations enacted during lynching rituals confirm "the psychic castration [the racist] himself has received" (56) presupposes a transhistorical self. *McTeague*, however, forces us to acknowledge the historicity pertaining to structures of identity formation.

The novel foregrounds that neither is the identity of the subject simply structured against difference nor is ethnicity "a scene of negation" entirely (Spillers, "Mama's Baby" 456). Instead, as Lloyd insists, the possibility of identity "depends on producing precisely the internal difference that threatens it" (260). Thus while "the psychic structure of racism to a large degree depends . . . on projection," it is "the *insistence* of" precisely that "difference internal to the constitution of identity which underlies the cultural logic of racism rather than either the return or the projection of repressed material" (260–61). In other words: the image of the black rapist or sexualized other figures the internal otherness upon which all constructions of identity rely, yet which takes historically specific cultural forms. Despite their structural likeness, Norris's "other self" and Dixon's black rapist thus function quite distinctly within a shared cultural narrative.

Having McTeague's better self win, Norris allows conscious will to triumph over animal instinct. (Dixon's black brute, belonging to the animal kingdom, knows no such battle.) McTeague becomes uncontrollably bestial, though, once his manhood is questioned or high quantities of alcohol awaken his "apelike agility" (288). As *McTeague* thus (re)constructs masculinity as a "continually" present (sexual) aggression, "tugging at its chain, watching its opportunity" (29), femininity in turn evolves as the desire to endure such aggression. Accordingly, as the main characters' sexual relations turn into eroticized patterns of abuse, the novel both registers and triggers transformations in the sex/gender system. At the same time, the text dramatizes the interdependence between sexual aggression and anxieties pertaining to (gender) identity. Conjoining male violence with women's empowerment (symbolized by Trina's economic superiority) and men's social competition (acted out in the relation between McTeague and Schouler), Norris's novel refigures dimensions of gender politics that inform racist romances as well. Focusing on relations between men, the text acknowledges remasculinization as an effect of what Eve Kosofsky Sedgwick calls the "crisis of homo/heterosexual definition" (*Epistemology* 1).

It is Trina's economic superiority and sexual autonomy, *McTeague* suggests—signpost of a sex/gender system out of bounds comparable to the upside-down world of Reconstruction—that cause her and her husband, representative of all other ethnic lowlifes, to stumble and fall. This new contingency between gender identity and economic power gets foreshadowed by the first closet scene, during which McTeague comes intimately close to his future wife as he invades her private space. After the "decisive" picnic at Schuetzen Park (66), the Sieppes invite Schouler and McTeague to stay overnight. As Trina "giv[es] up" her room to McTeague, the latter penetrates "his lady's bower," feeling "hideously out of place," "an intruder" with "crude, brutal gestures" (64). As he explores "her daily life, her little ways and manners, . . . her very thoughts," Trina's simple possessions stimulate his fantasies and recall the "confiding," "innocent," "infantile" woman he saw at their initial introduction (65). The scene climaxes—"he could hardly have been more overcome" (65)— when McTeague enters her closet and fondles the clothes as if they were her body and genitals.

> He went farther into the closet, touching the clothes gingerly, stroking them softly with his huge leathern palms. As he stirred them, a delicate perfume disengaged itself from the folds. Ah, that exquisite feminine odor! . . . the indescribably sweet, fleshly aroma that was a part of her, pure and clean and redolent of youth and freshness. All at once, seized with an unreasoned impulse, McTeague opened his huge arms and gathered the little garments close to him, plunging his face deep amongst them, savoring their delicious odor with long breaths of luxury and supreme content. (66)

The particular sensuality of the scene highlights how male desire and the ideals of female virtue interdepend. At the same time having McTeague penetrate Trina's "private parts," the novel stages an intense interplay of sexuality and economy, an economy of desire wherein greed and sexual "perversion" depend upon and figure each other. Though McTeague idealizes Trina's innocence, her true capital is not her virginity but her financial resources. Accordingly, the eroticized handling of female accessories feminizes McTeague, puts him in drag. The scene thus hints at "closeted" homoerotic desires, played out in the novel's many scenes of homosocial bonding and bodily conflict,[22] and foreshadows the economic and social failures that, in the course of the events, fundamentally compromise McTeague's gender identity. The very fact that McTeague eventually kills Trina in a closet at a kindergarten before returning to intense physical labor punctuates the "unnaturalness" of their "fruitless" alliance.

McTeague's aggressive sexuality is complemented by Trina's physical resistance, which, in addition to his conquest of her, proves him "a man of extraordinary ability" (71), capable of moving ahead in a universe of homosocial bonding. Unlike Charlotte Temple, who falters under Montraville's rhetoric, Trina withstands McTeague's "pleading—a mere matter of words" (70) yet succumbs to his physical strength and sexual lure. In fact, Trina's passion for McTeague is triggered by "the absolute final surrender of herself, the irrevocable, ultimate submission" that "merged her individuality into his" (145). Presenting this dynamic as "the changeless order of things—the man desiring the woman only for what she withholds; the woman worshipping the man for that which she yields up to him" (70), Norris's novel turns (hetero)sexuality into sadomasochistic power play and itself becomes "probably the first representation of masochism in American literature" (Michaels, *Gold Standard* 119). McTeague's use of physical force—the degree of which throughout the novel becomes a measure of masculinity—not only makes Trina give in fast; as her masochistic "second self" displaces her previously boyish, sexless nature, she also becomes keen on being brutalized. Her initial "intuitive feminine fear of the male" eventually "yield[s] . . . to that strange desire of being conquered and subdued" (Norris, *McTeague* 141, 141–42).

Presenting female desire as an effect of male aggression, Norris's fiction helps to generate what became the dominant model of heterosexuality, developed in the work of sexologists such as Havelock Ellis, Alfred Kinsey, and Masters and Johnson. Like Norris's naturalism, sexology presupposed a biologically inherent sex "drive" or "instinct" that is triggered by external stimuli and conditioned by social and cultural factors.[23] Its "hydraulic model" of sexuality reinforces the notion that male sexual desire "is either uncontrollable or, if repressed, causes neuroses or finds an outlet in sex crimes" (Jackson, "Sexology" 74)—assuming that the sexual drive of men surpasses, yet also complements, that of women. According to Ellis, the male sexual impulse is manifested in a "desire to pursue and conquer the female," while female sexual pleasure resides "in the pretence of resistance and . . . surrender to the male, perhaps after considerable persuasion or even physical force" (77). Reading this (im)balance as a biological fact, sexology made dominance and submission, power and violence, integral to common conceptions of heterosexuality, sexual "perversions" mere extensions of "normal" sexuality (80).

Resisting the conviction that violence informs all sexual activity, some feminists have in turn reduced male sexuality itself to "a 'perversion,' " as Margaret Jackson points out, that enforces male power (80). Thereby they even reject the plea (on the part of other feminists) for strong and active female sexualities because it supposedly replicates the dominant model of sexuality. Such views are debatable, though, since they fail to acknowledge that discourses of sexuality—including feminist versions of it—are historically constructed. Accordingly, with its claim that all heterosexuality amounts to rape, radical feminism reaffirms the very model of sexuality it means to dismantle. Likewise the belief that women's sexuality is nonaggressive by nature depends on the projection of an inherently aggressive male sexuality.

Norris's novel marks a particular moment in the history of sexuality. As the text employs sexual symbology to expose a "perverted" moral, social, and economic order, perversion gets located first and foremost in Trina's financial superiority and her increasing fixation on her little fortune, the growing physical excitement and sexual satisfaction she derives from toying with it. McTeague's "pleasure . . . in abusing and hurting her" rises in proportion (235), and the fetish objects (such as Trina's hairbrush) turn into instruments of torture (238–39). Most significant, though, is McTeague's strange habit of biting Trina's fingertips, "crunching and grinding them with his immense teeth," either to extort money from her or "for his own satisfaction." Arousing in her "a strange, unnatural pleasure in yielding," this practice reduces Trina's libido to "the passion for her money and her perverted love for her husband when he was brutal" (239). Greedily withholding her money, Trina also withholds her sexual services from McTeague, and once he disappears, money becomes her ultimate bedfellow: "One evening she had even spread all the gold pieces between the sheets, and had then gone to bed, stripping herself, and had slept all night upon the money, taking a strange and ecstatic pleasure in the touch of the smooth flat pieces the length of her entire body" (277). This scene (which recalls the narrative of Danaë ravished by Zeus disguised as a shower of gold) suggests that Trina's pleasure of ownership has displaced the passion aroused by McTeague's claims of ownership of her. Saving, as Michaels has it, has become "a kind of spending" (*Gold Standard* 141). Literalizing the interdependence of women's economic and sexual autonomy, Norris thus also projects the "perversion" of women's independence.

In this way the scene reflects back upon the significance of McTeague's sucking habit. As part of a persistent (phallic) symbolism that dramatizes castration anxieties, this habit suggests that (McTeague's) abusive behavior is symptomatic of a lack, not a surplus, of authority. Evidently, he targets the very body parts Trina employs to make her meager income (she whittles wooden toys). This correlation between McTeague's (sexual) violence and Trina's (economic) independence visualizes the threat inherent in the ongoing cultural transformation. Once (financial) power—as opposed to consensual gender roles—determines who is the "boss" (211), men are feminized, women masculinized. Accordingly, once McTeague withdraws sexually, Trina's hair turns into a "rat's nest," and she becomes a Medusa figure who deflects conventional femininity and amplifies McTeague's castration anxieties.

The key phrase expressing these fears—"[y]ou can't make small of me" (78)—echoes both during arguments with Trina (230) and when Schouler challenges McTeague at their local bar. Accordingly, the men's struggle capitalizes on two phallic objects. Infuriated by McTeague's lack of social graces, Schouler breaks his pipe and flings a jackknife past his head (113–14). Moments later, faced with the "golden wonder" purchased by Trina, "the Tooth—the famous golden molar," sign of his ambition and dream, McTeague is "over-powered" and "dwarfed" again: he "shrank and dwindled in the presence of the monster" (117), signpost of a dwindling Gilded Age, a corrupted American dream, and women's increasing potency. McTeague responds to these concerted blows with animal strength, tearing the sleeve off Schouler's shirt, biting his earlobe, and breaking his arm (180–85) or "making small" of Trina in the kindergarten closet in order to return to mine work and reanimate his manhood.

The continuous triangulation of McTeague's, Trina's, and Schouler's fates expose the crisis of homo/heterosexual definition that underlies and informs the cultural climate of remasculinization. Schouler—"the dentist's one intimate friend" (11)—drops in, for instance, when Trina desires McTeague to "[l]ove [her] big" (196). Keeping company with, yet not desiring, women, he is akin to Sedgwick's bachelor types. In fact, in an act of "heroic" generosity proving "[w]hat a fine thing was this friendship between men" (48), Schouler gives away Trina, the paradigmatic object of exchange and communication device, in a contract that "suddenly increased" "[t]heir mutual affection and esteem" "enormously" and allies Schouler and McTeague "for life or death" indeed. Right after this transaction Schouler reaffirms his superiority, though, cramming a billiard ball into his mouth "with a sudden, horrifying distension of his jaws" (49), challenging McTeague to do likewise. Following Schouler's lead, the latter makes "a veritable scene" as he tries to remove the ball and reaffirms his distance in the very scene of doubling (50). Stressing the characters' oral fixation and tendency to regress, this episode conjoins the drive of remasculinization ("having balls") with both an increased homosociality and (the disavowal of) homoeroticism.

In *The Clansman* this homoerotic subtext comes insistently to the fore as the rapist gets identified in the course of two curious experiments. Proclaiming "that nothing is lost from the memory of man," (witch) doctor Cameron traces photographic memory in his patients' eyes (313), enlarging on the retina of the victim's mother "the bestial figure of a negro" with "huge black hand" and "massive jaws and lips," the reflection of the violator Gus (313, 314). Suspecting that the image is in his father's eye, not in that of the woman (314), Cameron's son Ben, however, disqualifies the experiment as a projection and suggests that difference is internal to the viewer's identity. In a second experiment, witnessed by a group of clansmen, Cameron therefore manipulates Gus into reexperiencing the rape scene under hypnosis, to which fearful black men are believed to be particularly susceptible (213). Fear, however, dominates not so much the suspect as the clansmen themselves. As Gus rehearses his assault, "[s]trong men began to cry like children" (323). Afraid to lose their identity, to be emasculated, they "nervously grip . . . the revolvers" for reassurance (322). At the same time, the clansmen's "groans, sobs and curses" (323) echo the black man's primitive rhetoric. Provoked by Gus's ape-man performance, they manifest an agitation that mirrors his fury. One of them even reenacts Gus's final leap, "springing on the negro and grinding his heel into his big thick neck"; "[a] dozen more were on him in a moment, kicking, stamping, cursing, and crying like madmen" (323–24). "Some of the white men," the narrator adds, "had fallen prostrate to the ground, sobbing in a frenzy of uncontrollable emotion. Some were leaning against the walls, their faces buried in their arms." Gus in turn mirrors them as he is "bound, blindfolded, gagged and [likewise] thrown to the ground" (324).

This loss of control—a clear instance of male hysteria[24] and homosexual panic—culminates a scene of transgression, whose interplay of otherness and intense mirroring uncannily suggests a temporary breakdown of the barrier between self and other, the collapse of supremacist identity, and exposes the crisis of homo/heterosexual definition. This is no triumph of civilization over nature, nor is it the return of taboo sexuality, as Hoch has it (48, 54). As Gus reenacts the rape scene, homoerotic voyeurism surfaces, acknowledging the rapist as a figure of identification, an object of homoerotic desire, and, like Marion Lenoir, a medium of the disavowal of such desire upon which homosocial societies depend. Symbolically, this scene takes the place of the lynching scenario that the novel withholds—the scenario that, according to Wiegman, marks the limit of the homosexual/heterosexual binary and transforms the heterosexuality of the black assaulter into "a violently homoerotic exchange" ("Anatomy" 466).

The need to retain that binary partly explains why it is not the black rapist but Lydia Brown—the oversexualized mulatto mistress and housekeeper of Austin Stoneman, architect of radical Reconstruction—who emerges as the ultimate evil of postbellum politics. Stoneman, who "followed her catlike eyes[,] was steadily gripping the Nation by the throat," we are told (94). As Phil Stoneman confesses, commenting on his father's politics: "I believe the tawny leopardess who keeps his house influences him in this cruel madness. I could wring her neck with exquisite pleasure" (162–63). Most significant here is the recurrence of the novel's central image of rape, which presents both Stoneman and his son as sexual violators. But whereas the former enacts the "rape" of the South, the latter propagates (white-on-black) rape. Phil Stoneman is thus allied with the KKK, his father with the "negro regime" and its rapist legislators from whom he still distinguishes himself by his white "soul [which] had learned the pathway of the stars" (371). Mistaken in his belief that he could uplift Brown, Stoneman eventually dismisses her as a (castrating) "yellow vampire" into whose abyss he had been drawn (371). As a figure of otherness with diminished visible difference, the mulatto endangers, rather than enables, dominant identity. Where amalgamation turns out to be the ultimate threat to white supremacy, segregation remains the only solution to the "race problem."

"A Tender Lamb Snatched from the Jaws of a Hungry Wolf":
Inversions of Rapist Rhetoric in Frances E. W. Harper's *Iola Leroy*

African American novels such as Harper's *Iola Leroy* and Griggs's *The Hindered Hand* directly engage the racist rhetoric of rape and identity formation. At the same time, this rhetoric preordains black writers' own rape narratives to some degree. Just as the discourse of seduction informs and delimits the slave narrative, the racist romance enables its own contestations, while also imposing their restrictions. "The Negro is comparison," Frantz Fanon famously claimed (211). As a consequence, African American rhetoric is a revisionary, a signifying, practice, somewhat belated, marked by inversion and mimicry as well as by a (gender) difference within.

Merging elements of seduction novel, slave narrative, and domestic as well as realist fiction, yet addressing a black audience first and foremost, Harper's best-selling *Iola Leroy* is the first postbellum African American novel. Focusing on the portrayal of "noble, earnest men, and true women" (172) who are African American, it attempts to refute the stereotypes and myths projected by racist Southern romances. The novel follows, as James Kinney summarizes, the fate of the fair-skinned mulatto Iola Leroy during the Civil War and after, recalling her childhood via flashbacks. Raised in ignorance of her racial background, Iola refuses to pass as white after having been reduced to slavery. Working as a nurse, she rejects the proposals and protection offered by white Dr. Gresham and instead, after the war, returns to the South in search of her mother. Having succeeded in reuniting her family, she eventually marries a Dr. Latimer, who himself turned down a fortune by refusing to pass as white. Together they continue their race work in the field of medicine while Iola's brother Harry marries a "pure" African with whom he pursues a shared life-work in education. As in Dixon's *Clansman*, marriage here figures as a solution—albeit a different one—to national conflicts.

Both Harper's and Griggs's texts shift focus from African American men's supposed violation of white women to white men's violation of black women.[25] Like the slave narrative, they appropriate the sexually exploited victim as a (rhetorical) figure to battle racism. Harper's text—a "conversation full of . . . recollections of the days of slavery" (*Iola Leroy* 169)—does so by way of a rhetoric of inversion: it portrays, on the one hand, superior, desexualized characters who appear white yet insist on their blackness, and, on the other, white men who resemble savages. In this context the choice of a near-white mulatto heroine, ignorant of her race and raised in an aristocratic, slaveholding culture, is ingenious. Abolishing the visual evidence of racial difference, Harper's text disrupts "the law of verisimilitude that governs the metaphorical system of racism" (Lloyd 261). Redesigning black womanhood according to Victorian ideals, Harper manifests likeness where the slave narrative located difference, and claims the cult of true womanhood and its generic conventions, including the "reader-I-married-him" happy ending, as a code of emancipation.[26]

In this way, Harper's novel temporarily cancels slavery's system of sexual control, which obstructed kinship relations and legally invalidated slave marriages. Sexually innocent and culturally enlightened, Iola makes for a perfect witness attesting to the degradations of bondage and the misconceptions pertaining to miscegenation. As a mulatto, she embodies amalgamation and moves it center stage. Treating racial hybridity matter-of-factly and exposing its many paradoxes,[27] yet resisting the tragic-mulatto formula, Harper enters a debate of historical and national scope. She interrogates both derogatory fictional depictions of mulatto women and the belief that sexual assaults against white women were usually committed by mulattoes.[28] Subjecting Iola herself to sexual harassment only after her racial heritage is disclosed moreover allows Harper to highlight her heroine's virtue as well as the correlation between rape and race. Iola's preference of death to sexual violation affirms the dominant ideology of rape; the fact that she does not faint—a recurrent sign of sexual violation—reassures the reader that no such violence, hinted at by a master who threatens to have her whipped for turning him away, was inflicted (41). Nor is this a tale of seduction: she was "[t]ried, but not tempted," Iola insisted (115). Informing her reader that Marse Tom, intent "to break [Iola] in" (38), "tried in vain to drag her down to his own level of sin and shame" (38–39), Harper inverts the dominant racist rhetoric: in Dixon's *Clansman* Lydia Smith is said to drag down Stoneman. Likewise when Iola is rescued, with the assistance of white authorities, from threats of "cruel indignities" physically unharmed (114), the narrative employs elements from racist fiction to elevate its heroine and officially recognize black women's sexual exploitation. Accordingly, Iola's escape figures as the liberation of "a trembling dove from the gory vulture's nest" (39), as the fate of "a tender lamb snatched from the jaws of a hungry wolf" (273).

Instead of elaborating Iola's history of sexual harassment, though, the text concentrates on the discrimination she faces in the workplace. And as it displaces sexual subjection by economic exploitation, the novel deploys a very particular silence. Highlighting the "defenselessness" of enslaved women (39), Harper depicts sexual violence against black women as a phenomenon of the past (as when Uncle Daniel recalls that "de overseer used to cruelize dem so bad" [19]), of an economic system wherein female beauty was a "fatal dower" and woman were "liable to be bought and sold, exchanged and bartered" (74), "a system darkened with the shadow of a million crimes" (86). At the same time Harper opens a new feminist perspective on male sexual violence. Iola's "theory" is "that every woman ought to know how to earn her own living. I believe," she claims, "that a great amount of sin and misery springs from the weakness and inefficiency of women" (205).[29] Talking of "sin," "misery," and "unhappy marriages" (210), Harper timidly suggests that "every woman" is prone to sexual exploitation as long as she is economically dependent, and thus insists on black and white women's gender sameness.

In accordance with her feminist agenda, Harper's reconstruction of (supposedly savage) black womanhood corresponds to deconstructions of (supposedly superior) white manhood. Frequently, the author unsettles Iola's girlhood ideal "of high, heroic men, knightly, tender, true, and brave" (110) by way of white man's voice. When Alfred Lorraine, for instance, calls "beautiful" slave girls "the curse of our homes" and "willing victims," Iola's father objects that "[i]f it is cruel to debase a hapless victim, it is an increase of cruelty to make her contented with her degradation."[30] Though he himself considers female slaves "the bane of Southern civilization," Eugene Leroy insists that "they are the victims and we are the criminals" (70), thus recognizing himself as other. Iola reinforces this point: "I was abased," she admits, "but the men who trampled on me were the degraded ones" (115). Here it is the white slaver who, inflicting a "lawless brutality . . . upon innocent and defenseless womanhood" (39), is demonized (41). Likewise, Eugene Leroy describes the violator of his wife Marie, this "beautiful and defenseless girl," as "a reckless man, who, with all the advantages of wealth and education, had trailed his manhood in the dust." As Harper depicts both slaver and lyncher as criminal, beast, and satanic seducer, she ascribes to white men the very marks of racial difference Southern culture projected on African Americans to justify their lynching.[31] Both sexual assault and lynch violence attest to the moral inferiority of the "superior" race. Neither Professor Gradnor, one of "the earnest men . . . deeply interested in the welfare of the race" (246), nor former slave Robert Johnson knows of any "civilized country on the globe, Catholic, Protestant, or Mohammedan, where life is less secure than it is in the South" (250), "where men are still burned for real or supposed crimes" (224)—supposed crimes meaning "the one crime" (Griggs 136) or, as Mark Twain calls it, " 'the usual crime' " (278).

The continuity Harper establishes between the uncivilized lawlessness of sexual violence and lynch murders remetaphorizes lynching as a kind of rape and puts black women and black men in a similarly subordinate female position. Linking antebellum rape with postbellum lynchings, she, just like Keckley, insinuates that black identity, both male and female, is "dispersed across categories of property, injury, and punishment" (Hartman 552). Black women's physical violation during slavery turned into postbellum economic discrimination; black men's economic and political emancipation was canceled by physical violation. Yet as lynch violence displaces sexual violence, the perpetrator remains one and the same. Thus "[t]he problem of the nation . . . is not what men will do with the negro, but," as Dr. Gresham insists, "what will they do with the reckless, lawless white men who murder, lynch, and burn their fellow-citizens" (Harper 217).

Such nonironic inversions are characteristic of African American women's writing[32] yet generally of limited effect, as they tend to reinforce their (racist) literary precursors. This is the case partly because model and inversion depend upon a temporal trajectory that constitutes racial difference by situating dominant and racial subject in distant moments within cultural evolution (Lloyd 249–50). More precisely, Harper's aim of racial uplift conforms to the logic of assimilation that, as Lloyd argues, "constitut[es] the colonial subject as a divided self, one part constituted by acculturation as 'modern,' the other identified by the racist judgment as permanently lodged in a primitive moment incapable of development" (262). Accordingly, Harper adheres to the notion that, owing to both its origin in "heathen" Africa (217) and the oppressive system of slavery, the black race is arrested in an earlier stage of civilization.

At the same time, though, "the order of development is radically disrupted," Lloyd argues, "[w]here whiteness is suddenly, forcibly conjoined with the metaphors of difference" (261). The same applies where blackness is conjoined with metaphors of (gender) sameness; or where white culture itself is said to be out of sync, divided, as Harper claims, between its "mental and material progress" and its regressive "moral [and sexual] life" (250); and where the black man, lagging behind in education and material progress, is—owing to his moral superiority—deemed capable of synchronizing civilization, "not by answering hate with hate, or giving scorn for scorn, but by striving to be more generous, noble, and just" (249). Just like Jacobs's Linda Brent and Toomer's Karintha, Harper's heroine suffers through "adult" experiences in her adolescent years and thus is "prematurely old" and (morally) ahead of her time (272). But since this superiority rests on experiences and memories of intense pain and a subject position disseminated between a pain-ridden past and hopes for a promising future,[33] Harper's inversions remain local disruptions. Likewise, Iola's final plea for a fuller application of Christianity to national life (216), her projection of a transcendent solution (259) postponed to "a brighter day" (249),[34] inverts the temporality of racial difference without canceling it. Just like her adherence to the vanishing ideals of Victorian womanhood, her appeal to spirituality relies on a "feminized" middle-class morality that American culture, its black male critics included, was in the process of discarding. Griggs, for instance, considers spirituality and "the Gospel of peace" (310) "the Negro's greatest curse," a means of cultural deformation that "unmanned" the "great fighting race" (37, 310). This notion of deformation, in turn, bespeaks a sense of authentic blackness both avowed and disavowed by Griggs's practice of mimicry—a practice that characterizes much of African American males' cultural expression.

"The One Crime" and "the Real 'One Crime' ": Rape, Lynching, and Mimicry in Sutton E. Griggs's *The Hindered Hand*

The compromised position of the black male subject—his "hindered hand"—is the crucial target of Griggs's novel; it is dramatized by the author's figuring political and economic competition as a struggle over black womankind. "The world at large has heard," Griggs's narrator remarks, "that the problem of the South is the protection of the white woman. There is," he adds, "another woman in the South" (71). Note that "the problem" implied is not merely the continuing sexual exploitation of black women by white men but black men's inability to grant their protection—an inability that, in the logic of Southern chivalry, amounts to a lack of manhood. Thus contemplating "his position as . . . protector" of his fiancée Foresta, Bud Harper feels humiliated by "his utter helplessness" (128). Learning about the lynching of Foresta and Bud, Ensal Ellwood exclaims: "Poor Negro womanhood! Crucified at the stake, while we men play the part of women" (139). Violations of black women by white men consequently expose black men's powerlessness.[35] Whereas KKK atrocities supposedly serve civilization (317), any black man's attempt to "defend . . . himself and his home," as Pauline Hopkins put it, has been considered a "race riot" (271).

Accordingly, lynchings in Griggs's text are retaliations against either minor offenses or black men's interference with the exchange of black women across the color line, yet never against black-on-white rape. Quite the opposite: Griggs calls it a "well understood dictum" among Southern whites "that the Negro man and the white woman are utterly oblivious of the existence of each other" (12). Opening his novel on this note, he foregrounds how the racist agenda has deformed interracial relations. In a culture that reads a black man's "attempted flirtation with a young white woman" as a rape attempt (14), segregation has been fully enforced. Flirtation, Griggs insinuates, is consequently taboo, and any attention white women pay to black men is suspected to be a trap. As a result "nowhere in the world," Griggs claims, "does woman get more instinctive deference from men than what Negro men render to the white woman of the South" (311).

The Hindered Hand is set in Almaville, capital of an unnamed Southern state, during and after Reconstruction, which, aimed at "re-enslav[ing] . . . the race" (321), Griggs considers "the most pathetic page" of African American history (315). Pondering interracial relations and miscegenation, Griggs, unlike Harper, finds no benefit coming from the "mulattoism . . . forced upon" the race during slavery (313). Engaging Dixon's belief that intermarriage is "the highest ambition of the cultured Negro man" (312), Griggs in fact interprets miscegenation with reference to Douglass as treason and a trigger of alienation (313). Accordingly, Tiara, who comes to Almaville to start over, vehemently rejects Douglass as a potential new surname (40), thereby revealing "the very core of her life's troubles" (43). Whereas Harper makes mulattoism a narrative device mediating "the relationship between white privilege and black lack of privilege" (Carby, *Reconstructing* 89), Griggs employs it as a figure of racial disintegration (313). Accordingly, his protagonists dismiss assimilation and, echoing W.E.B. Du Bois, call for an "adjustment of the white to the darker races" instead (198).

Griggs's belief—that interracial contact does not enlighten but dissipates the black race by accelerating their regression—pushes beyond Harper's rhetoric of inversion. Blacks, he suggests, are naughty not by nature but by being acculturated into white "savagery" (171). They consequently enact the dominant projections of uncivilized blackness, which in turn mold their targets successfully. The novel's excessive convolutions thus bespeak irony as much as "literary Garveyism" (Moses). Viewed from an Irigarayan perspective, such use of irony, parody, and mimicry aligns the (speaking) position of African American male authors with that of women in the (American) symbolic order. Like his characters who, being white, apply blackface to investigate black crime (112) or, being black and female, pass as male for the sake of mobility (127), Griggs's text practices a kind of mimicry that rhetorically enacts assimilation, "the process of being made white" (198). This textual practice links Griggs's novel with Wright's *Native Son*, John Edgar Wideman's *The Lynchers* (1973), Ishmael Reed's *Reckless Eyeballing* (1986), and the performativity of gangsta rap. Unlike gangsta rap, though, Griggs exposes, rather than playfully enacts, cultural deformation and directly responds to Dixon's *Leopard's Spots* (1902), the precursor informing Griggs's own rhetoric. Displacing the set-piece conversation that Griggs originally used to attack Dixon by a supplementary, separate review entitled "A Hindering Hand," the third edition of *The Hindered Hand* not only blames Dixon for "pick[ing] the degenerates within the Negro race and exploit[ing] them as the natural type" (311), for "picturing the Negro race, as a race prolific with the assaulters of women" (312). It also compromises Griggs's own authority by acts of mimicry.

The plot of Griggs's novel is somewhat bewildering. Its major figures include Mr. and Mrs. Seabright, who—passing as white—arrive in Almaville accompanied by their daughter Eunice. Ambitiously intent on inscribing herself into history through race work, Mrs. Seabright marries her daughter off to the influential politician H. G. Volrees in order to manipulate racial politics, yet Eunice escapes before this marriage is consummated. Much darker in complexion, the Seabrights' other daughter lives apart under the name Tiara Merlow. Their son, Percy Marshall, passes as a white minister. Central to the convoluted story line are, moreover, three mulatto men, all Spanish-American War veterans who advocate civil rights: Ensal Ellwood, minister and moderate in his political convictions, who falls in love with Tiara; radical Earl Bluefield, the illegitimate son of Volrees, who eventually passes as white to further his political ambitions, takes on the name Johnson, and marries runaway Eunice; and Gus Martin, who holds the most militant views on the race problem. All three befriend Foresta Crump and her fiancé Bud Harper, whose fate centers the novel's depiction of (sexual) violence—an issue Griggs addresses much less delicately than does Frances E. W. Harper.

The story of Foresta and Bud shows quite dramatically how male and female violation and the criminalization of the black subject interdepend. After Foresta's little brother is killed by a mob, her father dies of shock, and her mother becomes indebted to her husband's employer, businessman Arthur Daleman, Daleman forces her into domestic work and soon enough craves her sexual services too (71). Foresta pleads ignorance of his motives and reproduces her silence when, in Linda Brent fashion, she lets her mother in on the situation:

> "He had dark purposes, mama," said Foresta.
>
> "Yes," said Mrs. Crump, rather feebly, fearful of what was to come.
>
> Foresta, detecting considerable anxiety in her mother's voice, looked up quickly.
>
> "Now, mama, don't look so scared and troubled; it isn't anything awful, now."
>
> So saying, she buried her face again and continued her recital. "He pretends to love me, mama. He has tried many times to kiss me. I knew what kind of a sword he held over you, and while I resented his advances, I sought not to enrage him for your sake." (95)

In her attempt to downplay the danger, Foresta passes the sword—both metaphor for Daleman's "weapon" and metonymy for its potential effect—on to her mother. Moreover, as she compares her own situation to that of white women, the focus shifts and the violation of black men comes to predominate over that of black women: "You know a colored girl has no protection," she explains. "If a white girl is insulted her insulter is shot down and the one who kills him is highly honored. If a colored girl is insulted by a white man and a colored man resents it, the colored man is lynched" (96). Accordingly, throughout the text economic and sexual exploitation, sexual violence, and lynching figure as the many sides of the same racist coin, blurring the difference between rape and lynching while exposing the death threat inherent in all sexual assaults.

This point gets dramatized in yet another of the novel's perplexing episodes. On the very night Foresta elopes with Bud, Daleman's daughter Alene uses Foresta's room and is accidentally murdered by Bud's brother, who wrongly suspected Foresta of having an affair with her boss. Having Alene take over Foresta's bed, Griggs literalizes (and thus ironizes) the claim that the shift of attention from black to white women's violation serves to cover up white men's continued sexual abuse of black women.[36] As Bud's brother directs his aggression against the black victim (as opposed to the white violator), he buys into the notion that black women are wanton, and denies their sexual violation. Resorting to murder and effacing his victim in the process (103), he reenacts the dominant projections of black masculinity. For Daleman Sr. and Jr. the murder of Alene consequently stirs an "awful unnameable fear, involving the motive of the crime." As their anxiety proves unsubstantiated, they are oddly relieved, almost joyful: "The horror was less" (104).

Escaped to Mississippi, where Bud buys a farm and Foresta engages in race work, the two fugitives (like the person falsely suspected of killing Alene) are eventually lynched for killing a white neighbor in self-defense. In this way, Griggs's novel underlines that lynching is not for "the one crime" but for "the crime of being black," as one Southerner nonchalantly admits (136). Both the black male *and* the black female subject, Griggs insists, are recognized as viola-tors of law, as "gangstas" only, and he dramatizes this insight in all its absurdity. When Ramon Mansford, Alene Daleman's fiancé, in search of Alene's mur-derer, stops a black woman "rushing along at full speed," his concern is not whether she herself is in danger, but whether she has "murdered some one" (109). Similarly ironic is the case of Eunice, who after her escape marries another man. As she learns that she is black, she reads the legal authorities' refusal to convict her for bigamy as a discriminatory act. The charge does not apply because law does not recognize intermarriage (236); a conviction would affirm her whiteness, grant her equality, recognize her identity—albeit an iden-tity based on the violation of law. Wright's Bigger Thomas, who establishes his identity by enacting this projection of blackness, thus reenacts the very ironies generated by Griggs's earlier novel.

Whereas the conception of the black subject as criminal applies to both genders, gender difference dominates the scene of Foresta's and Bud's torture, whose excessive brutality provoked critics to question the text's verisimilitude and, like the story of Eunice, motivated Griggs to comment upon its authentic-ity.[37] The tearing of Foresta's clothes and the penetration of her breasts with a corkscrew insinuate rape; the removal of her hair and fingers symbolizes cas-tration, as do the attacks on Bud's extremities. While both silently endure the ordeal, the singular mark of agency is Bud's involuntary gaze upon Foresta's ravaged body. Forcing Bud to witness her mutilation and concluding the scene with a focus on his dislocated eyeball, the text comes down on the side of maimed black manhood. Whereas the metonymic link between lynching and black women's sexual exploitation revises the dominant paradigm of rape and lynching and its inherent causality, their metaphoric alliance makes lynching displace rape as the dominant figure of racist violence. As gender difference is subordinated to (racial) identity, that identity becomes even more intensely marked by negation.

Griggs's Pan-Africanist solution is geographic separation. In contrast to Harper's continuous inversions of divided black subjectivity, such nationalism "offers to suture this division," to quote Lloyd again, "by relocating the institu-tions of the modern state on the very terrain that the colonizer regards as primitive. It restores continuity to the interrupted narrative of representation by reterritorializing it within the newly conceived nation. Nationalism, in other words, accepts the *verisimilitude* of imperial culture while redefining its pur-view" (262). And as the "verisimilitude of imperial culture" is being accepted, racist essentialism is reinforced.

This is exactly the effect foregrounded in Griggs's "supplement," which, intended to attack Dixon's authority, epitomizes the strategy of mimicry. Whereas Dixon's fiction is replete with racial prejudice, Griggs expresses clear class bias. Competing with slaves, he proposes, poor whites developed "the strongest sense of compulsion" against African Americans (303). Both Nathan Bedford Forrest, the leader of the founders of the KKK, and Dixon, he notes, hailed from this class where racism was hereditary (304–5). Calling Dixon a "literary exotic," Griggs takes on Dixon's own strategy of othering. As he traces the success of Dixon's demagogy to a cultural climate set for "unified Saxon-dom" (327) and to his secure "grasp upon the emotions of men, his ability to arouse and sway their feelings" (329), Griggs in turn finds Dixon guilty of "borrow[ing black] power" (328), a power he locates in "the highly emotional nature" of the "Negro race" (329). That Dixon "breath[es] the Negro air of emotionalism," Griggs considers an "irony of fate! Mr. Thomas Dixon, Jr., beyond doubt owes his emotional power to the very race which he has elected to scourge" (330).

In his "final word" on the author he presents Dixon as someone not quite on the beat, in one sense regressing, in another pushing ahead the "ultra radi-cal element of Southern whites."

> The coming of this radical of radicals before the bar of public opinion, clothed in his garb of avowed prejudice of the rankest sort, means that the self-satisfied isola-tion of the past is over, that even the radicals desire or see the need of sympathetic consideration from other portions of the human family—decidedly a step forward for them. The coming to the light of this type where civilization may work upon it is in this respect one of the most hopeful signs of America's future. Soberly the great world consciousness will deal with this enemy of the human race, and the universal finger of scorn that will surely in the end be pointed toward him will render it certain that no other like unto him shall ever arise. (332)

The tone here is curiously hybrid. Turning the tables by othering Dixon while, like Harper, appealing to a transcendent power, Griggs differs from Harper in degree (or "garb") of ironic display. Associating Dixon with the ultraradicals, he marginalizes him and his like. Using the term "type," Griggs cancels this marginalization to a certain degree yet also assigns Dixon the very status the white author had assigned to black assaulters of white women. Most conspicu-ous are his echoes of Christian rhetoric ("coming," "shall ever arise"), which ironize the faith African Americans put in a transcendent solution to race conflicts. Griggs himself finally proposes another solution. Anticipating "the coming better days of the world," he buries Dixon alive, so to speak, and even provides "the chiseler of the epitaph" with lines for his tombstone.

[L]et him carve thus:

"This misguided soul ignored all of the good in the aspiring negro; made every vicious offshoot that he pictured typical of the entire race; presented all mistakes independent of their environments and provocations; ignored or minimized all the evil in the more vicious element of whites; said and did all things which he deemed necessary to leave behind him the greatest heritage of hatred the world has ever known. Humanity claims him not as one of her children." (332–33)

Dixon's identity is purely negative here. He will be remembered as outcast, degenerate, criminal, and subhuman, as the epitome of his own projection of blackness. No surprise that Dixon is prematurely "lynched" in the final passages of Griggs's text.[38] Most significant, though, is the insight into the interdependent processes of black and white identity formation pertaining to Griggs's mimicry and his point on "borrowed power." While Griggs explicitly acknowledges "the fact that the Anglo-Saxon and Negro races are producing in each other modifications of many of their racial characteristics" (328), he also takes these assigned racial characteristics as facts, thus canceling his own sense of their detachment from black and white bodies. In fact, whereas Griggs's rhetoric ironically questions such essentialism, his politics of "race pride" and Pan-Africanism depends upon (projections of) racial difference, of a "truth" behind the "vile misrepresentations" of African Americans.

"A THING NOT TO BE FACED": RAPE AS ROBBERY IN UPTON SINCLAIR'S *THE JUNGLE*

In some sense, Griggs's novel compares to Sinclair's *The Jungle*—a text where sexual violation symbolizes class conflict and the rape of the protagonist's wife, Ona, by her boss reads as an assault against Jurgis, her husband, or "owner." The analogy between capitalism and slavery is central to Sinclair's text and works primarily by focusing on the worker's physical environment. At the same time the novel holds that economic oppression of poor immigrant populations has not displaced but in fact surpasses the cruelties of the slave system. The situation that Jurgis and his family escaped from resembled conditions of enslavement—Marija was regularly beaten by her employer (23), Old Antanas attacked by his own father for his reading exercises (60). The gruesome working conditions in the Chicago slaughterhouses, by contrast, are compared to the "medieval torture chamber" (112). The resulting criminalization and imprisonment of workers foreground the continuity between their "accursed" labor and their petty existence, "[a]ll life ha[ving] turned to rottenness and stench in them" (168). The brutal management of the "Beef Trust" (112) not only wipe out whole families or, as in the case of Jurgis's Lithuanian kin, its weakest members. They transmute men as confident, strong, and responsible as Jurgis Rudkus into criminals (likened to the novel's black characters), complicit opportunists, and convinced socialists (at best). The more debased the protagonist becomes, the more he reincarnates his wife's Irish rapist and the bestial black lowlifes at the bottom of Sinclair's ethnic hierarchy. Accordingly, Ona's rape functions differently from black women's sexual violation in African American texts. Whereas the latter associate rape with lynching, Sinclair subdivides capitalist exploitation along gender lines. Though, like slavery, capitalism doubly endangers working women, Sinclair focuses on their physical and sexual exploitation: "women's bodies and men's souls were for sale in the marketplace" (168). Both men and women are "struggling for life under the stern system of nature" (214), yet only women embody nature throughout the novel.

By employing slavery as a trope for the oppression of impoverished immigrants by industrial trusts, Sinclair revises notions of slavery and its "vices." The latter include white prostitution of black women, which looms large as slavery's major legacy in Griggs's text as well as in Faulkner's *Sanctuary*. Sinclair's novel re-presents rape as prostitution, which the nineteenth century considered a social illness more than an individual problem (Sander L. Gilman 242). Ona's forelady, Miss Henderson, for instance, was running a downtown "bawdy-house" under the aegis of the department and its superintendent, "a coarse, red-faced Irishman" (108). Consequently, "there was no place," the narrator comments,

> a girl could go in Packingtown, if she was particular about things of this sort; there was no place in it where a prostitute could not get along better than a decent girl. Here was a population, low-class and mostly foreign, hanging always on the verge of starvation, and dependent for its opportunities of life upon the whim of men every bit as brutal and unscrupulous as the old-time slave-drivers; under such circumstances immorality was exactly as inevitable, and as prevalent, as it was under the system of chattel slavery. Things that were quite unspeakable went on there in the packing-houses all the time, and were taken for granted by everybody; only they did not show, as in the old times, because there was no difference in color between master and slave. (109)

By distinguishing decent girls from prostitutes—who embodied both disease and passion, were marked by particular physical features, and merged with lesbian and black women[39]—this passage downplays the fact that female workers, just like slave women, did not—in fact, could not—consent to but were forced into prostitution. Moreover, the focus on the invisibility of "things" "unspeakable" recognizes a cultural effect rather than the painful individual experience. Accordingly, the depiction of Ona's rape centers the immorality of the capitalist economy and questions of male authority and ownership. Like slavery, Sinclair suggests, capitalism destroys institutions fundamental to civilization, partly, though, by making marriage and family themselves appear like slavery (141), and by encouraging prostitution as a family's final resort

(285, 287). Capitalism thus makes any man, no matter how down-and-out, a master/owner of his wife and her "honor." Jurgis's sense of losing the power to "protect [his wife]" (76) at the same time diminishes his manhood. Witnessing how the "accursed work" makes Ona deteriorate into physical "monstrosity," Jurgis is feminized ("a wounded animal"), "becom[es] half hysterical himself, which was an unbearable sight to see in a big man" (143). Ona's "ravishment" and forced prostitution suggest that, like a black man, Jurgis had no entitlement to his wife. Accordingly, the reconstruction of Jurgis's self-esteem, like that of the African American male, comes to depend on female violation. After Ona's death in childbed, he wanted "no more tears and no more tenderness . . . —they had sold him into slavery! Now he was going to be free, to tear off his shackles, to rise up and fight" (207).

Corrupted by the system, distrustful Jurgis makes Ona's rape meaningful by violently enforcing its confession. When he suspects that her nightly whereabouts have been "somewheres downtown," "[i]t was as if he had struck a knife into her. She seemed to go all to pieces" (150). As she "totter[s] forward and stretches out her arms to him," "he stepped aside, deliberately, and *let her fall*" (150, my emphasis). The following "hysterical cris[i]s" (150) shaking Ona's body is one of a series of crises and physical tortures figuring capitalist "robbery," yet, in Jurgis's eyes, bespeaking her guilt. "[F]ear and anguish building themselves up into long climaxes," "[f]urious gusts of emotion," "shaking her as the tempest shakes the tree," "as if some dreadful thing rose up within her and took possession of her, torturing her, tearing her" (150–51), a "shaking and twitching," "sobbing and choking" that climaxes "in wild, horrible peals of laughter" (151) substitute for the "unspeakable" sexual violation yet also put the blame on Ona herself. While she keeps reassuring Jurgis of her love, insists that "no harm" was done and he need know no more (152), Jurgis holds her captive (151), "seizes her by the throat" and forces out "the terrible truth," "[h]is breath beat[ing] hot in her face." "[H]e did not understand," the narrator (mis)interprets Ona's physical contortions, "that it was the agony of shame" (153). Instead, Jurgis's furious fit casts him as both violator and victim of the assault on his honor/Ona. Envisioning the subsequent loss of their house and other valuables (159), he reads rape as robbery and himself takes on the status of the rape victim.

The "assault" of Jurgis is launched by Ona's confession itself. Once she reports that Connor raped and forced her into prostitution, Jurgis "pant[s]" and "shak[es] so that he could scarcely hold himself up" (153). Speaking "as if in a trance," Ona herself is reanimated. As she starts "to breathe hard again," Jurgis falls silent, "killed" by his wife's words. Like forelady Henderson, Ona appears to collaborate with her violator. The insistence of the pronoun "he" throughout her confession, however, capitalizes on Connor as master plotter:

> It was all—it was their plot—Miss Henderson's plot. She hated me. And he—he wanted me. He used to speak to me—out on the platform. Then he began to—to make love to me. He offered me money. He begged me—he said he loved me. Then he threatened me. He knew all about us, he knew we would starve. He knew your boss—he knew Marija's. He would hound us to death, he said—then he said if I would—if I—we would all of us be sure of work—always. Then one day he caught hold of me—he would not let go—he—he——

Substituting a double dash and an account of her prostitution for the sexual violation, Ona finally "lay still as death" (154).

Rape thus remains a matter between men, as is most evident in Jurgis's attacks on Ona's violator, this "big, red-faced Irishman, coarse-featured, and smelling of liquor."

> Jurgis, lunging with all the power of his arm and body, struck him fairly between the eyes and knocked him backward. The next moment he was on top of him, burying his fingers in his throat.
>
> To Jurgis this man's whole presence reeked of the crime he had committed; the touch of his body was madness to him—it set every nerve of him a-tremble, it aroused all the demon in his soul. It had worked its will upon Ona, this great beast—and now he had it, he had it! It was his turn now! Things swam blood before him, and he screamed aloud in his fury, lifting his victim and smashing his head upon the floor. (155)

Lacking another formula, Sinclair's image of the capitalist/rapist resembles the sexual aggressor in Norris and Dixon: after all, the novel's ethnic hierarchy positions the Irish just slightly above the "stupid black negroes" (262). Here, though, capitalism, not black primitivism, constitutes the "jungle" wherein workers are caught; "wilderness" is no longer located on foreign territory but encountered by foreigners in American city districts (178), in an economy of rank growth breeding weed and vices (214). Jurgis's "flood of rage" (270), his "blind frenzy" (271), just like the criminal acts Griggs depicts, are effects of deformation and mimicry.

Like the clansmen's fight with Gus, Jurgis's attacks on Connor repeat the act of rape. His final attempt at retaliation figures as an act of vampirism both resonant with Dixon's rape scenario and foreshadowing Bret Easton Ellis's mutilation scenes. Sinking "his teeth into the man's cheek," Jurgis comes away "dripping with blood." The "little ribbons of skin . . . hanging in his mouth" (156) hint that Jurgis himself was maltreated (166)—a feminine wound inflicted on him—"fucked," so to speak, by the capitalist system: "this wild-beast tangle" (168) with its "raped and stolen power" (298) into which "men had been born without their consent," against their will (168), and which reproduces its own subjection devices. In fact, Jurgis's sense of manhood seems restored by his "raping," that is, feminizing, physically diminishing, his wife's rapist. Rape thus spells robbery, indeed. Accordingly, Jurgis finally diminishes Connor's offense to a misdemeanor, calling the rapist "a man that did me a mean trick once" (271).

Though Jurgis expects lynch violence (160), he is put on trial; during the proceedings Ona is significantly absent. As a matter between men rape lacks appropriate discourse. This has little to do with the immigrant's modest command of English—which, as the narrator comments, does not extend to "the statement that some one had intimidated and seduced his wife" (168); nor is it a translation problem. Throughout the text "rape" in the sense of sexual violation remains a foreign term. The word "intimidation" captures aspects of nonconsent and force yet equivocates the sexual aspects of rape; the term "seduction" does away with its nonconsensual nature yet gets employed whenever Ona's fate is referenced. Connor becomes "[t]he man who had seduced [Jurgis's] wife—who had sent him to prison, and wrecked his home, and ruined his life," Sinclair rhymes (270). Ona's rape thus metonymically figures her husband's ruin.

Owning to the judge's partiality, as well as the social hierarchy of the parties involved, the violence of rape evaporates during the trial. After he learns that Connor "had taken advantage of [Jurgis's] wife's position to make advances to her and had threatened her with the loss of her place" (170), the judge blames the victim for her own violation. "Well, if [the boss] made love to your wife," he addresses Jurgis, "why didn't she complain to the superintendent or leave the place?" This proposition is purely rhetorical: it whitewashes the plaintiff's offense that motivated the crime of the defendant; it overexaggerates the victim's position and the weight of her voice; and it ignores the "shame" any such confession involves for the violated woman and her "guardians" (Griggs 101). Jurgis's point that his family depends upon his wife's work is dismissed as fiction: "It is very unpleasant," Connor claims; "they tell some such tale every time you have to discharge a woman." "Yes, I know," the judge responds, "I hear it often enough" (171). Reading Ona's account of rape as a ploy, this gentlemen's agreement manifests a significant change in the sense of female sexuality.

For Jurgis himself the "monstrous" and "horrible" knowledge of Ona's rape and prostitution was "a thing that could not be faced," a matter he could not identify with, thus projected back on Ona, alienating her in the process: "[S]he would never be his wife again. The shame of it would kill her—," he claims, "there could be no other deliverance, and it was best that she should die" (158). For him Ona had already died while confessing. Her subsequent death in childbed just cashes in on his predicament. Bearing a premature dead baby, Ona is once again "being torn to pieces" (184). The repetition of this phrase, which previously referred to the pain Ona experienced confessing the rape, metonymically suggests that this "fruitless" pregnancy, the "abortion" of mother and child, results from the earlier violation. Implied in this causality is a prospect for the development of the human race under capitalist conditions. At the same time, the rhetorical echo identifies birth, rape, and forced prostitution as part of the same irrevocable "lot of woman" (184).

This lot is a separate sphere indeed: Jurgis is kicked out of the house (184) and must helplessly listen to the "monstrosity" of Ona's cries. Separation is further inflicted during the jail term, yet another consequence of Ona's rape that impacts on the family structure. In prison Jurgis restores his mind and body, while Ona physically deteriorates (172). Her death rehabilitates her, proves her superior virtue, and provokes Jurgis's further fall and final rise as a politicized man. Her rape thus bears his new activist identity and, like rape in classical myths, generates change. In fact, Ona's rape triggers the novel's central turning point. "[F]reed" from family ties, Jurgis first ceases to struggle against the "slave system." Having internalized its values, he actively supports its institutions, cooperates with those who tore his own wife/life to pieces (249, 253), and degenerates into a morally polluted (black) "wild beast." As he drinks excessively and engages with prostitutes, this "beast rose up within him and screamed, as it has screamed in the jungle from the dawn of time" (214).

Sinclair's condemnation of the capitalist "slave" system consequently does not eliminate but reinforces racist notions of racial difference. The supposed debasement of "negroes" even supports his argument: first "savages in Africa," then "chattel slaves," and finally "held down by a community ruled by the traditions of slavery" (267), they have developed into stupid criminals, lazy bums, and corruptible strikebreakers (263). Throughout the novel's latter part, African Americans serve as threatening images of the end result of dehumanizing exploitation, the very mud that breeds miscegenation, venereal disease, and the death of civilization (266–67). Like the slave narrative, Sinclair's novel employs women's sexual violation to epitomize its politics yet reinscribes racial, class, and gender differences in the process. The text thus rewrites rape as a parameter of economic hierarchies afflicting the lower classes primarily. Accordingly, the implicit assumption is that socialist or truly democratic societies dispense with sexual violence (as well as gender conflicts)—a belief that we reencounter in left-leaning (feminist) antirape discourse of the 1960s and 1970s. Oftentimes, though, such visions, like that of Gilman's utopian *Herland* (1915), dispense with sexuality altogether.

"Unconscious Penetration": Manners, Money, and the Primitive Man in Edith Wharton's *The House of Mirth*

My final examples—Moody and Wharton—do without rape. Like Norris, though, they compose scenarios of rape to construct sexuality and redraw the boundaries between consent and nonconsent. Generally there seems to be little sexual violence in white women's turn-of-the-century fiction. Even though Chopin, Gilman, and Wharton prominently figure the alienation of female sexuality and the terms of women's circulation, rape is rarely thematic where "ladies," not lower-class women, are involved. Yet like Gilman's *Herland*, Wharton's *House of Mirth* acknowledges that a culture which projects middle- and upper-class women as asexual, and supposedly ignorant of the sexual economy underlying social contracts, considers sexuality itself—capable of inflicting "social death"—a means of violence. This is why, I argue, Wharton dramatizes as a rape threat the very moment at which her heroine Lily Bart is forced to realize what she had so long disavowed: that a rising consumer society preoccupied with the gender-inflected activities of making and spending money no longer recognizes the codes of civilized, cultured society. To New York "high society," a figure like Lily had become an anachronism: the perfect "lady" whose capital is the beauty of her body, her mastery of manners, and her moral superiority—jewels of a vanishing Victorian age that society no longer trades in. Body and self have turned into objects of consumption *and* consummation, into fetishes, as Gilman argues in *Women and Economics* (1898), of male authority,[40] and consequently upper-class single women with their "helpless useless hands" (Wharton 166) find themselves in a state comparable to prostitution and prone to sexual violations other than those supposedly inflicted by black beasts jumping from the bushes.

Aware that her luxurious life depends on her securing a financially potent husband, yet unable to "sell" herself to affluent, yet unappealing, suitors, Lily approaches Gus Trenor for what she likes to believe is merely a small favor "any friend might do, or anyone [might] accept from a friend" (165). Familiar with the "vast mysterious Wall Street World of 'tips' and 'deals,' " Trenor could invest, she imagines, her limited means to facilitate an "escape from her dreary predicament" (100). Lily's apparent naïveté vis-à-vis the world of finances and her seeming reluctance to engage in its "indelicacy" correspond to and figure her ignorance of the sexual exchange she sets in motion by allowing Trenor to mediate her monetary business.

> In her inmost heart Lily knew it was not by appealing to the fraternal instinct that she was likely to move Gus Trenor; but this way of explaining the situation helped to drape its crudity, and she was always scrupulous about keeping up appearances to herself. Her personal fastidiousness had a moral equivalent, and when she made a tour of inspection in her own mind there were certain closed doors she did not open.

All indelicacies diminish as long as Lily disregards "the exact nature of the transaction" (101) and allows "the haziness enveloping the transaction [to] serve[] as a veil for her embarrassment" (104).

When she first approaches Trenor, projecting herself as "loveliness in distress," Lily makes calculated use of Victorian gender conventions. Likewise Trenor weighs gains against losses. While he would "protect [Lily] from the results of her disinterestedness," he knows that "she was left to bear the whole cost of her resistance" to potent, yet unappealing, suitors like Gryce (103). Accordingly, once the deal is done, Trenor makes his (physical) claims on Lily, "lean[ing] a little nearer." Such seemingly innocent, yet recurring, paternalistic gestures dismantle distance and physically affirm Trenor's entitlement to her body. In the beginning his touch "cost her only a momentary shiver of reluctance." This "was part of the game," the narrator comments upon Lily's motives, "to make him feel that her appeal had been an uncalculated impulse," while her "renewed sense of power in handling men . . . helped also to obscure the thought of the claim at which his manner hinted" (104). With others witnessing, though, Trenor's overtures begin to "vex" her: "what right had he to touch her?" (110). All the while she accepts Trenor's checks, Lily thus avoids close encounters, keeps him at arm's length, and snake-charms him with her rhetoric skills and prospects of intimate talks (137). Throughout, however, Wharton tropes Trenor's "shadowy claim" to her body by consistently phrasing the economic in terms of the sexual and vice versa. And once rumors, along with the "insistency of [his] gaze" (135) and touch, become increasingly "unpleasant" (136), "she wished she had a clearer notion of the exact nature of the transaction which seemed to have put her in his power" (135).

When Lily is trapped by Trenor into a private late-night encounter, knowledge is finally forced upon her. Significantly enough, this scene not only represents sexual violence. It also calls upon the image of the primitive rapist as a figure of male sexuality—a sexuality that, imposed in exchange for material provision, must seem aggressive to someone assuming that the world is free for the well-mannered. Expecting to meet Judy Trenor, Lily finds herself alone with Judy's husband in their residence. Intent on escaping this compromising situation, she is held captive. Instead of calling a cab, as she demands, Trenor blocks the door (162), the borderline between public and private space and a figure of sexual assault, squaring himself on the "threshold," letting Lily approach it "unimpeded" before "regain[ing] command of it" (163), pushing a chair between her and the door (164)—in short, physically enacting his financial power over her.

And yet: this is not a rape attempt but an argument cast as "fistfight." Whereas Charlotte Temple was overpowered by Montraville's rhetoric, Lily's rhetorical skills are her singular means of self-defense. Her ironic distance hurts Trenor like "an actual lash" (163); his crude tone, meant to cut through her mannered reticence, in turn hits her like "a physical blow." As Trenor's pitch levels to "steadiness and concentration," Lily realizes that "a quick swordplay of wit" will not "cover her retreat" this time (164). Feeling disgraced and feminized,[41] Trenor does not intend to sexually subdue Lily in private, though—even if he means to assure her he is "man enough" to do so and she "loose enough" to deserve it. Instead, Trenor is keen on upgrading his manly power, which, as Lily is well aware, does not carry much beyond his financial potency, "his show of authority" (104). This lack of authority, though, makes him all the more unpredictable. Just as Trina fears McTeague's aggressiveness, Lily is frightened of Trenor's "unmanageable mood," though it is prone to do social rather than physical damage (148). After all, Trenor does not merely claim his piece of the pie; keen on appearances, he desires that others see him swallow and digest it.

Accordingly, the disclosure of Trenor's true motives revitalizes Lily's favorite defense mechanism: the pretense of ignorance. Lily's shield of calculated naïveté, however, gives away her knowledge. She is well aware that talking to Trenor at this hour translates into sexual intercourse, diminishes her market value, and associates her with "fast girls" whose "excess of animal spirits" give away their lower-class status (146);[42] that any harm to her "reputation" accelerates her social decline.[43] For women's class status is registered on the basis of their (supposed) sexual relations.[44] Thus the threat of physical danger occurs only after Lily has stepped down the social ladder and engages with a sufficiently "dull" and "coarse" man, a McTeague-like character.

When Trenor finally attacks Lily physically, "[o]ver and over her the sea of humiliation broke—wave crashing on wave so close that the moral shame was one with the physical dread" (166). Note that it is not his body overpowering hers but her consciousness "drowning" in his mortifying discourse—"unconscious penetration" (112) indeed! "His touch," Wharton writes, "was a shock" to Lily, but "[t]he words—the words were worse than the touch" (166). Crushing her carefully constructed social self, his words lay bare her physical being, leaving her "heart . . . beating all over her body—in her throat, her limbs, her helpless useless hands," hands as unskilled for labor as for physical defense. This is no rape attempt but moral shame and "social death" refigured as rape, the closeted violence of the heterosexual economy written back into its social discourse.

Wharton's critique is compromised, though, by the fact that Trenor, the "cigar smoker" with a "puffing face" (99), comes to resemble the dominant figure of the rapist, "a brute," as he himself admits, "red," "massive," and reminiscent of Norris's crude dentist. This characterization once again ascribes sexual aggression to certain ethnicities and class contexts. When Lily finally realizes that her "recoil of abhorrence had called out the primitive man," Wharton, like Norris, even suggests that male "rage" and female resistance interdepend (166). Unlike Norris she holds, however, that the (female) pretense of ignorance triggers an innate male aggression that knows no class boundaries but informs all virility. Wharton's realism employs the figure of the "primitive man" not to put forth a particular ideology or ethos, a conception of the order of life, but to render her character's complexity, his contradictory psychic makeup, and inner conflicts. It is a trope for a state of mind or consciousness, not for a physical predisposition determining further action. And yet Wharton's realism is not of the kind that is merely, as Norris famously phrases it, "a formal visit, from which I may draw no conclusions"; it "does not bow upon the doormat and goes away" (*Responsibilities* 215–16). Instead, Wharton foregrounds to what extent notions of primitive masculinity had taken hold of the cultural imaginary, and, more specifically, how they already outlined notions of a "natural" aggressive male sexuality.

Leaving the scene while keeping up appearances, Lily regains control only to find herself, soon enough, "alone in a place of darkness and pollution" (167), facing a new, nakedly material self, a self stripped of its masks and manners. Lily—like McTeague—"seemed a stranger to herself, or rather there were two selves in her, the one she had always known, and a new abhorrent being to which it found itself chained" (167). Likewise Trenor is "humbled," violated in the end: "the situation loomed before him black and naked as the ruins of a fire. Old habits, old restraints, the hand of inherited order, plucked back the bewildered mind which passion had jolted from its ruts. Trenor's eye had the haggard look of the sleep-walker waked on a deathly ledge" (166). At a moment of cultural transition, those who trust "inherited orders" may easily find themselves in free fall. Accordingly, Lily is prone to violation, "a victim of the civilization which had produced her" (25). Civilization has produced in her the ability to make calculated use of restraining gender conventions and class bias while insisting on her right to transgress such conventions. Wharton's *House of Mirth* thus both reinforces and questions the dominant narratives of rape without being "about" rape.

"THE KIND WE CAN'T RESIST": THE LESSON OF WILLIAM VAUGHN MOODY'S *A SABINE WOMAN*

Moody employs the figure of the rapist to subtly suggest that fantasies of sexual violence hamper women's sexual desire. This is certainly not his main point. Moody's play *A Sabine Woman* (1906), after 1909 entitled *The Great Divide*,[45] pays tribute to classical mythology, which established the function of rape as a "generative event" (Bal, "Rape" 3). Meant to critique Puritan repression, Moody's drama presents the turns and twists of the (love) relationship between Stephen Ghent, a man of the "wild West"[46] and New England–born and – raised Ruth Jordan, between a potential rapist and his would-be victim. The play's romance plot follows the ancient rape narrative involving a woman who, married by force, overcomes her humiliation and learns to love her aggressor. It is crucial that Moody's realist text[47] appropriates a mythical rape scenario to forward its author's own philosophical and psychological agenda. Borrowing an established figure of change and liberation,[48] the play develops "modern" views of life and gender that favor remasculinization, resexualize womanhood, and eroticize sexual violence. Since the depiction of Ghent, the potential rapist, repeatedly centers on his resemblance to a native American, the events also refigure—or rather disfigure—the captivity narrative (where robbery, after all, is not identical with rape).

The plotline of Moody's adaptation runs as follows: trying to restore their dwindling family fortunes, Ruth, her brother Philip, and his wife Polly move to Arizona to establish a cactus-fiber industry. When after months of hardship Polly gladly accepts an invitation to San Francisco and is taken to the train by her husband, Ruth is attacked by three intoxicated men: a nameless "Mexican half-breed" and two Americans, "Dutch" and Stephen Ghent (27). Unable to fight off the intruders, Ruth offers her "life" (29) to the tallest under the condition that he protect her from the other two. Ghent accepts the deal, disables Dutch, pays off "the Mexican" with money, silver, and "a string of gold nuggets" (31, 32), and absconds with Ruth to make her his wife. Matrimony triggers Ghent's magical metamorphosis from wild, intemperate, and sexually aggressive animal into a civilized, chivalrous, generous family man. As such, he wholeheartedly embraces the Protestant work ethic, prospers as a principal shareholder of a thriving gold mine in the Cordilleras Mountains, and dedicates his life to making a wrong thing right, transforming "this bad business," as he puts it at the end of act 1, "into something good" (46). Bound by religious and moral conventions, Ruth, however, is unable to overcome her humiliation with a wink. Acts 2 and 3 thus follow the couple along their path from "bad business" through love and separate lives toward a happy ending, the triumph of Ghent's "natural ethic" (Maurice F. Brown 219) over Ruth's cultural constraint. So how and, most significant, *what* does Ruth overcome?

Faced with a rape threat, she manages to preserve her chastity and "honor" (Moody 73) yet cannot avoid degradation. Protection and matrimony, Moody suggests, come at the price of financial dependence and physical "captivity." Or, as feminism would have it, helpless vis-à-vis a horde of men, woman chooses the strongest rapist, who shields her from all other aggressors.[49] In Moody's text, however, emphasis is on economic rather than corporeal power. Whereas Ruth, having been purchased "like a woman of the street" (110), experiences marriage as prostitution (154), it is Ghent's take on the matter that finally triumphs: "Does it rankle in your mind," he inquires during the decisive final dialogue, "that I took you when I could get you by main strength and fraud? I guess most good women are taken that way, if they only knew it. Don't you want to be paid for? I guess every wife is paid for in some good coin or other" (161–62). The link between "good women" and "good coin" as opposed to "bad girls" and "dirty money" makes all the difference to Ghent. Accordingly, Moody's play is far from promoting feminist views and voices a modern critique of both (Ghent's) hedonist materialism and (Ruth's and her family's) Puritan/Victorian morality, which leaves the institution of marriage entirely unaffected. In fact, it celebrates the power of "good" institutions and good women.

Moody's main target is the Puritan "law" of "sacrifice and suffering" (161) that Ruth adheres to, torn between her love for life (40) *and* Ghent, on the one hand, and the moral and religious ideology governing her "familiar" existence, on the other. In her desire to be "cleansed" (166) of the sin in which her marriage originated, she accepts suffering as a way of life and suppresses her feelings for Ghent to make him repent. All the while she struggles for financial independence and manages to return the money he had paid for her, thus purchasing back her freedom. Having confessed her feelings and pregnant with their first child, she leaves for Massachusetts with her family. The couple reconcile after Ghent has suffered severely from Ruth's absence and Ruth has come close to insanity. Still resenting the fact that "whiskey, the sun, and the devil" triggered their union—whereas Ghent is "thankful on [his] knees for all three" (161)—Ruth finally converts to his future-oriented vision of life (163), eager to be taught and have their child taught how to embrace her husband's ways.

Moody's conclusion thus marks a triumph of what Mrs. Jordan, Ruth's mother, considers the "dreadful West" (122), of freedom, masculinity, nature, and sexuality over East, repression, feminization, culture, and misleading moralities; or, as Moody has it, of life over death. This—sudden and somewhat contrived—happy ending results from what Martin Halpern calls a "double reversal whereby Ruth submits to Ghent's view only after he has first submitted to hers" (129). More precisely, Ghent succeeds in winning Ruth over once he reformulates his ideology in terms of hers: her absence effects his suffering and "repentance" as well as his insight that their marriage has facilitated his "Second Birth" (157), his "awaking" as a "new man" (159) who easily dispenses with riches, realizing that love—or life—is all the religion you need.

In this narrative, Ruth is "a Sabine woman" indeed, mediating between discourses: in the rape scene, between the raw and the potentially civilized, and in the struggle between family tradition and marital alliance, between the religious and the secular. Being exchanged twice—first among the would-be rapists and second between brother and lover, between family real life and myth/fairy-tale romance—she negotiates conflicts between men and philosophies of life. The parallels between these transactions are striking and attest to Ghent's view of marriage, his notion that "most good women are taken that way." Twice Ghent asserts his "superiority" economically; first, by buying off his accomplices/competitors, and second, by generously easing the financial straits in which Ruth's family finds themselves. Both exchanges involve physical violence. In the former, Ghent shoots one of his rivals; in the latter, he himself is shot and critically wounded by Philip.[50]

Ruth, by contrast, bridges the "great divide" of religion, region, and class (93) and thus averts violence. She does so first when offering herself to Ghent, and second, by "throw[ing] herself in Philip's path" at the very moment her brother learns about the circumstances of her marriage (155). Philip's intense reaction bespeaks the defeat of his authority. This defeat is foreshadowed when, enraged by Ghent's presence, Philip breaks a paper knife his father brought from India, the "Far East" (130). The triumph of the heavyweight over the paper-weight prize fighter thus anticipates the final overturn of the

Puritan past—the "only way [Ruth] knew," "the only way [her] fathers knew" (166). Drawing on the Sabine myth at that very moment, Moody's narrative underscores that such forced disjunction facilitates rebirth and hastens the arrival of the future.

Significantly enough, the overturn of Puritan ethics figures as a defeat of the dominant ideology of rape. Embodied by Ruth's family, this ideology is voiced by her mother, who—appalled by her daughter's marriage to a potential rapist—claims that Ruth "ought to have died first" (154), "rather than accept life" (157). The fact that Ruth clings to her life instead questions the meaning of rape that informs the novels of Page, Dixon, and Sinclair. Now, unlike their heroines, Ruth, of course, has not been raped. The bestial violator is all in her mind, we are told. In fact, during confessional moments she admits that her worst struggle was not Puritan self-torture but her fight against the "hateful image [Ghent] had raised up beside [his] own image," "the Other One," "[t]he human beast, that goes to its horrible pleasure as not even a wild animal will go—*in pack, in pack!*" (109). Having the figure of the (black) rapist reappear here, Moody reconstitutes the trope as a fiction of misguided Puritan morality, as a figure of repressed female desires (Halpern 123). In this way Moody's text signifies a sharp change in the construction of female sexuality effected by the dominant rhetoric of rape. Once (white) male sexuality is cast as naturally aggressive, as " 'the life force' " (Gilman, *Herland* 134), dominant rape narratives and their bestial rapists turn out to be fantasy figures, projected, it is implied, by a paranoid, masochistic, and self-destructive mind. Evidently, such a view condones the denial of rape charges.[51] More than that, Moody correlates a person's sense of sexual victimization with his or her social position. Ruth succeeded in suppressing her "rape fantasy" while the couple is "poor and struggling" (110). Once the canyon "began belching its stream of gold" (110) and Ghent "began to load [her] with gifts," "to force easy ways upon [her]," she keeps remembering that she became his property, as Ghent puts it, "by blind chance and the hell in a man's veins," "by almighty Nature" (115).

Moody's text dismantles these fantasies by recalling ancient myths of rape that, implying that all history begins with such robbery or ravishment, support Ghent's point of view. Her sister Polly, though, offers two distinct readings of Ruth's situation:

> Here on the one hand is the primitive, the barbaric woman, falling in love with a romantic stranger, who like some old Viking on a harry, cuts her with his two-handed sword from the circle of her kinsmen, and bears her away on his dragon ship toward the midnight sun. Here on the other hand is the derived, the civilized woman, with a civilized nervous system, observing that the creature eats bacon with his bowie knife, knows not the manicure, has the conversation of a preoccupied walrus, the instincts of a jealous caribou, and the endearments of a dancing crab in the mating season. (132–33)

Significantly enough, both interpretations delete the threat of violence at the core of Ruth's and Ghent's first encounter. Moreover, they trace Ruth's feeling of victimization to her inability to "live in a state of divided feeling" (133), her failure to cope with modern conditions owing to a surplus of civilization. Polly herself figures as a modern woman. Considering Ruth and Ghent "predestined lovers" whose union was "made in Heaven" (137), she privileges romance over Puritan morality. At the same time, her appeal to the "primitive" woman, whose natural but repressed female sexuality matches aggressive manhood, proves her "negative capability." Thus, while considering men "*colossal brutes*" (134) and marriage—the very foundation of civilization—the result of their "savage propensity" (136), she still recognizes passionate, though "impossible" Ghent as "the kind we can't resist, any of us" (138). Every woman, Polly seems to suggest, loves a (potential) rapist, partly because of his very imperfection. Unlike Ruth's unsuccessful suitor Winthrop Newbury, who was "good," "gentle," and "chivalrous," but "finished," "all rounded off, a completed product," the man of her "dreams" is rough and raw "like this country out here," the "glorious unfulfilled" (15, 16). In this way the alliance between Ruth and Ghent also "solves" the communal conflict between "civilization" and "savagery."

As the struggle between cultural convention and natural impulses comes down on the side of passionate masculinity, Moody rewrites *McTeague*, presenting sexuality, to appropriate Foucault, as a "natural given which [the] power [of Puritanism] tries to hold in check" (105). Accordingly, Ghent comes to wear like a crown what Ruth considered the figure of her degraded existence: the string of gold nuggets marks the triumph of a new, "natural," aggressive masculinity complemented by an all but novel notion of the feminine as maternal and mediating "Sabine woman," resexualized and "primitive." Instead of effacing her body and self, Ruth is to express the "law" of "joy, and selfishness" that Ghent finds embodied in "the curve of [her] shoulder and the light on [her] hair" (161). Moody thus foreshadows the ideology of "sexual liberation" that brought as many new fetters as physical liberties.

"In little more than a hundred years," writes E. Anthony Rotundo, "the balance of bourgeois values has tipped from self-discipline to self-expression, from self-denial to self-enjoyment" (285). Moody's play is part of the discourse that triggered this turnover. Yet if "self-enjoyment" triumphs, what is defeated in the process? As for Moody's text, it dismisses, first of all, Ruth's toilsome struggle for financial independence—a crucial aspect of female emancipation—as part of the Puritan ploy of "wretchedness" and "self-torture" (166). Most significant, though, is the suppression of memory that reduces Ruth's feminist awareness of woman's condition to the trick of a misguided imagination, real and yet supposedly irrelevant. Thus Moody's text does not cancel the alienation of female sexuality that dominates other fictions of "realist" rape. Rather, it reconstructs "the great (gender) divide" in terms of a polar, yet complementary, economy of sexual desire where "warrior man" meets "Sabine woman" and "passionate" masculinity is greeted by a previously unacknowledged "natural" female longing for such "passion." This modern sexual economy reimagines woman's fear of sexual violation as her sexual fantasy and her desire for submission, rereads what Norris considered "perverse" as healthily natural.

The overall drive of turn-of-the century "realist" discourse on sexual aggression and aggressive sexuality is, on the one hand, to further sexualize (and criminalize) interracial encounters and to inflect sexuality according to class, race, and ethnicity. Sexual violence thus turns into a prominent figure of difference. On the other hand, intraracial and intraethnic sexual violence remains unmarked, insignificant, or missing, a denial triggering what Sedgwick calls "ignorance effect" (*Epistemology* 5). While black female sexuality and sexual violence among African Americans are silenced, sexual aggression on the part of white men tends to figure as aggressive male sexuality that white women either deserve or desire.

All this figures prominently, as Sedgwick has shown, in Margaret Mitchell's *Gone with the Wind* (1936). While the novel grants no signifying power to either white or black sexual aggression against black women, the attempted robbery of Scarlett by a black man has "the entire machinery by which 'rape' is signified in [American] culture roll[] into action" (9). White-on-white rape, by contrast, is shown in graphic detail yet not called by its name. Rhett had "humbled" Scarlett, we are told, "used her brutally through a wild mad night and she had gloried in it" (chap. 54, qtd. in Sedgwick, *Between Men* 10). Thus sexual violence is both ignored—an ignorance, as Sedgwick writes, "in which male sexuality receives careful education" (5)—and misrepresented as "marital bliss," privileging male perspectives in the process.

Ignorance thus indeed proves as potent as knowledge. Complicit with the dominant rhetoric of interracial rape, the silence on intraracial sexual violence maintains both the supremacy of "white people, including women . . . at the expense of Black people of both genders" (Sedgwick, *Epistemology* 32) *and* the subjection of (white) female sexuality and personhood within white dominance.[52] In turn one may argue that the ellision of black-on-black rape from the cultural text helps to evolve the figure of the lynching/"rape" of black men by white supremacy, which in turn marginalizes issues of (black) female sexuality and personhood. This is why even in prominent rape cases a sexual aggressor like Mike Tyson figures as a "victim" of rape,[53] and the actual victim—the lower-class victim in particular—almost vanishes from the scene.

At the same time, naturalist fictions of male dominance and female submission still inform contemporary feminist notions on sexual violence. Authors as diverse as Paglia and Dworkin reject the concept of female masochism yet accept the sadomasochistic sexual dynamic, first projected in American literature by Norris, as the order of things,[54] obliterating the difference between real rape and the ideology and aesthetics of what I have termed "realist" rape, between rape and the reality effects of its representations. While generating significant knowledge about the dynamics of gender relations, this line of feminist thinking has not only ignored the anxieties that triggered remasculinization and (mis)conceptions of imperial manhood and aggressive male sexuality. It also "unknows" the lessons of modernism.

—◦◦◦◦—

CHAPTER THREE

Rape and the Artifice of Representation: Four Modernist Modes

B Y 1910," MARK TWAIN WRITES in his essay "The United States of Lyncherdom" (1894), ". . . I shall see a negro burned in Union Square. For
murder? No, for being in the country against the country's will—like
the Chinaman in America and the missionary in China" (283). This bold vision bitingly analyzes a phenomenon Twain considers a national trademark of
transnational scope: projecting murder, not rape, as the legitimation for lynch
violence, Twain underlines that lynching reproduces the acts it condemns with
a comparable "bestiality." At the same time Twain's statement resonates with
the meaning of rape: echoing its legal definition ("the carnal knowledge of any
woman . . . against her will"), the author marks the violation of the country's
integrity ("Union Square") and willpower ("being in the country against the
country's will") as the true cause of lynch violence and thus underlines the
political significance rape has achieved, the symbolic ground that it covers. As
Twain extends to Asians the contempt in which African Americans are held,
he acknowledges that cultural anxiety is inflicted by multiple "others," that
American racism ties into xenophobia. Cynically likening the presence of foreign elements in the United States to American imperialism ("the missionary
in China"), Twain concludes that according to this logic proselytization becomes a kind of rape. Evidently, by 1894 rape is a complex figure for national
identity formation, for "the birth of a nation" indeed.

Projected as the time when racism and xenophobia need no longer hide,
1910 is also distinguished as the year during which, according to Virginia Woolf,
modernism was born. No matter whether we accept this time line, such synchronicity hints at the cultural bias of modernity and its aesthetics. After all,
even the success of D. W. Griffith's notorious moving picture depended largely
on cinematic and technical innovation. And, in another medium, F. Scott Fitzgerald's *The Great Gatsby* (1925) presents reckless, racist people triumphing
over Gatsby, the alien with an unknown past. In fact, Tom Buchanan, in one
of his "civilization-is-going-to-pieces" diatribes, casts himself as protector of
fair womanhood and family and Gatsby, by contrast, in the shades of emasculated black masculinity, as a potential black rapist passing for white.[1] Where
Twain's text projects, Fitzgerald's thus enacts the (modern) experience of

change, "the crossing or redrawing of boundaries," as Heinz Ickstadt puts it, "the ambivalent wavering between order and experience, between a need for hierarchy and the yearning for its dissolution" ("Liberated Women" 594).

Accordingly, in modernist cultural practice rape is no longer a central figure for social defects, economic and national conflicts, for gender trouble and other "cracks in the gilded bowl of Victorian culture in America" (593) that turn-of-the-century texts both register and mourn. Like realist narratives, modernist fiction responds to experiences of change yet does so not by negotiating cultural consensus anew but by translating or transforming cultural categories into textual ones (594). As modernist texts expose their own aesthetic strategies through an increase of self-referentiality, they come to interrogate the relation of rape and representation. In the process, modern fiction both foregrounds *how* rhetoric makes rape and its meaning circulate in opposite directions and further diffuses the dominant meaning of rape in multiple directions. Faulkner's *Sanctuary*, for example, projects rape through images of silence, blindness, and deafness, thus metaphorizing both culture's resistance to (the realities of) rape and rape's resistance to representation. Likewise Gertrude Stein's *Tender Buttons* (1914) and Barnes's *Ryder* foreground the violence inherent in acts of representation and codified by narrative conventions, thus acknowledging sexual violence as a systemic element of cultural sign systems, symbology, and civilization. At the same time the modernist rhetoric of rape ranges from Stein's deformations of mastery to an intense mimicry of literary precursors, a playful mastery of form that governs Barnes's *Ryder* as well as Wright's *Native Son*.

Modernist texts thus interrogate rape and representation in diverse ways, all of which, however, revise the established "realist" rape rhetoric and its codified dramatization of difference. Despite the greater openness about the body modernism displays, rape and the sexually violated body do not become more graphic. Nor do modernist texts simply deconstruct the inherited cultural codes and boundaries. Instead, modernist literature tends to blur the lines drawn by "realist" rhetoric, as do Faulkner and Wright when they dramatize intraracial rape. Whereas Faulkner employs (white-on-white) rape to foreground how Southern culture itself transgresses the borderline between savagery and civilization, Wright, by contrast, highlights how racialized sexuality served to erect and continually reerect intracultural boundaries. Modernist texts thus capitalize on the interdependence between representations of rape and the meaning a culture ascribes to real rape. In fact, they make visible the very media, conventions, and artifice of verisimilitude that realism tried to obliterate when putting the figure of rape to cultural work. In this way modernism has transformed not so much the dominant rhetoric of rape as our readings of it. In fact, as modernist fiction recognizes rape as a figure and form of representation rather than an event, it also hints that the insights of narrative theory and visual poetics I started out from are insights generated by modernism itself.

As a critique of realist traditions, American modernist writing moreover fills in some of their blanks, among which the sexual violation of the black female subject is the most blatant. Yet if modernism restores signifying power to maimed black womanhood, it does so in a highly mediated fashion. Stein's "Melanctha" (1909), McKay's "The Harlem Dancer" (1917), Theodore Dreiser's "Nigger Jeff" (1918), and Toomer's *Cane* (1923), among many other texts, may acknowledge as part of subjectivity those elements that "realist" narratives of identity have consistently othered. They also highlight, however, that the "[]other woman in the South" (Griggs 71) enters modernist discourse as the figure of ultimate difference upon which modern subjectivity comes to establish itself. As they symbolize intense sensuality, corporeality, and authenticity, blackness and the primitive are reconstructed as feminine in the process and deployed by both high modernist and Harlem Renaissance cultural expression. At the same time, wandering black female figures—be it Stein's Melanctha or Nella Larsen's Clare Kendry—are employed to challenge constructions of (black) female sexuality and "carnal knowledge." In this way modernist texts echo and interrogate the realist rhetoric of rape while aestheticizing the figure of the sexual and sexually injured black female body. As a consequence, the "way out" into an African American post-modernism itself involves a reengagement of realist and naturalist traditions, a revision highly inflected, though, by modernist strategies of mimicry. It led to Petry's novel *The Street*, which itself makes way for the fictions of Maya Angelou, Toni Morrison, Alice Walker, and Gloria Naylor. The preoccupation, on the part of contemporary African American women's fiction, with the incest trope, however, can itself be traced back to the novels of Barnes and Faulkner. And this is why I present Barnes's *Ryder*, Faulkner's *Sanctuary*, Wright's *Native Son*, and Petry's *The Street* as paradigms within modernist representations of rape here: to my mind these novels are paradigmatic because, first, they engage the established rhetoric of rape, highlighting its forms, aesthetics, and meaning construction, and, second, in the process evolve paradigmatic aesthetic modes that set the tone for post-modernist fiction and its repoliticization of rape.

"SOILED! DESPOILED! HANDLED! MAULED! RUMPLED! RUMMAGED! RANSACKED!": STYLES AND HYPERBOLES OF SEDUCTION, RAPE, AND INCEST IN DJUNA BARNES'S *RYDER*

Barnes's short-time best-seller *Ryder* is a carnivalesque imitation of the family chronicle. Presenting a tribe of picaresque figures engaged in transgressive sexual acts, including sodomy and incest, the novel challenges dominant rape narratives on both their textual and contextual levels: it touches upon such taboo zones as the patriarchal family and marriage, transmuting these institu-

tions into scenarios of sexual violation, while at the same time exposing established codifications of (literary) discourse and their power to mask and displace meaning. In fact, *Ryder* practices mimicry in excess, renders chapter-
length imitations of the Bible, Chaucer, and Rossetti, and presents, as Marie
Ponsot points out, a pastiche of genres, including the sermon, anecdote, tall
tale, fable, elegy, parable, bedtime story, satiric couplet, ghost story, debate,
aphorism, and emblem. Or, as Paul West puts it with a wonderful Irigarayan
twist: "Writing fiction, she was a woman applying lipstick again and again
to the same place" (244). Unlike the mimic practice characteristic of African
American texts, Barnes's frame of reference is not American realism and naturalism, though. Instead, she combines, as Sheryl Stevenson notes, a pre-twenti-
eth-century aesthetics with modernist disruptions of plot and narrative structure. Displaying an "extravaganza of literary styles" and written in the manner
of parodists such as Rabelais, Fielding, Sterne, and Joyce, *Ryder* thus remembers the past yet does away with realism entirely ("Writing" 81). Accordingly,
reading *Ryder* for reference—and, in particular, for real-life reference to
Barnes's own family history experiences of sexual exploitation[2]—is bound to
miss the mark. It is not the gruesomeness of real rape that the novel capitalizes
on, but the grotesqueness of a whole tradition of rape and seduction tales.

Stripped of its heteroglossal hyperbole, *Ryder* boils down to the story of
Wendell Ryder, whom Barnes depicts as the ultimate patriarch.[3] Chapter 1
introduces him in Old Testament prophetic rhetoric as a mock savior promoting free intercourse ("Jesus Mundane"), as "philosopher of polygamy," and
self-proclaimed father of all things, "whose relentless goal is excessive prog-
eny," the extension of " 'his race through mighty and illegal prodigal dissemination" (Stevenson, "Writing" 81).[4] In the poor rural home he shares with his
divorced mother, Sophia Grieve Ryder, Wendell has fathered eight children—
two families, one with his wife Amelia and another with his mistress Kate-
Careless—creating a universe of too much relation, too much intimacy. Accordingly, images of bodily processes and childbearing abound.

Set in the late nineteenth century, the text begins by sketching a family line:
in chapter 2 the reader is introduced to Sophia's parents; chapter 3 focuses on
Sophia herself; chapter 4 elaborates on Wendell's early years, establishing him
as a figure who both transcends gender[5] and engages a philosophy of hyper-
masculinity mocked throughout the text. By chapter 5, though, Barnes dispenses with all pretense of chronology and proceeds with fragmentary portraits of family members punctuated by her own quasi-antique illustrations.
In fact, it is the "Rape and Repining!" chapter, the fifth of fifty, that suspends
the plot with an excess of rhetoric heavily reliant on Renaissance literary styles
and echoing, among many others, Milton, Ben Jonson, and Fielding. Since
the chapter follows the first manifestations of Wendell's anti-Puritan hedonist
position and anticipates the depiction of his own "occupations" (chapter 10),
it carries a structural significance that surpasses the parodic, playful carni-

valesque. The end of chapter 4 erects a symbology that expresses male authority through male sexuality; "Rape and Repining!" mocks the (literary) discourse that has legitimized this male sexual economy.

Read from the perspective of (French) feminism, the text therefore cuts two
ways: on the one hand, it debunks male "erection" by privileging female laughter over male pretense and pompousness, a laughter personified by Wendell's
wife, Amelia, and Molly Dance, who "consumed one after another some hun-
dreds of shilling shockers, laughing with hearty delight when a knave got his
mouth clean slitten, or a damsel suffered rape: 'For at least,' she said, 'it never
hurts in the reading' " (193). On the other hand, Barnes's text also registers
that such accounts of rape equivocate women's pains and "misfortunes" (180).
"Rape and Repining!" dramatizes these equivocations by way of a hysterically
hyperbolic discourse replete with capitalizations, exclamations, imperatives,
and questions, a style whose artificiality tops all other parts of the novel.

RAPE AND REPINING!

Lock windows, bolt doors!
Fie! Whores!

What ho! Spring again! Rape again, and the Cock not yet at his Crowing! Fie,
alack! 'Tis Rape, yea, Rape it is, and the Hay-shock left a-leaning! Ah, dilly, dilly,
dilly, hath Tittencote brought forth a Girl again, no longer what she should be,
but forever and forever To-morrow and yet another day!

'Sblood's Death! Is it right, m'Lords? Ravished, and the Cream not risen in the
Pantry! Ravished, and the Weather Fork not turned twice upon its Vane! Ravished,
and no Star pricked upon its point! Can Hounds track her down to Original
Approval: the Law frame her Maidenly again; the not-oft-occurring-particular-
Popish dispensation reset her Virginal? Can Conclaves and Hosts, Mob and Rab-
ble, Stone her back into that sweet and lost condition? Nay, nor one Nun going
down before the down going Candle, pray her Neat.

A Girl is gone! A Girl is lost! A simple Rustic Maiden but Yesterday swung upon
the Pasture Gate, with Knowledge nowhere, yet is now, today, no better than her
Mother, and her Mother's Mother before her! Soiled! Despoiled! Handled!
Mauled! Rumpled! Rummaged! Ransacked! No purer than Fish in Sea, no sweeter
than Bird on Wing, no better than Beasts of Earth! (21)

The exclamatory epigraph prepares the reader for what is to come: its imperatives, juxtaposing a concern with the vulnerable, internal, private, feminine
(body) with a pretense of shock over women who openly market their bodies,
parodically expose the polarity that governs established representations of
rape. As it displays innumerable images of (locked) windows and (bolted)
doors and a whole cast of defenseless girls and maidens, the text suggests that,
once ravished, women turn whores, deserving, in fact calling for, their own
violation—a point both naturalists like Sinclair and Hubert Selby and modern-

ists like Faulkner make as they metonymically associate rape with prostitution. Unlike these authors, Barnes deconstructs this ideology of rape by deploying its styles and their historical trajectory. Accordingly, her rhyme of doors and whores, embedded in truncated syntax, does not capitalize on meaning and morality. Having Ryder identify himself as "whore" (164), Barnes even reengenders the term while blurring the difference between violator and victim, between consent and nonconsent, the difference that structures issues of rape. In this way, the epigraph sets an agenda: its stylistic excess dramatizes the constraints discursive conventions impose on the meaning of rape, suggesting to us that we are not making sense of rape, that rape escapes its aesthetics, gets disseminated along a chain of self-referential signifiers and tropes that catch our eyes and distract our minds.

The first three paragraphs of "Rape and Repining!" quoted above establish rape as untimely robbery. Images of early hour, unripeness ("repining" itself resonates with "ripening"), and early aging abound throughout the text. The self-infatuated rhetoric with its mock shock and regrets draws attention to its textuality and masks the status of victim and agent. With rape redefined as a season ("Spring again! Rape again"), the girl's youth comes to equal rape, and responsibility is relocated within a victim turned criminal. Personified as a carnivorous animal ("[r]ape has stalked abroad and found one capable of alteration" [23]), rape turns into "rapeability." The secondary meaning of the capitalized "Cock" itself, crowing throughout Renaissance and romantic poetry, marks a trace of the violator.

Reduced to prematurity ("forever and forever of To-morrow and yet another day") and finitude (once "ravished," "her Days are numbered, and her Nights are timed" [23]), the victim's identity is draped with metaphors of farming. Such figures recall blazoned depictions of femininity, the breast like "a bowle of cream uncrudded," for instance, exposed in Spenser's "Epithalamion" (1595). They also present rape as economic loss and lack of productivity ("the Hayshock left a-leaning!," "the Cream not risen in the Pantry!"). Accordingly, the perpetrator is not some singular villain but a whole village ("Tittencote"), a community that gestates its victims; rape becomes a public act of communal identity formation ("bring forth") defined by secular and church authorities ("m'Lords," "Popish," "Nun") and a juridical discourse mocked throughout Barnes's text: "The Unlawful, Carnal Knowledge of a Woman (before she is teachable)," we read, "has been gained, the Lad, in the full Legal sense (being but fourteen) incapable, but for all that, a Satisfaction and a Regret" (23). While it renders the exemptions of rape law that determine the ages of consent and intent, this passage obliterates the fact that knowledge is gained against woman's will. Its passive construction even insinuates that she herself wants to prematurely know. Moreover, the enigmatic conclusion ("but for all that, a Satisfaction and a Regret") recalls that legal definitions can in principal reverse

the irreversible act yet cannot practically "reset her Virginal," restore ignorance, "that sweet and lost condition" of girlhood (whose "sweetness" is itself
a product of "bitter" rape).

Accordingly, woman's insight into "carnal knowledge" is no gain but a
stigma and stain that Barnes's text assigns repeatedly with great pleasure:
"Soiled! Despoiled! Handled! Mauled! Rumpled! Rummaged! Ransacked!"
While the enumerative stampede suggests similar meanings, the terms themselves are by no means identical and connote physical harm, aging ("rumple"
means *wrinkle*), and (the seducer's) knowledge ("ransack" means *investigate*).
Infatuated with names and sounds, Barnes substitutes for rape a series of terms
that circumscribe a condition, not an act: rape equals spring and ravishment,
a state of knowledge (21), "Mourning" (23), or exile; it involves a loss of "Filament or Film," the text suggests, echoing Emily Dickinson, of "Difference"
(23), and turns "Ill Luck" (24) into "Ill Fame" (25). By insisting on "call[ing]
a Spade a Spade!" (23), the text both glosses its own evasiveness and urges us
to read literally, to take "Filament or Film" *as* "Filament or Film," to acknowledge how meaning is both compromised *and* heightened when its materiality,
medium, and intertextuality are highlighted.

Consequently, the text renders the victim's supposed responsibility for her
own violation, her fateful curiosity, in a highly absurd rhetoric that draws
attention mainly to itself:

> Hath the Leg drawn on the Tight Boot! La, what a Wicked Wakeful Waking for
> a Lass! . . .
>
> Girl, hast fornicated and become Wanton before thy Time? What Presage had
> you of it! Woke you early to the Madman's Bell, and his cry of "Six o'clock, and
> all Good People to the Brook!"? Or was your Back from the Cradle seeking for the
> Soft Grass, and your Neck for the Warm Arm? Who told you, Hussy, to go ramping
> at the Bit, and laying about you for Trouble? What thing taken from your Father's
> Table turned you Belly up? What Word in your Mother's Mouth set your Ears
> outward? Bawd! Slattern! Slut! Who gave you Rope to turn on! Slain you are of
> Slumber, and your Family mown down before that Sword of Sorrow. Thy Brother
> weeps amid his Diapers, and thy Father behind his Beard! No longer has thy
> Mother Pride in the Century-old *pro ocreis Reginae*; for the Annual Rent paid to
> the Queen, to keep her in Leggings, cannot make Tittencote smack of Tittencote,
> and you gone slipping down to Hell! (23)

Figuring the sexual act as a leg stuck in a tight boot—a trope recurring in
Sanctuary when Tommy sticks his big hand into Temple's small shoe—this
passage fashions all the stalking going on in the text into images of intercourse
enforced not by the lad but by the little lady herself. This is neither rape nor
seduction but fornication, belly-upness (which may lead to belly-outness),
ears-outwardness, strange physical contortions turning the body inside out,

provoked by parental misguidance, foul food, and foul words. Heavily alliterative, the paragraph teases out a trial interrogation, the outcome of which is predictably the slut's "slipping down to Hell!"

In the following paragraph, which mocks the Bible as much as it does classical mythology, rape turns from family affair to national event:

> Great things by Little are thus brought to Dust. Fair Rome sees Men come buttoning up her Appian Way, and an Ass brays over Babylon. Strong Nations rise and come to Flower under the Hee of one Emperor, and are brought low by the Haw of the next. And here, in the Heart of excellent small things, a County over which no Blood has been shed, save once in a Slip of History, a Girl has brought the very Rafters and Pinnacles of her House about her Ears, her one Nocturnal Tear bringing down many in the Morning.
>
> Yes: Is it not a Woman's quickest way of laying herself open to Legend? . . .
>
> But all of this, what can be said to better purpose than that she is Raped, yea, Horrid Raped! Oh, Beastly Stale! All the World knows no thing so Mad, so Daft, so Poisonous, so Balmy Glut of all Ill Luck! Doth not the Shudder of it crack the Paint of Historic Beds? (23–24)

This passage turns on the fact that cultures aggrandize the rape trope while at the same time trivializing the experience of rape. It debunks the grandiosity of such rhetoric by highlighting the corporeality of the act ("buttoning up," "Ass"); by avoiding statement of the obvious ("to Flower" suggests "deflowered" as opposed to the indistinct "are brought low" chosen here); by comparing imperial action to *hee-hawing* (thereby connoting the primary meaning of "Ass"); by juxtaposing the violent bloodshed of warfare with the "slipperiness" of sexual desire ("Pinnacles," "Nocturnal Tear"); and by literalizing rape metaphors ("laying herself open to Legend"). The verbose statement of indignation ("But of all this . . .") betrays sense by syntax; its erotic touch ("Glut," "Shudder") is canceled once we spot the "crack[ing] Paint of Historic Beds."

The text goes on to bemoan the frequency of rape ("Is there not a Stench of the matter in every Breeze, blow it East, West, North or South?" [24]), sharply foregrounding its materiality ("Stench"), and soon enough interrogates the victim, focusing on the "pleasure" involved in sexual violation:

> "And how was it, my Pretty Love?—Box her Ears, the Dirty Wanton!—and was it coming over the Stile, or was it this side of the Fence or the other? How went he about it? Did he lie to you, Frowsy Smelt? Said he that you had Sweet Chops and a Winter Eye? And you, how fared you at that Moment? Were you easily bedabbled, or came you reluctant to the Filthing? Backward looking, or leaping at the Bait? Leaping it was, I warrant me, and I'll give my Neighbour here my second Best Rolling Pin, and I'm not in the Right of it! Or were you, Little Cabbage, in a State of Coma, wherein a Man may step, the Beggar, and find you all he would, though nowhere Yourself! 'Tis a Pox of a Pity that a Woman's Wits may be as scattered as

Chaff, yet her Chastity well enough in one Place to bring her to Damnation! Out then! What will your Mother say to this? And what will you do from now on for a Life! (24–25)

Sounding her cheekily saucy tone at high pitch, Barnes retells the paradigmatic seduction tale, complete with the seducer's sweet talk ("Sweet Chops"), the ambivalence of the seduced, and the definite interpretation of the outcome ("Leaping it was"): the woman's unconsciousness may signal nonconsent yet will not prevent her social death. By shifting the subject to economics ("Though art less than a Farthing, and may be spent at one Ale House"), the text, in the following paragraph, projects her next "step upon the Stoop of Ill Fame." Here prostitution figures as "Philosophy ready risen for the Deed," developed by women "who think their Wits are better for the vending of their Wares." However, such "Wits" breed not good fortunes but criminal acts. Their agents are "such who Poison Wells, and make the Hackle rise on every Pubic Inch, and do split the very Bells by which we tell the Time!" (25).

The text keeps working by pull of association and metonymy. Significantly enough, the very moment "Logicians, from Seneca to Plato" are ushered in, the text's multiple voices are identified as "a Council of Women." Seneca thus also references the first American women's convention at Seneca Falls in 1848. This Council is no alternative, feminist authority, though, but performs a repetition of the same (as does the Seneca Falls "Declaration of Sentiments"). Accordingly, it holds that "[t]here is a 'No' with a 'Yes' wrapped up in it, and there is a 'No' with 'No' enough in the Weave, and we have been sorry amiss that our Girls have not learned of it." Thus girls must "learn how to say 'No!' with Fitting Intonation, for both Dish of Porridge and for Dish of Love," for either can make you "fat." Soon enough all this climaxes into "knots" of mock rhetoric: "Thus the Bobbin fats with Knotted Thread, and when it comes to sewing, what Garment shall be stitched of it, that shall not rip in Open Places and shame the Leg?" The Council's advice is merely accusations, discriminating "Better women [who] have refused" from the "unmannerly" engaged in deeds "Stinking, Large," "Awful," and dark ("in one Night you have changed the Complexion of all Nights"). The ravished maiden, we are told, proceeded by deceit: having appeared "True Coin," she turns out "false Metal," "Lead," or "Alloy" (26). "[N]one shall commerce with you," the Council claims, conflating the discourses of economy, politics, and intimacy, "without first turning you over to see where the Die stamps Treason" (27).

The final pages pretend to offer an array of different perspectives ("Or put it thus" [26], "Or thus," "Or so" [27], " Or better" [28]) but in fact amplify the text's hysterical hype, bemoaning the "corrupt[ion of] a Whole Body" (politic) (27) and the disruption of linear temporality ("What Nation has the Son first and the Mother second? What Tree springs up before the Orchard, saying, "Orchard, Orchard, here is the Tree!" [28]). So severe is the guilt of the fallen woman that she can only be exiled, positioned in a realm that, according to Irigaray, *is* woman's place indeed.

> Thou art Witless Whey, and should be Scourged! Flayed! Whipped! Stocked! Cried against! Howled over, and spent quickly, that you get from out our country and over the Border and into some Neighbouring Land, there to lie, until some Blithering, Scabby Potsherd mends a Stewpan with you, or lays you between Hot Iron and Hot Iron, and so melts you down, to make a Cap for his Heel. So shaken loose, so cutpursed that the Uncertainty is out of you, so set back as Current Coin. . . .
>
> And I myself ask no better Portion than that you fall to me, for then should all Eyes behold the Bone of Truth, the Marrow of Justice! For I'd have all Destruction in you well destroyed before the Striking of another Midnight Bell!
> Or thus:
> It is Spring again, O Little One, the Waters melt, and the Earth divides, and the Leaves put forth, and the Heart sings dilly, dilly, dilly! It is Girls' Weather, and Boys' Luck! (28–29)

Playing upon the figures and styles deployed throughout "Rape and Repining!," these final paragraphs also increase the amplitude of violence, the "scratch, slap, pinch, pull" of its rape rhetoric. Echoes of the chapter's opening bring the reader full circle, and as one enumeration ("Scourged! Whipped! Stocked! Cried against!") mirrors another ("Soiled! Despoiled! Handled!" etc.), the text dramatizes woman's double violation. The rhetoric of melting and molding literalizes her deformation in the aftermath of rape; the allegory of iron smelting elaborates on woman's economic value and devaluation: her reconstitution as "Current Coin" and "Honest Flesh" resituates her within the sexual economy, fixes her in the "certainty" of reproduction, thus resolving the case of rape, which appeared "a Riddle still and not a Certainty" (26). Or to put it differently: ravishment enforces woman's exile to a lower class, a different caste where, functioning as a "Cap for his Heel," she sustains and accelerates man's progress while spending her own currency. Lowered in that way, she will have no "Father behind his Beard" continuing to weep; public opinion ("we") has long taken over, making of her what it will, against her own will.

Proposing a complicity, on the part of the Council of Women, with the symbolic order, Barnes, like Irigaray, sees woman as mimic who, caught in patriarchal discourse and its logic, faces two alternatives: she can either choose to remain silent or else, as an interim strategy, mime, parody, paraphrase, and quote male discourse. Deliberately acting out the role that is historically assigned to women, reproduction, the female speaker exposes what she mocks and undermines the symbolic order and its representations of gender, in general, and of rape, in particular.[6] In Barnes's *Ryder*, though, reproduction is women's curse, male polygamy a philosophy and sexual practice enacted at the expense of women's bodies and minds. Accordingly, Amelia counsels her daughter Julie to "take warning by my size and don't let a man touch you, for their touching never ends, and screaming oneself into a mother is no pleasure at all" (95). Stevenson goes so far as to read *Ryder* as Barnes's "statement against woman's enslavement to reproduction" ("Ryder" 104), to being the breeder of (Ryder's) race. Barnes's concern with "breeding" as the flip side of sexual intercourse, be it enforced or consensual, thus also needs to be seen in the context of the 1920s, a decade that encouraged women's sexual expression yet left issues of contraception highly contested.[7]

At the same time, Barnes's focus on breeding, most explicit in "Ryder—His Race" (chapter 46), relocates rape and ravishment in a "racialized" context. Slavery institutionalized black women's premature sexualization—and polygamy, if you will—in order to reproduce property, and *Ryder* subtly identifies slavery as the historical reference point of Wendell's philosophy of free intercourse. Significantly enough, Wendell was born in 1865. Accordingly, the plea, on the part of the Council of Women, that ravished women ought to be "Scourged! Flayed! Whipped! Stocked!" borrows from the antebellum rhetoric of rape, as does the "Portrait of Amelia's Beginning" (chapter 6), which relates that Amelia's father occasionally "chased" her with a long horsewhip (30). Where female figures speak plainly of their lives, by contrast, headlines ("Amelia Hears from Her Sister on the Misfortunes of Women," chapter 42) and epistolary style echo the late-eighteenth-century novel. Set at the turn of the nineteenth century, yet engaging a rhetoric of rape that predates the realist paradigm, Barnes's mimicry refocuses on the fallacies of the female body.

Barnes's concern with incest and sexual abuse of under-age children at the same time underpins conceptions of middle-class sexuality. The middle class has created notions of "childhood," as Wilson argues, that "ward[] off sexual threats to children perceived as coming from class or racial others or from the child's own lascivious nature" (53). Accordingly, as Missy Dehn Kubitschek points out, the Euro-American tradition "seldom examines intrafamilial rape," displays "a reluctance to associate patriarchal family structure and rape" (49). Like the interventions of the contemporary incest-recovery movement, Barnes reveals such abuse and relocates its "source . . . from outside the class to within the class" (Wilson 53), from outside the race to within the race, from outside the family to within the family. In this regard *Ryder* compares with Faulkner's *Sanctuary* and anticipates Morrison's and Walker's daring texts on intraracial rape.

With Walker's *The Color Purple* Barnes's *Ryder* moreover shares a history of censorship—imposed not for her hyperbolic rape rhetoric or intimations of incest, though, but for passages preoccupied with body fluids and functions. And this makes perfect sense. For Barnes's text does not, as West suggests, "plead . . . for freedom of imagery" (244). Instead, *Ryder* highlights the limits of discourse and insinuates that whenever we talk about rape and sexual abuse, we "plunge headlong," to appropriate Jacobs's words, into a prepatterned, codified textual universe that prevents us from thinking, perceiving, speaking rape anew. Even at its most transgressive—pondering the grotesque, monstrous body, its taboo sexual practices, its physical convexities and openings, its processes of eating and defecation, copulation and pregnancy, childbirth and physical decay—Barnes's text re-members her (Rabelaisian) precursors. Thus she forces us to recognize how forms of representation and their "dilly, dilly, dilly" generic conventions monitor meaning, how the tales of seduction overshadow the significance of rape and incest.

Like Barnes's tales of "soiled" and ravished youth and beauty, Sanctuary—Faulkner's "darkest" book, as Fiedler claims (Love and Death 323)—interrogates the "conspiracy between female flesh and female season" (Faulkner, Sanctuary 13). Projecting Barnes's hyperboles onto a metonymic plain, Faulkner explores the relation of rape and representation without dispensing with (realist) narrative. Thus he engages "the myth of the South" (Allen Tate)—a myth established in part on the basis of rape narratives—exposing not so much the discourse of mythmaking as its prominent deletions, one of which is (the figure of) incest.

"THAT LITTLE HOT BALL INSIDE YOU THAT SCREAMS": RAPE'S RESISTANCE TO REPRESENTATION, THE RESISTANCE TO RAPE, AND THE TRANSGRESSION OF BOUNDARIES IN WILLIAM FAULKNER'S SANCTUARY

Even though Faulkner's fiction is replete with transgressive sexual acts such as pedophilia, necrophilia, incest, and bestiality, Sanctuary was his only book initially refused by its publisher. Employing rape as its "sensational pivot" (Matthews 258), the novel seemed a hastily written "pot-boiler" to Faulkner himself (Seed 73) and a chilling "shocker" to many critics (Allen Tate 427). Outselling all Faulkner's previous works, Sanctuary thus became his " 'pop' novel"—located, however, according to Fiedler, not at the periphery, but at "the very center of his achievement" ("Pop" 77).

For my reading of rape Sanctuary is central not only because Faulkner's fiction revises the popular and populist rhetoric (of rape) produced by romances of the Page/Dixon kind. Sanctuary, in particular, addresses the Southern myth in a manner that foregrounds its most uncanny subtexts and inner conflicts; it reveals what Harper considered the savagery of a supposedly supreme civilization as the "defilement" of cultural artifice by natural forces; and it ponders the proximity of "good" and "evil," of justice and crime. Accordingly, the novel's crucial motif of transgression, border crossing, and passing informs semantics as well as style. Sanctuary blends several of the 1920s popular genres, including the detective story, gothic fiction, comedy, and (sadomasochistic) pornography.[8] Dramatizing rape as enforced transition from a state of innocence to a state of corruption, Faulkner employs sexual violence as a trope for struggles interior to both the individual subject and Southern society. And he insists that this struggle is captured best not by "authentic observation," as Allen Tate claimed (421), but by modernist aesthetics.

This also explains why the text is "essentially voyeuristic in its appeal" yet—doing without "dirty" words and explicit depictions of sexual acts—ranks as the "softest of soft porn" (Fiedler, "Pop" 91, 90). Rape is not a fixed moment in time here but a process of transgression and transition. Constantly shifting between disclosure and concealment, and highly elliptical in structure—with rape as its central deletion—*Sanctuary* underlines that rape cannot be named, just as the line between innocence and evil cannot be located. Moreover, by metonymically linking rape, as John T. Matthews convincingly argues, to (Benbow's) incestuous desire, the novel interrogates the relation of nature and culture, savagery and civilization. While both incest and rape remain nameless throughout the text, rape becomes Faulkner's master trope of transgression. And rape's very resistance to representation inspires the reader to imagine the deleted transgressive acts. Filling in the textual gaps, we supplement our own rape fantasies, so to speak, necessarily misconstruing the moment. Thus we deform the face we assign to rape to the extent that the text effaces its forms of representation. The reader is as ignorant of the actual moment of violation as he or she is about its medium, the corncob—substitute for Popeye's "dysfunctional" penis, phallic symbol, and sign for deferred representation all in one. *Sanctuary* thus is also a text about representation and reading in general and a text about representing and reading rape in particular. Whether reading *Sanctuary* in turn amounts to raping, as some critics have claimed, is yet another matter.

Diane Roberts, for instance, claims that "SANCTUARY IS ABOUT RAPE" (21), that "*Temple Drake is raped over and over again*" (26) and that "in *Sanctuary*, the threat of rape enclos[es] all bodies" (34). Such an "all-inclusive" reading illustrates that rape has become a composite, indistinct figure for rather diverse violations and systemic violence. At the same time, though, Roberts remains unconcerned with the "discourse of rape" that she locates at the basis of Southern society, and the sexual violence she claims it condones (31). Instead, her reading, like that of Laura Tanner, is overdetermined by a (feminist) concern with real rape[9] and tends to disregard the ("realist") textual precursors Faulkner's modernist aesthetics and ideology build upon. Reading *Sanctuary* as a tale of women's exploitation, both critics fail to see that Faulker also deconstructs the myth of a prelapsarian South. Moreover, while Faulkner employs rape as a figure of transgression and process, parts of feminist criticism read rape as an act of penetration pertaining to analytical pursuits as well as physical violence. Walter Benjamin compared such pursuits to the task of the surgeon and the cameraman (as opposed to the magician and the painter), who cut into the patient's body, thus diminishing the distance from reality, penetrating its web, and generating a picture "of multiple fragments which are assembled under a new law" (234). This analogy may apply to the way *Sanctuary* introduces Benbow's fragmented self, and authorizes the gaze that is put to work throughout the text.[10] But does it also illuminate the meaning the novel assigns to rape?

Transgression and penetration differ in that the former is a process while the latter designates a moment in time. A person can be raped or penetrated repeatedly; he or she crosses certain borderlines only once and, in case of rape, without ever returning to a state of "innocence" or inviolacy. By equivocating the actual moment of rape and pondering the processes of transformation effected by (threats of) rape instead, Faulkner locates violence in the passage from one state of existence to another. He therefore does not withhold the horrors of rape. In fact, the novel captures rape as a life-threatening experience that destroys the victim's subjectivity by destroying the boundaries of her self. In this way *Sanctuary* signifies the difference between subject positions. Contemporary readers, however, tend to read for the rape itself: finding the moment of penetration suppressed, they turn around to discover rape in the text's every loophole, including the ways it builds up suspense or positions its readers.[11] Rather than deconstructing the rapist ideology of the novel, such readings enact its major points. For rape as represented in *Sanctuary* does not so much enclose all bodies as it reveals the complicity between the body politic and the rapist. Lacking the figure that "realist" rape identified so clearly, *Sanctuary* thus dramatizes the dissemination of the meaning of rape. And it is this dissemination that interpretations of the novel tend to reproduce.

My own reading instead capitalizes on how Faulkner's re-presentation of rape plays upon the insight that rape is "by definition imagined" and exists "as experience and as memory, as *image* translated into signs" only (Bal, "Reading" 142). Rape in *Sanctuary* is indeed deferred, displaced, and never present. Yet it is both retrospectively remembered *and* foreshadowed. Or, as Matthews puts it: "The language of *Sanctuary* preenacts the violation of Temple, making her deflowering a passage that can be presented only as already accomplished" (261). Thus the meaning of rape does not emanate from the act of penetration (which likens it to consensual intercourse), but from the before and after and their difference or distance. Accordingly, Faulkner does not zoom in on the pain inflicted *by*, but focuses on the initial fear *of*, rape and the subsequent denial that protects Temple from the damage done. Readings that emphasize Temple's complicity in her own violation, by contrast, disregard her furious attempts to fight off violation, prior to and after the fact. Even Temple's false testimony against Lee Goodwin bespeaks her desire to sever the experience of rape from her sense of self. And it is this desire that structures Temple's own retrospective account of her violation. Rape's resistance to representation thus corresponds to Temple's resistance to being raped and to acknowledging having been raped.

Temple resists her violation rhetorically, mentally, and physically. Her body is increasingly immobilized, paralyzed during the onset and the aftermath of rape. Her muscles "cramped" (86), her senses pulling back for protection, she retreats into a state of numbness, the "formal feeling" that Dickinson depicts, and that comes before *and* "[a]fter great pain" here (#341), dissociating body from mind. In this way, the experience of rape creates a kind of sanctuary indeed. Conventionally, sanctuary refers to sacred or consecrated places, to churches, churchyards, or temples, if you like. Faulkner's novel employs the term ironically to designate "the most sacred affairs of that most sacred thing in life: womanhood" (284), the figure of a self-fashioned sacrosanct South whose desecration we witness throughout the text. Yet sanctuary takes on another meaning in Faulkner's *The Town* (1957), redefined by Gavin Stevens as "a rationality of perspective, which animals, humans too, not merely reach, but earn in passing through unbearable emotional states like furious rage and furious fear" (qtd. in Arnold and Trouard 3). Having passed through "unbearable emotional states" of (fear of) sexual assault, it is "rational" for Temple to crave the very (sexual) aggression she has learned to ward off. Accordingly, in response to Popeye's renewed attempt to overpower her, Temple "cring[es] upon herself in as complete an isolation as though she were bound to a church steeple" (158). Sexual abuse therefore does not initiate Temple into sexuality, as has been suggested, but alienates her sexuality.

Foreshadowing and Remembering Rape

Faulkner's novel relates Temple's rape from three different retrospective angles. The first, rendered by Benbow, focuses on the moment the rape actually happens; the second is Temple's own account of her violation, presented to Miss Reba and Benbow; and the last is the trial scene which reveals that Temple's rapist employed a corncob. This is account number one, depicting Popeye as he approaches Temple in the crib:[12]

> He turned and looked at her. He waggled the pistol slightly and put it back in his coat, then he walked toward her. Moving, he made no sound at all; the released door yawned and clapped against the jamb, but it made no sound either; it was as though sound and silence had become inverted. She could hear silence in a thick rustling as he moved toward her through it, thrusting it aside, and she began to say Something is going to happen to me. She was saying it to the old man with the yellow clots for eyes. "Something is happening to me!" she screamed at him, sitting in his chair in the sunlight, his hands crossed on the top of the stick. "I told you it was!" she screamed, voiding the words like hot silent bubbles into the bright silence about them until he turned his head and the two phlegm-clots above her where she lay tossing and thrashing on the rough, sunny boards. "I told you! I told you all the time!" (102)

Shifting from disclosure to concealment, this scene displays the novel's dominant modes of sense making. Popeye's "waggling" pistol evokes the rape scene in Dixon's *Clansman* yet suggests the tail of a puppy dog rather than an erect, thrusting penis. The "released door yawn[ing] and clapp[ing] against the jamb" depicts Temple's apparent consent and complicity as well as her exposure, defenselessness, and some degree of force. In fact, however, full of fear and fury, Temple has just been through a series of attempts to either close doors for protection or to open them for escape—all to no avail. As Popeye unexpectedly enters through a trapdoor in the ceiling, Tommy's guardianship—like that of Temple's drunk date, Gowan Stevens—turns out to be a farce, the chivalric code a failure.

Still Temple experiences her violation seemingly detached, like a fish in a glass bowl, resigned to her fate in an apathetic posture—"hands limp and palm-up on her lap" (102)—she will assume once again when testifying against Goodwin (284). As Popeye kills her ineffectual "bodyguard" Tommy, Temple registers the gunshot as "no louder than the striking of a match: a short, minor sound shutting down upon the scene, the instant, with a profound finality, completely isolating it." This shot not only insinuates that Popeye's "fire" is consumed before the rape, that he is impotent, "the pistol behind him, against his flank, wisping thinly along his leg," like a "match" indeed (102). It also "shut[s] down the scene," barring it from direct view like a curtain or screen ("Moving, he made no sound at all"). At the same time Temple's sensibility is enhanced: as silence inverts into sound, she perceives the imperceptible and detects in the "thick rustling" of Popeye's movement the noise of the corn shucks that externalizes her mute inner violation. Literalizing synesthesia, the scene thus establishes translation as fundamental to the representation of rape. And just as such transformation is processual, Temple's own words scatter her violation across time: what happens "was" foretold, "is happening," and "is going to happen." The text thus comments on its own narrative procedure, its suspense of violence further suspended by its elliptical rendering of rape.

Temple's repeated "I told you" pinpoints her foreknowledge while also foreshadowing her act of telling, the disjunctive narrative she relates during her captivity at a Memphis brothel. Here, however, Temple addresses a deaf and blind old man physically present yet incapable of functioning as either witness, protector, or violator, thus embodying the dysfunctional supremacist Southern system and its pretentious codes. Aligning Pap with both Judge Drake (whose authority Temple repeatedly, yet vainly, invokes) and Popeye (whom she finally adopts as a surrogate father figure [236]), Faulkner's novel thus exposes the paternal complicity in the violation of daughters. Most significant, this alliance between inefficient fathers and impotent rapist redefines Temple's violation as incest, as a "family affair." As it overruns the boundary between nature and culture guarded by the prohibition against incest, Faulkner's *Sanctuary* discloses the Southern discrimination between savagery and civilization as self-deception. Diminishing the distance between (teasing) Temple, her (impotent) violator Popeye, and her (dysfunctional) defenders, the novel thus underlines how fictions of innocence and violation interdepend, how constructions of cultural supremacy require stories of culture invaded by nature (such as Page's and Dixon's). The representation of Temple's rape in turn acknowledges that the "actual moments of crossing thresholds," however, escape representation (Matthews 258).

The trial scene represents rape metonymically, exposing its medium. " 'I offer as evidence,' " the district attorney addresses the jury, " 'this object which was found at the scene of the crime.' He held in his hand a corn-cob. It appeared to have been dipped in dark brownish paint" (Faulkner, *Sanctuary* 283). Presenting the phallic "object" without naming it, the attorney invites people to interpret what it is evidence of. Its brownish color invokes the (black) male body and the paradigmatic rapist "savage" (yet emasculated) Popeye is associated with throughout (10). Misreading the trace of Temple's injury as "paint," the narrator insinuates both the artifice of Southern womanhood and the "artificiality" of the "realist" rapist. Accordingly, Popeye's face is compared to a "mask," his hands appear "doll-like" (5), his attire "like a modernist lampstand" (7).

Whereas the district attorney does not solicit Temple's explicit testimony, we get the most telling account of the rape when Miss Reba urges Temple to confess to Benbow (215). However, as she reimagines the events at the Old Frenchman place, Temple indulges in strategies of rhetorical evasion. In fact, the text translates into tropes the very psychic defense mechanisms that rape victims rely upon in order to work through the unsettling, traumatic experience, mechanisms ranging from splitting-off, denial, regression, and suppression to autoaggression and guilt, introjection and identification (and opposed to the strategies of compensation, sublimation, and rationalization that characterize Benbow's defenses).[13] These tropes render the memory of rape as monitored by someone who does not want to remember.

Temple's inconsistent, jumpy, mad as much as maddening account therefore shuns verisimilitude and reflects a victim's attempt to reduce fear and to steer the mind away from the injury. While fear results from confinement and causes one's breath to stall, Temple's tales translate that "inner scream," those "words like hot little balls," into narratives that ease the pain and scaffold a demolished psychic structure. As such, they split off and externalize the experience and its unsettling effects, and in the process reerect the boundaries of subjectivity that were violently transgressed. Temple thus generates a text that simultaneously accounts for her violation and acknowledges the processes of mediation, translation, and transformation that generate the distorted image of her former self. Therein Temple's "carnal knowledge" crystallizes into highly irritating scenes, oscillating between a desire to restore innocence and ignorance and the impulse to use that new knowledge against her aggressor, to turn the tables and reestablish herself in a position of power.

That position, however, lacks substance and figures as "a thin ghost, a pale shadow moving in the uttermost profundity of shadow" (148). Constantly reapplying her makeup, Temple attempts to retain control, to maintain "normalcy," yet reduces femininity to artificiality and "parrotlike" performance: her cosmetic efforts soon enough resemble tribal arts, providing the mask and costume of a primitive, sex-crazed condition. This impersonation says little about female sexuality, though. Instead, it bespeaks the space and meaning that Southern society assigns to "despoiled" womanhood, the position open to women who, unlike her (white) "foremothers," survive their violation.

In addition, Temple's rape narrative echoes in the depiction of Benbow's delayed physical reaction to it. The scene that shows him, after his return home, vomiting into the toilet, turning his insides out, metonymically aligns Popeye's rape of Temple with Benbow's own incestuous desire for his stepdaughter Little Belle. It thus reaffirms the complicity between Benbow and "black man" Popeye, a complicity that in turn makes Temple's abuse a case of interracial rape and a transgression of miscegenation laws. Incest thus emerges as the "other" of miscegenation; their alliance exposes the fear of savagery invading civilization as an inner rather than an external conflict. The analogy of rape and incest in turn renders miscegenation as a family affair, as the inner conflict of Southern culture. The novel thus recovers the past (of the slave economy) in the present, figuring the enforced, "incestuous" interracial relations in the extended "plantation family." Accordingly, Narcissa, scolding her brother Benbow for running out on his wife (and in to her), calls him "nigger" twice (108, 117). Likewise, Temple's self-identification as "nigger boy" (219) reinforces the proximity of rape, incest, and miscegenation. This proximity both reveals and conceals a "carnal" knowledge pertaining to constructions of (racialized) sexuality and sexual violence, underlining that such constructions depend as much on a will to knowledge as on a will to ignorance and a deployment of silence.

Temple first focuses on the night "she had spent in comparative inviolation" (215). Her narrative of resistance thus evokes the crime just as the phrase "comparative inviolation" evokes "violation": by literally negating and, figuratively, externalizing an act happening inside. The reader experiences the rape ("it") by way of Temple's mobile consciousness—a consciousness locked in an immobile body ("I just sat there"), yet moving along metonymic strings of association and generating curious similes, metaphors, and a seemingly "bright, chatty monologue" (216) that oscillates between fairy-tale fantasy and noise that borders on hysteria. Throughout this monologue, rape is marked as movement and sound, as an invisible phenomenon devoid of substance and rendered by slipping pronoun references that trigger the turns and twists Temple's rhetoric takes. The scenario of a "darkness full of movement" (218)

Temple depicts thus outlines rape as a structure and culminates in the chapter's final figure of rape, the image of "a flat car moving at speed through a black tunnel" (223).

Temple clearly remembers her silent breathing that made the shucks of her bedding rustle, thus "voicing" the movement of Temple's body and the corncob moving within it. When Popeye's "nasty little cold hand" (218), she recalls, had

> got down where my insides begin, and I hadn't eaten since yesterday at dinner and my insides started bubbling and the shucks began to make so much noise it was like laughing at me. I'd think they were laughing because all the time his hand was going inside the top of my knickers and I hadn't changed into a boy yet.
>
> That was the funny thing, because I wasn't breathing then. I hadn't breathed in a long time. So I thought I was dead. Then I did a funny thing. I could see myself in a coffin. I looked sweet—you know: all in white. I had on a veil like a bride, and I was crying because they had put shucks in my coffin. I was crying because they had put shucks in the coffin where I was dead, but all the time I could feel my nose going cold and hot and cold and hot, and I could see all the people sitting around the coffin, saying Don't she look sweet. Dont she look sweet. (219)

The "bubbling" of Temple's insides recalls the "thin eeeeeeeeeeeeeee sound like bubbles in a bottle" (99) released when she detected Goodwin outside the crib, possibly in anticipation of her false testimony. Imagining the shucks mocking the "unnaturalness" of Popeye's corncob act, Temple distracts her attention from the abuse and recapitulates the mental precautions she took prior to his uninvited touch. Scared into strategies of evasion, the first "funny thing" Temple contemplates is "to make like [she] was a boy" (216) by intensely looking at her legs, thus returning to a position of "inviolation" indeed.

At the same time, this fantasy refigures associations of rape and metamorphosis looming large in classical myths as well as in T. S. Eliot's *The Waste Land* (1922), which, like Faulkner's fiction, is preoccupied with cultural disintegration and decay. Whereas in myth (as in racist romances and in Moody's play) rape triggers cultural and political transformations, Temple's imaginary regression into boyhood allows her to mentally disentangle herself from the moments of violation and the transformations they effect. (Accordingly, her account repeatedly "races ahead of the event"). On a more abstract level, metamorphosis enacts the translation that Temple's rape narrative and our interpretation thereof involve. This is neither a translation of fact into fiction, as Roberts suggests (34), nor does Temple's tale "fulfill male fantasies and expectations" (Pettey 80). Rather, Temple sabotages such expectations (therefore Benbow experiences her account as a "monologue" that excludes him). Voicing her violation by expressing her resistance to it, she underscores that rape is as much a mental as a material matter, provoking physical and psychic defense mechanisms which in the act of re-membering rape transform into a rhetoric of evasion.

Accordingly, projecting her sex-change fantasy, Temple's mind wanders off into strange similes ("You know how you do things like that. Like when you know one problem in class . . ." [216]), weird associations ("I'd think about what they tell children, about kissing your elbow, and I tried to" [216–17]),[14] and inadequate actions (such as "count[ing] fifty" [217]). Temple not only wishes to dispose of her female body, particularly those legs that " 'd gotten [her] into this" (217). As a figure in transition, she opts for regression, just as Benbow does when he longs to recover the innocence of his boyhood. The difference involved, though, is that between subjectivity and subjection. While Benbow flees sexuality to avoid violating the most fundamental paternal law, Temple wishes to escape the effects of violent sexualization. Her rape is no "sexual awakening" (Seed 84), no "birth of sexual passion" (Matthews 258) but its stillbirth or death.

Temple is initiated into a sexuality indistinguishable from sexual violation, a sexual aggression of which she is both object and subject. In her final encounter with Red, Temple herself figures as rapist: "When he touched her," Faulkner writes, "she sprang like a bow, hurling herself upon him, her mouth gaped and ugly like that of a dying fish as she writhed her loins against him" (238). Provoked by Red's touch, Temple's sexual aggression recalls her own sexual violation ("dying fish"). With an impotent, emasculated rapist and a rape victim turned rapist, boundaries between victim and violator have become brittle. Accordingly, in her recollections Temple repeatedly engages in rape-revenge. Remembering a chastity belt a female friend had once seen in a museum (217), Temple (rape-)fantasizes that "maybe it would have long sharp spikes on it and he wouldn't know it until too late and I'd jab it into him. I'd jab it all the way through him and I'd think about the blood running on me and how I'd say I guess that'll teach you! I guess you'll let me alone now! I'd say. I didn't know it was going to be just the other way." Evidently these imaginary scenes are triggered by fear, not desire, and the "blood running on" Temple is the very "blood in her veins" she could hear when "feeling Popeye approaching"; it is the trace of a violation subtly insinuated by "the little muscles at the corners of her eyes cracking faintly wider and wider," the "nostrils going alternately cool and warm" (218).

Temple's retrospective account, privileging images of transformation, evasion, and revenge, slips back and forth over the pivotal moment of violation, never touching upon it. It thus reenacts her attempt to either escape her aggressor's touch or to get the thing over and done with and—ironically reversing the Sleeping Beauty tale—simply go to sleep. Accordingly, in her memory of the event, she even cheers Popeye on, thus changing from object to agent: "So I'd say," she tells her audience, "You're a coward if you dont! You're a coward if you dont! and I could feel my mouth getting fixed to scream, and that little hot ball inside you that screams" (218). Temple's cheerleading posture not only mocks Ruby's notion that sexual aggression makes a "real man" (59).

Like the "laughing" shucks it inverts, it (mis)translates an inner sensation of outermost discomfort, fear, and fury into self-aggrandizing sounds. Temple's "nymphomania"—an effect of her abuse—becomes a defense strategy meant to turn the tables, yet reinforcing her subjection.

When Popeye's "nasty little hand" reaches underneath her raincoat, "it was like alive ice," Temple recalls, "and my skin started jumping away from it like those little flying fish in front of a boat. It was like my skin knew which way it was going before it started moving, and my skin would keep on jerking just ahead of it like there wouldn't be anything there when the hand got there" (218–19).[15] This is carnal knowledge redefined: shedding her skin, Temple separates sensual perception from consciousness and hints at her metamorphosis. At the same time, the simile employed here ("like those little flying fish in front of a boat") depicts her abuse as an encounter between (female) nature and (male) culture and elaborates on the "fear and loathing" of female sexuality. Throughout the text female flesh, skin, and blood exhale "foul" (271), fishy smells and resonate with decay and death.[16] To my mind this insistence underscores that the text exposes—rather than propagates—a cultural imaginary that figures female sexuality as defilement only. Benbow himself nourishes the "romantic illusion" that it is "[b]etter for [Temple] if she were dead tonight," that the "only solution" is to simply blot her out, and along with her "Popeye, the woman, the child, Goodwin" (221). Accordingly, Temple's self-portrait as white, sweet, and dead parodies the paradigm of rape and death. The shucks in her coffin, however, blur the line between innocence and corruption that this paradigm sets out to symbolically reinstall.

In her final episodes, Temple, infuriated "because he was so long doing it" (219), aspires to regain control through a self-empowering rhetoric. However, its paratactical, repetitive, and illogical syntax and mockery of reason ("Because I'd say . . .") pulverize more than reconstitute her subject position:

> I'd talk to him like the teacher does in school, and then I was a teacher in school and it was a little black thing like a nigger boy, kind of, and I was the teacher. Because I'd say How old am I? and I'd say I'm forty-five years old. I had iron-gray hair and spectacles and I was all big up here like women get. I had on a gray tailored suit, and I never could wear gray. And I was telling it what I'd do, and it kind of drawing up and drawing up like it could already see a switch. (219–20)

Here Temple tries to ward off violation by refashioning herself into a virile *and* bosomy maternal authority figure in the face of whom the sexual aggressor is racialized and diminished. Soon enough she stars as "an old man, with a long white beard, and then the little black man got littler and littler and I was saying Now. You see now. I'm a man now. Then I thought about being a man, and as soon as I thought it, it happened. It made a kind of plopping sound, like blowing a little rubber tube wrong-side outward. It felt cold, like the inside of your mouth when you hold it open" (220). Like Temple's raincoat the "rubber tube" underlines that the "sexual practices" depicted here are nonreproductive—in fact, seen in the light of Benbow's subsequent vomiting, abortive and "unnatural." More important, the simile connotes an obsolete theory on the development of the male sexual organs delineated insightfully by Thomas Laqueur. Based on the assumption that male and female sexual organs are homologous, it was long assumed that penis and testes "pop out" of the male body because of its heat. This unenlightened conception of the evolution of primary sexual characteristics corresponds to the "naive" mode of Temple's rape narrative and handily bolsters her fluctuating sense of gender. Accordingly, as Matthews points out, her sex change both produces and feels like a cavity ("like the inside of your mouth"), thus connoting femininity and the threat of enforced defloration, which exposes her insides ("open"), ruptures her physical and emotional boundaries, tears her mentally and physically apart. And yet, reimagining rape, Temple projects herself on top of the situation:

> It felt cold, like the inside of your mouth when you hold it open. I could feel it, and I lay right still to keep from laughing about how surprised he was going to be. I could feel the jerking going on inside my knickers ahead of his hand and me lying there trying not to laugh how surprised and mad he was going to be in about a minute. Then all of a sudden I went to sleep. I couldn't even stay awake until his hand got there. I just went to sleep. I couldn't even feel myself jerking in front of his hand, but I could hear the shucks. I didn't wake up until that woman came and took me down to the crib. (220)

Seemingly self-satisfied, Temple applauds her own little drag performance. Yet when Popeye's hand catches up with her head, so to speak, she loses consciousness, leaving it to the shucks to voice her sexual violation. The multiple meanings of "crib"—denoting, variously, a cradle or cot, the nativity scene, a cheating aid, a plagiary, a manger, and finally, "a prostitute's small, often closet-sized room in a brothel" (Arnold and Trouard 86)—record Temple's departure and "destiny," render her passage in a single sign.

Temple reexperiences her violation during a medical examination that breaks down her defenses: as the physician "put[s] out a thick, white hand bearing a masonic ring," "[c]old air slipped down her body, below her thighs; her eyes were closed. Lying on her back, her legs close together, she began to cry, hopelessly and passively, like a child in a dentist's waiting room" (150). While Temple finally acknowledges her abuse, the conclusive simile—a distant echo of *McTeague*—restores her "inviolation" ("like a child"). Rape and its meaning thus keep circulating in different directions. Ring and dentist resurface in a scene involving Temple's initial violator. As Popeye puts his hand over Temple's mouth to choke the mockery of his maimed manhood (231), his "thick ring" feels to Temple "like a dentist's instrument" (232). Such an instrument prevents patients from closing their mouths and here recalls her medical examination ("her legs close together"). Relieved that the "imprint of his fingers cold on her jaw" does not show, Temple remembers her violation by recontextualizing its trope: " 'Shucks,' she said, 'it didn't leave a mark, even;' drawing her flesh this way and that. 'Little runt,' she said, peering at her reflection. She added a phrase, glibly obscene, with a detached parrotlike effect. She painted her mouth again" (233, my emphasis). Temple impersonates, wears like a mask ("parrotlike"), the very identity she was violently initiated into, throwing it back at her aggressors.

Rape and Incest, Rape as Incest

Temple's captivity at a Memphis brothel literalizes her social death. While Miss Reba acknowledges her pain (220), Benbow, preoccupied with his own marriage and his incestuous attractions to Little Belle and Narcissa, does not. Instead of "digesting" and acting upon Temple's disturbing account, he merely reacts to it, literally spews it out "unassimilated" (221). Like Temple in her failure to eat, to internalize her ordeal, Benbow refuses the "carnal knowledge" her rape narrative carries, yet for different reasons: his own incestuous longings affirm his proximity to Popeye.

The novel's alliance of rape and incest culminates in Benbow's vomiting. Having returned to Jefferson and faced with a photograph of Little Belle, he is overpowered by his illicit desire. "Ejaculating" the coffee that "lay in a hot ball on his stomach" (221), his body rebirths "that little hot ball inside you that screams" and externalizes its inner sounds.

> Then he knew what that sensation in his stomach meant. He put the photograph down hurriedly and went to the bathroom. He opened the door running and fumbled at the light. But he had not time to find it and he gave over and plunged forward and struck the lavatory and leaned upon his braced arms while the shucks set up a terrific uproar beneath her thighs. Lying with her head lifted slightly, her chin depressed like a figure lifted down from a crucifix, she watched something black and furious go roaring out of her pale body. She was bound naked on her back on a flat car moving at speed through a black tunnel, the blackness streaming in rigid threads overhead, a roar of iron wheels in her ears. The car shot bodily from the tunnel in a long upward slant, the darkness overhead now shredded with parallel attenuations of living fire, toward a crescendo like a held breath, an interval in which she would swing faintly and lazily in nothingness filled with pale, myriad points of light. Far beneath her she could hear the faint, furious uproar of the shucks. (223)

Through the subtle suggestion of indefinite pronoun reference ("her," "she"), the whole scene—complete with "swoon" and "shucks"—uncannily intermingles Temple's rape with the "seduction" of Benbow and the sexualization/rape of Little Belle. As Benbow reenacts the rape scene, taking on the position of sexual aggressor, it both recalls and consumes what he had wished to expunge from his memory: his day trip to Memphis—this "dream filled with all the nightmare shapes it had taken him forty-three years to invent, concentrated in a hot, hard lump in his stomach" (222).

Symbolically performing what Popeye was incapable of, Benbow acknowledges his complicity in the crime and his kinship with its perpetrator. We are introduced to Benbow, Pettey notes (74), on the novel's first pages, while he drinks from a spring near the Old Frenchman place as Popeye watches on. "In the spring," reads Faulkner's third paragraph, "the drinking man leaned his face to the broken and myriad reflection of his own drinking. When he rose up he saw among them the shattered reflection of Popeye's straw hat, though he had heard no sound" (4). Having "hatless" Benbow (3) recognize Popeye's hat/head as part of his own cubist mirror image, the novel establishes its main point of view as a narcissistic *and* fragmented modernist position. It thus literalizes what Allen Tate calls the narcissistic perspective of sentimental Southern literature "in which the South tried to define itself by looking into a glass behind its back: not inward" (420).

As the text aligns Benbow and, implicitly, the law with the bootlegger-rapist and violations of law, it establishes their kinship as one between self and other. Depicted as a dysfunctional, feminized rapist, as "object-like, in-human" (Pettey 74), and "black," as an "ape" (Faulkner, *Sanctuary* 49) and a "gorilla," Popeye embodies difference within the self-conception of both Benbow and the segregated South.[17] He thus is a figure of substantial weight and cultural significance, a "black presence," as Benbow sees it, "lying upon [the Old Frenchman place] like the shadow of something no larger than a match falling monstrous and portentous upon something else otherwise familiar and everyday and twenty times its size" (121). Associated with art and artificiality, with modernism, urbanization, and gangsterdom, Popeye darkens, fragments, and disfigures Benbow's vision of natural identity and family. This "radical intimacy between Horace and Popeye" not only suggests that "nature is interior to culture, not simply prior to it" (Matthews 263). It also underlines that the fear, loathing, and violation of female flesh is triggered not by a surplus but by an absence of potency and authority, by physical, emotional, and moral weakness rather than strength. Faulkner thus uncovers the fictions of remasculinized chivalric manhood and black bestiality as farce and interprets the "extreme corporeality" projected on black masculinity to be a conflict within (Southern) whiteness.

Benbow confronts (t)his self-division in encounters with Little Belle, one of which is particularly noteworthy. Objecting to her indiscriminate choice of male acquaintances, Benbow finds his masculinity challenged as his stepdaughter labels him "Shrimp! Shrimp!" (14).[18] " 'Then she was saying," he recalls,

" 'No! No!' and me holding her and she clinging to me. 'I didn't mean that! Horace! Horace!' And I was smelling the slain flowers, the delicate dead flowers and tears, and then I saw her face in the mirror. There was a mirror behind her and another behind me, and she was watching herself in the one behind me, forgetting about the other one in which I could see her face, see her watching the back of my head with pure dissimulation. That's why nature is 'she' and Progress is 'he'; nature made the grape arbor, but Progress invented the mirror." (15)

In Benbow's perspective, the superficial beauty of nature ("grape arbor")—like that of women—deceives; nature clearly equals violence, death, and decay here. By contrast, the surface of mirrors—like the self-reflexivity of men—searches, reveals, and embraces truth. The novel's first paragraph, though, has already done away with this neat opposition: nature itself provided the mirror for Benbow's self-inspection. Masculine and feminine self-deception and self-reflection are inextricably entwined. Faulkner himself evidently provided Allen Tate's metaphor for sentimental Southern literature. Part of this literature, as I have shown in chapter 2, acknowledges that the recognition of one's self, the construction of identity, always depends on both the assignment and the subordination of difference. By literalizing these structures of identity formation, Faulkner externalizes the inner conflict of the South. By metonymically aligning rape with incest, he unmasks the dominant projection of that conflict—miscegenation—as a family affair. Accordingly, we repeatedly find Benbow in one particular position: bent over a watery surface or looking directly into a mirror from which the object of his incestuous desire stares back at him.

The loaded symbolism, syntactical indeterminacy, and highly metonymical narration characterizing the scene of vomiting both reveal and conceal these subtexts. Visions of the inseparability of savagery and civilization, the interpenetration of laws and their violation, open up and dissolve as the boundaries between self and other are redrawn, reconstructing the other as an other identity made up of two others mirroring one another. The portrayal of Temple and Little Belle as composite martyr figures reminds us that rape, in Southern myth, metonymically relates to suicide as much as to murder. Accordingly, as it recalls Benbow's early sensation that Popeye "smells black"—"like that black stuff that ran out of Bovary's mouth and down upon her bridal veil when they raised her head" (7)—Bovary's reappearance suggests the complicity between Southern womanhood and its violators, a complicity counterbalanced by the polar imagery of dark and light employed throughout the scene. This alliance of Bovary and Popeye foreshadows the "kind of suicide" Popeye commits "by refusing to defend himself against the charges of having committed another murder of which he is innocent." This "complicity in his own death," Fiedler concludes, reconfirms Popeye's "ambiguous relationship with the woman whose lying testimony has seemed initially to deliver him from hanging" ("Pop" 87).

The image of the car roaring into the tunnel that climaxes the depiction of Benbow's vomiting fit blurs the boundaries between rapist and raped. While it literalizes the synchronicity of movement and sound that runs through Temple's rape account, its concreteness diminishes its potency as a figure of rape. Instead, the reader visualizes Temple/Little Belle "bound naked on her back on a flat car moving." If we identify the car with the thrusting penis/corncob, this image of transport merges rapist and raped, roaring into a vaginal tunnel which leaks that "black and furious" something reminiscent of Bovary's "black stuff" and Temple's blood. At the same time, the "blackness streaming in rigid threads overhead" visualizes the rapist's body as it moves back and forth over that of the victim. The preorgasmic moment ("a crescendo like a held breath") echoes Temple's own sensation that she stopped breathing/living during her rape, once again diminishing the distance between violator and violated. Benbow himself is a composite figure here, "pop-eyed voyeur, impotent father, ravishing lover, ravished victim" (Matthews 265). The release of (his) tension situates Temple in an interval of timelessness ("nothingness"), in a position between one identity and another ("an interval in which she would swing . . ."). The "pale, myriad points of light" that fill this void (of meaning) recall the "broken and myriad reflection" of Benbow's own self, attesting to his complex involvement in Temple's violation and the significance of his rape/incest fantasy. As the scene concludes, emphasizing "the faint, furious uproar of the shucks," which itself echoes the "black and furious . . . roaring" that "go[es] . . . out of her pale body," closure once again excludes Benbow and disavows his involvement.

Assembling Little Belle, Benbow, Temple, and Popeye in an intricate scenario of reflections, the vomiting scene blurs the boundaries between violator and victim, innocence and corruption, good and evil, dark and light, and crystallizes—in "an interval of timelessness," one could say—what turn-of-the-century Southern romances dramatize as conclusive linear narratives. Aligning interracial rape with incest, Faulkner makes sexual violence familiar to Southern culture in new ways. Accordingly, "the entire machinery by which 'rape' is signified in [American] culture" (Sedgwick, *Between Men* 9) operates in a dysfunctional manner here. Popeye goes free to be unjustly convicted and hanged for the murder of an Alabama policeman. Goodwin is lynched for a crime he never committed—a crime his lynchers would themselves have gladly engaged in ("I wouldn't have used no cob" [294]). Such lynch violence is officially legitimized. Once rape is involved, the district attorney claims, the case is "no longer a matter for the hangman, but for a bonfire of gasoline" (284). The very history of such bonfires racializes Temple's rape.

Defense attorney Benbow himself is, quite literally, up for grabs. "Do to the lawyer," we hear from the mob, "what we did to [Goodwin]. What he did to her. Only we never used a cob. We made him wish we had used a cob." Suggesting that Goodwin himself was raped (by an object other—larger, longer, bigger—than a cob), the text bespeaks the homosocial, homoerotic, and homophobic subtext of the racist romance. In the context of Faulkner's moral universe, such an "unnatural" act indicates a Southern Sodom, a community out of bounds, uncivilized, oversexualized. As Benbow escapes, he once again fails to acknowledge his own part in this tribal clansmanship: "Horace couldn't hear them. He couldn't hear the man who had got burned screaming. He couldn't hear the fire, though it still swirled upward unabated, as though it were living upon itself, and soundless: a voice of fury like in a dream, roaring silently out of a peaceful void" (296). The figures employed here—the fire, the roaring, the fury, the void—clearly resonate with the imagery pertaining to Benbow's own illicit desires and complicity in sex crime. Once again, however, the implications remain "unassimilated," silent, dreamlike, seemingly inconsequential, the "void" indeed guarding Benbow, as Matthews suggests (265), just as Temple desperately wished herself away from the scene of violation. Even though innocence is unmistakably lost, its dream persists—as does the myth of the South, Faulkner suggests, in a dysfunctional, destructive manner.

Such insights seriously unsettle analogies Faulkner's readers have drawn between the acts of looking, raping, reading, investigating/detecting, and interpreting. According to Roberts, the victimization of Temple "by male verbal attacks and the intrusive masculine gaze" anticipates her sexual violation. As a consequence, the author claims, "almost all the men in the novel"—including intoxicated Gowan Stevens (29)—"are potential rapists" (30). In fact, for Roberts, even Ruby qualifies as a rapist—an interpretation comparable to Sanchez-Eppler's reading of Jacobs's Mrs. Flint. As they "reduc[e] a woman to a kind of sexual addict," Ruby's "words" constitute "Temple Drake's first violation: rape by language" (28). Rape obviously serves as a metaphor for sexual harassment here, dissolving their difference. To Roberts's array of rapists Tanner adds the reader, who "conspires in an act of imaginative assault . . . not merely as a voyeur but as a violator" (*Intimate Violence* 27). Pettey not only holds that "*Sanctuary* entices the reader to participate in scenes of voyeurism, exhibitionism, and rape" (73); he also claims that "rape is Faulkner's master trope for the process of interpretation" (83). Finding readers "inculcated into a culture of rape—social, psychological, textual—from which we cannot escape any more than Temple could" (74), he even reconceives "us" as rape victims.

Reading closely, though, I cannot quite see why Faulkner should take "looking" to be primarily a "sexual act, a prelude to more aggressive physical appropriation" (Seed 75). Focused on two men "look[ing] at one another" (Faulkner, *Sanctuary* 5), the novel's opening scene instead constitutes the gaze as a means of projection, authorization, and identity formation, of self-knowledge as well as self-deception, and only in this way pertaining to the reading process. Nor can looking be reduced to a primarily male strategy of self-affirmation. Gender difference is not due to the fact that men do, while women do not, possess the gaze. It results from the different degree of authority assigned to male and female gazes. Temple's gaze, for instance, is repeatedly depicted as "blank" (30, 284). Instead of foreshadowing Temple's rape, the indeterminate act of looking thus manages to increasingly fix and immobilize her in the position of the other. Rape, by contrast, is a figure of transformation and transience in *Sanctuary*, mediating the passage from one position to another. The reader's expectation of the act is built up through the familiarity of a situation that pictures a "vulnerable young girl isolated in a ruined house" populated by five lower-class men (Seed 76), a situation that we have encountered in numerous captivity narratives, gothic and horror fiction, and Westerns. Yet Faulkner also defamiliarizes this scenario: Temple mistakenly believes herself to be safe among men with competing desires (Matthews 257). Uncannily akin to her violator, she is fooled by the weakest masquerading as the strongest.

Moreover, neither are voyeurism and exhibitionism identical with rape, as they manifest an entirely other dynamic of desire. Nor does the reader literally violate or rape anyone by reading. Re-presenting rape as a process, the novel instead makes the reader aware that his or her collaboration works by way of interpretation, aware of the seductiveness and titillation of narratives that disclose as much as they conceal, and consequently aware of his or her complicity in the *silencing* of rape. This, however, is an effect of representation, not an act of the reader. "At best" the reader is *like* a voyeur: trying to peep through the holes in Faulkner's narration, he or she can imagine how the corncob penetrates Temple. And yet, as Fiedler points out, reading pornographic texts such as *Sanctuary*, "we do not typically identify with its erotically active characters, rapist or raped; but with the Peeping Tom author, who compels us to keep our eye glued to the keyhole, ashamed but unable to withdraw" ("Pop" 91–92). What we discover is not some naked truth, though, but a "reflexive voyeurism" that for Fiedler figures as "the subject as well as the mode of apprehending the novel." The "climax" of that voyeurism he locates at the scene "in which Popeye slobbers over the bed in which Temple and Red copulate at his command." Reported by a black maid who watched Popeye watching, this scene puts "us as readers in the position of voyeurs at a fourth remove" and makes *Sanctuary* a "piece of metapornography" (92). Temple Drake thus may indeed have a "powerful story" to tell (Roberts 21). Her story does not, however, empower the feminist claim that texts are not "only words" (MacKinnon) but acts, and that our efforts at reading mark our complicity in acts of rape. Instead, Temple's story empowers us to see how texts that equivocate violence in turn beget fantasies of violence, how deletion and disavowal do their cultural work of generating interpretations.

At the same time, the perfunctoriness of explicit violence is literally central to Faulkner's text. In its original version, *Sanctuary* opened with a passage that recalls how a "negro murderer" had severed his wife's head. In its final version this scene is moved to the beginning of chapter 16, the very center of the novel:

On the day when the sheriff brought Goodwin to town, there was a negro murderer in the jail who had killed his wife; slashed her throat with a razor so that, her
whole head tossing further and further backward from the bloody regurgitation of
her bubbling throat, she ran out the cabin door and for six or seven steps up the
quiet moonlit lane. He would lean in the window in the evening and sing. (114)

Nowhere in the text is violence as unconcealed and straightforward as in this
decapitation scene; nowhere else is murder a mere peccadillo. The very non-
chalance of this rendition bespeaks this act's lack of "signifying power" as well
as its centrality for Faulkner's text: whereas prohibitions bar the transgression
of nature into culture, among "savages" there is no transgression. At the same
time, the "bubbling throat" of the decapitated woman, echoing Temple's rape
narrative, subtly suggests that each figure is implicated in the story of the other.

"Not What One Did to Women": Enacting Projections and Constructing the Racial Border in Richard Wright's *Native Son*

In view of the construction of blackness in American culture, it comes as no
surprise that many of the most prominent twentieth-century African American novels are preoccupied with sexual violence and rape. Among these,
Wright's *Native Son* has probably been the most controversial. Whereas early
readings capitalized on the novel's negative view of the "black community"
and the stylistic "weakness" of its politics, critics have more recently focused
on its treatment of black women in general, and on the rape and murder of
Bessie Mears in particular. To my mind such readings, though well-intended
and politically correct, are slightly off the mark, since they misread the novel
as realist or naturalist fiction. *Native Son* may go through the motions of realism and naturalism, yet it constitutes an ultimate form of mimicry, parodically
enacting the racist projections of black masculinity. James Baldwin's view that
Wright reduces character and theme to "simplistic formulae" (Robert Butler
9) is therefore quite trenchant. So is Michele Wallace's sense that "Bigger
Thomas was nothing more than the American white male's fantasy/nightmare/
myth of the black man thinly disguised, expanded upon (albeit brilliantly),
endowed with the detail of social reality and thrust back in the white man's
face in a form recognizable enough to connect with the old terror" (*Black
Macho* 86). And to my mind this reductive view of black masculinity is the
text's very strength, not its weakness. For Wright lets Bigger Thomas locate his
sense of self exactly where dominant culture has fixed it: in stories and acts of
(sexual) violence which are the sole signs of subjectivity registered by a culture
that identifies blackness with the violation of cultural taboos and transgressions of the racial border—a border constructed as "sexual border" (JanMohamed 109).

Whereas Faulkner's *Sanctuary* employs rape and incest to figure the interpenetrability of supposedly separate realms (such as nature and culture) and

to show that prohibitions are reinforced the very moment we acknowledge their transgression, Wright underlines how projections of "rapist" black masculinity serve to (re)erect and keep intact racial borderlines, borderlines that deny or destroy inter- *and* intraracial kinship. The novel's supposed "premise" that Bigger, through rape and murder, both becomes a "man" and overcomes the racialization of subjectivity (JanMohamed 108) is merely a racializing "promise" of dominant culture, meant to reaffirm the image of the African American male as violator of the racial border. Nor would I hold, as Abdul R. JanMohamed does, that the novel shows that assertions of black manhood necessarily replicate male violence against women. *Native Son* rather interrogates the racial inflection of such violence. It therefore does not merely invert the abuse of black women by white men (103); nor does Bigger emancipate himself by laying claim to a white power position (111). Instead, *Native Son* (re)enacts the construction of the racial-sexual border by dramatizing the power of its discourse and its will to "knowledge." The novel insists that Bigger's crimes "existed long before" they happened (Wright 361), or, more precisely, that they do not have to happen at all in order to exist. In fact, it is not the case that the crime exists before its event, as we are told; what exists is a rhetoric that results in crime.[19] Accordingly, the signifying power of the *story* of Mary Dalton's "rape" constructs and partly cancels the meaning of Bessie Mears's violation.

As JanMohamed aptly observes, *Native Son* characterizes sexuality and rape as paradigmatic modes of crossing the racial boundary and defines "the racial border as the zone of rape" (109). Interracial relations in *Native Son* are (metonymically) structured and (metaphorically) signified by the term "rape" and seem to involve black men only. Positioned at the threshold of the racial border, the black male subject delineates that border by transgressing it, changing himself in the process. When Bigger first approaches the Dalton home, for instance, he wonders how they "expect him to come in," aware that his moves are to follow a predesigned script. Assuming that his "wandering in a white neighborhood like this" translates into his "trying to rob or rape somebody" (Wright 45–46), he acknowledges that his presence registers only as violation of law. Accordingly, where laws have ruled out miscegenation involving African American men and white women, each of their encounters reads as rape (threat).

The conflation of robbery and rape testifies that dominant rape narratives emerged under conditions of economic competition. Bigger's meditation on the robbery of Blum's Delicatessen thus sets the interpretive frame for the events that will ensue:

> They [Bigger, Gus, G. H., and Jack] had the feeling that the robbing of Blum's would be a violation of ultimate taboo; it would be a trespassing into territory where the full wrath of an alien white world would be turned loose upon them;

in short, it would be a symbolic challenge of the white world's rule over them; a challenge which they yearned to make, but were afraid to. Yes: if they could rob Blum's, it would be a real hold-up, in more senses than one. In comparison, all of their other jobs had been play. (17–18)

"Crime for a Negro was only," Bigger later reflects, "when he harmed whites, took white lives, or injured white property" (307). Thus the "story" of the rape of Mary outweighs the "real" rape of Bessie, the latter merely serving as evidence for the former (306) and other unsolved sex crimes (283), as a means "to determine the exact manner of the death of Mary Dalton, who was slain by the man who slew Bessie Mears" (306). The reverse scenario is outright unthinkable.

At the same time as he oversteps sacrosanct borderlines, the perpetrator qualifies for cultural recognition. Wondering why black people live under inhuman conditions, Bigger concludes that it is possibly "because none of them in all their lives had ever done anything, right or wrong, that mattered much" (100). Crimes, transgressions of boundaries, violations of taboos do matter, have signifying power. "IF YOU BREAK THE LAW, YOU CAN'T WIN!" State Attorney Buckley addresses the (black) crowd in a campaign poster, positioning its reader as potential criminal, in terms of negation (16). Accordingly, "Negroes are rarely mentioned in the press," Wright notes (parenthetically), "unless they've committed some crime" (xv). Placed in such a no-win situation, Bigger comes to recognize his crimes as acts of self-creation. His employment at the Dalton home thus indeed offers him the chance, as his mother has it, "to . . . make a man out of yourself" (97)—a *black man*, to be sure. It enables him to enact the identity dominant discourse has molded and to wholeheartedly accept that identity of negation and death as his "true self." Bigger's self-creation therefore is a re-creation, an act of mimicry that appropriates the very position American culture has assigned to black male subjectivity, a creative act of liberation (364, 366) that turns out to be self-destructive loss, an "end [that] swallowed him in blackness," "in darkness" indeed (178, 253).

The murder, dismemberment, decapitation, and burning of Mary give birth to Bigger's new identity: "He had murdered and had created a new life for himself" (101), felt "[l]ike a man reborn," "risen up well from a long illness" (106). "[A]ccepting the deed" is the tribute he pays for recognition by a culture in which "timid" blackness (102) remains invisible, insignificant. The central irony of Bigger's identity formation is that while he does commit atrocious crimes, he becomes noteworthy—and newsworthy—for a crime he neither commits nor confesses (311–12), an act that cannot be proven or disproven, but whose very "staunch denial" indicates "that he may be hiding many other crimes" (328). Bigger's "rape" of Mary is a missing moment, a gap in the plotline filled by the acts that follow and by their consensual interpretations. Bigger's efforts to wipe away traces he never left are acts of simulation, themselves triggering traces that affirm more than cover up the uncommitted crime and supplement the "forbidden story" he never wrote.

This performance of a mimicry of mimicry necessarily empties out the meaning of rape, which partly explains why Bigger comes to believe that "rape was not what one did to women" (214), but what a supposed rapist feels pressed to do to "fulfill" his preconceived identity. As in Faulkner's *Sanctuary*, rape in *Native Son* is thus the process of an enforced passage from one identity to another, not an act of penetration. This very passage turns Bigger himself into a victim of rape, both violator and violated. In the process rape is associated with lynching and castration and recovered as a trope for disempowered black masculinity. Accordingly, Bigger's trial is observed by a kind of lynch mob, clearly kin to Dixon's clansmen and Faulkner's drummers. Leaving the courthouse, "[o]ut of the shrill pitch of shouts and screams" Bigger catches the phrase ". . . give 'im what he gave that girl . . ." (309). Unlike Faulkner, Wright capitalizes on the hysteria and homosexual panic involved here, a hysteria that mirrors Bigger's own and is characteristic of encounters of black and white masculinity at the racial border. Rape as (a figure of) violence and disempowerment of (black and white) women in turn gets dismissed, deleted, sacrificed, dis-figured along the way, and culminates in images of (Mary's) decapitation and (Bessie's) effacement.

In accordance with his mimic posture, Bigger does not speak for himself but through a narrator who interprets his acts and feelings. The discrepancy between Bigger's limited, unskilled voice and this narrator's eloquence reflects the novel's performative mode and underlines how Bigger's acts mean in ways he is incapable of shaping.[20] Likewise dominant discourse sets a limit on his engagement in the "real" by interpreting his acts and emotions for him. Bigger's reflection on his "rebirth," for instance, resonates with an identity that, as Wright explains, "came, not so much from Negro life, as from the lives of whites" (xvi). Such identity forms particularly well where its other remains sufficiently "alien," where the interpenetrability of different worlds is denied. Bigger's knowledge of white culture is as limited as the Daltons' knowledge of the "community" they financially support yet politically and physically sever off. To him whiteness is an indistinct domain of laws and prohibitions, a "territory" of "wrath," "a sort of great natural force, like a stormy sky looming overhead, or like a deep swirling river stretching suddenly at one's feet in the dark" (Wright, qtd. in Tanner, "Uncovering" 135). As a result " 'Bigger and his kind,' " writes Tanner, ". . . do not partake of the narrator's superior vision or capacity for self-expression; their wordlessness creates a vacuum in which he can construct a reality which their silence is said to affirm" (135).

Bigger's own speechlessness, the silences imposed on him, and his lack of access to what his lawyer Max labels "highly crystallized modes of expression, save that of religion" (365) allow other voices to predominate. Never is Bigger the "author and narrator of his own text" that Tanner claims he becomes in the end ("Uncovering" 145). Rather, as he echoes the voice of Max, who him-self echoes that of the narrator,[21] he accepts as his own the narrator's interpre-tation of his sense of self, thus becoming an effect of pure mimicry.

> "What I killed for must've been good!" ... "When a man kills, it's for some-thing. ... I didn't know I was really alive in this world until I felt things hard enough to kill for 'em. ... It's the truth, Mr. Max. I can say it now, 'cause I'm going to die. I know what I'm saying real good and I know how it sounds. ... I feel all right when I look at it that way. ..." (392)

Bigger may have "become adept at the storytelling competition" (Tanner, "Un-covering" 145), yet the story he tells is not his own. To Bigger, the narrator explains, "[e]vents were like the details of a tortured dream, happening without cause" (187). And like the narrator, Bigger's lawyer provides a story line, a narrative, a "reality" to the nightmare. Bigger simply "sounds," repeats, mimes Max's courtroom speech, which itself echoes the narrator's voice. As he rein-terprets his criminalization, he translates his insight that "he was black and he had done wrong" (206) into the belief that because he was black, doing wrong was the right thing to do. In this way the image of the "helpless, bewildered" man (201) whose body was wrapped in a "sheet of fear" (205) achieves whole-ness in a death-bound identity. This identity may put an end to flight and restlessness yet itself marks not a beginning but an end.

The crucial question here is how rape functions in this pattern of identity formation. After all, as Bigger grows to fit the familiar mold of (black) rapist and murderer, he keeps redefining rape, concluding that it "was not what one did to women" (214). What, then, is rape to Bigger? And what does "one" do to women instead? In Bigger's sense of the situation rape may indeed never have occurred. While Bigger never raped Mary, he comes to accept that he did the very moment Bessie confronts him with her acute sense of how the events will be interpreted ("They'll say you raped her"). As he acknowledges the delib-erate misreading/misnomer of his murderous act ("it was not until now that its real meaning came back" [213]), he concludes that rape was "not what one did to women." If (the) murder (of Mary) means rape, then rape is not merely a crime against women. Likewise, while Bigger undoubtedly rapes Bessie, ac-cording to the conception of rape he arrives at right before the act, what he does to her hardly qualifies as rape. Significantly enough, this inversion of rape affirms the opposed directions in which rape and its meaning have come to circulate. It reinforces a cultural symbology that grants great signifying power to black-on-white rape (even if the act never occurred), yet hardly any to black-on-black rape (even when it is blatantly evident).

Accordingly, the rape and murder of Mary Dalton boost and build Bigger's negative identity, while the rape of Bessie is depicted as his "fall." Bigger is mistaken, though, in assuming that "Bessie did not figure in what was before him" (220). As her remains provide "the raped and mutilated body" of "evidence" (306) in the rape/murder trial, his identity is in part achieved at her expense. Wright thus underlines that not only does the signifying power pertaining to narratives of black-on-white rape partly depend upon the veil of silence that dominant culture *and* the "black community" pass over the abuse of African American women. Bessie's maimed black flesh also adds the juicy evidence that Mary's dry white bones cannot provide.

This interdependence figures prominently in parallel depictions of the violence to which Mary and Bessie are subjected. At the same time, these repercussions pinpoint the function of Bessie's rape for Bigger. Since her insights into the significance of his acts ("They'll say you raped her") resonate with the voice of white culture and its prohibitions, her violation triggers Bigger's self-re-creation. Likewise, Bigger's conception of rape evolves from Bessie's reasoning:

> They would say he had raped her and there would be no way to prove that he had not. That fact had not assumed importance in his eyes until now. He stood up, his jaws hardening. Had he raped her? Yes, he had raped her. Every time he felt as he had felt that night, he raped. But rape was not what one did to women. Rape was what one felt when one's back was against a wall and one had to strike out, whether one wanted to or not, to keep the pack from killing one. He committed rape every time he looked into a white face. He was a long, taut piece of rubber which a thousand white hands had stretched to the snapping point, and when he snapped it was rape. But it was rape when he cried out in hate deep in his heart as he felt the strain of living day by day. That, too, was rape. (213–14)

If the murder of a white woman by a black man metonymically means rape to white culture, rape, Bigger infers, is an act—in fact, *any* act—committed in self-defense, motivated by fear or by the experience of excessive abuse ("stretched to the snapping point"). And his own fear may result, at least to a considerable degree, from the murder of his father by racist Southerners. Rape thus is a "metonymy of the process of oppressive racist control" (JanMohamed 109). Redefined as a form of fear as well as a rebellion against powerlessness, rape at the same time emerges as a metaphor for a sense of identity that depends on interracial encounters and involves processes of mirroring and projection ("every time he looked into a white face"). This also confirms what both Dixon's *The Clansman* and Faulkner's *Sanctuary* suggest: that the obsession with the black rapist figure is triggered by fear of recognition and self-knowledge on the part of dominant culture.

The overall effect, though, of Bigger's discontinuous redefinition (". . . when he snapped it was rape. But it was rape when . . .") is that it disseminates the meaning of rape and inverts subject and object of sexual assault. Feeling powerless, feminized, scared, and cornered, Bigger himself figures as the victim of an (emasculating) attack who, "full of hysteria" (194), reacts like Faulkner's Temple. When surprised, while burning Mary's body, by the (catty) "white blur," "[h]is mouth opened in a silent scream and his body became hotly paralyzed" (90). When Bessie reminds him of his murderous act, "[t]he world of sound fell abruptly away from him" (129) and it "seemed that he was not breathing at all" (130). Forced to "rape," he threatens his victims (any "white face") with decapitation/castration rather than sexual aggression, lashes out with knives (at Gus) and hatchets (at Mary), and desires to "lam" shovels across people's heads (203). With its signifying power stretched to the snapping point, rape indeed ceases to be "what one did to women." When this reassessment of rape snaps, though, it backfires not at the white oppressor but on black women like Bessie, hitting home, so to speak. In this way, Bigger's "insights" into the meaning of rape themselves turn out to be a twist of mimicry, a strategy that exposes *and* reinforces the cultural work of dominant discourse.

Bigger's redefinition of rape is prefigured in his violent encounter with Gus (39–44), in gestures that have been read as "fellatio, castration, and rape" (JanMohamed 110). In a conflict hinging upon male authority—Gus shows up late for the robbery of Blum—Bigger threatens Gus with a knife ("I'll slice your tonsils") before mounting and forcing him to lick his weapon (41). Yet while castration and rape eventually mingle indiscriminately in Bigger's identity politics, they do not dominate the narrative here. The threat of having one's tonsils sliced may—symbolically and phonetically—come close to the threat of castration (to having one's testicles sliced). The symbolism of enforced fellatio, however—a figure of circularity and self-containment—dramatizes the synchronicity of emasculation and silencing.

Moreover, we are not at the racial border here, but within the bounds of black masculinity. The specularity that characterizes this encounter—throughout the scene Bigger projects his own fear onto Gus—figures the black male subject held at bay, immobilized by a circle of anxiety and aggression. At the same time, as Bigger's anxieties pertain to the projected transgression of the racial border—Bigger prefers to "fight Gus and spoil the plan of the robbery" rather than "confront[ing] a white man with a gun" [44])—the scene figures the dynamic of that border internalized and reenacted. It mimes, for instance, the subjection of Dixon's rapist Gus.[22] The geopolitical landscape of the racial border thus gets reproduced in the intraracial context, within black male subjectivity. In turn, "going among white people," Bigger relies on his (phallic) weapons—his knife and his gun—for a "sense" of equality, "of completeness." In symbolic terms, Bigger thus is as impotent a rapist as is Popeye. Accordingly, the scene ends in a mockery of masculinity and its props, which are literally thrown back at disempowered Bigger: first hit by a billiard ball Gus throws at him, he finally slips on a cue stick, engaging in a slapstick performance that unmasks his authority as pitiful posture, as "power game" indeed (41–42).

Cast as a violent, yet disarming, encounter, this scene foregrounds how the construction of black masculinity affects and structures relations between black men. The circularity suggested by the figure of fellatio echoes when Bigger, in another threatening gesture, "put the tip of the blade into Gus's shirt and then made an arc with his arm, as though cutting a circle. 'How would you like me to cut your belly button out?' " (41). Reminiscent of Morrison's *Song of Solomon*, the kind of surgery suggested here targets marks of (maternal) origin and lineage and hints at a person cut loose from the history and memory of familiar bonds. At the same time, it enacts a neglect of the (black) female body which insinuates that black manhood, no matter how disempowered, both depends upon and reaffirms the negation of black female subjectivity. Such negation, running throughout Wright's novel, often figures within the context of a dismembered family, a family supposedly dominated by "masculinized" black matriarchs. Accordingly, when Bigger's mother interferes on his behalf, it is rape, too: "paralyzed with shame; he felt violated" (280).

Given Bigger's disposition and conception of rape, what *does* "one" actually do to women? Bigger evidently does not rape Mary; nor does he "attempt" rape, as Alan France claims (417). Instead, Bigger is sexually aroused by Mary's (intoxicated, weak-willed) body—a body "smaller" and "softer" than Bessie's (83), "her lips touch[ing] his, like something he had imagined" and his fingers "tighten[ing . . .] on her breasts" (84). As in *Sanctuary*, this scene is "witnessed" by someone incapable of seeing, by Mrs. Dalton, depicted as "a white blur . . . silent, ghostlike." Bigger chokes his illicit desire—seized by "a hysterical terror . . . as though he were falling from a great height in a dream"—by literally choking its object. What in fact Bigger performs on Mary is decapitation, depicted at gruesome length (90–91) and anticipating Ellis's narratives of dismemberment. Attended by yet another dysfunctional witness, capable of seeing, yet unable to tell—the Daltons' white cat, "a white blur" "star[ing]" at Bigger—this "lynching" scene is metonymically linked with the "rape" scenario, thus substituting for the crime Bigger does not commit. The cat's whiteness mirrors both Mary's "white face hanging limply from the fiery furnace door" (90) and the Daltons' "white hair," "glisten[ing] like molten silver from the pale sheen of the fire" (189). Leaping onto his shoulder during police investigations, emitting a "long whine"—as Bessie does during her rape—it eventually "give[s Bigger] away" (190).

As a symbolic act of self-empowerment Bigger's decapitation of Mary does not target the "real" power, political or sexual, she holds over him. Meant to obliterate the "evidence" of a crime never committed, her dismemberment aims at the signifying power she embodies. Lashing out at cultural symbology, Bigger repeats both the act he and his kind have always been accused of *and* the act of retaliation that has served to reconstitute white supremacy: "The knowledge that he had killed a white girl they loved and regarded as their symbol of beauty made him feel the equal of them, like a man who had been somehow cheated, but had now evened the score" (155). At the same time, it is exactly the gravity of this violation that makes Bigger assume he will not be suspected: "They might think he would steal a dime, rape a woman, get drunk, or cut somebody; but kill a millionaire's daughter and burn her body?" As he identifies rape with such misdemeanors as stealing dimes or getting drunk, Bigger not only ridicules fictions of black crime (and facts of real rape). He also fashions Mary and Bessie (who habitually drink) as ordinary black criminals, as common as any run-of-the-mill black rapist. Here, once again, rape is what women do to black men. Bigger is mistaken, though, to assume that he could "act like other people thought you ought to act, yet do what you wanted" (108). He misreads the significance of rape, downplays the conjunction between rape and death/murder and the desire, on the part of public discourse and law, to retain that link. This is dramatized as his incapacity to acknowledge the material "evidence" of Mary's death. Staring at her bones, "he could stand and look at the evidence and not know it" (220).

Bigger's murder of Bessie is motivated by the same impulse that triggers the violence against Gus and Mary: fear. Unlike Mary, though, who knows too little (about blacks), Bessie knows too much (about the construction of blackness). She asks uncomfortable questions, provides unrequested analysis, questions Bigger's gangsta posture, and breaks his new "stride," holding before him a mirror that makes him remember how and what blackness means in American culture. While Bessie thus triggers Bigger's reassessment of rape, her own rape amounts to "business as usual." What he considers a relation of fair trade ("She wanted liquor and he wanted her. So he would give her the liquor and she would give him herself" [132]) reeks of sexual exploitation to her: "All you ever did since we been knowing each other was to get me drunk so's you could have me" (215). This conflicting view of the—consensual or nonconsensual—nature of their sexual relation and Bigger's re(de)fined notion of rape dominates the representation of Bessie's rape.

Bigger quite literally overrides Bessie's will, drowns her repeated declarations of nonconsent in silence. In accordance with his redefinition, however, the text figures her rape as an act of self-defense, as aggressive sexuality which climaxes the very moment that Bessie's resistance and nonconsent reach their climax ("*don't don't don't Bigger*"). Bigger's act is first motivated by "[a] huge warm pole of desire," "insistent and demanding" (219), turning Bessie away, "still, inert, unresisting, without response," almost dead, "[h]er head lay[ing] limp" (just as Mary's head did, refusing to fit into the furnace), her "don'ts" and moans punctuating his unwelcome advances. These moans, though, are residues of screams Bessie is forced to choke back when entering the place of her violent death:

> They stopped in front of a tall, snow-covered building whose many windows gaped blackly, like the eye-sockets of empty skulls. He took the purse from her and got the flashlight. He clutched her arm and pulled her up the steps to the front door. It was half-ajar. He put his shoulder to it and gave it a stout shove; it yielded grudgingly. It was black inside and the feeble glow of the flashlight did not help much. A sharp scent of rot floated to him and he heard the scurrying of

quick, dry feet over the wooden floor. Bessie sucked in her breath deeply, about to scream; but Bigger gripped her arm so hard that she bent halfway over and moaned. (216–17)

Replete with echoes from *Sanctuary* (including the "eye-sockets," the rat, the held breath, the symbolism of doors and windows) and foreshadowing Petry's *The Street*, this scene recalls the killing of Mary and prepares for the rape of Bessie.

Unlike Faulkner, who lets Temple voice her own disturbing story, Wright presents rape from the narrator's/Bigger's point of view. And Bigger reads Bessie's resistance as consent, her initial sigh as a sign "of resignation, a giving up, a surrender of something more than her body," a "prolonged sound that gave forth a meaning of horror accepted" (219). Bessie's explicit nonconsent ("Bigger. . . . *Don't!*"), rendered as "urgent whispers of pleading," comes "from out of a deep far-away silence," a voice almost cheering him on: Bigger, the beast unleashed, "[i]mperiously driven," committing the crime that performs and proves the "horrific," wholly imaginary rape of Mary.

> The loud demand of the tensity of his own body was a voice that drowned out hers. In the cold darkness of the room it seemed that he was on some vast turning wheel that made him want to turn faster and faster; that in turning faster he would get warmth and sleep and be rid of his tense fatigue. He was conscious of nothing now but her and what he wanted. He flung the cover back, ignoring the cold, and not knowing that he did it. Bessie's hands were on his chest, her fingers spreading protestingly open, pushing him away. He heard her give a soft moan that seemed not to end even when she breathed in or out; a moan which he heard, too, from far away and without heeding. He had to now. Imperiously driven, he rode rough-shod over her whimpering protests, feeling acutely sorry for her as he galloped a frenzied horse down a steep hill in the face of the resisting wind. *don't don't don't Bigger.* And then the wind became so strong that it lifted him high into the dark air, turning him, twisting him, hurling him; faintly, over the wind's howl, he heard: *don't Bigger don't don't.* At a moment he could not remember, he had fallen; and now he lay, spent, his lips parted. (219–20)

Sexual violence is no abuse of power here but the effect of a fear Bigger projects on Bessie, a projection that diminishes her nonconsent into "whimpering pro-tests." Rather than becoming equal to the white master whom he imitates, as JanMohamed suggests, rapist Bigger is both uplifted and bound to fall. Figured as "the face of the resisting wind," thus recalling his redefinition of rape ("He committed rape every time he looked into a white face"), Bessie's resistance embodies the limits that Bigger feels white culture imposes on him. Metonymi-cally aligned with that culture, Bessie becomes a castrating force, causing Big-ger's fall into feminization: "spent," spoiled, "his lips parted," "his legs wide apart" (220). In the process, rapist and raped shift positions; "rider" Bigger becomes ravished victim. Accordingly, he conceives of his murder of Bessie as self-defense ("He couldn't take her and he couldn't leave her; so he would have to kill her. It was his life against hers" [222]) and self-empowerment, an act of decapitation that disfigures her "black face"/blackface into "a sodden mass," "a wet wad of cotton, of some damp substance whose only life was the jarring of the brick's impact." "[O]ut of it all," Bigger concludes,

> ... there remained to him a queer sense of power. *He* had done this. *He* had brought all this about. In all of his life these two murders were the most meaningful things that had ever happened to him. He was living, truly and deeply, no matter what others might think, looking at him with their blind eyes. Never had he had the chance to live out the consequences of his actions; never had his will been so free as in this night and day of fear and murder and flight. (225)

Insofar as Bigger conceives of himself as (rape) victim rather than (sexual) violator, the rape of Bessie has no signifying power whatsoever in this newly established identity. Instead, it is murder that is meaningful here; decapitating Bessie, Bigger completes his new self.

The media coverage of the Dalton case in turn projects the murder of Mary as a sex crime ("AUTHORITIES HINT SEX CRIME"), a re-presentation that indeed "excluded [Bigger] utterly from the world": first, because it displaces his agency by their "authority"; and second, because the very "hint" of a sex crime "was to pronounce a death sentence" (228). Once the hint is articulated, the case is a "Negro's rape and murder," Bigger a "Negro rapist and murderer" (229), the three terms melting into one: negrorapemurderer. As the coverage turns racist diatribe, Bigger is cast as "ape," as "beast utterly untouched by the softening features of civilization," as at best "an earlier missing link in the human species" (260). Likewise Buckley insists that Bigger "killed [Mary] because he *raped* her," that "the central crime here is *rape*," and that "[e]very action points toward that!" (377). In other words: every one of his moves *figures* rape. Accordingly, his very motion insinuates penetration: leaving the courthouse, he is led through a "narrow aisle ... cleared for him" (309); at the Dalton house, he is "led ... through the gate," "led down the hall," "led ... into the room" (310). Bigger's position is literally reduced to a space known by the name of rape; the racial borderline is reerected and preserved as the boundary between savagery and civilization. Or as the media put it: "Residential segregation is imperative" (261).

Buckley's account of Bigger's crimes clearly draws on the dominant "realist" rhetoric of rape: they register as "two of the most horrible murders in the history of American civilization" (346), perpetrated by a "despoiler of women" (352), a "black lizard" (373), "this black mad dog" (374), "a bestial monstrosity who has ravished and struck down one of the finest and most delicate flowers of our womanhood" (373). As Bigger withholds his own story, Buckley's diatribe culminates in a fantasy of torture, rape, sodomy, and vampirism bursting with transgressions and illicit acts:

> "My God, what bloody scenes must have taken place! How swift and unexpected must have been that lustful and murderous attack! How that poor child must have struggled to escape that maddened ape! How she must have pled on bended knee, with tears in her eyes, to be spared the vile touch of his horrible person! Your Honor, must not this infernal monster have burned her body to destroy evidence of offenses *worse* than rape? That treacherous beast must have known that if the marks of his teeth were ever seen on the innocent white flesh of her breasts, he would not have been accorded the high honor of sitting here in this court of law! O suffering Christ, there are no words to tell of a deed so black and awful!" (376)

Despite his final disclaimer, Buckley deploys a sufficient range of discourse, drawn from the Bible, gothic tales, and racist romances and bespeaking both the homoerotic voyeurism and the homosexual panic involved in the matter.

To make his case, Buckley even calls upon Bessie once again, framing her fate in a sentimentalized naturalist version of the fallen-woman topos in order to punctuate the rape/robbery of Mary: "So eager was this demented savage to rape and kill," Buckley polemicizes, "that he forgot . . . the money he had stolen from the dead body of Mary Dalton. . . . He took the ravished body of that poor working girl—the money was in her dress, I say—and dumped it four floors down an air-shaft" (378). The murder of Bessie, this passage suggests, is primarily a waste of money and a metonymy for the robbery/rape of the value assigned to the Dalton daughter. In this way, the racial border is reerected in terms of sexuality and class. Buckley is thus mistaken when he claims that "we have but the bare word of this worthless ape to go on" (377). Bigger is an "ape," "wordless," "outside of the lives of men" not because "[t]heir modes of communication, their symbols and images had been denied him," though, but because these modes overdetermine and position him in the realm of silence, crime, and death, a position Bigger comes to embrace wholeheartedly.

At the same time the racial border remains semipermeable, as is hinted by a scene that echoes the drummers' talk about Temple featured in *Sanctuary.* After a glimpse at Bessie's dead body, one of the members of the posse chasing Bigger "wonder[s] what on earth a nigger wants to kill a white woman for when he has such good-looking women in his own race. . . ." Another one agrees: "Boy, if she'd let me stay here I'd give up this goddam hunt" (244). The first man's "wonder" identifies murder with rape and does so by substituting "to kill" where "to rape" would make more obvious sense. His statement moreover highlights that the term "rape" applies only selectively to interracial sexual encounters. Whereas black-on-white sexual relations signify rape as death and involve "niggers" forcing themselves violently upon "women," sexual relations involving black women are deemed to be consensual encounters with "good-looking," willing "brown gal[s]" who let men "stay" (243). Lacking power, black men, it is implied, cannot but consent to such exchange of black women across the color line. The passage thus monitors racialized notions of sexuality that, on the one hand, deny the kinship between blacks and whites. On the other, they deny any knowledge of how this demarcation is violated by whites.[23] Wright thus exposes "the highly selective permeability of the racial border" (JanMohamed 99) as well as the strategic silences pertaining to racialized sexuality.

Like Bessie, Bigger achieves clarity of vision right before his death. Whereas she acknowledges her dependence on him, though, he registers how rape and murder—the enactment of racist projections—set him free of all responsibility: "They say that black men do that [rape]. So it don't matter if I did it or if I didn't" (323). Having accepted mimicry as his position, Bigger finds his death sentence simply a "natural" disposition (331). At the same time, he recognizes how significant the dominant rape rhetoric is for the maintenance of the racial border. Interrogated by Max as to why he both "hated" and "felt like having" Mary, he phrases his insights in his own clumsily suggestive manner:

> "Yeah; I reckon it was because I knew I oughtn't've wanted to. I reckon it was because they say we black men do that anyhow. . . . They say we rape white women when we got the clap and they say we do that because we believe that if we rape white women then we'll get rid of the clap. . . . Jesus, Mr. Max, when folks says things like that about you, you whipped before you born. What's the use? Yeah; I reckon I was feeling that way when I was in the room with her. They say we do things like that and they say it to kill us. They draw a line and say for you to stay on your side of the line. . . . And then they say things like that about you and when you try to come from behind your line they kill you. They feel they ought to kill you then." (325)

Bigger's analysis of the black male disposition—"you whipped before you born"—puts it in a nutshell: the figure of whipping reappropriates the trope that slave narratives had substituted for rape and thus traces his disempowerment back to slavery. Syntactically reduced, the passive construction "you [are] whipped" equivocates both the agency of the master/violator and the passivity of the slave/victim. In this way, the phrase hints that the black male is whipped as well as that he whips and abuses/rapes because he himself been abused/raped/lynched/castrated. Extending its meaning, such refiguration of rape at the same time disseminates its significance. In fact, rape and its meaning are segregated in the process. Accordingly, Max insists: "Let us not concern ourselves with that part of Bigger Thomas' confession that says he murdered accidentally, that he did not rape the girl. It really does not matter. What matters is that he was guilty *before* he killed" (369). Bigger was a rapist long before he was born. Along the racial border, rape has liberated itself from reference, displaced by an interpretation that overdetermines real rape. Houston Baker is thus mistaken when he takes Wright's revisionism as "history repeating itself as parody" ("On Knowing" 221). What *Native Son* parodies is not history but the prominent fictions of rape, written over and over by American cultural practices. By 1940, the equivocation of black women's sexual violation has become a convention of these fictions, a convention mocked by the depiction of Bessie's rape as an act of self-defense. Enter Petry's Lutie Johnson.

FIGHTING "FORCED RELATIONSHIP": RAPE AND MANSLAUGHTER IN ANN PETRY'S *THE STREET*

"Women would rather be killed," Dworkin claimed during a discussion of her novel *Mercy* (1991),[24] "than fight back and kill their attackers." Dworkin's words certainly do not apply to Lutie Johnson, the protagonist of Ann Petry's 1946 best-selling novel *The Street*[25] who kills Boots Smith, the second man who in the course of a few days attempts to rape her. Though both would-be rapists are black, the reader witnesses two very distinct kinds of sexual assault, driven by different desires and invested with specific meanings. The first is staged as the attack of a sex-crazed social underdog, apartment supervisor ("super") William Jones, on a clearly nonconsenting, socially superior victim. The second incident inverts the social hierarchy of assaulter and assaulted and involves two parties with mutual, yet nonmatching, interests. What Lutie, somewhat like Lily Bart, considers a (financial) favor, her aggressor Smith, somewhat like Trenor, deems an exchange of sexual favors for money. In a scene that recalls the late-night encounter between Lily and Trenor, Lutie first resists Smith's advances. After he hits her once, however, she strikes back and batters his head with a heavy iron candlestick until his face is "veiled" with blood, reducing the man to a "still," "motionless, bloody figure," "an awful faceless thing on the sofa" (431)—and leaving critics appalled that a woman could write such a violent book.[26] Provoked by "forced relationship," as Petry puts it, Lutie murders Smith not out of fear but in an explosion of rage directed against "everything she had hated, everything she had fought against, everything that had served to frustrate her" (429). Reconsidering her act, Lutie wonders:

> Had she killed Boots by accident? The awful part of it was she hadn't even seen him when she was hitting him like that. The first blow was deliberate and provoked, but all those other blows weren't provoked. There wasn't any excuse for her. It hadn't even been self-defense. This impulse to violence had been in her for a long time, growing, feeding, until finally she had blown up in a thousand pieces. (434)

In Lutie's perception, Smith had blurred into an "unstable triple vision," not an individual, but "a handy, anonymous figure" (429), personifying "the dirty, crowded street" (430), her unfaithful husband Jim, "the insult in the moist-eyed glances of white men," as well as the ultimate target of her violent outburst: "the white world which thrust black people into a walled enclosure from which there was no escape."

The paradigmatic reading of Petry's first novel acknowledges that (intraracial male) sexual assault provokes (female) manslaughter. It moreover emphasizes that both acts of violence result from a systemic, environmental violence to which the (black) perpetrators themselves have been subjected by dominant white culture, personified by Junto, one of Harlem's "white power broker[s]" (Holladay 586). For black men sexual violence against black women—previously a taboo subject—appears a means to self-empowerment but turns out to be self-disempowerment in disguise. Petry thus foregrounds the tragic irony of this dynamic by which an oppressive system manages to have its own violence reproduced without itself actively imposing more violence. (Accordingly, Junto himself never lays a "violent hand" [279] on anyone.) Where intraracial gender wars keep reducing African American men to "things," mere faceless objects, lynching has become obsolete. At the same time, this self-reproduction of violence legitimizes systemic violence and disciplinary control, which tend to further criminalize those subjected to violence in the first place.

These insights, of course, do not make a novel, nor are they all that new; we have seen them emerging in Griggs and Sinclair and being elaborated upon by Wright. In fact, *The Street* reflects a high awareness of the history of rapist rhetoric, calling upon Jacobs's narrative and turn-of-the-century racist romances as well as on Wharton's *House of Mirth* and Barnes's *Ryder*. Petry's novel thus highlights how notions of sexuality and sexual violence are framed by established racialized and class-inflected discourse. And yet *The Street* sets itself clearly apart from *Native Son*, a text to which it has repeatedly been compared. Wright and Petry share themes and generic qualities as well as political leanings. While Wright's focus on black masculinity as an enactment of dominant projections centers interracial relations, though, Petry's novel capitalizes on issues marginalized by Wright: the dynamics of intraracial gender wars and the deployment of physical and sexual violence against African American women in the privacy of their own home.[27] In fact, *The Street* is one of the first texts in which intraracial sexual violence looms large, not merely as an event that triggers narrative development, but as a consistent structural device corresponding to an acculturated dynamics of desire. In this way Petry ushers in a new era in the history of rape rhetorics, foreshadowing perspectives on sexuality and sexual violence further explored by post-modernist American fiction.

As she illuminates (attempted) acquaintance rape, Petry daringly disturbs the silence with regard to black male violence. Throughout her novel, such violence is triggered by a lack of economic power on the part of black men. What is presented as an "unnatural" state in *McTeague*—the wife's being the (economic) superior of her husband—proves to be the rule, not the exception, in Petry's African American "community." The fact that both of Lutie's would-be rapists are employed, however, even work in "superior" positions (Jones as apartment supervisor, Smith as bandleader), shows Petry's resistance to tracing sexual violations to external, economic conditions alone. Instead, her concern is the effects of economic and political discrimination on the psychosocial makeup of the black male subject. Nor is her text's position, as Calvin Hernton claims, that of "a pioneer Womanist Feminist novel" (*Sexual Mountain* 65). Taking her heroine to task for misconceiving reality and internalizing middle-class ideals, thus exploring her complicity in her own violation, Petry clearly lacks the unconditional bias of that perspective, instead providing insights into the "double consciousness" of black female subjectivity. The author thus touches upon issues of race and psychoanalysis, interrogating an alliance that, as Hortense Spillers underscores, has never gotten off the ground.

Accordingly, while its mock realist-naturalist mode makes Petry's novel appear a "historical document," a piece of "sociological criticism," as the cover of the 1974 Houghton edition announces, the text actually recontextualizes "realist" representations of sexuality and sexual violence. Featuring two closet scenes, for instance, Petry's novel forcefully invokes *McTeague* and spells out its homoerotic subtext. Literalization, in particular, is the ironic strategy by means of which Petry foregrounds the potential as well as the shortcomings of the (naturalist) symbology on which her novel heavily relies. The text, for example, accounts for underdog Jones's preoccupation with his physical desires by aligning him with his own (police) dog Buddy (110) and by emphasizing his life in dark basements, thus, on the one hand, reducing social difference to sheer materiality and downplaying the mental dynamic that drives Jones's sexual desires. By exploring exactly that dynamic, Petry's novel, on the other hand, reflects a fundamental change in the perception of the sexual violator, emerging from new studies of human sexuality and the growing significance of psychiatry, psychology, and psychoanalysis for the understanding of "sexual deviance."

In order to explore the complex mental theater accompanying acts and experiences of sexual violation, Petry adapts, for instance, Faulkner's technique of projecting central events (such as Lutie's first threatening encounter with Jones) through multiple perspectives and indirect discourse. While Lutie's point of view clearly dominates, it is itself not consistent but shifts between her desire, on the one hand, to construct herself as separate from and superior to other African Americans, as white, and, on the other, to legitimize the behavior and "base" desires of (other) "black folk" through sociological and historical reasoning. At the same time, Petry's rape narrative draws upon the paradigmatically modern medium of the moving picture.

Petry Goes to the Movies; or, Black Males and Blackmail

Petry's interest in the movies may be one reason why *McTeague* looms large in *The Street*. Norris's novel has frequently been praised for its strong visuality, which itself suggested Erich von Stroheim's endeavor to produce *Greed*, its

1926 screen adaptation. Petry's text in turn translates the visual into the textual—a tendency that comes to dominate the representation of sexual violence
in Ellis's *American Psycho*.[28] Petry recontextualizes the cinematic, for instance,
by assigning the movies a significant function in her texts,[29] emphasizing rapid
movement, paying close attention to lighting conditions, and focusing on the
gaze as a prominent means of social control, sexual pleasure, and identity
formation. Such emphasis on a paradigmatically modern mode of representation is in itself modernist. Petry's favorite locale—New York City—may even
recall John Dos Passos (who, of course, adapts film technique in rather different ways). More particularly, though, *The Street* translates into an African
American context Alfred Hitchcock's first sound film, *Blackmail* (1929).

Blackmail, Tania Modleski points out, "poses the issues of rape and silencing
of women with almost exemplary clarity" ("Rape" 304).[30] Shot in quasi-docu-
mentary style, the film presents the story of Alice White, a shopkeeper's daughter. After a lengthy, silent opening sequence, we see Alice meeting her fiancé
Frank Webber, the film's detective hero, outside his Scotland Yard office. At a
nearby café, she picks a quarrel with Frank for his lateness in order to keep an
assignation she had made with an artist named Crewe, who eventually lures
her into his studio. In the apartment, after Alice's attempt at drawing and
modeling—which allows for some timid pornographic titillation—Crewe
drags her to his bed; a struggle ensues, and she finally stabs him with a bread
knife, conveniently placed on the bedside table. As Scotland Yard enters the
case, Frank finds one of Alice's gloves in Crewe's apartment, while a mysterious
Mr. Tracy has secured the other and begins to blackmail the couple. When
Frank learns that Tracy was observed by Crewe's landlady on the night of the
murder and is Scotland Yard's primary suspect, he begins to threaten Tracy in
turn, transferring Alice's guilt onto him. While Tracy is pursued and finally,
on the verge of identifying Alice as the killer, plunges through a skylight at the
British Museum, Alice, paralyzed with guilt, decides to confess to the police.
At the chief inspector's office, she finds Frank, though, who manages to prevent her from doing so, while acknowledging her (sexual) guilt, which cannot
be transferred (Modleski, "Rape" 309). With such knowledge, he will be able
to blackmail—that is, silence—her for the rest of their lives.

While Hitchcock's heroine never gets to tell her story, Petry renders her
case of (attempted) rape and manslaughter through her protagonist's own
perspective. As Lutie gets her say, however, she cannot present "her own story"
but finds it interacting, being crossed out and overlaid, with readily available
familiar narratives. Like Hitchcock's movie, Petry's novel thus tells a story
of the silencing and refiguration of rape while simultaneously refiguring and
recontextualizing Hitchcock's silences. Interestingly enough, her text ends with
the very act that gets Hitchcock's movie going, with murder. Unlike Alice,
though, who loses her glove and thus allows the blackmail plot to unfold, Lutie
hides her blood-streaked gloves in her coat pocket, aware that "she was acting

as though murder was something with which she was familiar" (433). What she is in fact quite familiar with is that the law does not protect her.[31] Unlike Alice who, after having killed her assaulter, wanders the streets aimlessly, Lutie knows exactly what needs to be done: having a clear motive for murdering Smith, she needs to escape. And while the moving picture is framed by scenes that situate its heroine between two men, Lutie is on her own when we meet and part with her.

In the meantime Petry's novel follows "escape artist" Lutie Johnson (Holladay 49) in her brief "progress" along 116th Street (Petry, *The Street* 26, 85). Here Lutie, like Alice, is repeatedly positioned as the object of sexual exchange, as a communication device between Junto and Smith as well as between Jones and "mountainous" Mrs. Hedges (237), who occupies a position of male authority figured by her insistent gaze. Unlike Alice, however, who works in her father's business and is engaged, Lutie is a lonesome fighter, "freed" from family ties (as in fact all the other characters are), separated from husband and father and never mentioning her mother. Accordingly, Lutie cherishes the American dream of upward mobility, aspires to the seeming "perfection" of white suburban "Country Living" (50) she glimpsed working in the Chandler household—a family she knows to be dysfunctional, its members engaging in abuse of alcohol, marital infidelity, incest, and suicide. Petry thus echoes Harper, highlighting the "uncivilized" behavior of the supposedly civilized, the very lack of happiness of those who are alleged to have succeeded in its pursuit. Unlike Harper's heroine, though, Petry's Lutie is no latter-day saint but playfully self-fashions herself after Benjamin Franklin. She thus associates herself with Mrs. Hedges and Junto, who themselves have progressed from garbage collectors to neighborhood chiefs, and evokes Gatsby as well as his African American avatar, Larsen's Clare Kendry. Unlike Gatsby, Lutie, however, is both the "golden girl," the pursued, and the pursuer of a dream that becomes a nightmare. Likewise, unlike James Gatz, Lutie is bound to live on, leading a life, though, that is a matter of survival rather than fulfillment.

Like Hitchcock's Alice, Petry's Lutie kills her assaulter, thus "usurp[ing] the male prerogative of aggression against the opposite sex" (Modleski, "Rape" 306). Likewise both protagonists experience considerable guilt in hindsight, despite the fact that they acted in self-defense. Hadn't they willingly met with and accompanied their aggressors to their private spaces? In highlighting the heroines' own interest, both Hitchcock and Petry suggest that once culture acknowledges and accepts female desire—be it sexual, economic, or intellectual—the boundary between sexuality and sexual violence blurs so as to cancel out and veil sexual violence in new ways. In this context it is noteworthy that both film and novel portray their sexual violators as artists: Crewe, like Smith, plays the piano, and Jones, like Crewe, paints (the walls of Lutie's apartment) and draws (the pattern for his "master key"). He even authors a detective story in which he himself functions as police informant: under the pretense of assisting the police in a case of mail theft, he lures Lutie's son Bub into stealing letters from mailboxes in order to have him arrested. Jones's plotting recalls Hitchcock's—when Crewe takes Alice to his apartment, he first checks his mail—and in fact literalizes its title *blackmail.* Thus like the movie, Petry's novel suggests that the silencing of women results from a kind of blackmail.

Projecting the violators as artists, both texts moreover insinuate that the aggressors themselves create a context in which their assaults might be read as sexuality. Accordingly, Crewe, Jones, and Smith approach their victims pretending to make them part of an artistic process, to empower their acts of self-fashioning. When Alice sketches a women's head, though, Crewe adds her curved female body; likewise, having her pose as a model, he abuses this situation to sexually assault her. Similarly, Lutie wishes to have her apartment painted white to "shove the darkness back a little" (19), yet Jones colors it according to his own taste. Smith proposes that Lutie sing with his band, but frustrates her hopes of a solid income—hopes he himself had nourished. Such neglect of woman's interests and desires works her disempowerment. Accordingly, Lutie experiences both her disappointment by Smith and Jones's rape assault as a "blow" to her ambitions rather than to her body. This underlines that both heroines' desire (and thus their guilt) is not primarily sexual (as in Hitchcock) or not sexual at all (as in Petry). Alice's moves are motivated by her wish to retaliate against her fiancé's disrespectful behavior. Just as Frank legitimizes his lateness by the importance of his business—law enforcement— Alice's interest in Crewe is triggered in part by a desire to augment her own status. Lutie's interest in Smith is purely financial. Foregrounding the nonsexual nature of both women's "complicity," Hitchcock and Petry insinuate that their violation is an effect of their resistance to the position of sexual object. Both consequently consider themselves violators of (paternal) law, guilty of manslaughter as well as sexuality. As a cloak of silence is passed over their violation, both experience the law's complicity in the crimes to which they are subjected.

This silencing of violence is itself presented as a kind of art in a crucial scene in Petry's novel that resonates with Hitchcock's cinematic text. In chapter 8 Lutie stumbles into the text's singular incident of openly violent interracial crime. A poor young black man is killed with a bread knife by a white baker who claims that the boy had tried to hold him up. Lying on the sidewalk, "[p]art of his body and his face . . . covered with *what looked to be a piece of white canvas*" (196, my emphasis), the man is being identified by his sister. In a rare moment of unaccountable recognition Lutie identifies with the pain and loss experienced by this other woman, yet is distanced and angered once this expression is "replaced by a look of resignation, of complete acceptance" (197). As Lutie finds none of her own sense of the situation reflected in the news report, which refigures the "thin ragged boy" as a "burly Negro" deserving his fate, the canvas turns into a trope of invisibility and misperception, suggesting that art and media "cover" the "real" by covering it up. Recontextualizing the image of artistic perception (Crewe's canvas) and the metonym of violence (the breadknife), Petry implicitly drags the theme of rape and representation into the open to suggest that both intraracial intimate assault and interracial street violence are culturally equivocated, rendered invisible.

Accordingly, racial difference and discrimination are not merely matters of economy and class but depend upon cultural strategies that work and maintain their particular ideology. The most crucial—internalized and internalizing—strategy is figured, throughout Petry's text, as an insistent gaze which suggests that intra- as well as interracial hierarchies are imposed by a system of supervision. Supervisor Jones, for example, who constantly "stare[s] hungry-eyed" (89) at Lutie, at "women passing," and children "swarming" down the street (287, 297), is himself secretly supervised by Min, who registers him "almost eat[ing] [Lutie] up looking at her" (114) and herself feels paralyzed by his satanic, "black and evil" gaze. Jones in turn fears Junto (279) and Mrs. Hedges, whose "unwinking" gaze (289) or "queer speculative look" (385) manipulates and polices Jones's actions repeatedly (89), chasing him (289), crisscrossing his own gaze, reading his mind, imposing herself on his privacy, undoing his voyeuristic pleasures (288, 385). Both Junto and Hedges oversee a corrupt system, Hedges extending the white man's eye/I, her vision "still," "as malignant as the eyes of a snake," "flat eyes that stared at [Lutie]—wandering over her body, inspecting and appraising her from head to foot" (6). In fact, her gaze resembles less "the hostility in the eyes of the white women" than "the openly appraising looks of the white men" whose eyes penetrate [Lutie's] clothing, that "warm, moist look about their eyes that made her want to run" (57). The harmonious relation between Junto and Hedges—a relation freed from sexuality and based on mutual respect—stresses their functional identity. Junto himself is never object, always subject, of a gaze (275, 276) that reaffirms his dubious empire—the Junto Bar and Grill and its outpost, Hedges's whorehouse. Boots Smith, by contrast, occupies an unstable position: having "jumped" from "Pullman porter to Junto's right-hand man" (264), he is both servant (boots) and craftsman (smith), an enslaved self-made man or a self-made slave—in short, an oxymoron.

Accordingly, whereas *Blackmail* centers Alice as the object of male gaze and sexual desire, desire is polymorphous and sexuality a multifunctional means of pleasure and power in Petry's novel. Acknowledging sexuality and sexual violence as a continuum, the text renders their difference as highly dependent upon context, upon who does what to whom and for what reason. It thus reinterprets sexual aggression as an instrument of individual empowerment rather than a metaphor of political power. Seemingly empowered are several categories of people: sexually attractive persons (such as Lutie) who employ their charms for manipulation, yet who fall as they fail to see that they themselves are being manipulated (as Lutie, like Lily Bart, does, while, unlike Lily, she still survives); those who, like Hedges, no longer circulate as objects of sexual pleasure yet manage sexual services and exchange black women across the color line; and those who, like Junto, are willing and able to pay for being served. Likewise the denial of sexual services (such as Jones's neglect of Min or Hedges's rejection of Junto) empowers the one who denies. In turn, those who (like Jones and Smith) try to force sexual relations reveal their lack of authority.

In accordance with such class- and race-inflected notions of sexuality, throughout Petry's novel the difference between consensual and nonconsensual acts depends on context rather than form—penetration. In fact, sexual assault is quite effectual without rape here. More than that, sexual desires, fantasies, and fears are themselves presented as (de)formed by class and race inflections. By delineating Jones's sexual fantasies and Lutie's fears as complementary, albeit mismatching, texts, the novel illuminates how persistent projections of racialized corporeality affect the sense of sexuality of those who have been the target of such projections. Sex-crazed Jones thus not only confirms dominant views of black masculinity. His hypersexualization is further reinforced by Lutie's class-inflected, alienated sense of sexuality, which reduces sexual activity to the past and to economic conditions she aspires to escape. When she depicts segregated life, Lutie emphasizes lack of space and (leisure) time: "It was any place," Lutie claims, "where . . . [people's] bodies were their only source of relief from the pressure under which they lived; and where the crowding together made the young girls *wise beyond their years* (206, my emphasis). Echoing the timid diction of the female-authored slave narrative, Petry's heroine (who also calls Jones's aggressive sexual desire his "dark designs" [19]) reveals how the white middle-class ideology of sexuality keeps engendering both class difference and silence on intraracial violence among African Americans.[32]

Owing to Lutie's class-inflected sense of sexuality, the two rape attempts featured in the novel, though in many ways structurally alike, signify quite distinctly. Whereas Jones's assault is projected as uncontrollably driven, Smith's is cast as "normal" aggressive male sexuality involving Lutie as complicit victim. Driven by her own (economically motivated) desire—a desire akin to (Jones's) sexual desire as it feeds on daydreams and fantasy—she tolerates Smith's aggressive bodily presence, allows him to "baby," to diminish, her, and cashes in on her body's capital. Whereas "being nice" to white men, in her mind, amounts to prostitution, she considers being nice to Smith a legitimate business strategy, a means to the ends she craves, while ignoring the fact that she herself is being exchanged among Jones, Smith, and Junto. Thus while Petry's women transgress gender boundaries, they do not escape the limits set by their female bodies. "If the Victorian ideal divided women into the pure and the impure," writes Estelle B. Freedman, "modern ideas about sexuality blurred boundaries in ways that made all women more vulnerable to the risks once experienced primarily by prostitutes" (201). The fact that Lutie foreshadows both rape assaults in her mind attests that women fear rather than fantasize rape. The fact that she is violated at the very moment she least expects such an assault at the same time insinuates that women's acculturated fears are just as misleading as projections of female purity are inadequate to control male sexuality.

"Forced Relationship": Take One

Petry's portrayal of Jones echoes dominant turn-of-the-century discourse. In Lutie's perspective 116th Street is a "jungle" (8), Jones "something less than human" whose "dark" disposition results from his living in gloomy basements. Unlike Wright, who projects black masculinity as placeless, in flight, Petry's prototype is "chained to buildings until he was like an animal" (191). Accordingly Jones's dog anticipates his master's moves, throwing his weight against the door when Lutie first rings (9), approaching her "as though he were drawn toward her irresistibly," "head down, his tail between his legs" when she signs the lease (21). Having inspected the apartment, Lutie envisions Jones "snuffing on my trail, slathering, slobbering after me" (25). In one of her nightmares dog and master "become one," a whining, panting creature with a "building . . . chained to his shoulders" (191). Lutie, urged by Hedges to "[u]nloose him," has "her hand and part of her arm . . . swallowed up inside his wolfish mouth" (192), "felt the sharp teeth sink in and in through her shoulder" (192–93), until "[t]he arm was gone and blood poured out" (193). Visualizing rape as castration, as a threat to her sense of self, authority, and voice, Petry recalls the many twisted arms and bitten fingers featured in *McTeague*. Accordingly, while in her dream Lutie screams, during the actual attack "there was no sound anywhere" (236).

Like *Blackmail*—"one of the first of many Hitchcock films," Modleski points out, "to associate a room at the top of the stairs with sexuality and with danger and violence to a woman" ("Rape" 304)—*The Street* furnishes Lutie's apartment as the domain of potential sexual assault. Throughout the text inner space figures prominently, as in gothic tales: hallways are "reaching out for [Lutie]" (12); doors exhale a "soft, sucking sound" (11); stairs go "up steeply," suggesting "a newer and intricate—a much-involved and perfected kind of hell at the top—the very top" (6). Climbing the stairs followed by Jones, she feels "his eyes traveling over her—estimating her" (13). Her aggressor's "hungry" gaze is streamlined by the "long black flashlight" (11) he uses, one of the novel's insistent figures, which displace the guns and pistols erected in earlier rape narratives. By way of synesthesia—Lutie "think[s] the rod of its length was almost as black as his hand" (12)—the text identifies well-endowedness with blackness. Appropriately, as Jones focuses the light beam on his feet, he turns "into a figure of never-ending tallness" (14), going "up and up into darkness" (15)—"Jones, the Super" (278), "savage," "superhuman" (300), and Superman indeed. At the same time, the alliance between the "shiny black—smooth and gleaming" flashlight and hands of "dull, scarred, worn flesh" (12) seems in line with Lutie's notion that, among blacks, sexual gratification compensates for economic subjection. Accordingly, as Jones hands Lutie another flashlight he "fished . . . from his pocket" (13), the text hints at his emasculated sexual position. Scared of his reach, yet endowed with male power, Lutie "resolutely turns the beam of her flashlight on the kitchen walls." As Jones radiates his desire, "an aching yearning that filled the apartment, pushed against the walls, plucked at her arms," Lutie feels as if "he actually did reach one long arm out toward her, his body swaying so that its exaggerated length almost brushed against her" (15). This is flash/flesh against flash/flesh, one tall body against another "tall long-legged body" (27), arm(or) against arm(or), and gaze fighting gaze.

Significant here is Lutie's ambivalence about how to read the situation. Feeling like "an idiot, drunk on fear, on fatigue and gnawing worry," she is uncertain whether her sense that Jones is about "to leap upon her" is correct (15). Interrogating the image of the black rapist she herself has internalized, she calls upon its recent enactment: Bigger Thomas. In fact, Bigger resonates with Jones's nickname Super—a kind of superlative of Bigger—and surfaces every time Jones operates the furnace (97, 101, 288). Like Bigger, Super is a misnomer, though. Just like Dixon's Gus, Jones is a fearful, superstitious creature, less powerful even than either Gus or Bigger, because like Popeye he is incapable of rape while lacking Popeye's "ingenuity" to supplement for his lack.

Granting that it may have been "only [her] imagination upstairs" (25), Lutie retrospectively deems that she has entertained rape fantasies. Hearing "a queer, muffled sound from the Super in the living room," she startled so that

> she nearly dropped the flashlight. 'What was that?' she said sharply, thinking, My God, suppose I'd dropped it . . . and he'd turned out his light. Suppose he'd started walking toward me, nearer and nearer in the dark. And I could only hear his footsteps, couldn't see him, but could hear him coming closer until I started reaching out in the dark trying to keep him away from me, trying to keep him from touching me—and then—then my hands found him right in front of me—At the thought she gripped the flashlight so tightly that the long beam of light from it started wavering and dancing over the walls so that the shadows moved—shadow from the light fixture overhead, shadow from the tub, shadow from the very doorway itself—shifting, moving back and forth. (17)

Evidently, Lutie's "rape fantasy" is informed by Faulkner—Temple can hear but cannot see her attacker—as well as by Hitchcock, who likewise projects sexual assault as shadow dancing on the wall, moving figures on a blank white ground.

When Petry re-presents the scene through Jones's perspective, Lutie's "rape fantasy" turns out to be a complement of his own: while Lutie inspects kitchen and bathroom,

> he made himself stand still. For he knew if he followed her in there, he would force her down on the floor, down against the worn floor boards. He had tried to imagine what it would be like to feel her body under his—soft and warm and moving with him. And he made a choking, strangled noise in his throat. (99)

Unlike Lutie's parodic projection of the paradigmatic black rapist, this exploration of the mind of a potential rapist introduces a new conception of the sexual violator. Like Crewe, whose sexual assault on Alice seems out of character, Jones, the man with the "perfectly ordinary name," is in fact "unusual, extraordinary, abnormal" (25) and cast as a sexual psychopath.

This figure, which still dominates views on sexual violence, emerges, as Freedman points out, during "the sex crime panic of the thirties, forties, and fifties" (211). The panic was driven not so much by an actual increase in sexually related crimes as by demand from the media, law-enforcement groups, and organized private citizens that sex crimes be prevented (200). In 1904 the term "psychopathic personality"— first applied to criminals and persons with "unstable personalities," including prostitutes and homosexuals—came to connote sex crimes as a result of three convergent trends. First, the use of psychiatry had been extended beyond mental institutions to courts and prisons. Second, the social stress of the depression had disrupted the traditional family and drew attention to problems of male deviance. And third, as the study of sexuality became respectable, the influence of psychoanalysis, during the 1930s, on American psychiatry provided a base for a sexuality-oriented theory of crime (202). This development itself increased the authority of psychiatrists and the enactment of laws addressing psychopathology, which operated, as Freedman explains, alongside older penal codes that punished rape and murder with imprisonment or execution. In practice these distinct codes were applied with a racial bias: "white men who committed sexual crimes had to be mentally ill; black men . . . [were] believed to be guilty of willful violence" (209). Petry's black psychopath thus embodies an abnormal abnormality.

The concept of the sexual psychopath generated new categories of victims. Defined by the laws as someone incapable of controlling his sexual impulses and therefore " 'likely to attack . . . the objects of his uncontrolled and uncontrollable desires' " (qtd. in Freedman 200), the sexual psychopath posed a violent threat to children as well as to women (201). In fact, the concept of the sexual psychopath is driven to a substantial degree by fears of child abuse and by homophobia, which themselves hint at a renegotiation of sexual normality. "Ultimately," Freedman claims, "the response to the sexual psychopath helped legitimize less violent, but previously taboo, sexual acts while it stigmatized unmanly, rather than unwomanly, behavior as the most serious threat to the sexual order" (201). This tendency shows in Petry's depiction of Jones, which subtly hints at his homoerotic leanings, his "queerness" (114), a desire directed toward Bub—whom Jones targets systematically after his rape attempt fails.

Petry thus shifts ground in many ways. Exploring the mind-set of a would-be rapist, she takes issue with the dominant assumption that some men are born criminals, and highlights the significance of failed perception and acts of misreading for sexual aggression. The novel's insights into Super's obsessions are appropriately situated in chapter 4, following the depiction of Lutie's history (chapter 2) and her present life on 116th Street (chapter 3). Having observed that Lutie is "crazy about her kid" (87), Jones deems Lutie his equal and Bub his rival for the affection he himself craves. He thus affirms his ongoing adolescence and kinship to the psychopath that a 1937 article in the *Psychoanalytic Review* labeled " 'phallic man,' fixated at an infantile stage of boundless, bisexual energy" (Freedman 204). Well into his fifties, Jones is fixated on "young, well-built," "round" women (86, 87) and physically attracted to Bub, noticing the "roundness of his head, how sturdily his body was built, the beginnings of what would be a powerful chest" (88). (At the same time, Bub is frequently chased, humiliated as "whore" [346] by street-gang boys with "jeering eyes" and "hard, young bodies" [350].) The narrator legitimizes Jones's sexual preference and voyeurism with a social and emotional deprivation (85) that triggers his overactive imagination to take charge of his perception of the real: "dreaming of women," Jones would ". . . plan the detail of his love-making until when the dream became a reality . . . he went half-mad with a frenzied kind of hunger that drove the women away from him" (86). No longer attracting young women who put up with his "violent love-making" (87), Jones is stuck with his compulsions and lacks self-control as well as other men's respect (380). Even Bub's companionable "Supe" is a mere diminutive (300).

The sense of sexuality that informs Petry's portrait of Jones and his own view of the situation—he fears that his frustrated desire for Lutie may build up and eventually explode—correspond to the dominant heterosexual paradigm. "In this energy-control (or hydraulic) model," writes Martha Vicinus,

> sexuality is seen as an independent force or energy disciplined by personal and social constraints. Sex is always something to be released or controlled; if controlled, it is sublimated or deflected or distorted. But it is, for example, never simply part of a spectrum of mind-body images and feelings that can become more or less intense. Sexuality in general is defined in terms of the male orgasm; it is like a powerful force that builds up until it is spent in a single ejaculation. (136)

Employing this sense of sexuality to render Jones's crazed economy of desire, Petry redefines it as a model of psychopathic male sexual violence. In principle, though, this model also accounts for female desire: Min's (sexual) deprivation finds its release in an overflow of rhetoric, a seemingly endless stream of words (295); and Lutie's rage finally explodes on Smith.

Employing a phallic object, Lutie symbolically performs the very violence she manages to escape, whereby rape literally turns into murder and Petry's novel into a rape-revenge narrative. Like this mirroring between rape and manslaughter, the use of the term "dream" in the depiction of Jones's sexual economy supports the novel's subtle, yet insistent, alliance between Lutie and both of her aggressors, all of whom are incapable of reading their situation appropriately, "realistically." Lutie intensely desires to transcend color and imagines her progress to be a matter of "careful planning" (56, 63). Jones's assault on Lutie is a desperate attempt to make reality cohere with his misguided sense of it. Increasingly obsessed with the idea of "having" Lutie (87), he fails to see that this desire is not mutual, and imagines her body responding, "[h]er breasts pointing up at him" (97). Neither explicitly violent nor "perverse," the (fetishistic and voyeuristic) fantasies Jones projects onto the screen of his mind build up a tension that calls for matching experiences, experiences of which he gets a foretaste when he invades the emotional and physical space that Lutie occupies. Interrogating processes of (mis)perception and (mis)interpretation, Petry thus illuminates their effects on reality formation and shows how the "subjectivity of viewing," in Susanne Kappeler's words, "goes over seamlessly into agency in the world" (58).

Whereas Jones eagerly fantasizes heterosexual encounters, he goes blank on his more repressed sexual leanings, for which no rhetorical paradigms exist. Accordingly, Jones's homoerotic desires, transvestism, fetishism, and pedophilia draw subtly, though recognizably, upon Norris's *McTeague*. As in *McTeague*, homoerotic desire entangles males who are both buddies and rivals. Recognizing Bub "as an exact replica of his father—the unknown man who had held Lutie in his arms, caressed her breasts, felt her body tremble against him" (88), Jones sees in Bub what he himself desires to be: both Lutie's lover and her love object. Compulsively fantasizing Lutie's sex life, Jones recurrently positions Bub as the object of the homoerotic desire that his (indirect) discourse and fetishistic object relations insistently bespeak. Both a threat to Jones's virility and the object of a desire that Jones himself senses to be deviant, abnormal, Bub becomes his victim. Equally attracted and repulsed, Jones "by a prodigious effort . . . controlled himself" (89) or casts his victim as seducer and aggressor, akin to "the black bastard . . . that used to screw [Lutie]" (88).

In a crucial scene Petry metaphorizes the tension between Jones and Bub as a dispute over Lutie's lipstick that dramatizes the ownership of the phallus and its exchange between men. On a night Lutie visits Junto's bar to escape the "haunting silences of rented rooms" (147), Jones manages to explore the privacy of her bedroom and closet without her knowledge, against her will, so to speak. His very walk up the stairs, "deliberately making himself go slow when what he wanted to do was to run up them" (101), bespeaks his desire yet also recalls Lutie's reminiscences of her desire for Jim: climbing the stairs to their apartment, Lutie recalls that "she wanted to put off the moment when she would undress and get in bed beside him, wanted to defer it at the same time that she wanted to hurry it" (176). While Petry thus situates victim and aggressor within the same economy of desire, Jones's visit to Lutie's apartment is distinct as it wavers between fantasy and real time. Bub, who functions as agent of the latter, is repeatedly lured by Jones to adhere to the former. Keeping him busy relating the plots of detective movies, Jones disappears into his imaginary sex life with Lutie, "his mind . . . peering into the bedroom" and closet (104).

Before he actually enters that space—having sent Bub on an errand—he "almost involuntarily" picks up Lutie's lipstick from the living-room table. For the rest of the scene this item ("rounded from use" and red, with "a grainy look from being rubbed over her mouth" [105]) becomes the center of attention, a fetishistic object. "[T]he Marxist and Freudian fetishist," writes Linda Williams, "locates illusory and compensatory pleasure and power in the gleam of gold or the lacy frill of an undergarment" (104), constructs a "substitute object to evade the complex realities of social and psychic relations" (105). Accordingly, Lutie's lipstick substitutes for and evades her physical closeness. At the same time, toying with the "red stick," Jones also compromises his masculinity. When he is about to engage in a drag performance ("He raised the lipstick toward his mouth"), Bub, with "a swift, instinctive, protective gesture," gets hold of it and drowns it in his pants pocket, explaining that "Mom thought she'd lost it" (Petry, *The Street* 105). Bub is protecting not only Lutie but the phallus/himself here, an object he would not want to exchange. Robbed of the fetish, Jones fantasizes how "good" it would be "to hold it in his hands at night before he went to sleep," to "carry it in his pocket where he could touch it during the day and take it out and fondle it down in the furnace room," to feel it "lying deep in his pocket. He could almost feel it there now—," he claims, "warm against him" (106). Since this room is where Jones meets Bub, attempts to drag Lutie, and may fondle himself, the fetish centers all of Jones's desires, be they aggressively heterosexual, homoerotic, or autoerotic.

Like the dispute over the lipstick, the passage depicting Jones's sojourn in Lutie's bedroom is loaded heavily with sexual innuendo. Focusing first on Jones's excitement (hitting "his knee against a chest of drawers," he "stood there for a moment rubbing the place and cursing"), it presents this visit as an exploration of Lutie's private parts, suggested by the "strong," "sweet smell" from "a can of talcum" Jones imagines she "sprinkled . . . under her arms and between her legs" and the "flowered pink spread" that "covered" her bed (107). As he "open[s] the top of the can" (108), the reader recalls how he "pulled the top off" the lipstick (105) and perceives their complementary shapes. As he "sprinkle[s] some of the powder in his hand," his hand itself becomes the space "between [Lutie's] legs," suited to accommodate the "lipstick." As Jones "rub[s] his hands together," he dramatizes the specificity of female sexuality/

subjectivity Irigaray elaborated upon in "When Our Lips Speak Together" (1980; reprinted in *This Sex*).[33] Once Jones observes the powder "lay[ing] there dead-white against the dark paleness of his palm," the text awakens us to the violence of Jones's smooth operations. Turning toward Lutie's closet as he feels "the clothes bent toward him" and smells the talcum exhaled from her "thin, white" blouse—whose "fullness of . . . cloth . . . made a nest for her breasts to sit in"—he symbolically enacts that violence: "he crushed [the blouse] violently between his hands squeezing the soft thin material tighter and tighter until it was a small ball in his hands" (108). Significantly enough, Jones steps into the bathroom next, the very space that Lutie's flashlight had set shadow-dancing (17), recontextualizing Hitchcock's figure of sexual assault.

In the following, fantasy prevails: "[A]fter being close to Lutie like this" (109), Jones not only craves "to have her soon" (110), convinced that "[h]e couldn't go on just looking at her. He'd crack wide open if he did. There musta been some way he could have got that lipstick away from the little bastard." He also feels that he needs to get rid of Min and "set the stage for it by letting the door bang behind him so that the sound went up and up through the flimsy walls of the house until it became only a mild clapping noise when it reached the top floor." Aligning the image of self-division and "rape" ("crack wide open") with Jones's defeat in the struggle over the phallic fetish, the text insists that what is at stake here is Jones's masculinity. Accordingly, he seeks to reauthorize himself by violating the woman he deems dependent on him. Finding Min gone, he realizes that losing her would diminish "his chances with Lutie" (111). The traveling sound—sign of the interdependent and "warring" position (233) the women take in Jones's mind—suggests that his fantasies are inseparable from his acts, triggering an "itching to do violence to Min" (139).

Accordingly, he reenacts the closet scene with a wholly different twist, "pushing [Min's clothes] into a corner with a wide violent gesture of his arm as if by threatening them they would reveal whether Min had walked out on him" (112). The presence of a table wherein she hides her money reveals that she has not. Sexually deprived and, like Norris's Trina, no stranger to physical abuse, Min has taken to thrift, curiously enough with the goal of purchasing a set of false teeth (and, like McTeague, she owns a caged canary [296, 364]). As Min uses this money to leave Jones, the text underlines that economic dependence endangers women first and foremost. Lutie herself experiences the most severe sexual threat when she is in a financial fix. In fact, the very synchronicity between Lutie's seeming "progress" with Smith and Jones's invasion of her closet highlights that Lutie's economic progress comes at a sexual and emotional price she is unwilling to pay.

Jones finally puts his hand on Lutie in a scene resonant with echoes of their earlier encounter(s) and presented from a perspective that oscillates between Lutie's and Jones's. Once again, his move is encouraged by an act of misreading. As Lutie returns from Junto's bar, she "*seems*" to be "smiling at the sight of him and bending and swaying toward him," like the clothes in her closet. Jones himself "*seemed* taller than ever," his "wide open, staring" eyes and quick breathing giving away his sexual "excitement." Lutie, by contrast, first does not recognize her aggressor ("couldn't *see*"), "for the cellar door was in *deep shadow* and she could not separate the *shadow* and the movement" (234, my emphases). Whereas he sees too much (light), invests Lutie's mere presence with surplus meaning, overinterprets, she sees too little, does not understand, remains in the dark. All the while Petry employs shadow and movement as figures of attempted rape, playing upon *Blackmail* as well as her own previous citation of the cinematic text.

Just as perceptions mismatch, movements become asynchronic: as Lutie recognizes Jones walking toward her, "[s]he saw again the tight, hard wrinkles in her blouse and thought of how he must have squeezed it between his hands," becomes paralyzed, "unable to move," "her muscles . . . rebelling against any motion." When he "stopped moving," she feels an urge to "get past him now, quickly" and without acknowledging what is happening to her. Accordingly, speech falters. His "sweettalk" ("You're so sweet. . . . You young little thing" [235]) is hardly audible to her, "for he was so excited that his voice came out sick and hoarse," a "speech impediment" that echoes the scene that foreshadowed Jones's rape assault. Likewise Lutie's attempt to scream fails ("there was no sound anywhere in this"), which likens her experience to that of Temple Drake. Once her voice works, it travels "insanely shrieking" up and down the stairs "until the whole building echoed and reechoed with the frantic, desperate sound" (236). This imbalance of sound—either silence or overamplification—encapsulates the whole history of the representation of rape; its "insanity" hints that not Jones but Lutie, like Drake, is the sexual psychopath.

Not police force but Hedges's "powerful hands . . . wrench . . . [Lutie] violently out of the Super's arms" (236) to save her for Junto (240). Hedges imposes paternal law, orders Lutie to "[s]hut up," and threatens to have Jones "locked up" if he should "look at that girl again" (238). Both obey. Jones refocuses his gaze on Bub, and Lutie does not report the assault: she fears both Jones's "revenge" and the indifference of the police (308). Like Hitchcock's Alice, she takes the blame, wonders whether she herself had suggested the kind of "love-making" that has been forced upon her (240), dismissing the fact that Jones ignored her frantic resistance (235). His trust in his misperception thus corresponds to her distrust of her social literacy.

After the event, Jones finds his mind "swirling" (280). The "fragments of thought" his brain "spewed up" (281) all relate to the women around him: feeling threatened and abused by Hedges's "big, hard body," "her baleful eyes rammed practically into his face," Jones blames Min for his failure with Lutie yet is unable "to lay violent hands on her" (279). Soon enough Lutie's "small, yielding, pliant body" comes to mind, outbalancing the pain he feels where

Lutie has scratched his face. According to Jones's "analysis" Lutie just "hadn't understood that he wasn't going to hurt her" (280). He legitimizes her screams as caused by his dog's presence and by his misconceived ideas that she "was in love with Junto" (282), "belonged to a white man" (283), and "openly lived with white men" (293). Imagining himself winning her over with presents, Jones eventually settles on the belief that black men "weren't good enough for her" (282), and decides to "destroy her," "hurt her through the kid" (283), excited by his "sudden inspiration."

Jones's plot is highly resonant with figures and fragments from Hitchcock's cinematic precursor; it is as simpleminded as it is effective. The plan is to lure Bub into stealing mail and let him be caught, and at the same time to get rid of Min by involving her in the reproduction of the mailbox "master key" (291). Jones's plot is a seduction narrative with symbolism of lock and key looming large. The drawing of the master key itself—the one key "that seemed to em-body all the curves and twists of the others"—is not simply an act of copying but an erotically charged and intellectually stimulating endeavor, both "Jones's own creation" and an act of self-fashioning (292). Designed by Jones, the key is manufactured by the "key man" (291), purchased by Min, and handed over to Jones, who hands it on to Bub (just like the lipstick). It is an object of exchange both feminine ("she")—a "slender little thing," "so small and yet so powerful" (297), a miniature Lutie—and omnipotent, "stiff in the lock," in need of being "force[d . . .] a little." Making "the boy try it again and again until he began to get the feel of it" (299), Jones initiates Bub into black man-hood, blackmails/blackmales him into crime, and makes the conflation of fan-tasy and reality an essential part of the boy's self-perception. Having first re-fused to engage in Jones's detective plot, he soon enough finds his part "more thrilling, than anything he had ever done. . . . It wasn't make-believe like the movies. It was real, and he was playing the most important part" (342).

"Forced Relationship": Take Two

Like Jones's rape attempt, Smith's assault is "foreshadowed" by Lutie during their first meeting. Throughout, she senses his physical aggressiveness (151), driven not so much by sexual desire as by a need to "feel . . . superior"—a need he shares with white men (158) and Lutie herself, who longs to make swift progress, escape crowded, colored spaces. As she identifies with self-made man Smith, Lutie interprets his advances not as a sexual threat but as part of a mutual exchange. She herself "wanted something" (156) and wanted it "so badly that she decided to gamble to get it" (152). Yet their cravings are discon-gruent: she wants to move up; he "just wanted her" (263).

Like Jones's sexual "hunger," desire is again figured in terms of eating here. Lutie remains undecided, though, as to whether she is being hunted or engaged in civilized dining. She knows Smith considers her prey and has put a "bait" out for her; she also admits she's not "going to nibble" but will "swallow it whole" (151). Having eagerly accepted his invitation to go for a ride (152), she pictures the scene (of seduction) as "a pattern repeated over and over or the beginning of a meal," the course of which, however, is lined with dangerous tools or weapons, thus recalling the famous breakfast scene in *Blackmail*, which insistently deploys the word "knife."

> The table set with knife, fork, and spoons, napkin to the left of the fork and a glass filled with water at the tip end of the knife. Only sometimes the glass was a thin, delicate one and the napkin, instead of being paper, was thick linen still shining because a hot iron had been used on it when it was wet; and the knife and fork, instead of being red-handled steel from the five-and-ten, was silver.
> ... The soup plate would be removed and the main course brought on. She always ducked before the main course was served, but this time she had to figure out how to dawdle with the main course, appear to welcome it, and yet not actually partake of it, and continue trifling and toying with it until she was successfully launched as a singer. (156–57)

Playing on Hitchcock, this passage suggests that Lutie, like Alice, finds herself toying with food she does not crave yet may be forced to consume. When Smith parks the car in a remote spot overlooking the river, she not only realizes that "duck and cover" might not work this time. She is well aware that she "hadn't walked into this situation. She had run *headlong* into it, snatching greedily at the bait he had dangled in front of her." Echoing Linda Brent, who claimed to have "plunged headlong" into her life with Sands, Lutie projects Smith as white and still seeks "some plausible way of frustrating without offending him" when he begins to serve the main course. Feeling his mouth "so insistent, so brutal," she has no time to dawdle and escapes "his ruthless hands and mouth" (161) only by calling him back into real time (162), like Bub when he interferes with Jones's sexual fantasies.

Like Jones's assault on Lutie, Smith's advances are triggered by acts of misreading on his as well as on Lutie's part. Her fantasies of clean streets (151), her "bright optimism that had pictured a shining future," "[t]hose things that had become real to her" (305) compare to Jones's overexposed sense of reality and blind Lutie to the dangers of sexuality. Smith for his part, having "lost all sense of time and space," deems himself white and enjoying free access to black women's sexual services. Accordingly, "[i]t was more a matter of itching to lay his hands on her than anything else" (263). Forced to give up Lutie out of loyalty to Junto, he simply regrets "having lost the chance to conquer and subdue her" (275), having missed an opportunity to "uplift," to erect, himself.

Whereas Smith and Jones, unaware of how their minds conflate fantasy and fact, do not feel guilty of sexual assault, Lutie deeply regrets having allowed fantasy to overpower fact. As a consequence, she, like Alice, not only blames herself for her own victimization but even feels protective toward her aggressors, confirming their ignorance of their own status as violators (307). In other words: whereas the men in Petry's novel easily extend their fantasies into reality, no matter how unsubstantiated in fact they are, Lutie cannot acknowledge that her dreams have been nourished by her aggressor Smith, who had offered a "job," not "just experience" (304). Nor does she read her violation as an act of aggression; interpreting her subjection as a result of her own lack of "reason," she reduces it to a phantasma, a rape fantasy, if you like. As she reasons, the violence reemerges figuratively, intratextually:

> The world hadn't collapsed about her. She hadn't been buried under brick and rubble, falling plaster and caved-in sidewalks. Yet that was how she felt listening to Boots.
>
> The trouble was with her. She had built up a fantastic structure made from the soft, nebulous, cloudy stuff of dreams. There hadn't been a solid, practical brick in it, not even a foundation. (307–8)

To me, the bricks missing in Lutie's structure recall the brick that Bigger employs on Bessie, a piece of solid, concrete materiality that reappears in the rape scenes of, for instance, Raymond Carver's short story "Tell the Women We're Going" and Naylor's *The Women of Brewster Place*. Here, Lutie's denial of any "solid, practical brick" in her sense of the situation equals a denial of her violation. At the same time, Lutie reimagines the limits that white culture imposes on her as an "ever-narrowing space . . . built up brick by brick by eager white hands" (323–24). Eventually, she envisions Junto with "a brick in his hand. Just one brick. The final one needed to complete the wall that had been building up around her for years" (423).

Lutie's limited perception—her unwillingness to identify her violators as what they are, and the tendency to blame (white) stock figures instead—depends in part, as Petry underlines, on an established rape rhetoric focused on black women's exploitation by white men. Accordingly, when Crosse, a white man running the Crosse School for Singers, tries to trade lessons in "showmanship" (320) for "a coupla nights a week in Harlem" (321), Lutie finds analogies in slave economy, just as her grandmother would have. Resituating herself and Crosse "back in the days of slavery" (322), Lutie, like Smith, loses "any sense of space and time"; like Linda Brent and Iola Leroy she reads black beauty as a curse (321); and, like Harper, Petry highlights the inferiority of the supposedly "superior race." When Lutie "hurls" an inkwell "full force in [Crosse's] face," transforming his piglike countenance into blackface (322), she forces herself to acknowledge the black violator yet at the same time insinuates that all black aggressors are the product of white culture. Accordingly, her final act of manslaughter is cast as a kind of lynching, whose agent is black yet whose subject is white culture. Perception, Petry suggests, is thus inseparable from prepatterned interpretations and their silences.

This explains why, in the process of murdering Smith, Lutie's (sense of) self diffuses into "a thousand pieces" (434). As she kills her violator, intent on striking out at the white world that circumscribes her own, it becomes evident that both Lutie and Smith are victims engaged in self-destruction. Thus while shedding light on black men's—psychic as well as physical—violence against black women, Petry's novel also takes to task black women who prefer to blame themselves or the white "other" for their violation, rather than accusing the actual perpetrator, in this way facilitating male violence. Lutie is consequently a complicit victim indeed; her fault, however, is not that she "asks for it," but that she does not tell.

Accordingly, nowhere in the novel is the aggression against Lutie referred to as attempted rape. Rather, recontextualized as systemic violence, it is—literally and figuratively—naturalized as the effect of a physically hostile environment. When we first encounter Lutie, for instance, she is struggling against "a cold November wind" (1) that lifts her "hair away . . . so that she felt suddenly naked and bald" (2). And yet it is not on "that goddamned street" (where Lutie is strong, striding, and safe) but inside their own homes that persons—and women in particular—are violated, by their own kin and acquaintances. After a violent fight with his former lover Jubilee, for instance—a scene echoing Hitchcock and foreshadowing his final encounter with Lutie[34]—Smith himself wonders why "with all that noise and screaming no one had tried to find out what was going on. He could have killed her easy and no one would even have rapped on the door" (270). He himself is killed, without anybody's noticing or telling, in a private room "alive with silence—deepening pools of an ominous silence" (433).

In contrast to most readers' claims, however, Petry does not hold (as Smith and Lutie do) that intraracial violence results from interracial oppression, but that this perspective itself serves to reproduce a system based on silence. Thus when Lutie finally flees Harlem, we no longer perceive the hostilities of a racially segregated culture as violent natural forces:

> The snow fell softly on the street. *It muffled sound.* It sent people scurrying homeward, so that the street was soon deserted, empty, quiet. And it could have been any street in the city, for the snow laid a *delicate film* over the sidewalk, over the *brick* of the tired, old buildings; gently *obscuring the grime* and the garbage and the ugliness. (436, my emphases)

This passage clearly underlines how culture (like nature) beautifies violence by way of silencing. Whereas in the beginning, weather conditions strip Lutie naked, here they provide a soothing overcoat, a veil (and a white one at that). So just like *Blackmail*, the final emphasis of Petry's novel falls on the "obscuring" of the attempted sexual crime/grime ("brick"), which pinpoints the film's very paradox. Hitchcock's first sound film, *Blackmail* at the same time "muffle[s] sound." Likewise Petry's novel, one of the first to explore intraracial rape head-on, concludes "mufflingly," thus exposing the self-destructive dynamic of such muffling. It therefore comes as no surprise that those figures who profit most from the silence cloaking intraracial (sexual) crime have themselves built their identity on "muffled sounds." Both Hedges and Junto obscure their past and the wounds and scars it inflicted, disfiguring body and mind (253).

Black-on-black assault, Petry underlines, is "muffled" partly because black-on-white rape has been loudmouthed. Accordingly, the term "rape" is employed with reference to interracial violence and in a parodic mode only. Reminiscing about his work as a porter, Jones rehearses the dominant notions on black masculinity he was faced with: "Niggers steal. . . . Niggers lie. . . . Niggers rape. Cover yourself up. Didn't you see that nigger looking at you?" (264–65). Interestingly enough, the term "rape" occurs in yet another "interracial" context—the German Nazi regime and the U.S. involvement in World War II. Like Bigger, Jones had refused to "[g]o . . . fight . . . the white folks' war for them" (255), "[b]ecause no matter how scared they are of Germans"—who supposedly "cut off baby's behinds and rape women and turn men into slaves"—"they're still more scared of me" (258). Whereas throughout the novel domestic gender wars and local power struggles put the war in Europe at a distance, the trope of rape realigns American and European efforts at nation formation. Thus Smith's parodic picture of the German as child molester, rapist, and slaver readdresses the history of his own subjection by way of "othering" it. His refusal to fight German rapists/slavers is therefore a refusal to engage in interracial conflicts he deems to be a losing battle. Accordingly, Smith (like Bigger) targets not Junto but Lutie.

In contrast to Hitchcock's movie, which ends on the note of male laughter over a joke cracked at Alice's expense, nobody wins or laughs at the end of Petry's novel. Underdog Jones, defeated early on in the race, succeeds in violating yet also chases Lutie away and "secures" Bub behind bars. As Smith fails to turn the tables by "having" Lutie before "master" Junto manages to, Junto finds his authority reinforced but his desires frustrated. Stifling man's laughter by committing manslaughter, Lutie reaches no happy end either. Instead, there is more rage and anger than had ever before appeared in African American women's writing. Anger, as Modleski points out, "for women continues to be, as it has been historically, the most unacceptable emotion" ("Rape" 310). African American women, in particular, have historically been forced to deny or repress anger. Allowing for anger not just to surface but to predominate and direct Lutie's sense of self, Petry not only anticipates the tone and temper of Anglo-American 1970s feminist writings, that "era of eros and anger," as Elaine Showalter has it ("Rethinking" 238). Just as Petry reappropriates the (paradigm of the) black rapist as a "family member"—and thus rearranges the racial border and draws her attention toward the space on her own side of it—she also rewrites African American female subjectivity.

"Intrusive" Desire, Transitional Subjects

The originality of Petry's text results partly from a shift in perspective, from a kind of psychological realism that explores the desires, fears, (rape) fantasies, and frustrations of both victim and assaulter. Following the lead of Larsen's *Passing*, Petry's novel thus interrogates alliances between race and psychoanalysis that, according to Spillers, "constitute the missing layer of hermeneutic/interpretative projects of an entire generation of black intellectuals now at work."[35] "[O]nly a handful of writers of fiction"—among them Ralph Ellison and Morrison, so Spillers suggests—have staged ". . . the mental theater as an articulate structure of critical inquiries into the 'souls of black folk' " (" 'All the Things' " 76). Petry, I would argue, belongs among those authors. She not only explores African American subjectivity as a disposition constructed within ethnicity as well as across and between races and ethnic groups. Her texts also interrogate what it means to be a subject constructed by violence, "dispersed across categories of property, injury, and punishment" (Hartman 552), in terms of psychic reality and reality perception.

For Spillers the absence of psychoanalysis in the debate on race is partly due to the focus of social sciences on the collective social and economic situation (83–84). As a result, the African American subject seems determined almost entirely by outside forces. This tendency also dominates readings of African American literature and, in particular, "naturalist" novels such as *The Street.* Petry herself strongly objected to critics' dismissing the text as "a novel of social criticism": "a special and quite deplorable creation of American writers of the twentieth century," as she claims ("Novel" 32). Rather, interrogating (mis)perceptions of reality, Petry's text provides the very element, according to Spillers, that is missing from "[t]he three dimensions of subjectivity offered by Lacanian psychoanalysis, the Symbolic, the Imaginary, and the Real" (which, according to Lacan, is not the real). These categories do not account for "the 'reality' that breaks in on the person," but Petry adds the "fourth register" that establishes " 'reality' (of the dominated political position) as the psychic burden, acquired post-mirror stage" (Spillers, "All the Things" 82). Monitoring this "reality" through multiple perspectives that are in themselves divided, Petry practices what Spillers calls a strategy of "*interior intersubjectivity*" (83). Her protagonists do not view the world from the margins of an oppressive system; they are not merely "synecdochic representation[s]" of a so-called black community (100). They are figures "in discourse crossed by stigmata" (103) and yet central to themselves, subjects that are self-divided (though in specific, racialized ways) and yet one and individual (as opposed to many and communal). They are agents as much as they are acted upon, possessors of the gaze as much as its objects, violators as well as violated.

At the same time Petry's protagonists also lack what Spillers defines as missing from African American cultural analysis as such: self-reflexivity, self-knowledge, and a sense of desire as a secret that has to be spoken. Where desire remains secret, sexual violence is all there is. Consider Lutie and Min, for instance, who both take action after having been abused yet, misreading this abuse, "escape" into similar situations. Willing to exchange domestic labor and physical favors for free lodging, Min invites the very abuse she has just left behind. Fleeing Harlem for Chicago, Lutie is bound for just another "goddamned street." As a consequence, both experience desire, to appropriate Spillers's words, "as intrusive, as the estranged, irrational, burdensome illfit that alights between where she 'is at' and would/wanna be" (107).

—◦ᴥ◦—

Voicing Sexual Violence, Repoliticizing Rape:
Post-Modernist Narratives of Sexuality and Power

MODERNIST AMERICAN cultural practices generated rape as one of
their dominant tropes. In contemporary popular culture, though,
rape seems even more rampant, recurring in the lyrics of rappers
and "girl groups," in the visual arts, and in cinematic texts from *Straw Dogs*
to *The Accused* and *Pulp Fiction*, among many other places. At the same time,
it is modernist representations of rape themselves that hint why such deployment of rape says little about the frequency of real sexual violence. Whereas
turn-of-the-century texts employ figures of rape and the rapist to mark differences and redraw boundaries, modernist aesthetics exposes the media and the
making of these divides, at times even unmaking them on the local level of
textuality. Yet while modernist texts thus lay bare the ideology that informs
rape narratives, they do not follow specific political agendas. Post-modernist
fiction in turn retranslates the textual categories of modernism into cultural
ones and in the process repoliticizes the rape trope. In doing so, however, it
both retains modernist insights into rape and representation and interrogates
the divides and differences that turn-of-the-century texts established. And as
rape turns into a trope of (identity) politics, it monitors two prominent tendencies within contemporary American culture: the rising significance of sexual matters as markers of subject position and the displacement of activist
politics by what Ross calls a "politics of symbolism" (163).

At the same time post-modernist re-presentations of rape correlate with
modern conceptions of sexuality and changing sexual mores, without which
the explicitness of, say, Selby's *Last Exit to Brooklyn* (1957) would be unthinkable.[1] This explicitness in turn reflects the inversion that the rhetoric of rape
has undergone since the rise of the novel and the slave narrative: antebellum
texts limit the cultural significance of sexual violation to abolitionist or moral
arguments, while their particular aesthetics retain the displaced meanings that
transcend these political contexts. Now that rape is depicted graphically, its
cultural significance is being displaced. Rape and its representation thus still
circulate in opposite directions. Unlike its precursors, though, post-modernist
fiction disseminates not the representation of rape but its meanings. As a consequence this fiction reinforces the tendencies within modernist texts to align

rape with incest, to dissolve the distance between rape and lynching, and, most significantly, to project rape as systemic violence.

In fact, post-modern texts draw intensely on their precursors and recontextualize both realist and modernist paradigms. Accordingly, the aesthetics of post-modern rape narratives can be divided, albeit broadly, into two modes, one of which amplifies modernist parody (as Kathy Acker's texts do), while the other further develops the realist lines within modernism (as do Naylor and Carver, for instance). Both modes, however, foreground their own rhetoricity as well as their intertextual leanings: affirmative post-modern texts like Robert Coover's *The Public Burning* (1977), Reed's *Reckless Eyeballing* (1986), or Acker's *The Empire of the Senseless* (1988) reframe rape in hyperboles of mimicry and self-referentiality. Alternative post-modern fiction, as well as texts ranging from Selby's *Last Exit to Brooklyn* across Joyce Carol Oates's "Where Are You Going, Where Have You Been?" (1966) to Carver's "Tell the Women We're Going" and Naylor's *The Women of Brewster Place*, reinscribe rape within a realist tradition, a tradition whose sense of the real they simultaneously challenge.

What aligns these two aesthetic modes is that they both self-consciously employ rape as a trope of power relations. Take, for instance, Selby and Acker, both of whom ponder the established association of rape and prostitution. Selby's "Tralala" chapter challenges this association by creating causal alliances among premature sexualization, a woman's sense of her body and self, and sexual exploitation, between aggressive sexuality and sexual violence. In the process, the text reassesses common notions about consent. Having disappropriated her body and sexuality as commodities, Tralala may consent to the carnivalesque orgy of "drinking and screwing" she herself helps to initiate (125). She does not consent, though, to having her teeth knocked out and her lip split by a beer can. Thus while the split in her lip, on the one hand, figures her sexual violation, it also draws a line between scenes of consensual aggressive sexuality and nonconsensual sexual and physical abuse. Accordingly, it is at this point in the narrative that Tralala loses consciousness and along with it, as Tanner points out, the ability to consent (*Intimate Violence* 93). Selby's text thus acknowledges that sexual intercourse may transmute into rape, that consensual and nonconsensual sex are separated by only a fine line.

The scope of this insight, though, is limited to a particular historical moment, a certain "region," and a lower-class environment. Rape in *Last Exit to Brooklyn* is what demoralized lowlifes do to loose women and perverted queers, thus bespeaking their own degeneration. At the same time, the experimental aesthetics of Selby's rape scene diffuses all historic specificity: as the ordeal accelerates into its fatal finale, parataxis predominates and punctuation goes out the window—and along with it, the text suggests, all that is left of structure, order, and civilization. In this way, matters of sexual violence merely contribute to the novel's general critique of the American dream turned nightmare, a critique that employs rape as one of its crucial figures.

Acker's *In Memoriam to Identity* (1990), by contrast, parodically rehearses Faulkner's *Sanctuary*, oftentimes verbatim, disengages Temple's story from its Southern context, and playfully appropriates it as a paradigmatic tale of female initiation. Presenting woman's move into the symbolic order as "rape by the father,"[2] her position within that order as prostitution, Acker spells out Faulkner's subtleties while echoing Barnes's hyperbolic style. Reading rape as the entrance ticket to the symbolic order, she recognizes and reemploys rape as a trope for the female condition. No surprise that rape is indeed rampant in Acker's writing. At the same the author by no means embraces, but mimes and mocks, feminist perspectives that drive home similar messages yet fail to acknowledge the historicity of their own discourse and the parodic effects of its continuous rehearsal.

Making reference to their modernist precursors, some post-modernist (rape) narratives thus implicitly challenge the sense of mimesis promoted by antirape discourse. Whereas MacKinnon in *Only Words* holds representations of rape to be continuous with acts of real rape, Carver, for instance, privileges Faulkner's metapornographic mode, which seduces the reader into participation by deleting, eliding, the act of rape. This is how rape figures in the final lines of Carver's short story "Tell the Women We're Going":

> [Bill] looked and saw the girls. He saw them crouched behind an outcrop. Maybe they were smiling.
>
> Bill took out a cigarette. But he could not get it lit. Then Jerry showed up. It did not matter after that.
>
> Bill had just wanted to fuck. Or even see them naked. On the other hand, it was okay with him if it didn't work out.
>
> He never knew what Jerry wanted. But it started and ended with a rock. Jerry used the same rock on both girls, first on the girl called Sharon and then on the one that was supposed to be Bill's. (66)

Carver's minimalist depiction throws the reader back on his or her own imagination to visualize the unexpectedly violent encounter that the gap in the narrative both insinuates and disavows. Zooming in on the means of violence (a "rock"), the text at the same time disrupts the movement of the pornographic mind, desexualizes, de-eroticizes rape, and enlarges the injuries inflicted in the vicinity of sexual violence. In the process Carver subtly dissects the (gender) ideology of clear-cut subject and object positions conducive to such violence: the rock, we are told, is being "used on" two girls, one of whom "was supposed to be Bill's." Here sex happens—if it happens—merely in the reader's imagination.

The very title of Carver's tale recalls Oates's story "Where Are You Going, Where Have You Been?" Presenting the passage from girlhood into womanhood as a seduction into "voluntary rape," Oates makes a point delivered more bluntly in "Airplane," Acker's parody of *Sanctuary*, whose narrator nonchalantly claims: "taken her virginity or raped her, it didn't matter which" (*In Memoriam* 115). Unlike Acker, though, who revels in a post-modernist hyperbole and mockery of feminist commonplaces, Oates's text literalizes Faulkner's symbolism of rooms and doors (which echoes its own precursor texts). The screen door that separates Connie's family home from her pathetic aggressor, Arnold Friend, symbolizes the space she has to give up simply because there is no other way "out" into the world of womanhood. Oates's tale thus teases out the subtleties lost on a feminism that reads all heterosexuality as rape; at the same time, the story ridicules the male "seducer" and his pitiful ploys. Readdressing rape and seduction in this way, Oates underlines that as long as we formulate the problem of sexual violence (and sexuality) by distinguishing rape from seduction, we "necessarily block[] the attempt to found a sexuality without victimization, a sexuality which is not finally reduced by the active/ passive distinction" (Rooney 1272). And it is exactly this reduction that is exposed by woman-authored rape-fantasy fictions prominent in the 1970s.

Thus while both echoing and literalizing its literary precursors, post-modernist fiction illuminates some of their blind spots too: it addresses intraracial rape head-on (as Baldwin, Angelou, Morrison, Gayl Jones, Walker, and Naylor do); exposes same-sex sexual violence (as do Selby, John Rechy, James Dickey, Dennis Cooper, and Califia); explores rape fantasies (as do Erica Jong, Gould, and Ellis); or, like Naylor's *The Women of Brewster Place*, renders the moment of physical violation from the victim's own perspective. Contemporary American literature thus refocuses, recontextualizes, and often politicizes matters that modernist texts negotiate subtly, aesthetically, and in this way transforms (modernist) textual categories into cultural ones. At the same time, post-modernist rape narratives generate their own blind spots.

The alliance of rape and incest, for instance—a central trope within modernist refigurations of rape—recurs as a theme in post-modernist texts preoccupied with race matters. Harper Lee's novel *To Kill a Mockingbird*, for instance, reveals a case of incest behind what is publicly presented as a case of (black-on-white) sexual assault. It thus suggests that the hierarchical social order of the South, upheld by boundaries of race, region, class, gender, and tradition, is in fact based on crimes against fundamental laws of civilization. Like Harper long before her, Lee thus inverts the dominant rapist rhetoric. Unlike Faulkner and again like Harper, Lee at the same time envisions a transformation of civil society, the motor of which is the exemplary (white) person, embodied by lawyer Atticus Finch, whose saintly ethics is passed on to his (protofeminist) daughter Scout. Lacking female role models, Scout, like her father (and Lee herself), aspires to the legal profession, which allows her to challenge the codes of Southern chivalry, charity, and chastity. Lee thus highlights the difficulties of (white) female identity formation yet leaves black women's marginal, albeit idealized, position unchallenged. In presenting black women primarily as domestics and surrogate mothers, her novel, dedicated to the struggle for racial equality, suppresses the (gender-related) concerns of those who have triggered that struggle.[3] Lee's novel instead allies the movement for the civil rights of black men—featured, in her novel, as ministers and handicapped workingmen wrongly accused as rapists—with (white) women's liberation. The text thus repoliticizes rape with a race bias.

Several 1970s and 1980s novels written by African American women, by contrast, appropriate the incest trope to redefine sexual assault as a family matter, thereby suggesting that racism, once internalized, results in autoaggressive acts within the "black community." In the context of African American culture, such reassessment of one's own racial "family" as "site of oppression" was a new and "defamiliarizing strategy" indeed (Butler-Evans 167). It violated the established "cult of secrecy" and stirred up a fair amount of "plain black [gender] trouble," to appropriate the words of Bessie Mears. In fact, black women's fiction instigated unprecedented debates among African American male and female writers—controversies that are believed to have triggered a genuine African American feminist criticism. Thus, curiously enough, as contemporary black feminism emerges from a critique that reassesses the "myth of the black rapist" and takes issue with the dominance, within black liberation movements, of the trope of lynching over that of rape, the history of this feminism itself follows the narrative structure of classical rape myths. Here, as in classical texts, the trope of rape functions as a motor of change and transformation.

Meanwhile many white female authors, by contrast, were preoccupied either with narratives of rape-revenge or with fictions that engage rape fantasies.[4] This (racialized) difference within recent American women's writing, to my mind, is due partly to precursors that construct white women's sexual desire almost exclusively in contexts of sexual aggression. Throughout my argument we have encountered a whole cast of characters, including Norris's Trina, Moody's Ruth, Faulkner's Temple, and Mitchell's Scarlett, who seem to enjoy "violent love-making" (Petry, *The Street* 87). The censorship imposed upon fiction depicting female sexual pleasure, like Wharton's "Beatrice Palmato" or Chopin's "The Storm," has further reinforced the prominence of the female "masochist."[5] Since women have always remained marginal to the construction of sexuality, especially their own, any attempt to enter into the struggle over sexual definition—be it by way of women's pornography or rape-fantasy fictions—is highly momentous.[6] And yet we cannot expect such attempts to be earthshaking. Dependent on a well-established codified discourse on female sexuality, no *ars erotica* (in the Foucauldian sense) will dream up an *other* economy of desire. In fact, as Claudia Gehrke emphasizes, female desire does not necessarily "look as we would hope it would," is not inherently politically correct, "for it is not untouched by reality. To say that therefore it cannot be desire (and thus should not meet the public eye)," she claims, "is political propaganda that hardly helps the fight against sexual violence" (17). Nor does such "propaganda" help to evolve a female sexuality that is not guilt-ridden.

And these are exactly the issues that arise in rape-fantasy fictions. As my reading of Gould's *A Sea Change* and Jong's *Fear of Flying* (1973) shows, neither do these texts assume female sexuality to be natural, yet repressed, nor do they demonize male sexuality as intrinsically violent. Instead, they present rape fantasies as products of a historically developed discourse on sexuality, a discourse that generated fantasies of rape as one of its crucial tropes. Thus unlike Faulkner and Petry, who insist that female reflections on rape are as much a defense mechanism *against* sexual violation as an effect of fear, they foreground what has emerged as rape fantasy. The "phantom men" haunting the imagination of Isadora Wing, for instance, are not of the rapist kind. They are playmates partaking in imaginary, noncommittal, casual sexual encounters projected by a (post-modern) heroine with a knack for what singer-songwriter George Michaels calls the "religion" of "fast love." Thus if we read rape-fantasy fictions as dramatizations of an essential female desire to be violated, we nullify the reciprocity pertaining to the discursive construction of female sexuality and sexual violence. Most significant: such a reading literalizes what is meant to function figuratively. After all, fictional rape fantasies are in fact metafantasies, forcing us to confront the function of their own fictionality.

Among the various rape narratives that have emerged in recent American fiction and have advanced rape into a master trope of sexuality and power, I chose to concentrate on those synchronically emerging, yet distinctly racialized, fictions authored by black and white women. This allows me to pick up on the issues discussed in the first chapter and to readdress both the development of women's writing and its complex relation to feminist criticism. Unlike their antebellum precursors, rape-fantasy fictions and African American narratives that treat rape as a "family affair" directly engage matters of masculinity and the male body. Marginalized by the seduction novel and the early African American autobiography, yet central to realist and naturalist literature, constructions of manhood turn out to be crucial to representing and reading rape.

Accordingly, I frame my analysis of recent women's writing with two male-authored rape narratives, Himes's *A Case of Rape* (1965) and Dickey's *Deliverance* (1970). Dickey ponders what some consider the "last taboo" (Mullen): male-on-male rape. Re-presenting rape as what is (literally) done to men, his action novel reassesses the "myth" of the South and the male anxieties that inform its rapist rhetoric. Himes's *Case of Rape*, which turns out to be no rape case at all, in turn illuminates how that rhetoric has affected relations among black men. All of these texts highlight that the inversion representations of rape have undergone since antebellum times involves a fundamental reversal of their function: whereas rape narratives, none of which made the violent act particularly explicit, once served to construct differences of race, gender, or class, the explicit portrayal of rape in recent fiction mediates a disturbing journey into the complexities of identity and difference.

"Mankind's Greatest Crime, Man's Inhumanity to Man": Chester Himes's *A Case of Rape*

The translation of Himes's virtually unknown *Une Affair de Viol* appeared in 1980, in a limited American collectors edition of 350 copies, with the title *A Case of Rape*; it was republished by Howard University Press in 1984. Like *Native Son* and *To Kill a Mockingbird* the novel deals with the trial of an accused black violator of a white victim. This, it seems, is where parallels end. Himes's pseudodocumentary narrative reports on the alleged rape of Elizabeth Hancock by four black men from largely, yet not exclusively, middle-class background, one of whom, Scott Hamilton, was once romantically entangled with Hancock. What looks like "a case of rape" and murder, though, turns out to be a series of curiously contrived circumstances leading to a fatal accident in Hamilton's hotel room, where the five people had gathered.

Setting the novel in the expatriate scene of Paris's Latin Quarter, Himes frames his "case" as a transatlantic affair, thereby interrelating American racism with French colonialism, American civil rights struggles with "French politics on the heels of France's setbacks in Indo-China and Morocco" and its "hopeless war against Algerian nationalists" (27). As he pinpoints the effects of the established rhetoric of rape and race on common conceptions of consensual interracial relations, the author focuses on the harm resulting from "positive" essentialist notions of (racial and gender) difference and from the attempt, on the part of both (educated) blacks and whites, to appear tolerant and beyond racial prejudice. Involving a group of black men whose interests conflict, *A Case of Rape* demystifies notions of racial solidarity, foregrounding the preconceptions that African Americans have come to hold concerning one another. In fact, it is the novel's ultimate irony that the verdict wrongly convicting four African American men results partly from a tendency among blacks to stifle intraracial tensions and struggles of male authority. Accordingly, the novel's rhetoric itself is highly ironic; the work is by no means a "somber, almost documentary examination of racial injustice," as Robert Skinner suggests (30). Rather, mocking Wright as well as the documentary mode that typifies African American race politics and ideology, Himes's text ponders the psychic makeup of black men in a parodic mode.

Divided into fifteen parts, the text first presents the reader with "The Charge," "The Defense," "The Summations," "The Verdict," "The Sentence," and "The Fourth Estate" (i.e., the coverage of the case by the international print media). It goes on to unravel the details leading up to the rape-murder conviction, delineating first the work of "investigator" and "American Negro writer, Roger Garrison" (27; parts 7 and 8), and second the narrator's own insights into the liaison of Hancock and Hamilton (parts 9–13)—insights that complement and correct "Roger's Findings" and "Roger's Errors" (parts 9 and 10). In part 13 the novel discloses "The Missing Evidence" upon which our full understanding of the case depends. What we get is consequently three versions of the same story, varying in perspective and style.

The first version is delivered in a blunt, mock-documentary, pseudo-objective mode. "The Charge" introduces the protagonists, Hancock and Hamilton, as well as his African American friends Caesar Gee, Theodore Elkins, and Sheldon Edward Russell; the location where the alleged crime took place; the state in which victim and violators presented themselves at the scene; the results of the autopsy (which revealed both Hancock's four "sexual employments" and traces of a powerful aphrodisiac in her blood). "The Defense" focuses on the relation between Hancock and Hamilton and explains why the five persons met on that particular afternoon: Hancock had wrongly accused Hamilton, whom she had given a half interest in work that she was going to publish, of informing her publisher that her book was in fact ghostwritten. Denying this charge, Hamilton wanted his closest friends to testify that he was telling the truth. In the course of the afternoon, Hancock had some sherry, got tired, lay down, and after waking poured herself another drink from a similar bottle that contained a blend of sherry and the aforementioned aphrodisiac, given to Hamilton "by a white American journalist . . . who had laughingly suggested that he employ it to perpetuate one of great American myths" (20). As a result, she became "mentally deranged," tore her clothes, screamed, tried to jump out the window (15), "gasped and died" (16). Despite some incongruities of evidence, the court finds the accused "guilty on both counts," rape and murder, and the media reports—not incorrectly, yet insufficiently—that Hancock "had died from the combined effects of an overdose of an aphrodisiac and repeated sexual employment" (25).

Investigator-writer Garrison, by contrast, elaborates on the politics of the case:

> He saw in the verdict a perfect example of the racist-political ends served by all such convictions of Negro men for raping white women.
>
> According to his considered opinion, the very essence of the trial was that of an inquisition to reestablish the inferiority of the entire Negro race. (27)

The narrator's irony and loaded diction foreground the author's concern with readings of rape cases (as opposed to "cases" of rape) and, more specifically, insinuates that Garrison's conspiracy theory itself makes for another "great American myth." Just like the French court, which pays little attention to the details of the case, Garrison's own preconceptions make him oblivious to questions that would have emerged if this were not a case of interracial conflict. Such conflicts have generated, so Himes suggests, two dominant interpretative paradigms: that of rape *and* lynching and that of rape *as* lynching. Like Wright, Garrison may be right in observing "that the virtues of Negroes were never determined from the true nature of their motives, but only from the construction placed upon their motives for racist expediency; that their vices were never presented in the framework of good and evil, but only in their application to the opinion of whites in their judgments of blacks" (30). The very same, though, Himes underlines, goes for Garrison's own sense of the virtues and vices of whites.

Garrison himself resists the fact that "his own fame and failure" as a writer was promoted for political expediency. In the United States, the author (whose name commemorates William Lloyd Garrison) had projected himself in a familiar (Richard Wright–style) fashion: "born on an Alabama plantation, one of twelve children of poverty-stricken Negro sharecroppers," he had joined the Communist party, which marketed his writings and prodded him into writing his autobiography—"as do most American Negro Writers," the narrator sarcastically adds, hinting at the constraints of "black literature" effected by the predominance of the slave narrative.[7] While Paris seemed to promise freedom from such constraints, France in turn employed his resignation from and subsequent critique of the Communist party in "rightist" propaganda, celebrating him as the one "great genius of his race" (32). Now Garrison craves to have his work "evaluated on merit," "to assume his true position among the writers of the world." This being his "major motive," he also "knew," we are told, that "he could have been convicted of rape and murder too" (34). The paradox here is, of course, that Garrison seeks to transcend the limits of race by playing the race card. As he founds his work on "investigation" (as opposed to imagination), he performs a mimicry of mimicry. Quite appropriately, the narrator concludes that our investigator-author "had discovered nothing that was not already known or assumed" (64).

Accordingly, Garrison's insights into the defendants' lives mock the familiar fictions of black subjectivity. He concludes, for instance, that Caesar Gee—a cross between a (great black) Gatsby, complete with bootlegging background, and a bohemian artist (whose paintings displayed "a rare violence" and were "devoted entirely to sex")—"was more likely to have been raped than to have committed rape" (40). Likewise, "handsome" and "popular" Sheldon (Shelly) Edward Russell "was the kind of *Uncle Tom* who did it for free, to have the good will and personal liking of cultured and intelligent white people, preferably of the upperclass" (47). Echoing Bigger Thomas, Garrison capitalizes on black men's "effeminacy" (48). Moreover and most significant, "[h]e committed the customary error of white persons who assume that Negroes love one another" (68).

Similarly one-dimensional are Garrison's notions of womanhood, no matter what shade. He depicts the only African American woman featured in the text, Hamilton's former wife Stella Browning, as "a full-bodied, *café au lait*, black haired piece of red hot sex, rotten to the core," as an irresponsible unwed mother working as a singer and "amateur whore and sleeping free with three men. But she had a voice" (59–60, 60). By contrast, Hancock, in his view, "was like all other American white women lusting after Negro men" (70). A "descendent of a passenger of the Mayflower" (61) and "the John Hancock who had signed the *Declaration of Independence*" (73) she epitomizes Americanness, being both a worldly young woman and "appallingly ignorant of the most rudimentary knowledge relating to sex" (74–75). It is this (American) inno-cence, the narrator suggests, that made her vulnerable to the wooing of the man who became her husband, the dentist André Brissaud. Like his lower-class colleague McTeague, Brissaud is projected as hereditary evil incarnate, "imbued with an ingrown, refined evil of generations of decadence," an evil, however, "termed by Americans as *continental.*" Unlike McTeague, who "pene-trates" Trina by way of dental surgery yet manages to put the brakes on his sexual "drive," Brissaud "could not have her without surgery," which he had "performed by three friends . . . and had her immediately afterwards. He truly thought she would enjoy the pain" (76). Rewriting rape as surgery, Himes literalizes the trope of surgery as rape. As it involves four men altogether, this rape scene foreshadows the alleged violation in Hamilton's hotel room.

In the context of Himes's sharp parody it comes as no surprise that Han-cock's own devilish Nazi-collaborator husband (77) turns out to be the rapist who had chased her into Hamilton's arms, where she expected to find what her marriage was lacking. The alliance between Hancock and Hamilton is driven, we learn, by their common (middle-)class background as well as a mutual sympathy with each other's victimization. Hancock was, we are told in a mock-feminist mode, "as much a casualty of racism as [Hamilton]—an inverted sort of racism that perpetuates the dominance of the male." Pre-senting both Hancock and Hamilton as victims of such dominance, Himes, like Wright, casts rape as a crime against black men and at the same time ponders its subtexts, homoeroticism and homosexual panic. (Hamilton in fact deems Brissaud to be homosexual.) However, just as the portrait of Brissaud resonates with its precursors, Hancock and Hamilton fail to see beyond the codified "black-and-white" images they project of each other. Whereas Hamil-ton idealizes sophisticated Hancock and wishes to "heal" her "hurt soul" (83), she wants to "lose herself in the dark night of his love" (85). Guided by ra-cialized misperceptions, though, they lose themselves "in the maze of racial barriers," erected here by a set of positive stereotypes. Wrongly assuming that Hancock expected him to support her, Hamilton "contracted all the forms of mental illness . . . he had meant to cure in her," "suffered all the fears and frustrations and anxieties and paranoia she had first suffered" (86), even reex-periences her rape trauma. At this point, Hancock reunites with her husband, lured by the strongest of all aphrodisiacs (according to Henry Kissinger, that is): power.

The "missing evidence" is revealed, like Faulkner's corncob, at a later moment in the narrative, and it partly explains Hancock's condition when she meets with Hamilton and his friends: she is both physically exhausted from an excessive sexual encounter with her ex-husband and mentally drained by the fact that "spiteful enemies" wrongly accuse her of having engaged a ghost-writer. What medical experts interpret as signs of gang rape turns out to be traces of repeated consensual intercourse prior to the victim's meeting with the defendants. The final ironic twist, however, occurs as the focus shifts from the overdetermining interracial relations to the "underreported" intraracial tensions. Jealous of what appeared to be Hamilton's enjoyment of "life's benefits without struggle" (94) and feeling "unmanned" by what he considered contempt on Hancock's part (95), investigator-writer Garrison himself turns out to have misinformed Hancock's publisher. The "errors" of his investigation consequently result from his own petty personal quarrels. Likewise, Hancock's death is effected by a "joke" played upon Hamilton, the group's apparently most powerful male, by its weakest member, Theodore Elkins, who resented Hancock's paying less attention to him than to the other men present.

"It was fear," the narrator explains, that made the defendants withhold Ted's motive—sheer "spite"—which "no one outside of the American negro race would believe" (100). Interracial relations, so Himes insists, lack a conception of "individual guilt"; "the crimes of one Negro" are always—synecdochically—attributed "to the entire Negro race." The very testimony against Ted "would have been tantamount," the narrator reasons, "to confessing they had given her the aphrodisiac for the purpose of raping her. No one would believe they had not actually raped her." Rather than "try to explain the degree of his guilt," to deny "any charge" was therefore best for "any Negro" (101). Likewise, Hamilton could not reveal his knowledge of Hancock's sexual encounter with her ex-husband because such detail would have compromised his own position. "Was he her father confessor? Was he a homosexual who could share her ecstasies vicariously?" (102). His sense that Brissaud is homosexual thus bespeaks his own compromised position. Accordingly, throughout this section the potential testimony pertaining to Hancock's sexual history goes by the name of confession, the admission of Hamilton's own guilt. This guilt, it is suggested, boils down to a (latent) homosexuality, to effeminization. Unlike Bigger, who deems himself raped and victimized by systemic racial discrimination, Hamilton feels himself to be a transgressor of the boundaries delineated by normative heterosexuality. Like Bigger, he suffers from the effects of internalized racism.

Accordingly, A Case of Rape does not reveal its "tragically ironic metaphor of rape" in the fact that, as Hernton claims, prosecuted by a jury who would not believe them, "the minds and emotions of the four black men were raped—just as the bodies and minds and emotions of all black people have been raped by centuries of 'man's inhumanity to man' " ("Postscript" 139–40, quoting from Himes, *Case* 105). Unlike Wright's novel, Himes's narrative does not displace one misconceived trope—all "Negro men . . . *are potential rapists*" (105)—with another: "all Negro men are being raped." As it foregrounds homoeroticism and homophobia, Himes's parodic tale goes one step further: it discloses the crucial function of the rape trope in what Sedgwick has called the "chronic, now endemic crisis of the homo/heterosexual definition, indicatively male, dating from the end of the nineteenth century" (*Epistemology* 1). The issue at stake in Himes's "case" of rape is constructions of (black) masculinity, and the novel quite appropriately ends with a note on relations between men. If the "missing evidence" were revealed, the narrator "speculates" in conclusion:

> Men would have then been influenced to consider whether the greater crime was rape or the conviction of innocent men for rape on racial preconceptions.
>
> Perhaps this might have forwarded the precept of all men of whatever race to bear some measure of the guilt for mankind's greatest crime, man's inhumanity to man.
>
> And this is how it should be. We are all guilty. (105)

Significantly enough, this "grand finale" and final plea, reminiscent of earlier African American novelists' appeal to a humanism transcending matters of race and rape drowns the novel's insight into the anxieties and silences among black men in a deployment of generic mankind. Along with it, it submerges the charge of "plain black (gender) trouble" leveled by black women against black men. Protesting "the subjection of Black feminist discourse to the politics of race" (Butler-Evans 37)—a subjection that Himes's text both enacts and mocks—African American women's fiction of the 1970s and 1980s addresses that charge under a new name: incest. Ultimately at issue in these narratives are matters of black female subjectivity—Himes's parodic "black haired piece of red hot sex" and song in search of her own body and self, her own voice and history.

"Plain Black (Gender) Trouble": Intraracial Rape, Incest, and Other Family Feuds

"The American black woman is haunted," Wallace wrote in *Black Macho and the Myth of the Superwoman* (1978),

> by the mythology that surrounds the American black man. It is a mythology based upon the real persecution of black men: castrated black men hanging by their necks from trees; the carcasses of black men floating face down in the Mississippi; black men with their bleeding genitals jammed between their teeth; black men shining shoes; black men turned down for jobs time and time again. . . . Every time she starts to wonder about her own misery, to think about reconstructing her life, to shake off her devotion and feeling of responsibility to everyone but

herself, the ghosts pounce. She is stopped cold. The ghosts talk to her. *"You* crippled the black man. *You* worked against him." (30)

Rewriting black gender relations as horror fiction, Wallace insists that black women, haunted by the "myth of the black rapist," have come to accept the myth of the superwoman and accomplice of white supremacy. Accordingly, like Wallace's text, the literary work of Morrison, Angelou, Ntozake Shange, and Walker has been criticized for accepting "the fruit of feminist knowledge" offered by white women (McDowell 79), for being seduced, that is, into denouncing black men, for airing "dirty laundry" in front of a white audience eager to use the fictional texts as evidence to support its own race politics. Such a practice of reading, which mistakes fiction for social documentary, has been just as common among African American male critics, though, and is the effect of an all-too-comfortable binarism between black and white, between oppression and liberation[8]—a binarism that not only dominates historical and sociological views of the African American condition but also reduces that condition to the historical and sociological. Following the lead of Robert Staples, manifesting little concern for aesthetics and style, and taking tropes of rape and incest literally, many African American male critics have consequently preferred to ignore how black women's writing exposes the fictions pertaining to the racial family and its condition.

Relying upon the generic tradition of the slave narrative and African American autobiography, contemporary black women's fiction re-members the very idiosyncrasies pertaining to African American gender relations. Central, yet marginalized, in this sex/gender system is a female subject circumscribed by sexual exploitation, by an economy that managed to place African American women *"out* of the traditional symbolics of female gender" (Spillers, "Mama's Baby" 480). Making room for this different—social and psychic—subject, African American women's fiction also forces its readers to "disremember" (Morrison) that rape is "not what one did to women," that rape equals the lynching of a black man.

African American women's fiction achieves this in part by exploring the very violations that nineteenth-century literary convention allowed, in fact "almost demanded," as May Henderson notes, to "be named but not described" (314). It does so by finding new ways, as Morrison's *Beloved* does, to relate "proceedings" considered "too terrible to relate" (Morrison, qtd. in Henderson 314) and thus to overcome the continuing impulse to "beat . . . back the past" (Morrison, *Beloved* 73). This required, among other things, that "the mantle of silence" wrapped around gender trouble among African Americans (Keckley 50) be lifted. Reimagining this trouble by way of the incest trope, contemporary black women's fiction at the same time drives further into the interiority that Petry began to engage, fusing memory with experience. In the process, their fiction reconstructs African American kinship relations, portraying truly dysfunctional families. They also deconstruct the myth, applied as an antidote to the legendary black rapist, that black men don't rape. The re-presentation of rape in recent African American women's fiction thus is bound by multiple generic conventions, including the female-authored slave narrative, the dominant rapist rhetoric deployed in "realist" texts, and modernist precursors such as Faulkner's and Petry's fiction. My rereading of Morrison, Angelou, Walker, and Naylor thus focuses on how this history of discourse affects contemporary visions of black female subjectivity.

Sexual violation looms large throughout Morrison's work, beginning with *The Bluest Eye* (1970), running through *Tar Baby* (1981), and returning with particular vehemence in *Beloved* (1986), a text literally haunted by the history, memory, and trauma of rape.[9] Likewise Walker has written extensively about both interracial and intraracial rape. In her short story "How Did I Get Away with Killing One of the Biggest Lawyers in the State? It Was Easy" an adolescent rape victim kills her aggressor, robs his safe, and "gets away with it," because— unlike Bigger Thomas—a little black girl in the vicinity of the big white lawyer simply remains invisible. "Advancing Luna—and Ida B. Wells," by contrast, problematizes the difficulties black and white women have in communicating about (interracial) rape. Issues of sexual violence are thus employed to interrogate feminist loyalties and the limits of "sisterhood." Walker's most controversial text on the issue, however, remains *The Color Purple* (1982).[10]

The adaptation of the incest trope links *The Color Purple* with Morrison's first novel and Angelou's *I Know Why the Caged Bird Sings* (1969), all of which present (step)fathers or family friends as sexual aggressors. In *The Bluest Eye* protagonist Pecola Breedlove is raped by her father Cholly; and whereas the slave narrative emphasizes survival, here the severity of the experience figures in the victim's madness and premature death. This does not so much confirm that "the truth of women's total defeat by rape," as Kubitchek suggests, "had to wait to emerge in literature until the truth of the survival and even triumph had been established" (47). Rather, Pecola's death foregrounds that internalized racism eventually defeats the community, and the incest theme tropes internalized racism as a form of self-mutilation. Accordingly, whereas 1970s rape-revenge novels, for instance, launch angry attacks on patriarchal oppression and "compulsory heterosexuality" (Adrienne Rich), African American women's writing expresses a certain sympathy with the disempowered perpetrator. *The Bluest Eye*, for instance, depicts the father's sexual aggression against his daughter as resulting to a considerable degree from his own troubled first sexual experience. "Overseen" and enforced by white spectators, thus embedded in a scene that visualizes the denial of privacy and the racialized construction of black sexuality, this experience breeds not love but illicit family relations. In Morrison's depiction of Pecola's rape, rendered through the perspective of a powerless aggressor, the reader even senses a certain degree of empathy for this victim-turned-violator. In fact, the destructive act is framed by intimations of tenderness that, unable to be communicated appropriately, cause an irreparable breach.

Interrogating racialized constructions of gender (like the idealized beauty of white womanhood) and cultural myths (passed on in fairy tales or school primers), Morrison's novel at the same time dramatizes the interplay between cultural imaginary and literary imagination, underlining the reality of both. The same goes for Angelou's autobiographical narrative, which renders and interprets traumatic experiences by way of texts as culturally significant and sacred as the Bible and Shakespeare. Its central disorienting event is the rape of narrator Maya at age eight by Mr. Freeman, the (emasculated) lover of her mother. This abuse has an intensifying foreplay: in the first instance, Freeman masturbates in Maya's presence, performing an act the child cannot understand while also extending a tenderness she thoroughly enjoys ("Finally he was quiet and then came the nice part"). In fact, as Freeman holds her "so softly," Maya "wishe[s] he wouldn't ever let me go" (61). Since her abuse is accompanied by pleasure and female pleasure is aligned with whoring ("they would stone me," she projects, "as they had stoned the harlot in the Bible"), Maya fails to mention the encounter during the trial against Freeman. Any such confession of her own transgression would invalidate her testimony on the rape itself.

In addition Freeman himself had imposed Maya's silence before his violent act: "If you scream," he threatens her, "I'm gonna kill you. And if you tell, I'm gonna kill Bailey," Maya's beloved brother (65). The narrative enacts his command by shifting from first- to third-person point of view, from a limited, naive, and personal perspective to a detached ethical one. Presented by way of proverbial biblical wisdom, the latter perspective monitors Maya's violation through a worldview informed by a principle of retributive justice.

> I could tell he meant what he said. I couldn't understand why he wanted to kill my brother. Neither of us had done anything to him. And then.
>
> Then there was the pain. A breaking and entering when even the senses are torn apart. The act of rape on an eight-year-old body is a matter of the needle giving because the camel can't. The child gives, because the body can, and the mind of the violator cannot.
>
> I thought I had died—I woke up in a white-walled world, and it had to be heaven. But Mr. Freeman was there and he was washing me. His hands shook, but he held me upright in the tub and washed my legs. "I didn't mean to hurt you, Ritie. I didn't mean it. But don't you tell . . . Remember, don't you tell a soul." (65–66)

Framed by the rapist's command, the sexual assault is rendered in a matter-of-fact and seemingly rational manner. The text thus enacts the tearing of the senses, the rape—a disjunction of body and mind, the body/"needle" giving in while the mind gives up, caves in—by a shift of tone. Moreover, by adapting and literalizing the first, metaphorical part of the wisdom Jesus passes on to his disciples—his insight that a camel is more likely to pass through the eye of a needle than a rich man to enter the kingdom of God—the text capitalizes on the physically improbable to foreground that rape "on an eight-year-old body" is an act beyond human understanding.[11] The act is incomprehensible even to its perpetrator, who, figured as a misguided and stubborn mind, in the aftermath concentrates merely on the cleansing of Maya's silent body. At the same time, the "matter" of camel and needle triggers acts of remembering and recontextualization on the reader's part: by reconstituting the deleted part of the proverb, we recover the "wisdom" of Maya's naïveté and the text's uncomfortable ironies. Assuming that she has crossed beyond heaven's gate, Maya affirms both her innocence and her loss, the loss of a "possession," of riches that she had never conceived of as such. Accordingly, in contrast to the balanced world of proverbial wisdom where "many that are first will be last, and the last first" (Matt. 19:30), Maya's real-life experience knows no real justice. As Freeman is sentenced, yet released, and subsequently lynched by Maya's uncles, she blames herself for her rapist's fate: having withheld the first "pleasurable" part of his abusive behavior, she has lied in court. Convinced that her words have the power to kill, she falls silent for a year.

As Christine Froula points out, this particular conjunction of rape and silence not only recalls the Philomela rape myth. It also foregrounds Ovid's retelling of it, which entwines rape with incest. "Tereus," Froula observes, "watching Philomela cajole her father into allowing her to visit her sister Procne, puts himself in her father's place: 'He would like to be / Her father at that moment, and if he were / He would be as wicked a father as he is a husband' " (636). According to Froula such an alliance between rapist and father dramatizes the "law of the father" and his ownership of daughters, which is extrapolated into an ownership of all females with whom he is allied by kinship or marriage. What is more: like the appropriation of proverbial wisdom, the employment of myth highlights how literary codes and conventions inform contemporary representations of rape. The same goes for Maya's reemergence from silence into sound: her voice revives during a recital of Shakespeare's *Rape of Lucrece*. Unlike Froula, though, I do not read this as a fall from literal into literary silence (636); nor would I hold that "[t]he black child's identification with an exquisite rape fantasy of white male culture" simply "violates her reality" (637). Rather, these fantasies *are* her reality. Along with the slave narrative that keeps molding African American fiction, they attest to the limitation as well as the potential of generic convention.[12] As she gives voice to Shakespeare—her "first white love" (11)—Maya, on the one hand, begins to overcome rape by means of defamiliarization. Employing an established poetics of rape for her tale of identity formation, Angelou, on the other hand, suggests that "rape of an eight-year-old (black) body" surpasses the traditional codes of representation.

Like Angelou's autobiography, Walker's *The Color Purple* makes the telling of violation a means of self-authorization. Both texts in this way rehearse the slave narrative, and even though they substantially rewrite their literary precursor, they also reinforce its dominant effect: the conflation of black female subjectivity with sexual violation. Just like Linda Brent and Maya, Celie establishes her new sense of self on the narrative of such violation. Owing to the censorship imposed by her father/violator ("You better tell nobody but God"), this narrative figures as confession, with God himself being the confessor (thus recontextualizing Puritan beliefs quite uncannily). At the same time, Celie's confession does not so much bespeak her own deviance as it echoes Temple Drake's sense of something "happening to [her]." And unlike Brent, Celie is both prematurely sexualized *and* sexually violated, and her very account of that violation underscores the prematurity of this experience: "First he put his thing up gainst my hip and sort of wiggle it around. Then he grab hold my titties. Then he push his thing inside my pussy. When that hurt, I cry" (3).

Significantly enough, Walker's novel employs both the conventions of the slave narrative and the aesthetic mode of the epistolary novel. Like the sentimental novel, *The Color Purple* establishes its authority on illusions of authenticity and appeals to emotions as a means of moral insights. Appropriating an aesthetics that traditionally engenders tales of seduction and female fall, the text insists upon the parallels pertaining to interpretations of black and white intraracial rape. Thus whereas in Jacobs's text the recurrent seduction motif tends to undermine the author's particular agenda, here it serves to clearly separate Walker's perspective—the focus on intraracial rape and its predominant interpretation as seduction—from that of Jacobs. Critics who, like Joanne M. Braxton and Hernton, read *The Color Purple as* a slave narrative in turn retranslate black gender trouble into master and slave relations.[13]

In accordance with the novel's hybrid aesthetics, the black rapist denies the difference between seduction and rape, between appropriate sexual initiation and sexual violation. As he "choke[s]" his victim, in the course of the act of rape, advising that she "better shut up and git used to it" (3), silence becomes "an integral part" not only "of the rape itself" (Boesenberg 301) but of its telling. Thus whereas sexual violation and initiation into (hetero)sexuality are joined in silence, Walker in turn associates the breaking of that silence and the emergence of female "authority" with the recognition of a genuinely female "jouissance," another economy of sexual desire. This development becomes a main drive of her text: the healing of Celie's incest experience corresponds to her defiance of silence and to an initiation into a "lesbian continuum" (Adrienne Rich), a woman-oriented existence, with Celie's sister Nettie as emotional support system and her (second) confessor Shug as friend and lover. In this context the epistolary form of the novel accommodates an intimate communication that establishes the subject's own "voice" in communion with an other, an addressee.

The depiction of this sea change calls upon the Philomela myth, which structures the alliance between Celie and Nettie. As their epistolary connection is cut, the latter temporarily loses her voice, authority, and subject position. While Nettie regresses to the state of silence, Celie, by contrast, comes close "to silencing Mr.," as Eva Boesenberg puts it, "by cutting his throat with a razor" (304), thus, like Petry's protagonist, turning the tables. Displacing Petry's muffled manslaughter with a figurative killing, in the course of which Celie's voice strikes Mr. dumb, Walker realigns speech with liberation and life. Accordingly, Celie's ability to assert her presence ("I'm here" [176]) in her own vernacular voice finally triumphs.

It is thus quite ironic that a novel which celebrates the overcoming of silence has itself been silenced repeatedly. Again and again *The Color Purple* has been removed from libraries and school curricula because it supposedly rehashes stereotypical images of blackness.[14] Interestingly enough, it is exactly these stereotypes that the work of contemporary young African American artists— which I discuss, albeit briefly, in my conclusion—reproduces in order to newly engage the realities of African American history and subjectivity. To address cultural traumas by exposing their "evil images," however, was never Walker's intention. Rather, *The Color Purple* means to suggest "that the trauma of incest-rape can be overcome, that the victim's voice may yet prevail over the rapist's censorship" (Boesenberg 306), and that such triumph requires the resurrection of the black female body as a desiring body. The ongoing censorship of the novel thus, on the one hand, conduces to a tendency within American culture to make victimization a central parameter of individual and national identity formation.[15] On the other, it prolongs the silence pertaining to black female sexuality.

At the same time, *The Color Purple* attests that the discourse of an other desire is hard to come by. In Walker's novel the destructive pattern of heterosexual relations vanishes behind a life-asserting female universe replete with images of pre-Oedipal identity. In this highly idealized female space mutual maternal nurturance prevails; art and music thrive. Female jouissance, however—the pleasures of the "button," as Shug has it, as opposed to the "hole" associated with penetration and pain—is eventually subsumed within a wholistic philosophical framework reminiscent of Emersonian transcendentalism and Whitmanian pantheism. Thus "elevat[ing] the erotic to [a] spiritual plane," the text not only ". . . efface[s] its power" (Boesenberg 308).[16] As the perceiving self overcomes her alienation from the material world by communicating with a godly oversoul, Walker's novel repeats the transcendentalist paradigm of male mind subduing female matter and the rapist rhetoric through which it occasionally operates,[17] leaving the gender-inflected structure of subject/object relations intact. Like its generic hybridity, the novel's recourse to transcendentalism acknowledges that conceptions of sexuality and sexual violence, of authority and silence, remain deeply interdependent.

Like Walker's novel, Naylor's narrative "The Two," one of the seven episodes that make up *The Women of Brewster Place*, leads into a feminist-inspired survivor discourse. At the same time, like Morrison's Pecola, Naylor's rape victim does not survive and, what is more, takes along with her another innocent person. The originality of Naylor's narrative depends in part on its context—the gang rape of Lorraine is an instance of gay bashing, perpetrated by a group of black men who share the Brewster women's homophobic mind-set. Disempowered, these men are by no means pitied as an "endangered species," though: "They only had that three-hundred-foot alley," we read, "to serve them as stateroom, armored tank, and executioner chamber. So Lorraine found herself, on her knees, surrounded by the most dangerous species in existence—human males with an erection to validate in a world that was only six feet wide" (170). This "six feet wide" world recalls the scene of attempted rape in Page's *Red Rock*. Like Page ("there was no way of escape. The bushes on either side were like a wall" [254]), Naylor creates a cul-de-sac situation. Unlike Ruth, who is rescued, Lorraine makes the "fatal mistake" (167) of crossing gang territory at night and is brutally raped.

Most significant, the reader witnesses Lorraine's violation through the eyes of the victim, who fragments and reduces her aggressors into a modernist collage, featuring "a pair of suede sneakers" and "a face" with "flared nostrils" and the "smell of decomposing food caught in its teeth" (169). Like Page, whose representation of Gus focuses on the aggressor's "grin," "yellow teeth and horrid gums" (254), Naylor ponders images of potency by depicting sexual violence as vampirism. Her point is, on the one hand, to let the reader experience the horror, the disgust, to make him or her smell the blood and semen on Lorraine's stomach and thighs, sense the biting pain, sympathize with her silence. On the other, her text capitalizes on the reproduction of violence within the "black community." As Lorraine regains consciousness, she targets the very first movement she perceives and hits Ben, her friend the janitor, a drunk and yet "a nice colored man who never bothered anybody" (3). As she smashes a brick "down into his mouth," his teeth "crumble[] into his throat" (172). Fragmenting Ben's body in this way, Lorraine's belated self-defense resonates with her own rape; it highlights how intraracial violence gets duplicated and creates novel alliances between rape and lynching. Accordingly, in a collaborative effort, the women of Brewster Place eventually tear down the wall stained with Lorraine's blood, symbol of the limitations intraracial violence imposes on black communities and, in particular, on black women's mobility.

In the eyes of black male critics such projections of intraracial female solidarity, situated within female-authored rape narratives, offend against the established contract of racial solidarity and disturb what Deborah McDowell labels "family romance": "the story of the Black Family cum Black Community headed by the Black Male who does battle with an oppressive White World" (78). In this scheme of things, "sexist behavior," as Staples sums up the matter, "is nothing more than men acting in ways which they have been socialized to behave" ("Myth" 27). In his essay "The Myth of the Black Macho" (1979) such men, by the way, appear exclusively as *others*, as lower-class men. And in the same text black women's cultural practices resemble lynching rituals. Watching a performance of Shange's play *For Colored Girls Who Have Considered Suicide When the Rainbow Is Enuf* (1975), for instance, Staples notes "a collective appetite for black male blood" (26). As he reverses the castration thematic, "displacing the Name and the Law of the Father," as Spillers puts it, "to the territory of the Mother and Daughter" ("Mama's Baby" 455), Staples also acknowledges that the issue at stake is paternal authority.

Accordingly, McDowell rightly points to "the critical double standard that glosses over representation of violence, rape, and battering in Richard Wright's work"[18] yet highlights such representations in *The Bluest Eye*, *The Third Life of Grange Copeland*, and *The Color Purple* (80). For McDowell the subtext of such bias is "an unacknowledged jostling for space in the literary marketplace" (83). In that marketplace tales of sexual(ly violated) black female bodies have done quite well. In fact, as I have argued, in texts by Douglass, Toomer, McKay, and Wright black women's experience of pain inflicted by an oppressive White World is a platform for (black male) subject constitution. Readdressing the pain of "plain (black) gender trouble," black women's post-modernist fiction thus reclaims a territory of subject formation and does so, significantly enough, without parodic distance. Whereas black male authors' rape narratives have established a tradition of mimicry leading from Griggs through Wright, Himes, and Reed all the way down to gangsta rap, African American women "employ narratives of progressive emergence," "of self-assertion and autonomy," as Brook Thomas points out, without "necessarily ironically inverting them" (58). It is both historically consistent and highly ironic, though, that these narratives still follow the tradition of their early precursors, presenting the black female subject as a solitary victim, fighter, and survivor.

The infamous Anita Hill–Clarence Thomas episode is another case in point here. The hearings situated Thomas in the position of race/blackness and assigned Hill the realm of gender/whiteness, where she engaged in a kind of "rape ploy" manipulated by dominant feminist politics. The episode was thus refashioned as an interracial conflict or, as Thomas himself repeatedly suggested, as a case of "lynching" for which he was not going to "provide the rope" (qtd. in Mayer and Abramson 83). Defeated, Hill relates her Washington experience in her book *Speaking Truth to Power* (1997), which employs the familiar framework of the African American autobiography. In this way she reappropriates the subject position historically assigned to black women— that of the violated body—and reconceives her personal history within the established narrative of black "liberation," having made her way up from an Alabama family farm via Yale University to Washington, D.C. Accordingly, in public discussions of the text, she recasts herself as victim-survivor who left the capital "badly bruised, "badly beaten," "badly wounded."[19] "Set on surviving the experience" of sexual harassment—an experience she claims to be ongoing (as, for instance, by way of phone calls invading her voice mail), she turns that struggle into a permanent position, "choosing a life of challenge," as she puts it, "over one of complacency." In view of the tradition that, as Kubitschek notes, from the slave narrative to the novel of the 1980s "encourages the rape victim to survive" (49), Hill has refashioned herself as such a victim. At the same time, casting her narrative in the generic frame of the slave narrative, she also whitens her black aggressor. Accordingly, like Linda Brent before her, Hill confesses to her audience—the potential buyers of her book— that she has refrained from revealing the titillating details of the case, refrained from retelling the self-defeating tale.

The discursive framing of the Hill-Thomas case reaffirms Gillespie's critique (which I discussed at the end of chapter 1), her claim that among African Americans "that particular four-letter word only seems to draw our outrage when the penis being wielded like a sword is white and the victim Black, or vice versa. Then rape becomes a race issue, conjuring up ugly stories of women raped on slave ships and in cotton fields, plantation houses and slave cabins." We may add to this observation, though, that even when both weapon and victim are black, the same ugly stories and the pressure of generic convention prevail. So what are writers to do? Gillespie herself opts for irony. At the end of her article, she bluntly states: "Tick, tick, tick—every six minutes a woman is being lynched" (93). In this way, she reappropriates both the trope that has overshadowed the sexual violation of African American women and the strategy of mimicry that characterizes the cultural practices of African American men. Recontextualizing the established term, Gillespie at the same time reintegrates white women and men into the matter of rape. What, however, was happening to white women's writing all the while?

"PHANTOM MEN" AND "ZIPLESS FUCKS": RAPE FANTASIES AND THE FICTIONS OF FEMALE DESIRE

The seventies, as Showalter puts it, were "an era of eros and anger" ("Rethinking" 238). Whereas the 1950s and 1960s woman's novel—like much turn-of-the-century fiction—"too often ended in the heroine's madness or suicide, it now ends in her rape, assault, or murder" (239), or in her rape-revenge.[20] Examples of such texts include Muriel Sparks's *The Driver's Seat* (1970), Judith Rossner's 1975 bestseller *Looking for Mr. Goodbar,* many female-authored science fiction novels, and Gould's *A Sea Change,* which will be my focus here. For Showalter these novels' violent plots reflect both "the social reality of rape and women's intense concern with rape as a sexual problem in American culture" (239). And indeed, the early seventies mark the beginning of a continuing preoccupation, on the part of feminist criticism and theory, with rape and sexual violation, and an overdue revision of rape laws.[21] It is noteworthy, though, that rape becomes the most urgent issue of feminist debate at the very time women reconsider the demands of the "sexual revolution"[22] and attempt to rescue, from beneath the hype past and present, their bodies and selves.[23] The very moment the term "sexual harassment" evolved, women were also probing "the myth of the vaginal orgasm" (Anne Koedt) and aggressively claiming reproductive rights.

This synchronicity of "eros and anger" is certainly no coincidence. Nor is the preoccupation of (white) women authors' texts with rape fantasies. Instead, this tendency reflects that part of the difficulty in rediscovering "our bodies, our selves" is due to the fact that (white) female sexuality has been constructed primarily in contexts of sexual violence or threats thereof. Accordingly, just as men's castration anxieties do not necessarily express, as Haskell trenchantly notes, a desire to be castrated, women's rape fantasies do not prove that women crave sexual violation ("Rape Fantasy" 94). Instead, such fantasies are a means women (writers) employ to renegotiate the fictions of—a supposedly masochistic—female sexuality deemed to complement an aggressive male sexuality. As such, they are imaginary interrogations of gender identities, sexualities, and power relations that turn-of-the-century discourse—the fictions of Norris and Moody, as well as Freudian psychoanalysis[24]—successfully established as facts. Just as we need to distinguish real rape from representations of rape, we therefore need to separate real rape fantasies from rape-fantasy fictions that reflect a double awareness of their own fictionality. What, then, is the function of rape fantasies in women's texts? And what shape do such fantasies take in the first place?

To explore these questions I concentrate on Gould's puzzling *A Sea Change* and Jong's playful *Fear of Flying*, two texts that instrumentalize rape fantasies in seemingly incomparable ways. Yet just as Jong's playfulness becomes highly irritating at times, there is plenty of parody and play in Gould's phallic "gunman" fantasy. Gould's heroine Jessie Waterman, the victim of—fantasized or actual—robbery/rape, rids herself of her black-gunman fantasy by taking on her rapist's garb, by adopting the initials of the figure that haunts her imagination, taking B. G. as her first name and "Kilroy" as her last. Referring to a cartoon character (who is "watching you" yet gone once you have detected its signature) and voicing the imperative to "kill Roy" (Roy being her husband's name), this new surname embodies the significance of the black-gunman fantasy for Jessie's life: helping to dethrone her husband, it allows her to leave, to be gone. B. G. literally—and violently—initiates the "sea change" we witness, Jessie's attempt to repossess a sexuality that is not so much female as mutable and multiple. At the same time, such a name should warn us not to take things at face value, because, like Kilroy, meaning is always absent, deferred, gone once you get there.

In fact, both Gould and Jong project a considerable degree of ironic distance, toying with their dominant precursors while appropriating the drag of realist "verisimilitude" (Jong xiv). Jong's "zipless fuck" fantasy revels in imaginary decontextualized sexual encounters, mocking male womanizing and its four-letter-word discourse in the process. Gould's narrative, by contrast, echoes the captivity narrative, the Western, and the racist romance. Choosing an eroticized *black* gunman, the author in fact literalizes the lore that " 'All White Women fantasize being raped by Negroes' " (Haskell, "Rape Fantasy" 94). At the same time, the text employs rape as a trope of inspiration, transformation, and change, a trope prominent in ancient myths and adapted by such modernist texts as Eliot's *The Waste Land*, Edgar Lee Masters's *Spoon River Anthology*, and William Butler Yeats's "Leda and the Swan." Rape fantasies in Gould's novel thus evolve as a complex figure with strong intertextual resonance, a figure of the fictional itself, far from "the *Daily News* rape, with the physical pain of ripping your vagina open" (Gould, qtd. in Haskell, "Rape Fantasy" 85).

The motif of transformation through rape gets established in an epigraph that elaborates on "sex reversal" in a certain species of fish.

> Males of *Labroides dimidiatus* control the sex reversal within social groups. Each group consists of a male with a harem of females among which larger individuals dominate smaller ones. The male in each harem suppresses the tendency of the females to change sex, by actively dominating them. Death of a male releases this suppression and the dominant female of the harem changes sex immediately. (7)

Like these female fish, Jessie disposes of the male figures dominating her life and herself takes on maleness in the process. In fact, however, it is not bodies that matter here but their cultural significance; Jessie claims no new sexual identity but another gender as she sheds her female skin/name, transmutes into "something rich and strange," as this second epigraph, from Shakespeare's *The Tempest*, anticipates.

> Full fathom five thy father lies;
> Of his bones are coral made;
> Those are pearls that were his eyes:
> Nothing of him that doth fade
> But doth suffer a sea-change
> Into something rich and strange.

Echoed in Dickinson's poem "She rose to His Requirement" (#732) this passage hints at the "Pearl, and Weed" that matrimony breeds as it forces woman to "drop[] / The Playthings of Her Life."

The novel's opening scene visualizes the female position as immobile and captive, depicts woman as unable to communicate adequately or liberate herself from her entanglement. Rendered at a highly parodic pitch, the first paragraphs already hint that ahead is neither "feminist utopia" nor an "ironically absurd reversal" of dominant gender relations (Heller 267). Rather, this is a narrative that mocks feminist positions by inhabiting them.

> Jessie Waterman lay in a neatly folded pile beside her bed, a supplicant without a prayer, like a figure in one of those malignant contemporary sculptures that represent hell as a shock of recognition. Stone-age woman staring at a color TV. Plasticine man with newspaper shoes, wine bottle and stained pants. Statutory rape (metal, acrylic, plaster and hair) in a battered hot rod with New Jersey plates. Robbery victim in blue bedroom.
>
> In Jessie's case the artistic version would pay reverent attention to minute details; the knotted strips of torn nylon pantyhose binding wrists and ankles behind their back; the crossed bare feet; callused soles upturned like the tender parts of unfortunate animals.
>
> She had been in this position long enough to plot a series of spectacular escapes. Rolling to the window and hanging out like a lumpy package, bound fingers grasping the ledge. SOS notes written with a pencil grasped in the teeth and then spat out into the street. Whoever finds this I love you; please excuse handwriting.
>
> But the nylon knots had been tied in such a way that Jessie's slightest move to free herself, or even to roll around with extreme caution, caused them to slip gently into a tighter hold upon her—a fine subtle paradox that no one would expect her to appreciate under the circumstances.
>
> Useless to struggle, she decided finally, and sighed with relief, as if her victim's license had been automatically stamped VALID after a routine examination. Who was to say that non-struggling, like non-violence, wouldn't be better for both of them in the long run. (How very Jessie that was, always considerate, thinking not only of herself but also of her captor, the black gunman. Was it okay to call him B. G. from now on? They were on fairly intimate terms.)
>
> Of course the plan worked. B. G., utterly tranquilized by her clever use of non-struggle, which he took as abject surrender, wandered off to seek his fortune elsewhere in the house. Whether he found riches beyond his wildest dreams, or only a couple of portable TVs and a digital clock, he might well be back any minute, lusting to commit some random atrocity in lieu of scrawling Kilroy or Stop Me Before I Kill More. (11–12)

This (post-)modernist installation ironically acknowledges the female captive/rape victim as a well-established topos of the arts. In fact, Gould's protagonist figures the feminine per se. Fashion model and privileged by the male gaze, Jessie stars as object ("neatly folded pile," "like a lumpy package") and female prototype. At the same time the narrator's ironic distance doubles the protagonist's attempt to detach herself, as Temple Drake did, from what is happening to her. "Detachment," we are told, "like the numbness in her hands and feet, gradually filled her mind, sealing it off from the physical shocks of fear that had been coming in waves for the past hour" (13).

In the face of such mental and physical immobility commonplace counselor advice (to rely on "non-struggle" strategies) appears utterly absurd. Instead, Jessie's passive resistance adds to the climate of consent ("intimate terms"); blurring the boundaries between intimacy and intimate violence, it leads into the novel's most irritating moment, wherein Jessie reimagines her violation as an erotic encounter:

> . . . B. G. had caressed her breast with the gun. She had taken a black lover. Called it Roy and let it do with her what B. G. willed. How easily. How cocksure it had been, gliding in as if it lived there. As if Roy had come home. Something clicked into place. Roy had come home. Never mind, B. G. said. Leave it in. Let's show him how you do. He would see her like that, Roy would find her like that with the gun. Watch her explode. Ahh. B. G.'s laugh, short, a dog's barking. He said Roy could have a turn next. Only fair, he said. Roy could either use the gun or watch B. G. use it. Roy had a choice. Perhaps he couldn't choose. Down in the darkness, she had sighed, finally. Ahh. As if she did not care what they did. (121)

This re-presentation of the novel's opening "event," asserting complicity and homoerotic tension between rapist and husband, undermines the novel's apparent realist mode. Yet at no point will the reader be "cocksure" whether rapist/robber B. G. is for real or imagined, his gun an ambiguous Dickinsonian figure of Jessie's new life and identity; whether rape simply amounts to an ironic rhetorical device for whatever stuns Jessie into recognition, silence, and eventually "liberation."

The silence with which Jessie veils her violation, on the one hand, echoes the silences we encounter throughout the history of rape rhetorics. On the other hand, silence breeds power and change here. Held captive, Jessie is preoccupied with writing imaginary telegrams to her homeward bound husband ("STOP ROY [STOP] SAVE YOURSELF [STOP]"), her words turning into a "silent scream," rolling into "a ball, squeezed dry" (15), comparable to "that little hot ball inside you that screams," the fear that tortured Temple Drake (Faulkner, *Sanctuary* 218). Here, however, we have "[l]oaded words ready to be fired, and she [Jessie] had never fired a word in her life. But now she could hear them, rolling, bursting—dumdum words tearing jagged holes in the dark (STOP)" (15). These words, tearing at her center just as scientists' instruments "would probe the source of her [Minerva's] energy, the vortex at her core where she was most violent, screaming and whirling" (73), release her own energy, get her "loaded-gun-life" going. Like the speaker in Dickinson's famous poem, Gould's protagonist thus possesses the power to both kill and live on.

The narrative strategy at work here is the literalization of established tropes, most significantly B. G.'s phallic gun as a sign of phallic power, and hurricane Minerva, the symbol of female energy. When Jessie finally adopts B. G.'s identity so that he can protect her female center, the figures of Jessie's twofold self become characters. The process of this "sea change" takes us on a journey, triggered by a series of break-ins and a general sense of "something, askew," a "sense of displacement, or of never having been placed" (22). *A Sea Change* therefore follows Jessie's attempt to place herself apart from the familiar spaces of career and "comfort station; home" (67). Jessie eventually "liberates" herself from B. G. ("I'm free of you, B. G." [175]) by removing herself and her two daughters to an island even more remote than their family ("funeral") home, Andrea Island (49). Exchanging her telling name Waterman for B. G., Jessie settles down in a community that believes her to be "an artist who fished for relaxation, a builder who had taken up painting, or a fisherman" (187). But how does she get there? And what happens to B. G.?

Throughout the text robber/rapist and husband are allies and counterparts at once: B. G. is a productive, Roy a destructive force, even though, like Barnes's Ryder, Roy engages in "casual breeding habits" and successfully reproduces his genes (19). Jessie herself produces miscarriages, references decay, and

> nurs[es] her secret which grew inside her like a tumor or a monstrous child: hating Roy, hating Jessie. She felt it constantly, an oceanic current pulling at her, stretching and tearing from within. Sometimes the pressure made her weak; she would sink to the bed in a near-faint, or run out of the house, gasping for air, to climb a high rock and lie there outstretched like a captive seal, bleating and panting. . . . *What was happening to Jessie.* (25, my emphasis)

As Gould recontextualizes the trope of captivity, B. G.'s robbery/rape turns out to be the source of both Jessie's fury and her energy. And as something "was happening to Jessie," as it was to Temple Drake, Jessie's rape (fantasy) is similarly outlined as a process, not as a singular moment of violation.

In that process, Jessie comes to question "the identification of 'man' with phallic unity" (Bordo 265). Sucking Roy and "thinking Phallus," she can hardly discriminate "the real one," the penis—instrument of pleasure and danger—from its phallic re-presentations: "So hard to remember," she reflects. "Everything they make to remind you—buildings, cars, bombs, crucifixes. All weapons that control or hurt" (29). She also realizes, though, that such icons of male potency merely cover up male anxieties. The "real one" (Roy's penis) is "[s]oft, vulnerable. Nothing like a gun, really. Nothing like the words. Buildings, guns, words. Blown up out of proportion, so you forget how soft, how vulnerable" (30). Engaging feminist commonplaces, Gould's novel underlines that "actual men are not," as Susan Bordo puts it, "timeless symbolic constructs, they are biologically, historically, and experientially embodied beings; the singular, constant, transcendent rule of the phallus is continually challenged by this embodiment" (265). In fact, as Bordo adds, "[t]he phallus is haunted by the penis," which "[r]ather than exhibiting constancy of form . . .

is perhaps the most visibly mutable of bodily parts; it evokes the temporal not the eternal" (266). Highlighting that difference between phallus and penis, Gould explores what Haskell, intent on qualifying Brownmiller's "grim and monochromatic portrait of male villainy and female victimization," calls "the gray areas of social intercourse," the fact that "power in a relationship is not invariably on the side of the male" ("Rape Fantasy" 86).

Accordingly, the narrative ponders symbols of female power. While her friend Kate jokes about Venus's-flytraps and *vagina dentata*, Jessie dismisses such things for their lack of "self-starting power. That's what makes them seem female," she insists. "They never go off by themselves"; yet "[t]hey're men's nightmares about what women could do to them, even if they carry guns." Kate herself suggests "[a] sponge, maybe. Or some kind of suctorial device": "All the natural destroyers use female energy—quakes, volcanoes, whirlpools, cyclones. Even ocean currents. Powerful sucking devices in a female form" (53). Such energies, Jessie adds, "[m]en can't control," cannot "adapt . . . for practical use. They shoot bombs into volcanoes, and it makes them worse" (54). "Gang rape," she calls it, "as a tool of basic research" (74).

In light of Jessie's oral performance on Roy (29–30), the celebrated "sucking devices" work an ironic reversal, hinting that men "never go off by themselves." At the same time, Gould's novel exhausts and ridicules the well-worn imagery that distinguishes destructive phallic powers from "natural" female energies. Where science equals rape, we lose sight of rape and its meaning, and figures of male violence (such as B. G.) and female energy (such as Minerva) become quite literally signs of self-fashioning. Like Jessie, Minerva was "remarkably photogenic" and "still changing her shape, arranging herself artfully, her curving white arms reaching out" (73). Like Minerva, Jessie experiences an "implosion of hate inside her" (68) and a "bursting inside" that coincides with a "gang bang" fantasy.

> There was a sharp sudden sound, a bursting inside, something running red and black. B. G. had laughed. Jessie exploding red-black, red-black running down. Stop *Roy*. B. G. had laughed, voice like a dog barking Do it man, do it here I'll show you. And Roy would not stop, couldnotwouldnot. Come on, man, don't ever stop B. G. said nobody ever stops B. G. But it was Roy no don't come like that Roy *stop*. Roy had come, exploding laugh was that his laugh too, dog sound. Roy had come Ah, Jessie, Ahh, red-and-black, her blood and B. G.'s cock/gun Roy had come exploding finally Ah Jessie Ahh. (142–43)

Taking into account the trop(e)ical universe of Jessie and Kate, a "symbolic order" where male power destroys female energies, such imagined teamwork of rapist/robber and husband corresponds to the research that scientist do on volcanoes and hurricanes—hurricanes like the one that passes over Andrea Island. Accordingly, while chapter 11 terminates with Jessie's rape fantasy, the opening of chapter 12 presents us with Roy's daughter Diane, hanging "suspended from her tree branch, like a drip-dry rag doll," trying to see through the fog that envelopes a "ruined landscape" (144), the "lay of the land" (Annette Kolodny) so to speak.

The novel thus persistently shifts between levels of reality perception that within feminist consciousness appear to be analogous. Jessie's transformation itself is effected by a narrative strategy that literalizes the tropes governing feminist ideology and thus takes this analogous thinking to an extreme. I am in fact reminded here of the line Rich uses, in "Snapshots of a Daughter-in-Law," to rephrase Yeats's "Leda and the Swan": "The beak that grips her, she becomes"—a line preceded by the claim "A woman sleeps with monsters" (*Snapshots* 22). In *A Sea Change* woman indeed opts for such monstrous bedfellows. Yet as in Rich's poem, the monster is a *figure* inhabiting woman's mind here. As Jessie becomes the figure of her fantasies, she necessarily turns into something else, moves from a position defined as stereotypically female, helpless, and silent to one that is likewise stereotypically male, self-sufficient, outgoing, and expressive. Once the paradigmatic object of the male gaze, she comes to embody that gaze; once captive and tied in nylon nets, she/he now catches fish and escapes into the isolated outdoors, a "pioneer" existence. Jessie has longed for such "separate peace" (25), which she happens to find exactly where Hemingway, among many others, located it. Literalizing rape fantasies, Gould's novel thus engages both the dominant cultural imaginary and feminist consciousness, parodically exposing their limits.

"Catharine MacKinnon says," Roiphe recalls, "don't read *Hustler* or fantasize about rape." Roiphe herself rejects such imperatives as "part of the effort to regulate and control the way we think about sex" (*Morning After* 170). Engaging (sexual or rape) fantasies, she seems to suggest, in turn liberates that thinking. Gould's novel, it seems to me, clearly puts such faith into an ironic perspective. Exploring the impact of fantasies of sexual violence on women's (sexual) imaginary and taking that impact to its literal extreme, *A Sea Change* addresses, in all its ambivalence, the paradox of 1970s feminism, whose attempt to recover a strong female self by way of the female body at the same time raised a growing concern with and fear of sexual violence. Gould's novel thus dramatizes, in a troublingly direct and yet highly mediated manner, how women's increasing awareness of sexual aggression has partly canceled out their "liberation," effecting an unprecedented sense of helplessness, vulnerability, and anxiety. The clear-cut discrimination between (female) victims and (male) violators, the text also seems to suggest, has hampered rather than helped the evolution of new bodies and selves.

Jong's *Fear of Flying* has been read as a picaresque, a romance, a female bildungsroman, and the feminine version of *The Catcher in the Rye* and *Tropic of Cancer*. To my mind, this tendency to categorize Jong's novel in terms of other literary texts and genres is telling. For Jong's novel is not simply a success

story of female emancipation whose heroine "reach[es] out for independence
and [does] not die as a result of her hubris," a heroine who "would go home—
chastened, changed, empowered, and redeemed by her adventure—and life
would go on" (Jong xiii). As its protagonist playfully talks about men, marriage, masturbation, menstruation, and female desire, about hidden, horny,
and limp genitals, among many other things, Jong's novel makes all too clear
what holds women captive: fictions of gender in which women do not survive
and female sexuality is a no-no, a nuisance, or a construct of male fantasies;
fictions which even insinuate that "[t]he fear of the intruder is the wish for
the intruder" (276).

Accordingly, *Fear of Flying* foregrounds throughout that women's expectations of life, love, sexuality, and, most significant, the "phantom men" that
populate their minds (277) are the products of fictions ranging from Shake-
spearean drama to popular Freudian symbolism and Italian movies. The main
point of the narrative is not to exorcise these fictions and phantoms, as Heller
has it (251), but to acknowledge them as what they are: fictions and phantoms
that take part in constituting our sense of the real. Thus literary texts and
characters, as well as their authors' lives, build Isadora's frame of reference
(166) and generate the "images rush[ing] into [her] mind" (275), the ground
against which she projects the figures of her own adventures.

Frequently Jong's heroine detects correspondences between her own existence and the lives of "real and imaginary people"—"D. H. Lawrence running
off with his tutor's wife, . . . Romeo and Juliet dying for love"[25]—correspondences that occasionally uplift her: "I was one of *them*! No scared housewife,
I. I was flying" (171). Yet even though these comparisons hardly hold, Isadora's
flight is no trip from a fictional never-never land to the realities of gendered
existence. Rather, she moves from a place where fiction equals fact and woman
awaits "Prince Charming to take her away 'from all this' " (11) to a position
where she recognizes how these fictions structure women's lives according to
well-established patterns and plotlines. "In nineteenth-century novels, they get
married. In twentieth-century novels, they get divorced. Can you have an ending in which they do neither?" (311), Isadora wonders at the end of the novel,
soaking her body in a bathtub. By that time she has not only come to like that
body. She also realizes that, even though "seduced and abandoned" in Paris
(263), she will "never be a romantic heroine" who dies for love, but prefers to
"stay alive" (300). Life itself, however, turns out to be a plotless journey, a
post-modernist text taking twists and turns for which fear and self-loathing
are inadequate travel companions (311). Survival is a key term here, and so is
courage. Fallen heroine turned "Hemingway hero" (310)? I wonder. Is *Fear of
Flying* yet another novel of sea (and sex) change?

A great part of the text roams through fictions about sexuality that Isadora
considers an essential part of her upbringing. Here is some of that 1950s lore:

A. There is no such thing as rape. Nobody can rape a woman unless she consents at the last minute.

(The girls in my high school actually used to repeat this piously to each other. God only knows where we got it. It was the received wisdom, and like robots, we passed it on.)

B. There are two kinds of orgasm: vaginal and clitoral. One is "mature" (i.e. good). The other is "immature" (i.e. evil). One is "normal" (i.e. good). The other is "neurotic" (i.e. evil).

This pseudohip, pseudopsychological code was more Calvinistic than Calvinism.

C. Men reach their sexual peak at sixteen and decline thereafter. . . .

Brian was twenty-four. No doubt he was over the hill. Eight years over the hill. If he only fucked me once a month at twenty-four—imagine how little he'd fuck me at thirty-four. It was terrifying to contemplate. (195)

Mocking the discourse of scientific truths, this ABC of 1950s sexology, revisited in the aftermath of the "sexual revolution," literally grounds its insights into female and male sexuality on the premise of rape denial. Point A still applies to women who flaunt their looks: men try to pick up Isadora, her second husband Bennett suggests, because she conveys her " 'availability,' " "dressed too sexily. Or wore my hair too wantonly. Or *something*. I deserved to be attacked, in short. It was the same old jargon of war between the sexes, the same old fifties lingo in disguise: *There is no such thing as rape; you ladies ask for it. You ladies*" (273).

The denial of women's sexual violation is linked here to definitions of sexuality that measure female sexuality in qualitative, male sexuality in quantitative terms. The hydraulic model according to which (male) sexual potency peaks and is reduced in the spending grants men a particular license. While sex-starved Isadora develops "all the classic symptoms of the unfucked wife," including "fantasies of zipless fucks with doormen, derelicts, countermen at the West End Bar, graduate students—even (God help me!) professors" (194), her first husband Brian falls from one extreme (sexual abstinence) into another, panic sex or, in fact, (marital) rape, were there such a thing as rape (see point "A" above).

He wanted to prove he could satisfy me. He hadn't screwed me in about six weeks, but now he wouldn't stop. He fucked like a machine, refusing to succumb to an orgasm himself but urging me to come again and again and again. After the first three times I was sore and wanted to stop. I begged him to stop but he wouldn't. He kept banging away at me like an ax murderer. I was crying and pleading.

"Brian, please stop," I sobbed.

"You thought I couldn't satisfy you!" he screamed. His eyes were wild.

"You see!" he said, lunging into me. "You see! You see! You see!"

"Brian, please *stop*!"

"Doesn't that prove it? Doesn't that prove I'm God?"

"Please stop," I whimpered.

When he stopped at last, he withdrew from me violently and thrust his still-hard penis into my mouth. But I was crying too hard to blow him. I lay on the bed sobbing. What was I going to do? I didn't want to stay alone with him, but where could I go? For the first time I really began to be convinced he was danger-ous. (201)

Preoccupied with his own self-esteem, Brian does not realize that all the while he fucks himself into godlikeness, he is committing rape. Neither does his wife, who, considering her husband a psychopath, simply reaffirms point A: under "normal conditions" there is indeed "no such thing as rape."

These realities of Isadora's married life are, from the very beginning, coun-terbalanced by her "zipless fuck" fantasies, her response to "those other long-ings which marriage stifled," that "itchiness" for both sex and solitude (10). The zipless fuck, Isadora explains, "was more than a fuck. It was a platonic ideal," depicted here in Whitmanesque transcendentalist diction: "Zipless be-cause when you came together zippers fell away like rose petals, underwear blew off in one breath like dandelion fluff. Tongues intertwined and turned liquid. Your whole soul flowed out through your tongue and into the mouth of your lover" (11). The "true, ultimate zipless A-1 fuck" must be brief and anonymous, with no facial contours, no personal histories disclosed. Inspired by movies rather than firsthand experiences, it "has all the swift compression of a dream and is seemingly free of all remorse and guilt," of "talk," "of ulterior motives," and of "power game[s]." It is sex at its "purest" (14), desired by a woman well aware of the morals, conventions, and ideals of female sexuality: a woman who cannot recognize herself in the codes of female sexuality handed down, who grew up "measur[ing her] orgasms against Lady Chatterley" until it occurred to her "that Lady Chatterley was really a man" (24)—or a male fantasy of female sexuality—and that "sex is all in the head."

Jong's novel is consequently of interest here not because her protagonist entertains rape fantasies, but because she learns to discriminate fantasies of female desire from desirable sexual encounters. Isadora's imagined "zipless fuck" engages the most common of these fantasies: the sexual encounter with a stranger,[26] which in "real life" takes the name of "rape." Thus at the very moment sexual assault is officially recognized as a crime involving acquain-tances rather than strangers, sexual encounters with total strangers are ac-knowledged as stimulating sexual fantasies. Accordingly, Jong clearly discrimi-nates Isadora's "zipless fuck" fantasy from notions of female masochism, from the belief that "Every Woman Adores a Fascist" (15). Adopting this line from Sylvia Plath's poem "Daddy," Jong highlights how we shape our desires in the patterns of predominant fictions: for Isadora, who is Jewish, her European adventures, "en route to the congress of dreams" (1), for instance, involve a return to Germany with her second husband and start off with a night she "dozed fitfully amid dreams of Nazis and plane crashes" (23). Making love in their German hotel room, Isadora "kept pretending Bennett was someone else" and, echoing Plath, wondered who was this faceless "phantom man who haunted my life? My father? My German analyst? The zipless fuck? Why did his face always refuse to come into focus?" (24). Throughout the novel this faceless phantom remains a blank, never takes shape.

Isadora's "zipless fuck" fantasy, in particular, turns out to be a fraud once it takes shape in the realm of the "real": first, in the figure of Adrian Goodlove, "the real zipless fuck," the "real primitive," "natural man" who makes the entire lower half of Isadora's body "liquify" (72) until his face and history show; and finally in the young train attendant who "grab[s her] by the snatch" (302), a scene that transposes the original cinematic version of the zipless fuck into an instance of sexual assault. Accordingly, unlike Gould's Jessie, Jong's Isadora undergoes no sea or sex change. She gives up her "zipless fuck" fantasy yet remains the woman of "male desires." As her body soaks in the bathtub— "[t]he pink V of my thighs, the triangle of curly hair, the Tampax string fishing the water like a Hemingway hero" (310)—the irony that informs a female subjectivity framed by male fictions and figures prevails. In fact, the hyperboles of Isadora's diction, the proliferation of four-letter words as well as the self-portrayal as "unfucked wife," are a new version of Barnes's *Ryder*, a version that echoes the lingo of a more recent literary tradition.

Susan Rubin Suleiman is one of the few critics who recognize the self-irony and mocking tone in which *Fear of Flying* is soaked. Jong's book, she claims, has an "ironic awareness of [its] own unconventionality," of the "flaunting use of obscenities in a novel signed by a woman and published by a major press." Suleiman reads Jong's use of obscene language as "a self-conscious reversal of stereotypes, and in some sense a parody of the tough-guy narrator heroes of Henry Miller and Norman Mailer," calls her "reversal of roles *and* of language" a usurpation of "both the pornographer's language and his way of looking at the opposite sex" (9). No wonder Miller considered Jong the sensation of the year and draws analogies to *Tropic of Cancer*.[27] Suleiman moreover reminds us that the figure of flying is not simply one of (sexual) liberation. It also appropriates the term that French feminists have employed as an "emblem of women's writing: flying, *voler*, which in French also means to steal" (10). It is this kind of robbery and rape that explains Jong's significance here. Read through the lens of Irigaray, *Fear of Flying*—triggered by what Jong considered her interest "in the illusion of total verisimilitude" (xiv)—turns out to be a case of mimicry, woman's interim strategy of miming, parodying, paraphrasing, and quoting male discourse while herself remaining "elsewhere."[28] Puzzling over the question "What do you women want?" writes Jong, Freud "never came up with much" (24). Neither does Isadora Wing. In fact, I can detect little of the "streamlined optimism" Roiphe discovers in Jong's novel (*Morning After* 168). Instead, like Barnes and Acker, Jong highlights the difficulties involved in rescuing female subjectivity and sexuality from the debris of prepatterned discourse that allows, at best, only for faceless phantoms of female desire. At the same time, she underlines that "the ability to ghost-dance freely between the factual and the imaginary is," as Elizabeth Young argues, "an essential strategy for contemporary psychic survival" (88).

"An Obscene Posture That No One Could Help": Sodomy, Male Anxiety, and the "Crisis of Homo/Heterosexual Definition" in James Dickey's *Deliverance*

Male-on-male rape is labeled the "last taboo" (Mullen) because sexual violation seems to reaffirm a woman's femininity yet emasculates the male victim, enforcing a shift in gender position. The distinct status of sexual violence perpetrated by and against men is evidenced by the fact that, in legal terms, male rape for a long time did not exist. Subsumed under the rubric of sodomy, both consensual homosexual acts and sexual acts enforced by men on men were historically considered a crime against nature (D'Emilio and Freedman 30–31).[29] At the same time, the figure of Sodom, which crystallized Puritan fears of failure and doom, has loomed large in the American cultural imaginary since the days of John Winthrop.[30] In chapter 2 I myself argued that both the naturalist novel and the racist romance shape male anxieties into images of disavowed homoeroticism and homophobia, images that foreground the emerging crisis of homo/heterosexual definition as a subtext of rape (and remasculinization) narratives. Accordingly, (threats of) male-on-male sexual assault occur predominantly in texts set in all-male environments, where rape serves to establish and reinforce hierarchies. Meanwhile, owing to the rise of gay fiction from Rechy to Cooper, sexual violence perpetrated against and by gay men can be called a topos, dramatizing homophobia as well as conflicts of gay identity.

Male-on-male rape, however, remains a predominantly "heterosexual offense" (Mullen 14). One such offense marks the crucial moment in Dickey's novel *Deliverance* (1970), the first novel of the Georgia-born poet, who always considered himself a Southern writer with leanings toward the Fugitives and the Southern Agrarians. Dickey's text is of particular interest here because it renegotiates a central topos of American literature—men's flight from civilization and femininity into nature—by interrogating the postures and performativity of American manhood. Unleashing the homoerotic and homophobic tensions that inform the American quest novel, the text exposes the vulnerability and mutability of masculinity and does so most graphically in a scene of male-on-male rape. In this way, so I argue, *Deliverance* literalizes the very anxieties that figure erratically, hysterically, in *McTeague* and *The Clansman*. By recontextualizing this racialized conflict between men within the classic American tale and its flight from civilization into nature/savagery, *Deliverance* at the same time realigns the myth of the South with the great American myths. In some sense *Deliverance* thus refigures *Sanctuary*. The discomforting insights into human nature generated in the course of its narrative are handed down, though, as a secret between men. All the furious action that ensues after bachelor Bobby is raped serves but to cover up an unspeakable sexual violation. Bobby does not "want this to get around" (112), imposing a silence that eventually advances witness Ed to a stage of higher knowledge, elevates him as the owner of a secret not to be revealed.

My reading of *Deliverance* is highly indebted to Linda Ruth Williams's illuminating interpretation of John Boorman's 1972 movie adaptation, a reading focused on the cinematic aesthetics of the visual and the gaze, and unconcerned with the novel's particular poetics. Wittily entitled "Blood Brothers," Williams's 1994 essay[31] insightfully argues that the "power" of the cult film lies "in what it tries not to show, how it plays with what you saw and didn't see, what it denies you as well as what it offers up" (19). The power of the novel, by contrast, lies in how it aestheticizes and poetically reinscribes what it disavows so explicitly. In fact, its very poetics makes Dickey's action thriller quite unlike many texts of its kind.

Deliverance belongs to the genre of the rape-revenge novel. Four city guys from Atlanta—Ed who works in advertising, the quiet Drew, sales supervisor of a big soft-drink company, and salesman Bobby, cheered on by pseudophilosopher Lewis's diatribes about survival in the wilderness—set out to canoe down the last wild "unfucked-up" river in the South, right before a monolithic power company is to commit ecological "rape," as Lewis has it, on this (feminized) waterway. Along with this last frontier, its inhabitants, a community of genetically deficient backwood folks with whom the adventurers soon come into conflict, are, as Williams puts it, "on the brink of displacement, if not extinction." The novel in this way reengages the history of colonization that Joseph Conrad reimagines in *Heart of Darkness* (17) as well as the "lay of the [American] land" and the subjection of Native and African Americans. Here this history figures as a sexual assault, perpetrated by socially superior city dwellers on primitive country folk.

Accordingly, the rafting trip turns nightmare as the repressed (history) returns with a vengeance: Bobby, the popular bachelor with his occasional "rage of a weak king" (Dickey 11), is anally raped by one of the mountain men, while Ed is forced to look on and barely escapes oral rape when Lewis kills Bobby's assaulter. During the turbulence that ensues in the aftermath of this event, Drew dies under dubious circumstances, only to resurface as a horrific corpse that needs to be buried again; Lewis, the most physical of the four men, is seriously hurt and resigns his authority to Ed, the first-person narrator and crucial eyewitness—with "eyes made for seeing in this blackness" (77)—who eventually shoots his (suspected) would-be rapist with an arrow. "The three survivors," Williams sums up, "escape to an unnerving safety built on a cover-up story which disavows not only the double murder they have committed but the shame of male rape and the uneasy circumstances of Drew's death" (17). How, then, does rape figure and function in this drama of masculinity?

Let us first consider how *Deliverance* subjects central American myths to a fundamental reversal: here the flight into nature does not amount to a withdrawal from the familiar and the sexual. Instead, nature turns out to be the site of sexuality, albeit a transgressive kind, the habitat of a Southern breed that is "too close to nature," and whose home is the very space of (ecological) rape and incest. As in Barnes, Faulkner, and more recent African American women's fiction, the family is revealed as a "staple source for horror, as breeding site for psychosis, indulged taboo desires" such as "interbreeding" and "literal motherfucking." The heroes' journey into nature itself emerges as a trangressive act, nature not a "redeeming," but a "deforming," site (L. R. Williams 17). Just like the mountain men, who lack fingers, brain power, and skin color—as albinos they seem inverted black rapists—Lewis finds his potency compromised. The case thus is not one of civilized city slickers versus bestial hillbillies; not difference, but likeness and "familiarity" are at issue here. The problem is indeed not, as Williams underlines, the death or the absence of family but "relatives all over the place" (Dickey 107), entangling the protagonists "in a sticky, genetically intensified web made by *too* much family," "of relatedness run wild." For whereas family done right facilitates conformity, "family done wrong breaks open the membrane of civilization" (L. R. Williams 17). In this way Dickey refigures, literalizes Faulkner.

In the rape scene, Dickey's narrative suggests, we have moved way beyond the line separating civilization from bestiality. Both Bobby and Ed are stripped to animal-like femininity. Ed is robbed of his web belt, knife, and rope and is tied to a tree; his coveralls are "zipped . . . down to the belt as though tearing me open" (98). Threatened with having his "balls cut off" and feeling a knife scraping across his hairy chest, Ed admits that he "had never felt such brutality and carelessness of touch, or such disregard for another person's body" (98). Bobby, by contrast, is forced to undress and display his hairless body, "plump and pink, his hairless thighs shaking, his legs close together" (99), "in an obscene posture that no one could help" (100). Why help, however, and help in what way? I wonder. The reader experiences the rape as it is projected by Ed, who almost mistakes Bobby's scream for his own. Bobby's sounds of "pain and outrage," "wordless," high-pitched, and "carrying," provoke Ed to "let all the breath out of [him]self" (100). As Ed's breathing punctuates Bobby's screams, his eyewitness position is synchronized with that of the rapist. At the same time, his superior, voyeuristic pleasure likens him to the rapist's companion, who threatens to rape him orally.

The rape scene thus, on the one hand, anticipates the fantasy of rape, castration, and decapitation Ed engages after he hunts down and kills his own would-be rapist. On the other, it insistently focuses on Drew, whose mysterious death

will draw the reader's attention from the actual events of rape and rape-revenge, and from the transgressive fantasies these events generate. Accordingly,
during the rape of Bobby, Ed searches the river for Lewis and Drew and sees
both disappear.

> At last he [Bobby] raised his face as though to howl with all his strength into the
> leaves and the sky, and quivered silently while the man with the gun looked on
> with an odd mixture of approval and sympathy. The whorl-faced man *drew back,
> drew out.*
>
> The standing man backed up a step and took the gun from behind Bobby's ear.
> Bobby let go of the log and fell to his side, both arms over his face.
>
> We all sighed. I could get better breath, but only a little.
>
> The two of them turned to me. I *drew up* as straight as I could and waited with
> the tree. (100, my emphases)

The repetition of the word *drew* in the context of Bobby's rape is curiously
significant. It not only hints that Drew's later death/suicide indeed serves to
cover up the unspeakable violation Lewis refers to as sodomy (104). It also
subtly aligns Ed with the rapist; after all, it is he who enforces the silencing of
the rape.

> I went over to Bobby and Drew, though I had no notion of what to do when I got
> there. I had watched everything that had happened to Bobby, had heard him
> scream and squall, and wanted to reassure him that we could set all that aside;
> that it would be forgotten as soon as we left the woods, or as soon as we got back
> in the canoes. But there was no way to say this, or to ask him how his lower
> intestine felt or whether he thought he was bleeding internally. Any examination
> of him would be unthinkably ridiculous and humiliating.
>
> There was no question of that, though; he was furiously closed off from all of
> us. (104)

The focus of Ed's description on matters of position defines the rape of Bobby
as a violation of male subjectivity. Accordingly, silence is the only antidote;
while Ed reflects on Bobby's violation as a medical problem, its crucial meaning—the destruction of his sense of manhood—remains unmentioned. Such
equivocation cannot undo Bobby's marginalization, though: he transmutes
into a separate species, seems prematurely aged ("twenty years older" [108]),
and eventually becomes a drifter. Set apart, he is associated with Drew, who
will be sacrificed—or sacrifices himself—in order to secure silence and the
appearance of "absolute inviolation" (Faulkner). After all, it is Drew who insists that sodomy legitimizes retaliation, and threatens to give away the unspeakable secret, to "[t]ell [the highway patrol] the whole story":

> "Tell them what, exactly?" Lewis asked.
>
> "Just what happened," Drew said, his voice rising a tone. "This is justifiable

homicide if anything is. They were sexually assaulting two members of our party at gunpoint. Like you said, there was nothing else we could do." (106)

When Drew's dead body finally resurfaces, his twisted physique recalls the contortions of Bobby's assaulted body. As in the Southern "historical" romance, rape is thus displaced by Drew's inexplicable death, translated into suicide or murder. The men's concerted efforts to bury the corpse; the police authorities' unsuccessful investigations and search for Drew's body; and the gentlemen's agreement between Ed and Sheriff Bullard (221), who is well aware of the incongruities of Ed's story, of a secret (desire) not to be spoken—all of these dramatize a systematic denial of knowledge, the systemic ignorance that, as Sedgwick convincingly argues, is just as fundamental to culture as is the deployment of particular discourses. What is more, the novel insists that culture depends as much upon the homo/heterosexual division and the taboo of homosexual desire as on the incest taboo.

At the same time, in *Deliverance* Bobby's rape and the rape threat against Ed give rise to a "superior" kind of knowledge pertaining to the "essence" of the human condition, a knowledge projected by the novel's epigraphs:

Il existe à base de la vie humaine un principe d'insuffisance.

GEORGES BATAILLE

The pride of thine heart hath deceived thee,
thou that dwellest in the clefts of the rock,
whose habitation is high; that saith to his heart,
Who shall bring me down to the ground?

OBADIAH verse 3

Dickey's novel, on the one hand, spells out what Bataille's "principe d'insuffisance" has meant to American culture: the gap between "Me" and "Not-Me," culture/civilization and nature/savagery, an alienation that one can overcome, as transcendentalism proposed, by perceiving, reading, translating nature's sign language. Dickey echoes Whitman's poetics in particular, a poetics that projects the fusion of self and other in a homoerotic love-act.[32] On the other hand, *Deliverance* dramatizes the longing to overcome incompletion and lack by pondering sexualized acts of transgressive violence and translating the homoerotic and homophobic subtext of homosocial rituals into theme. Ed's intimate and secret confrontation with the corpse of his aggressor thus to a certain degree refigures the transgressive moment of rape-revenge in Dixon's *The Clansman* or the vampirist attacks Sinclair's protagonist launches against the violator of his wife, moments during which the juxtaposed parties physically fuse. Yet unlike his precursors, Dickey has his narrator retaliate against a rape that he actually witnessed, as the rapist's companion did, with "an odd mixture of approval and sympathy" (100). Accordingly, Ed's crucial transgression is framed not merely as a "frenzy of violence" (Heller 174); it figures as a (homo)-sexual fantasy too:

> I had thought so long and hard about him that to this day I still believe I felt, in the moonlight, our minds fuse. . . . If Lewis had not shot his companion, he and I would have made a kind of love, painful and terrifying to me, in some dreadful way pleasurable to him, but we would have been together in the flesh, there on the floor of the woods, and it was strange to think of it. (154)

This imaginary scene of unfamiliar ("strange") "lovemaking," the fusion of (victim and violator) identities, materializes into a rape-revenge fantasy after Ed shoots his aggressor and hurts himself in the process:

> I crawled over him and picked up the knife. I put it in his mouth and pried at the gums, and a partial upper plate began to come out. . . . I took the knife in my fist. What? Anything. This, also, is not going to be seen. It is not ever going to be known; you can do what you want to; nothing is too terrible. I can cut off the genitals he was going to use on me. Or I can cut off his head, looking straight into his open eyes. Or I can eat him. I can do anything I have a wish to do, and I waited carefully for some wish to come; I would do what it said. (170)

Recalling diverse precursors, including Dixon and Wright, this eroticized vision of a sexual(ly violent) encounter takes on a larger cultural significance: as Ed works on his victim's gums, we may remember how images of black rapists focus on teeth and mouth, suggesting sexual prowess as well as fear of castration. *Deliverance* thus dramatizes the conflict at the center of both the American male and the American nation.

To a certain degree, Ed's journey into another man's body parallels the "surgical" mutilation and dismemberment Ellis's psycho killer practices on his female playmates. A crucial difference, however, pertains to the significance of these (imaginary) dissections: in Dickey's fiction the encounter between killer/castrator and victim is both erotically charged and symbolically loaded, projecting Ed's penetration of physical surfaces as a sexual act, an identity practice, and an exploration of a higher truth, thus making the physical, the cultural, and the metaphysical interpenetrate. Ellis's text, by contrast, lacks eroticism, metaphysics, and substance, offers "no catharsis," "no deeper knowledge" about identity (377). There is only "surface, surface, surface" and a "hero" who is none: "there is an idea of Patrick Bateman, some kind of abstraction, but there is no real me, only an entity, something illusory . . . *I am simply not there.* . . . Myself is fabricated, an aberration" (376, 377). Unlike *American Psycho, Deliverance* maintains the illusion of the real and the "reality" of deeply ingrained American mythologies while turning its subtexts inside out. Imagining how he might "cut off the genitals he was going to use on me," Ed explicitly envisions the mutilations practiced during lynchings. He also hints, though, that he would not have minded being used sexually by the other man, and that part of his revenge results from frustrated desire, thus revealing the subtext of these ritual killings. This subtext thrives in the paragraph that follows:

> It did not *come*, but the ultimate horror *circled me* and *played* over the knife. I began to sing. It was a current popular favorite, a folk-rock tune. I *finished*, and I was *withdrawn* from. I *straightened* as well as I could. There he is, I said to him.
>
> The problems came back, one by one, in sequence. I would rather *drag* him, than carry him. . . . (170, my emphases)

Why "withdrawn," why "straighten," and who is "he"? we may wonder. Soon enough, Ed mirrors himself in his would-be rapist's eye/I, just as Dixon's Gus is reflected in mother Lenoir's eyes, or as Benbow and Popeye mirror each other throughout *Sanctuary*: "He looked lazily straight up into the sky. One open eye had been poked into by a branch or a twig, and was cloudy, but the other was clear blue, delicately veined in a curious, uneyelike pattern; I saw myself there, a tiny figure bent over him, growing" (172). Just as the poked and the clear eyes mark the double position of the other as both rapist and raped, so Ed is both his aggressor's potential victim and his violator. More than that: the desire for and fear of an other who is also the same are inseparably entangled here. Since Dickey frames Ed's trangression in terms of Bataille's metaphysics, though, he not only disavows his novel's own daring. Advising us to read the homoerotically charged fantasies of rape and castration as a regression into a precivilized, primitive condition, a process from which we emerge with a higher knowledge, the text adds to the silence imposed in the plotline a metaphysics of silence that covers up violence as well as the mutability of manhood. And it is this mutability and not the recovery of an "Iron John" manhood that emerges as a higher knowledge from Dickey's novel.

Accordingly, when asked by the only "real" black figure in the text, the "Negro ambulance driver": "What in this world happened to you, man?" Ed replies: "The river happened to me. But I'm not the one. I'm just the only one that can move" (197). Echoing Temple Drake, Ed suggests that he was "raped" by the river, while also insisting that he was least compromised in his masculinity. And yet, as he observes the workman dragging the river for Drew's dead body, Ed has to admit: "I understood the full horror of the phrase I was always seeing in the newspapers, especially in the summer: 'drag the river for the body.' Drag was right." Drag is the mot juste indeed because it acknowledges the instability of manhood and the anxieties it breeds, a fact that is horrific, a knowledge that needs to be denied.

Interestingly enough, feminism itself has reinforced this denial when—following Brownmiller's lead—it reads rape as a sign of male dominance and power and, in order to regain control over male sexuality, refashions women as passive, passionless victims. Like Timothy Beneke's illuminating book *Men on Rape* (1982), recent studies instead emphasize that acts of sexual violence are triggered by a sense of powerlessness. But this does not mean that we are to pity the sexual violator. In fact, as Margaret Atwood's hilarious short story "Rape Fantasies" suggests, "feeling sorry for the guy," believing that "there has to be something *wrong* with them," is as much a rape fantasy as expecting "handsome strangers coming in through the window" (106). Instead, men need to break what came to be seen as the contract of masculinity, to refrain from doing what a man's gotta do, or, as John Stoltenberg puts it, to refuse to be men.

This, of course, is no short-term agenda and by no means a new suggestion. Bell Hooks, for instance, has argued that "[m]en must begin to challenge notions of masculinity that equate manhood with ability to exert power over others, especially through the use of coercive force." Making the end of (sexual) violence dependent upon a rejection of "capitalist patriarchy" and its values (*Margin* 122), Hooks—like Angela Davis—projects an agenda as utopian, though, as Harper's well-intended Christian humanism.[33] Likewise Stoltenberg's own argument is firmly grounded in the gender binarism that informs radical feminist perspectives. In fact, his position imitates the Dworkin/MacKinnon view of male aggressiveness. Dedicating *Refusing to Be a Man* (1989) to "Andrea," Stoltenberg implicitly addresses all "other" (that is, heterosexual) men as rapists, while, like his feminist allies, refusing to touch explicitly upon issues of race, ethnicity, and class, upon what American culture conceives as otherness.[34] Sexual assault among women, by contrast, has only recently been acknowledged—and only with much embarrassment.[35] Is it time, then, for a new master trope?

—⟨*∂/∂*⟩—

Challenging Readings of Rape

IT HAS BEEN the premise of this book that if we want to understand the deployment and significance of rape in contemporary American culture, we need to begin with the rhetoric of sexual violence and its history. I have furthermore claimed that, on the basis of such insight into the cultural imaginary, it may be more productive to challenge our readings of rape than to either celebrate (as free speech) or censor (as "evil images" and acts) its possibly disturbing representations. Accordingly, I want to dedicate these final pages to challenging the readings of three rather diverse 1990s re-presentations of sexual violence, representations that recognize the ongoing transformation of talk about rape, as well as its historical trajectory.

The 1990s have seen, among many other matters, the publication of Ellis's notorious *American Psycho*, a novel deemed—by both rape-crisis feminism and fundamentalism—to be conducive to rape; the emergence of incest narratives as what Roiphe calls America's "latest literary vogue" ("Incest Scene" 65); and the controversies around a group of young African American artists who parodically reemploy stereotypes of blackness to visualize the realities of an (African) American imaginary. To be sure: I am not suggesting any particular relation among these phenomena. Yet each one of them reconsiders dominant moments within the American rhetoric of rape; and each one, in its own way, implicitly challenges antirape discourse. Ellis's supposed "realism" has provoked readings that make one wonder whether modernism ever happened. The proliferation of incest fiction, by contrast, not only marks a certain exhaustion of the cultural effect of the rape trope. It also downplays issues of race and does so, significantly enough, by borrowing a trope traditionally infused with racial significance. Current African American cultural practices in turn shift, to an increasing degree, from modes of disclosure and confession to modes of irony and, like Kara Walker's silhouette art, do so quite effectively.

For many a critic Ellis's 1991 novel, with its gruesome details of horrific sexual violations and its cast of dismembered women (and animals), amounts to a manual for the practicing "pervert." Yet why would the potential rapist (who is also assumed to be an ardent reader) prefer Ellis's *American Psycho* to, let's say, Dworkin's *Mercy*? After all, like Dworkin, Ellis neither glories in representations of rape nor propagates sexual violence. Exposing its own representational strategies, Ellis's novel, rather, resists eroticizing sexual violence and stages a drama of mutilation that indeed "offers . . . no pleasure whatsoever" (Norman Mailer, qtd. in Tanner, *Intimate Violence* 103), provoking extreme discomfort and nausea instead. Even though "shilling shockers" never hurt in the reading (Barnes 193), reading *American Psycho* is a painful experience because Bateman leaves pornographic titillation way behind us. Unlike Faulkner's *Sanctuary*, whose very lack of explicitness "compels us to keep our eye glued to the keyhole" (Fiedler, "Pop" 91–92), Ellis's novel forces us to turn our backs on that door, to put the book down, spent, exhausted. Rather than overriding the reader's resistance, thus performing a kind of rape, as Tanner suggests,[1] the text effects such resistance.

In my view neither of the dominant critical perspectives hits the mark:[2] the claim that, as a piece of art, *American Psycho* comes under the aegis of the First Amendment falls just as far short as the conviction that, like hard-core pornography and snuff movies, it provides the theory for the practice of rape and thus deserves to be censored. Nor can we simply dismiss *American Psycho* as a bad novel, as Roger Rosenblatt—among many others—did:

> So pointless, so themeless, so everythingless is this novel, except in stupefying details about clothing, food and bath products, that were it not the most loathsome offering of the season, it certainly would be the funniest. . . . Of course, you would be stunned to learn that the book goes nowhere. Characters do not exist, therefore do not develop. Bateman has no motivation for his madness. . . . No plot intrudes upon the pages. Bateman is never brought to justice, suggesting that even justice was bored. Nor is Mr. Ellis.

Curiously enough—and notwithstanding Rosenblatt's value judgments—this passage not only depicts Ellis's post-modernist aesthetics quite adequately. Rosenblatt's suggestion that both Bateman and Ellis should be legally prosecuted moreover reveals an affinity with certain feminist readings that identify the content of a speech act with the act it delineates.[3] In accordance with such views, Ellis's book is deemed not a description of (sexual) violence but (sexual) violence, not the depiction of an idea of (sexual) violence but a product that can be bought and used for sexual acts.[4] To my mind, however, Ellis's rapist rhetoric does not even depict an idea of sexual violence but delineates an idea of representation. In fact, *American Psycho* confronts the overheated American debate about sexual violence and censorship by questioning its mimetic notion of representation and the widespread belief that evil acts cease once we wipe out evil images. As a post-modern text that presents itself in the garb of realism, *American Psycho* projects unspeakable fantasies of violence with surgical and cinematographic precision—without, however, disclosing substance. Just like his colorful world of capitalist consumption, Bateman's chainsaw-massacre practices of torture and rape reveal no more than additional surfaces.

Owing to its meticulous use of detail, Ellis's novel may indeed initially appear realistic. As we read on, however, the text—and this distinguishes *Ameri-*

can Psycho from Oates's *Zombie* (1995), for instance—dispenses with its realistic garb and dons parody, keeping us guessing as to whether Bateman's excesses are in fact for real or plain fantasy. This set of alternatives, of course, is itself misleading. For as Young trenchantly observes, no matter whether Patrick Bateman's rapes and murders "are phantasies or not," "within fiction they are all fictional." We are consequently "forced by the author to confront the definition and function of fictionality itself" (116). For indeed *American Psycho* is no realist text; it does not obscure but illuminates its fictional artifice. Neither plotlines nor characters cohere, inconclusiveness abounds, and the narrator's ways of perceiving and commenting upon his world are oftentimes more comical than shocking. As videotapes, *The Patty Winters Show*, and pharmaceuticals cloud his senses and hallucinations take over, Bateman becomes increasingly unreliable, even loses his status as first-person narrator, becoming an abstraction, a cipher, "something illusory . . . fabricated, an aberration" indeed. Such self-reflectivity not only affirms the fictional status of the text. It also insists that reference here is first and foremost to other fictions, including gothic narratives, action novels, and, most significantly, film, thus monitoring the shift from a primarily verbal to an increasingly visual culture. Depicting a voyeurist hero whose (post-modernist) vision reduces reality to a cinematic text that withholds deeper sense and significance, Ellis, in *American Psycho*, makes the mediation of the real his main target.[5] Employing the cinematic and televised world both thematically and structurally,[6] the novel demystifies and mocks more than celebrates horror movie and hard core.

Accordingly, with the power of the visual in charge, Bateman's true obsession is not to simply "act out" but to dramatize and stage his fantasies like a movie director. Recording his excesses on videotape, he legitimizes his enterprises philosophically: "in an attempt to understand these girls I'm filming their death" (304). Like Dickey's *Deliverance*, *American Psycho* thus holds that threshold experiences offer insights into the *condition humaine*. "I'm . . . in touch with humanity," Bateman claims (341). Yet while Dickey, authorized by Bataille, propagates regeneration through violence, Ellis parodies his precursors, including Dickey and Bataille. Bateman not only renounces the truth he mockingly locates in the depth of bodily cavities, but reveals the belief in such truth as an illusion. Bateman opens up bodies but provides neither insight nor vision. This is why there is little difference between Ellis's depictions of Bateman's bathroom rituals and his murderous routines; why lists of labels and logos crisscross the scenes of his gruesome pastimes; and why Ellis is closer to Pynchonesque paranoia than to T. S. Eliot's cultural pessimism. His protagonist gets lost in the loops of his own projection, which are themselves projections of various cultural practices and discourses. And many of Ellis's readers follow along.

Somehow Cindy Sherman's 1980s series *Disaster Fairy Tales* comes to mind here. The deeper Sherman's camera moves into the realms that our body-conscious culture of fashionable surfaces marginalizes and excludes, the more it revels in the abject, the more artificial become the color and lighting of her photography, the more plastic the inner life that is excavated. Not the body but our phantasms and anxieties pertaining to that body and its abysses are disclosed in the process.[7] Ellis, however, forestalls that final step. Instead, his novel's deployment of "evil" images leads to their very death. In the process "voyeurism becomes white noise," and Bateman, as Tanja May appropriately puts it, "the terminator of his own pornographic fantasy and thus a parody of the pornophilic as such" (2). And still: *American Psycho* does not merely deconstruct the pornographic. The novel also makes us feel how painful such deconstruction can be. This pain, though, is far from the pain that real violence inflicts, a pain that necessarily remains absent from Ellis's explicit representation. And curiously enough, that pain returns in the movie adaptation of the novel. It seems most evident when the camera—instead of confronting us head-on with the scene of violence and its tortured victim—simply displays Bateman's blood-splashed countenance.

In my view, the persistent disregard of Ellis's post-modernist aesthetic repertoire attests to a resistance to modernist insights into representation. Images, so the lesson of modernism goes, do not literally mean what they represent, just as their absence—like Faulkner's deletion of the act of rape from *Sanctuary*—does not prevent the reader from supplementing meaning. Accordingly, *American Psycho* is not about sexual violence against women, even if it deploys its depiction. Instead, its explicitness recognizes that the meaning of rape has long been displaced. At the same time, this does not mean that the text cannot be put to (ab)use and trigger sex acts: when the Los Angeles chapter of the National Organization for Women, for instance, had telephone lines installed that sampled the text's most irritating passages and notorious scenes, they may indeed have serviced the practicing "pervert," as some would have it. Others would probably hold that such use of the text channels sexual aggressions. Still others would call such recycling of writing—the fragments torn from the textual body—rape. Especially if the victim was not *American Psycho* but *Mercy*.[8] The rape of a book. To be more precise, though: reducing fiction to content and translating writing into speech act, the *American Psycho*–hotline not only overrides both the novel's aesthetics and politics. Turning post-modernist text into phone sex, NOW also distances itself from Ellis's ethics, which comes closer to feminist morality than feminism would dare to acknowledge. For while Ellis complains that *American Psycho* has been taken at face value, too literally, he also keeps defending the novel as a satire of the insane violence of our time.[9]

Displaying an "iron-fisted denial of complexity and ambiguity" (Gaitskill 264) with regard to both sexual and texual practice, rape-crisis discourse stars as the Iron Mike of current cultural criticism, to appropriate Fluck's ironic trope for the (modernist) critique of realism's supposed lack of technique, its reduction of style. But just like realism, rape-crisis discourse, of course, has its own particular style—and a post-modernist style at that. Crucial to that rhetoric is the use of rape as a central trope that—taken literally—managed to draw new attention to the corporeality of female subjection. As part of the postmodernist repoliticization of rape, however, such deployment of rape as a master trope "for defining the violation of woman by patriarchy" (Warren Warner 13) could not help but diffuse the meaning of rape. This diffusion in turn diminished the figure's effectiveness.

Where it abolishes precision and indiscriminately covers phenomena as discrete as verbal aggression, pornography, and sexual assault, the term "rape" even trivializes actual sexual violence. Sexual harassment and hate speech meanwhile function as ciphers: in a culture that accepts oppression and (sexual) violation as the "natural" state of many of its subjects (and thus hardly even recognizes, for instance, the thousands of cases of real rape that I refer to at the opening of this book's introduction), the intervention into an individual's sense of sexual identity has become the event that pinpoints oppression most potently. Frequently such interventions allow the privileged to refashion themselves as victims. Oftentimes they involve children, the weakest of all victims. The example of some six- and seven-year-old boys who in 1996 were temporarily suspended from North Carolina and New York schools because they bestowed "sexist" kisses on their female classmates is just one of the more amusing among the telling cases in point. Amusing because the misogynist perpetrators were first-graders, found guilty not of carrying guns into schoolhouses but of extending an act of tenderness to a classmate—albeit without following Antioch rules and having their acts preapproved. Telling because such distorted perceptions of violence hint at severe uncertainties and anxieties pertaining to gender, race, and sexual relations.[10]

In view of an exhausted rape trope, a growing concern with underage victims, and the frequent alliance of rape and incest within (post-)modernist literature, it is interesting to note that rape has more recently been overdetermined and displaced by the trope of incest and child abuse. But whereas 1970s and 1980s African American women's fiction employed the incest trope in order to re-present rape as "family affair" and figure for internalized racism, the current focus on incest steers straight away from and passes by issues of race, class, ethnicity, gender, and age. In a "nation of raped children" (Sapphire, qtd. in Roiphe, "Incest Scene" 68) to be "rapable" no longer defines what a woman is, as MacKinnon claims; it defines anyone as a victim.

No surprise, therefore, that Roiphe—in a 1995 review of incest narratives authored by Oates, Atwood, Mary Gaitskill, and Marilyn French, among others—takes issue with this new "incest scene," with "novel after novel . . . grop[ing] for dark secrets" (65), with "the stock plot of a culture obsessed with sexual abuse" (71). Yet is it actually sexual abuse with which American culture is obsessed? Throughout this book I have shown that cultures do not articulate their obsessions directly, without mediation and ironic distance. What is more: the recent rise to prominence of the incest trope within (American) cultural symbology is part of a larger struggle over signifying power, a struggle that makes increasing use of particularly potent rhetorical figures. The current inclination to appropriate and recontextualize terms like "genocide" and "holocaust," for instance, in the discourse pertaining to AIDS or African American history manifests a tendency within American culture to project identity through parameters of violation and victimization, to redefine—and thereby racialize—subjectivity as survival.[11]

As we have seen, this sense of the subject as a survivor (of sexual violation) has its own particular history in American culture: it appropriates the position of the (sexually violated) African American woman and a rhetoric that evolved under conditions of institutionalized sexual violence. It is thus somewhat shortsighted to blame the "alchemy" of 1980s academia and politics for having created "a mainstream fascination with victims of all kinds" (Roiphe, "Incest Scene" 68). Instead, I would like to suggest that—not unlike the multiculturalist celebration of difference—the tendency within American (middle-class) culture to refashion subjectivity as victimization seems driven, at least in part, by a desire to transcend racial conflict and avoid issues of race. The current prominence of incest fiction thus is certainly more than a "modish plot twist" (71).

Accordingly, the irony that governs Roiphe's review of the "incest scene" reaches its highest pitch where race matters are concerned—and concerned she is, even if the author avoids talking about race explicitly. The "current trend" filling bookshelves "with stories of the family romance getting a little too romantic" (65), she claims, "blew north from the hot porches of Southern literature." The titillating timbre of Roiphe's voice not only mocks and eroticizes the fiction of Morrison, Angelou, and Walker, which she considers "the prototypes for the modern incest scene" (68). It also conjures up America's primal incest scene, the enforced "incestuous" relations within the extended "plantation family." It is this scene that current incest fictions uncannily remember. Thus "seeing this subconscious stuff dramatized," as Roiphe sloppily puts it, does not simply "appeal[] to our most primal fears and fantasies" (69). Current incest narratives also appeal to historically specific American fears and fantasies, the scope of which Faulkner has re-presented with so much subtlety. But unlike Faulkner's and Morrison's fictions, which transform history into memory, recent incest narratives make the recovery of memory an identity practice while dispensing with history.

The same goes for Roiphe's review. While Roiphe acutely observes that different novels recount the incest drama "in remarkably similar terms"—terms that in fact echo the incest scene on the very first page of *The Color Purple*—I am surprised to hear her find "pornographic precision" and "cinematic detail" in the recurrent poetics of "'hard thing'" and "'panties'" (70). What is more, detecting sex as "the selling principle" "[b]eneath the swelling prose," Roiphe presents the novel incest narratives as the pious pornography of our day, while outing herself as a porNO activist whose notions of both pornography and sex are certainly dubious. To my mind, though, the only common ground between, say, Walker's novel and pornography is that both have been accused of replicating hierarchies by rendering stereotyped views of race and gender relations and sexuality. "Stereotypes are stereotypes," Ferguson declares in "Pornography: The Theory" (1995), "because they reflect judgments of value, judgments that have particular force as implicit maxims because they claim the authority of what has been credited over what has not" (673).

This authority is being reclaimed, however, by those who have been subjected to stereotyping. Whereas both feminist and race work have aimed at eliminating stereotypical depictions of women and African Americans, the powerful silhouette art of Kara Walker deliberately romances stereotypes of blackness and sexuality and thereby reimagines interracial relations, exploitation, and sexual desire in an uncanny manner. Like fellow artist Michael Ray Charles, Walker thus resists the self-censorship that the "black community" has imposed on images of extreme corporeality. "There is a widespread conspiracy," Charles claims, "to keep those [stereotypical] images forgotten invisible. What," he adds, "if Jewish people never wanted to talk about the Holocaust?" (n.p.). This question not only suggests that the distorted images of blackness structure African American reality just as the dominant documentary and monumental re-presentations of the Holocaust have defined and thus also diminished "Jewish identity." Charles further implies that the Holocaust has become the stereotype of that identity—an insight that in no way questions the reality of the Holocaust. Instead, Charles dissolves the polarity of myth and truth, of imaginary and real. And accordingly Charles and Walker do not dismiss stereotypes of blackness as lies but parodically reemploy such imagery to insist that the myth indeed *is* the African American real. Breaking what Mel Watkins calls the "unspoken but almost universally accepted covenant" "to present positive images of blacks" (qtd. in McDowell 80), they instead evolve a new conception of African American subjectivity and redefine the real as well as our sense of realism.[12]

Walker claims to cherish "images of popular racism" "for their sheer strangeness, the almost open-endedness of meaning" ("(Like Home)" 102), and engages, blackens, those images that African American culture has left untouched and dismissed as lies traded by white culture. "[T]here is a clearly drawn blank space," she explains her practice, "defined here by all this denial." And it is this space she intends to visualize by means of "[her] black hole, [her] silhouette" (104), as she lovingly labels her art, echoing Alice Walker's distinction in *The Color Purple* between "button" and "hole," between clitoris and female jouissance, on the one hand, and penetration and pain, on the other. By penetrating this pain—including the pain inflicted by self-imposed

racism—in a highly seductive manner, Kara Walker, however, generates no definite, but double, meanings and makes the viewer aware of his or her own agency in this process of sense making. By presenting herself at her own art shows as "free Negress of noteworthy talent" (112), Walker takes on the stigma and wears it like a crown, thus—like the gangsta rapper—exposing its work by way of parodic performance. Acting out stereotypes, including "the tantalizing Venus Noir, the degraded nigger wench, the blood-drenched lynch mob," Walker wants "to seduce an audience," she explains, "into participating in this humiliating exercise/exorcise with me" (106).

Accordingly, the viewer, attracted to Walker's art by its seemingly innocent generic quality, notices only gradually what a mess he or she has gotten into. Anchoring, on the one hand, in a contemplative nineteenth century, while, on the other, dramatizing unspeakable fictions of race and sexuality, Walker's silhouettes translate imaginary links between seduction and violence into a

Left and above, *The End of Uncle Tom and the Grand Allegorical Tableau of Eva in Heaven,* 1995 (details). Cut paper. Collection Jeffrey Deitch, New York. Courtesy Brent Sikkema, NYC.

seesaw of pleasurable recognition and physical malaise. Reengaging subjects and objects of slave economy in this way, she interrogates cultural traumas in a daringly discomforting manner. Her scenes accentuate the reciprocity of physical and emotional exploitation, projecting such exploitation as mutual exchange of bodily fluids, the literal feeding/breeding upon each others' bodies, refigured as the sucking of breasts, thus suggesting nurturance, sexual gratification as well as abuse. As her figures tear at genitals, tear open bodily orifices, cut through each others' bodies as easily as Walker herself engages in her black-on-white shadow-and-substance art, the silhouettes indeed re-create, as Isaac Julien suggests, slavery as a sadomasochistic scenario, a ritual of consensual sexual violence.[13]

Despite its explicitness Walker's re-presentation of licit and illicit desires is not straightforward but deflects the pornographic and homoerotic gazes it constructs. Involving black and white women and men, Walker's art capitalizes on the interdependencies of human relations within the slave economy, fore-

African't, 1996 (detail). Cut paper. Collection Eileen and Peter Norton, Santa Monica. Courtesy Brent Sikkema, NYC.

grounding a shared desire for intimacy and interracial attraction that have customarily been disavowed. At the same time, her work dramatizes kinship within the extended "plantation family" as pedophilia and "incest." Walker's refigurations thus not only disclose the actual violence that the maintenance of the slave economy required. She also translates—oftentimes quite literally—the fantasies and traumas it generated. Accordingly, Walker sees her work in analogy to fiction, including the slave narrative, the sentimental novel as well as racist diatribes of the Dixon kind. In this way, she generates what Spillers finds lacking in much of African American cultural expression: moments of self-reflection and self-knowledge as well as a vision of an interior intersubjectivity, all of which do not come to a halt at the racial border.

Interestingly enough, the very popularity—and commercial success—of Walker's art has also revitalized the silhouette itself. I was somewhat struck, though, to find its aesthetics appropriated in a "call to action" by a Violence Prevention Working Group concerned with domestic violence.[14] After all, Walker has endowed the silhouette with the memory of a very particular "domestic violence." In the context of the reading of rape and its representations in American culture, however, it comes as no surprise that this memory looms large—and sells well—in the poetics of current identity practices.

While I started out with a case of real rape, I will conclude with a case of real rape-crisis discourse. At about the same time the Carpenter Center for Visual Arts at Harvard University presented Walker's controversial work,[15] Harvard students organized their 1998 spring "Take Back the Night" week. The organizers of this event issued a pin whose white lettering on stark red ground read: "RAPE HAPPENS AT HARVARD."[16] The production of this interesting artifact was inspired by the refusal, on the part of the university administration, to agree to the implementation of rape education and awareness classes as part of the official orientation for incoming first-year students. Hence the "awareness pin." Yet what, I wonder, does the statement "RAPE HAPPENS AT HARVARD" actually mean? Of what should it make us aware? Are we to be relieved that rape happens at Harvard too? Decontextualized from the administration's refusal, the phrase is not easily glossed: is it a good thing or a bad thing that rape happens at Harvard? What is the politics of that button—as opposed to, for instance, buttons worn thirty years ago, pins that insisted, "Stop the Rape of Vietnam"? Is it a "red badge of courage"? Or does the button, like the flyers posted by the Harvard rape hotline in the women's restroom of Harvard's athletic center, suggest that you "cannot walk alone at night," thus intimidating women and policing their access to public space?[17] If rape no longer happened at Harvard, would this mean a loss of territory, of a "control" over male sexuality that women have secured for themselves, for better or worse? Is it part of Harvard's (corporate) identity politics, as the pin is draped in Harvard's colors? Do we hear echoes of Temple Drake, who foresaw that "something" was going "to happen" to her? Probably all of these resonances and more come into play, just as the literary rhetoric of rape bears multiple meanings, foreshadowing fears and recollecting horrific memories, yet by nature giving away little of the experience of rape itself. Rape does happen indeed. Its re-presentation, its translation into signs, images, signposts, posters, and pins, however, is an altogether different matter, closed off by quotation marks from the unspeakable experience, the full horror that cannot but remain absent, elsewhere, and real.

Notes

1. I allude here to Susan Estrich's book *Real Rape*. Estrich employs the term in what she calls "an argument for change," for an understanding of rape that recognizes that so-called simple (acquaintance) rape is as real a rape as is any stranger rape (7). Aiming at legal reform, Estrich's argument insists on reading rape cases in new ways. I myself in the following use the term "real rape" when I mean to distinguish acts of sexual violence from their representation.

2. See also Terry.

3. On the "Southern rape complex" and the construction of race and gender, see also D'Emilio and Freedman 215–21.

4. As in the title to this introduction, I allude here to Raymond Carver's short story "What We Talk about When We Talk about Love."

5. For a trenchant analysis of race as a social construction and "its totalizing effect in obscuring class and gender," see Higginbotham (95).

6. In her article on interracial rape, Valerie Smith talks about the "inescapability of cultural narratives" ("Split Affinities" 285).

7. The term "rape culture" is used in sociological studies to differentiate so-called rape-prone countries (such as the United States) from countries where, according to official records, rape is a relatively rare crime ("rape-free" countries). See Peggy Reeves Sanday's essay "Rape and the Silencing of the Feminine," in Tomaselli and Porter 84–101. It has been adapted by feminist criticism to suggest a culture's general tendency to oppress women. See, for instance, Buchwald, Fletcher, and Roth.

8. The term "rape-crisis discourse" refers to a perspective dominant in parts of the feminist movement which holds that rape is a crime that has in recent decades been increasing to a hitherto unknown degree; it also implies a certain critique of or distance from that position.

9. I thank Ernst-Peter Schneck for drawing my attention to Bal's insightful essay.

10. I am indebted here to Peter Storey's chapter "Althusserianism" (110–18).

11. Lloyd himself partly relies on the argument that Colette Guillaumin makes in "Race and Nature."

12. Using a hyphen between "post" and "modern," I mean to suggest a particular understanding of postmodernity that does not limit the term to a particular aesthetics. Rather, I take post-modernism as a cultural condition that, like any other era, is characterized by what Ernst Bloch called the synchronicity of the nonsynchronic. On this issue, see Sielke, "(Post-)Modernists or Misfits?"

13. The amount of literature published on the subject since the 1960s attests to this deployment of discourse. Among the most significant texts belong Susan Griffin, "Rape, the All-American Crime" (1971); Diana Russell, *The Politics of Rape* (1974); Noreen Connell and Cassandra Wilson, eds., *Rape: The First Sourcebook for Women* (1974); Susan Brownmiller, *Against Our Will: Men, Women, and Rape* (1975); Susan Estrich,

Real Rape (1987); Liz Kelly, *Surviving Sexual Violence* (1988); Robin Warshaw, *I Never Called It Rape* (1988); Elizabeth Brauerholz and Mary Kowaleski, *Sexual Coercion* (1991).

14. This literary polylogue is due partly to the fact that I deal with different writing subjects, namely, Anglo-American and African American male and female authors who, dependent on their particular histories and subject positions, have responded to the issues at hand with literary practices that differ in both aesthetics and politics. And yet: just as their histories and subject positions interdepend, so their specific rhetorics of rape interrelate. The texts thus exemplify Bloch's conception of a synchronicity of the nonsynchronic. On similar grounds Andreas Huyssen distinguishes the affirmative post-modernism of, for instance, Robert Coover, Thomas Pynchon, and Kathy Acker, from the alternative post-modernism of, let us say, Toni Morrison, Adrienne Rich, and Ishmael Reed.

15. I borrow this phrase from Eve Kosofsky Sedgwick (*Epistemology* 1).

CHAPTER ONE
SEDUCED AND ENSLAVED: SEXUAL VIOLENCE IN
ANTEBELLUM AMERICAN LITERATURE AND CONTEMPORARY
FEMINIST DISCOURSE

An early version of this chapter appeared under the same title in a special issue entitled "The Historical and Political Turn in Literary Studies," edited by Winfried Fluck, *REAL* 11 (1995): 299–324.

1. This tendency has been criticized in particular by black feminist critics, e.g., Angela Davis and Hooks. Other authors redefine rape as a crime of violence as part of a general opposition to feminist rape-crisis discourse; unlike Brownmiller they do not see rape as a feminist issue but relate its rise to a general increase of violence in the United States. See, for instance, Bonilla and Sommers's chapter "Rape Research," in Sommers 209–26.

2. Cf. Dworkin, *Intercourse*.

3. Cf. also MacKinnon, *Sexual Harassment* 218–20.

4. For a discussion of these matters, see Strossen. Cf. also Sielke, "Drawing the Line."

5. According to *The Official Sexually Correct Dictionary and Dating Guide* (New York: Villard, 1995), the term "date rape" was coined in 1982 by *Ms.* magazine writer Karen Bechhofer. It is a concept that, owing to the absence of a "dating system," lacks a frame of reference in many European countries, including Germany.

6. October 13, 1994, John F. Kennedy School of Government.

7. Roiphe, in fact, makes this quite explicit. "Maybe the average college student's boyfriend has a copy of *Hustler* magazine, maybe they once rented a pornographic video to see what it was like, but the pornography industry that MacKinnon describes—with all of its diabolical machinations, the nude dancer under bright lights—takes place far from our world" (*Morning After* 152). Cf. also 157.

8. See Daniel Williams. These early rape narratives belong to the genre of criminal narratives, which were usually coauthored by ghostwriters and criminals. According to Williams, only the "most egregious crimes and criminals" got recorded, and their narratives became "unique commodities in the eighteenth-century print culture" (196).

9. While literary history traces the American seduction novel back to Samuel Richardson's *Pamela* (1740) and *Clarissa* (1747–48), Nancy Armstrong in turn traces the

English novel back to the captivity narrative. Like Richardson's epistolary texts, Armstrong argues, wherein the victim/heroine transforms from sexual object to subject of her own writing, the captivity narrative reaffirms the individual as author. See Armstrong, "The American Origin of the English Novel."

It should also be noted that the slave narrative is a hybrid rather than a genuinely African American genre. Braxton, for instance, refers to earlier studies, such as Stephen Butterfield's *Black Autobiography in America*, that "demonstrated the parallel development of the slave narrative with colonial and early federal autobiographies, journals, and diaries" (6). On the function of African American autobiography, see also William Andrews, "The First Century of Afro-American Autobiography: Notes toward a Definition of a Genre," *To Tell a Free Story* 1–31.

10. Cf. D'Emilio and Freedman 56 ff.

11. *History of Sexuality* 1:75–131.

12. This change of paradigm is convincingly argued by Laqueur.

13. Cf. Sander L. Gilman.

14. For an informative history of the seduction motif, see Jenny Newman's introduction to the *Faber Book of Seductions.*

15. I therefore hesitate to read, as Claudia Tate does, the "literary representations of black motherhood" in Jacobs's narrative and Wilson's *Our Nig* (1859) as part of female "discourses of liberation" (108, 107). Cf. also Berlant ("Queen of America") on Jacobs, Harper, and Anita Hill.

16. Cf. Ferguson, "Rape" 103. This view seems to reflect an older belief that conception requires orgasm, "heat," and the involvement of bodily fluids from both partners. See Laqueur, "Orgasm and Desire," in *Making Sex* 43–52. Such beliefs, though, are by no means eradicated. On April 28, 1995, for instance, WBUR Boston morning news reported that Congressman Aldridge from North Carolina had, during an abortion debate on April 27, claimed that rape rarely leads to pregnancy (and therefore does not need to be exempted from antiabortion statutes) because the "body fluids" are not activated so as to lead to conception. Pro-choice activists rightly pointed out that pro-life argumentation dispenses with even the most fundamental medical knowledge.

17. Shortly before her death, Charlotte refers to the sexual encounter in a letter to La Rue: "we both," she writes, "pardon me, Madam, if I say, we both too easily followed the impulse of our treacherous hearts, and trusted our happiness on a tempestuous ocean, where mine has been wrecked and lost for ever" (115).

18. See *Charlotte Temple*, chaps. 18 and 20, especially p. 78.

19. "The crime of rape," as Daniel Williams points out, "was not always a crime" (194). The Massachusetts Bay Colony's first code of laws omitted rape from its list of twelve capital crimes because no biblical sanction for its inclusion could be found. Only after a case of sexual abuse of three children was disclosed did the General Court pass "laws stipulating the death penalty for the rape of a child under 10 years of age and for the rape of 'any mayde or woman that [was] lawfully married or contracted' " (195). These laws, however, were not included in later legal codes. American rape law was instead developed in the second half of the seventeenth century on the basis of British common law, which defined rape as "carnal knowledge of any woman above the age of ten years against her will and of a woman under the age of 10 years with or against her will" (Lindemann 64). For the early development of rape laws in America, see

Daniel Williams, Lindemann, D'Emilio and Freedman 11, 18; on the subject of rape and the law, see also Brownmiller, Bessmer, and Tong.

20. Cf. D'Emilio and Freedman 31. Marybeth Hamilton Arnold, who investigated sexual assaults in New York City between 1790 and 1820, claims that rape "was overwhelmingly a crime of the poor" (37). This, however, contradicts more recent findings that sexual violence is a pattern of behavior occurring in all social strata. The particular treatment of a case, though, has always depended on the social status of both victim and perpetrator, and convictions have generally been more frequent the lower the standing of the perpetrator (Lindemann 80).

21. As Marybeth Hamilton Arnold points out, women "scraping by at the very margins of existence" were severely incapacitated for work by rape-related physical injuries and by pregnancies ensuing from rape. Therefore, lower-class women's complaints in rape cases concerned the physical rather than the sexual nature of an assault (47).

22. Cf. Lewis 719. This secularization taking hold in America as well as England is made explicit on the novel's very first page. Montraville and Belcour, we are told, "sauntered out to view the town, and to make remarks on the inhabitants, as they returned from church," yet do not themselves attend church (Rowson 3).

23. Limited employment opportunities were a major concern of women's groups during the nineteenth century; women's sexual exploitation by their employers was deplored in magazines such as *The Friend of Virtue* and the *Home Guardian*. Cf. Debra Gold Hansen 51, 76.

24. See, for instance, Cynthia J. Davis's reading of Jacobs's narrative.

25. Karen Sanchez-Eppler's reading of Jacobs's narrative thus exemplifies the practice of reading the violence back into texts by foregrounding the violence of representation. Concerned with "the ways in which rhetoric effaces and contains the real, not only with the physical and juridical violence directed against women and slaves, but also with the violence of represention" (8–9), her interpretations tend to obliterate the difference between rhetoric and "real." As Sanchez-Eppler concludes, for instance, that Jacobs's narrative "fails to displace the sexual experiences it describes," and instead "repeats them, as the act of telling this story results in rape, shame, contempt, and denial" (102), I wonder: how could rape be anything but a figure here? And as such what does it signify? And what, then, does it displace? Jacobs's experience after all was the threat of rape, not real rape.

26. On the subject, cf. Berlant, "Queen of America."

27. The question of whether Jacobs was indeed the author of the text preoccupied scholars up to the 1980s. While it was long assumed that editor Lydia Maria Child herself wrote the narrative, Jean Fagan Yellin's essay "Written by Herself," on the basis of the correspondence between Jacobs and Amy Post, conclusively demonstrates that *Incidents* was indeed written by Jacobs herself.

28. That image was partly reproduced by African American literature itself; cf. for instance, William Wells Brown's *Clotelle: A Tale of the Southern States* (1853) and *Louisa Picquet, the Octoroon* (1861) by Reverend Hiram Mattison, which portrays both black women and Southern whites as "carnally unrestrained" (Andrews, *To Tell* 245).

29. Cf. Rooney's discussion, 1274–75.

30. Women's sexual history keeps resurfacing as an issue in rape trials, despite the fact that reforms of rape law, first manifested by the passage of new rape statutes in Michigan in 1974, have established rules governing the use of the victim's prior sexual

history as evidence, restricting it to the victim's relationship with the defendant. See Temkin 28 and Tong 104–18.

31. In *Novels, Readers, and Reviewers* Nina Baym writes: "Even in novels where the wife or young woman remains chaste, some reviewers felt that the depiction of temptation or the unlawful love on the man's part was too immoral" (182). Through the era, she emphasizes, "reviewers were looking for novels featuring heroines who exemplified such virtues as self-sacrifice, self-control, and self-discipline" (189).

32. Cf. D'Emilio and Freedman 297 and Angela Davis's essay "Rape, Racism, and the Myth of the Black Rapist."

33. Sexual relations among slaves were—because they presumably belonged to a completely different order—beyond the reach of the common law. See, for instance, Hartman 554, Jordan 157, Brownmiller 162 ff.

34. Even though miscegenation laws supposedly regulated all interracial sexual relations, they were primarily designed to prevent the exchange of white women across the racial border, thus manifesting, as JanMohamed argues, the exclusion of blacks from the social order and, more generally, the "overwhelming determining role of juridical prohibitions" in the construction of racialized sexuality (102).

35. Similarly, in her reading of Sarah and Angelina Grimké's *American Slavery As It Is* (1839), Bell Hooks argues that the authors' concern with sexual exploitation was motivated by their concern with the souls of white man. "Many pro-slavery white women ultimately denounced slavery because of their outrage at the sexual barbarity of white men." Referring to rape as male adultery, they positioned the white wife and not the black slave as victim; white women in turn blamed black women for the state of their marriages (*Ain't I* 28, 54).

36. Cf. Taves 72.

37. This is a central theme in William Wells Brown's *Clotelle*, a tale capitalizing on the sexual exploitation of female slaves.

38. Cf. Hartman 546–47.

39. Cf. Jacobs, chap. 10 in particular, where Brent pleads: "O, ye happy women, whose purity has been sheltered from childhood, who have been free to chose the objects of your affection, whose homes are protected by law, do not judge the poor desolate slave girl too severely!" (54). Passages like these clearly conflict with efforts of the early women's movement to highlight women's vulnerability within the realm of marriage and family. They moreover foreground that white support and sympathy rely on clear assertions of racial difference. White feminist-abolitionists, by contrast, attempted to bolster their politics by obliterating such difference and appropriated slavery as a metaphor for female subjection. Angelina Grimké, for instance, famously insisted that "[t]he investigation of the rights of the slave has led me to a better understanding of my own" (qtd. in Winter 3). While black men, as I argue below, tend to erect their sense of self at the expense of the violated black woman, white women thus utilize the specter of black victimization for an assessment of their own subjection.

40. Examples of twentieth-century African American novels that employ the scar as a central figure include Petry's *The Street* (1946) and Morrison's *Beloved* (1987), where the trope of the tree transforms the scar into a sign of origin and power, both a trace of pain and a mark of strength. (For an excellent reading of Morrison, see Henderson.) The scar thus functions as an image which insists that African American personhood remains inextricably associated with an injured and violated body.

41. Eric Foner's claim that only "with freedom came developments that strengthened patriarchy within the black family and institutionalized the notion that men and women should inhabit separate spheres" (*Reconstruction* 87) has been questioned by feminist critics and historians who take the submission of black women as the basis of both black and white manhood. Hooks argues that black men's virility was always taken for granted in the assignment of gender-specific tasks (*Ain't I* 20–21). Cf. also Mann's work on gender-related divisions of labor and White's analysis of sex roles and status in the antebellum plantation South.

42. Criticizing "the failure of the law of sex equality to address sexual abuse," MacKinnon wants these abuses to be treated not as crimes or private violations, but as acts of sex discrimination ("Sex Equality" 378).

43. According to MacKinnon, "[t]he law of rape divides women into spheres of consent according to indices of relationship to men.... Daughters may not consent; wives and prostitutes are assumed to, and cannot but.... Virtuous women, like young girls, are unconsenting, virginal, rapable. Unvirtuous women, like wives and prostitutes, are consenting, whores, unrapable" (*Feminist Theory* 175). Donald A. Dripps, by contrast, argues that to preclude the constraints that matters of consent entail, sex should no longer be considered a matter of consent but rather be treated as a property of women.

44. Whereas MacKinnon's legal analysis accounts for the limited value of comparisons between racial and gender discrimination, she draws easy analogies between sexual assault and lynching ("Sex Equality" 380).

45. This suggestion was part of a speech to the National Association of Counties that criticized the plans of the Republican Party to overhaul the American welfare system, presented on March 7, 1995, and commented upon by WBUR Boston the same day.

46. Cf. "Sex Equality" 381–82.

47. Cf. Katha Pollitt's review of *The Morning After*, entitled "Not Just Bad Sex," 170–71.

48. See Paglia's essays on rape (*Sex* 49–54, 55–74).

49. About 90 percent of all rapes are intraracial. For statistics on rape, see, for instance, Sielke, "Gewalt gegen Frauen" 196, and Brodie.

50. See, for example, MacKinnon, "Sex Equality" 379.

CHAPTER TWO
THE RISE OF THE (BLACK) RAPIST AND THE RECONSTRUCTION
OF DIFFERENCE; OR, "REALIST" RAPE

1. For a discussion of the predominant images of black masculinity, see, for instance, Donald Bogle's "interpretive history of blacks in film" (1973), which distinguishes the religious, hardworking, loyal Tom from the happy-go-lucky coon and the violently virile buck.

2. According to E. Anthony Rotundo (whose study is focused on New England and unconcerned with blackness) the emergence of modern notions of aggressive masculinity results from the transformation of the colonial "communal sense of manhood" to a sense of "*self-made manhood*" (3) emerging in conjunction with late-eighteenth-century cultural and economic developments—a transformation that redefines manliness as a matter of individual success rather than public service. By the late nineteenth century, notions of a "new *passionate manhood*" (5) had developed that cherished male

competitiveness, aggression, and toughness, aligned physical strength with strong character, and made the body itself "a vital component of manhood" (6), yet still conflicted with Victorian notions of sexual restraint (286).

3. According to Daniel Williams, the rape crime narrative *The Life and Dying Speech of Arthur* (1768) features American literature's first black rapist (200). In these early narratives, rape constitutes a crime against family order and social structures, whose reaffirmation required that "the rapist's life [be] presented as a pathetic progression from rebellion to execution" (196). Rape crime narratives thus focused on the rapist as uncontrollable outlaw, as ethnic, racial, or political "other" (204). Frequently he was a slave who, according to generic convention, repented "for the sum of his vicious life rather than for the rape" (199) and was executed less for the sexual violation than for disrupting social order (200). Criminal rape narratives thus did not serve "to denounce the crime of rape, but to warn masters and servants to abide by their prescribed roles" (215).

According to Kinney, Virginia court records document at least sixty rape convictions of black men between 1789 and 1833. In twenty-six of these cases whites testified that the woman consented, and defended the supposed aggressors on the grounds that they were involved with women of "worst fame" (qtd. in Kinney 15). The "ploy of crying rape," Kinney argues, was provoked partly by heavy legal penalties imposed on the white woman who bore a mulatto child. Some women accused their black lovers of rape to avoid being indentured. At the turn of the nineteenth century, then, interracial rape was still handled by the judicial system and not by lynch mobs (15). Adultery of white women (who had relations with blacks) might have led the husband to file divorce before the Civil War, while in postbellum times it provoked "homicidal fury" (18). The anonymously published *The Fanatic; or The Perils of Peter Pliant, the Poor Pedagogue* (1846), Kinney claims, introduced the black rapist—shunned thereafter until Dixon made explicit use of him—to American literature (46).

4. My brief excursus into the function and aesthetics of realism is based on Fluck's illuminating study *Inszenierte Wirklichkeit*.

5. Naturalism, by comparison, combines its reality effects with moral analyses—in fact, creates reality effects, as Stefan Brandt points out, by articulating dominant ideologies (106), thus retaining elements of romance and sentimental novel. A similar blend of generic qualities also characterizes African American turn-of-the-century texts—texts that take issue with dominant ideologies, though.

6. As they reintroduce the fallen woman, naturalism and realism pick up on late-eighteenth-century narratives of sexuality and danger. Instead of pinpointing the (economic) dangers of premarital sexuality, however, they explore a new range of female identity and renegotiate women's economic dependence and sexuality, as well as the institution of marriage, all of which had remained untouched in the domestic novel. Kate Chopin's *The Awakening*, for instance, toys with the topos of seduction and fall, the seducer being the liberated self personified by the tempting and dangerous sea. "The voice of the sea is seductive; never ceasing, whispering, clamoring, murmuring, inviting the soul to wander for a spell in abysses of solitude; to lose itself in mazes of inward contemplation" (25). At the same time, fallen women (such as Stephen Crane's Maggie, Wharton's Lily Bart, and Theodore Dreiser's Jennie Gerhardt), as well as emancipatory figures (such as Chopin's Edna Pontellier or Dreiser's Carrie), signify a substantial cultural shift by readdressing women's sexual vulnerability in novel ways.

7. Earlier studies see lynchings as either aberrations of democracy (Cutler, in 1905) or as legitimate responses to abhorrent crimes (Collins, in 1918). Cutler defends lynch law yet admits that its practice is "our country's national crime," "a criminal practice which is peculiar to the United States" (1); Collins, who traces the black man's "stronger sexual passions" to his being "but lately removed from the jungle" (58) and defines "the Negro criminal as a race" (70), argues, against evidence recorded by Ida B. Wells and Mary Church Terrell, that lynching was undertaken mostly in retaliation against rape. Wells had shown that lynching was legitimized, first, as a means to repress "race riots," second, as a reaction to black men's attempts to exercise their right to vote, and, only as a third rationale, by the "cry of 'rape,' " which mobilized racist gender ideologies (Carby, *Reconstructing* 112–13). Collins defended lynching on the basis that American civilization holds "certain personal rights . . . even more dear than life itself. . . . Therefore, the average Southern white man does not believe that the innocent rape victim of a Negro should be obliged to endure further humiliation incident upon her appearance in a court of law" (55–56). At the same time, lynching was legitimized as an effect of human passions. Page, for instance, who opposed lynching, still insisted that "the stern underlying principle of the people who commit these barbarities is one that has deep root in the basic passions of humanity: the determination to put an end to the ravishing of their women by an inferior race" (qtd. in Fredrickson 274–75). Even Douglass—carefully avoiding the term "rape" throughout his 1894 essay "Why Is the Negro Lynched?"—granted that "the crime alleged against the Negro is the most revolting which men can commit," "a crime that awakens the intensest abhorrence and tempts mankind to kill the criminal on first sight." Douglass insists, however, that the discursive deployment of black-on-white rape "is plainly enough not merely a charge against the individual culprit, as would be the case with an individual of any other race, but it is in large measure a charge constructively against the coloured people as such" (495). Trudier Harris reassesses lynching as the "communal rape" of black men (qtd. in Wiegman, "Anatomy" 465). For an acute critique of Harris's perspective and its disengagement of lynching from rape, see Schwenk. On (African American) women's antilynching campaigns, see Hall, *Revolt* (1979), and Thompson, *Ida B. Wells-Barnett* (1990). For a recent analysis of lynch justice in the United States, see *A Festival of Violence* by Tolnay and Beck, who see lynching as an "integral part of the Southern economy and class structure that emerged during the 1870s and 1880s to replace slavery" (244).

8. Whereas, for instance, Hoffman's findings of 1896 affirmed "the large proportion of negroes connected with crimes against women and chastity," deemed African Americans responsible for 40 percent of the cases of rape in the country at large (230), and maintained that "[t]he lynching of colored men is usually for rape" (229), it has long since been ascertained that "[o]f the known victims of lynch mobs in the period 1882–1946, only 23 percent were accused of rape or of attempted rape" (Hall, *Revolt* 149), and that the actual figures for black-on-white rape were in fact insignificant.

9. Statistics on prison populations and arrests served as scientific "proof" of this theory. In 1896, Hoffman argued that while "[d]uring slavery the negro committed fewer crimes than the white man" (217), the percentage of imprisoned African Americans, both men and women, as compared with their percentage in the population, documented an "excess of negro criminality" (218). Acknowledging that deviance depends upon "conditions of life," Hoffman compares "negro" criminality with that of

other "foreign elements" to substantiate this claim. Since the extent of crime among the various immigrant groups "is almost always, excepting for the Irish, in proportion to population" (224) while "the criminality of the negro exceeds that of any other race," he concludes that "education has utterly failed to raise the negro to a higher level of citizenship" (228).

10. These are the words of a participant in the Montgomery race conference of 1900 (qtd. in Hall, *Revolt* 145).

11. Lynchings were practiced long before Jim Crow legislation, yet it was the postbellum era that redefined lynching (and therefore rape) "as a racially coded practice" (Wiegman, "Anatomy" 454) that declined only after "segregation was firmly in place" (Hall, *Revolt* 30). Underlying this practice are struggles over economic resources; accordingly, after 1919 the number of lynchings decreased, to rise again during the Great Depression (Hall, *Revolt* 133).

12. Since the Reconstruction regime, as Michaels argues convincingly, was read as an attempt to colonize the South, the politics of white supremacy is fundamentally anti-imperialist. "[S]ubjected to the greatest humiliation of modern times: their slaves were put over them—," writes Page, for instance, the aristocratic Southerners "reconquered their section and preserved the civilization of the Anglo-Saxon" (1). Cf. Michaels, "Souls" and "Race into Culture." African American novels such as Hopkins's *Contending Forces* in turn present the black female body as "colonized by white male power and practices" (Carby, *Reconstructing* 143), thus propagating an anti-imperialism of their own kind.

13. Shakespeare depicts "Tarquin's progress toward Lucretia's bedroom" as an "intercourse" through "a series of doors" (Fineman 40).

14. According to Douglass, it is this "heart-rending cry of the white women and little white children" to which rape has frequently been (metonymically) reduced ("Why" 502).

15. In Hopkins's *Contending Forces* (1900), Mabelle Beaubean, after having been kidnapped, raped, and forced into prostitution, is rescued and placed in a convent. Likewise Faulkner's Temple Drake is adrift after having been subjected to kidnapping, rape, and prostitution. See my reading of *Sanctuary* in chapter 3. In Allen Tate's novel *The Fathers* (1938) the rape of spinsterly (white) Aunt Jane Anne by (black) Yellow Jim is a relief for her family, who feared that she might marry and desert her domestic duties. In this way the novel foregrounds the multiple functions that the "Southern rape complex" takes in the (re)construction of gender. For a recent discussion of this—more or less forgotten—text see Kreyling.

16. In this sense, racist rape narratives are comparable to the news of the Ripper murders of late-1880s London, which "have achieved the status of a modern myth of male violence against women." Of course, the Ripper murders actually occurred and did not involve rape. Moreover, their message concerned urban spaces: "the city," they insinuate, "is a dangerous place for women, when they transgress the narrow boundaries of home and hearth and dare to enter public space" (Walkowitz 544).

17. This works effectively, as Michaels shows in "The Souls of White Folk," in *The Great Gatsby* (1925). Fitzgerald's novel does not simply kiss the American dream goodbye but discriminates neatly between those worthy to retain it (like the Carraway clan) and those lowlifes who will never embrace it: the mourners on Queensboro Bridge with their "tragic eyes and short upper lips of south-eastern Europe," the "negroes"

chauffeured by a white man, yet rolling "the yolks of their eyeballs . . . in haughty rivalry" as they pass Gatsby's car (75), and Gatsby himself, "Mr Nobody from Nowhere" (136).

18. On the discourse of the "masculine primitive," cf. Brandt 300–313.

19. Hugh J. Dawson explores McTeague as a type styled according to predominant scientific conceptions of ethnicity (such as Cesare Lombroso's theories of criminal anthropology), as well as to the treatment of actual crimes (such as the San Francisco murder case of Patrick Collins, an Irish laborer, from which Norris's novel supposedly took its inspiration).

20. I take this term from Brandt (96), who adapts it from Christopher Wilson, *The Labor of Words* (1985), and offers an insightful overview of the conception of the genre.

21. I am echoing Terry Eagleton's deconstructive analysis of the male-female binarism here (133).

22. Such latent homoeroticism, as Patrick Schuckmann observes with regard to contemporary buddy movies, is frequently countered by a "female character who confirms the men's heterosexuality and serves as a token object of exchange" (675). In *McTeague*, Trina serves a similar function.

23. The following excursus into sexology is indebted to the work of Margaret Jackson.

24. Cf. Brandt's chapter "Die Axt im Hause: Hysterische Männlichkeit als Zeitphänomen" (39–92). In contrast to the Freudian model of hysteria, the author defines hysterical masculinity as a rhetoric overdetermined by an exaggerated anxiety over self-loss. This anxiety, Brandt claims, manifests a fear of emasculinization and is frequently expressed by a loss of control.

25. As historians emphasize, sexual exploitation of black women did not cease after emancipation and was on the rise during the "blood tides" against black men (Giddings 25).

26. Feminist critics have recently reassessed the significance that postbellum black women's fiction assigns to domesticity and marriage. Both Ann duCille and Claudia Tate underline that marriage and its rites "were a long-denied basic human right—signs of liberation and entitlement to both democracy and desire" for African Americans (duCille 14), that they constitute "the very sign of social progress for black Americans," "a central prerequisite for a civilized society" (Tate 117). Unlike Carby, who discriminates *Iola Leroy* from the formulaic sentimental novel for its preference of partnership over romance (*Reconstructing* 79 ff.), Tate insists that black female authors' "preoccup[ation] with middle-class propriety, civility, domesticity, and commodity consumption" (106) should not be read as "mimetic representation" but as "allegorical narratives in which black female subjectivity is the sole proprietary authority"—thus as romances. According to Tate, the narratives of Jacobs, Harper, Hopkins, and Harriet E. Wilson, among others, "construct, deconstruct, and reconstruct Victorian gender conventions in order to designate black female subjectivity as a most potent force in the advancement of the race" (107) and claim "the inalienable rights of black people as the consummated rights of families. . . . For nineteenth-century black women writers," Tate concludes, "marriage and family life were not the culminating points of a woman's life but the pinnacles of a people's new beginning" (126).

The fact that the focus on family and marriage corresponds to the attempt, on the part of women's organizations and activists, to re-create black women as sexually virtuous and to counterbalance the image of the "unchaste" black male—which Collins, for instance, "substantiates" with figures on illegitimate births (95)—throws a different light on this argument. As the discussion about "unwed mothers" (who are generally deemed to be African American) is ongoing, I wonder about its political thrust. After all, as long as we keep considering marriage "a prerequisite for a civil society," all other private arrangements keep their taint of "savagery." Likewise I think that the current tendency to reread African American women writers' and activists' appropriation of Victorian passionlessness as "both a rhetorical device and a political strategy," "as a vehicle for female empowerment" (duCille 31), is to a considerable degree inspired by the ideology of sexual correctness. Accordingly, I do hold that the question whether late-nineteenth-century novels are allegories of liberation or tales of containment cannot be decided, since neither liberation nor containment captures the complexities of anybody's culturally embedded subject position.

27. "Isn't it funny," Harper's figure Robert Johnson remarks, "how these white folks look down on coloured people, an' then mix up with them" (27).

28. Cf. Fredrickson 277.

29. Harper's perspective on female employment conflicted with the widespread belief that black women's need to work outside the home attests to a lack of racial progress and endangers black women's morality (Harley 164, 170). Therefore many black women preferred unpaid domestic work and voluntary community or church service. Still, about 60 percent of all African American women held wage-earning jobs (compared to 80 percent of black men).

30. Hopkins makes a similar point in *Contending Forces*, when she cites Emerson both on the title page and in the text: "The civility of no race can be perfect whilst another race is degraded."

31. Cf. also Hopkins 269. Harper's depictions of black men in turn capitalize on their devotion and loyalty to mothers and masters. "Fragile women and helpless children," Harper repeats the current argument against the criminalization of black males, "were left on the plantations while their natural protectors were at the front, and yet these bondsmen refrained from violence" (9). Collins supports this point yet takes it as proof of the "happy condition" during slavery (31–32).

32. Cf. my citation of Brook Thomas (58) in chapter 4.

33. Harper thus suggests that African American experience, as Ralph Ellison puts it in *Invisible Man*, is "never quite on the beat. Sometimes you're ahead and sometimes behind" (8).

34. Projecting Iola as missionary, Moses figure, saint, and angel (256–57), as a person "beyond" body, gender, and race who finds the times too "serious" to engage in earthly pleasures (243), Harper's project of synchronization turns out to be utopian. Likewise Mary Church Terrell concludes her address *The Progress of Colored Women* "look[ing] forward to a future large with promise and hope," thus locating the "justice" and "equal chance" she pleads for at a considerable temporal distance (15).

35. Accordingly, Harper's figure Tom Anderson wonders whether he could "ever again glory in his American citizenship, when any white man, no matter how coarse, cruel, or brutal, could buy or sell [Iola] for the basest purposes" (39). Thus while the (sexual) violation of black women endangers the black male subject, the resistance against their exchange across the color line boosts his sense of self. "I don't spose she

would think ob an ugly chap like me," Tom comments on his rescue mission, "but it does me good to know dat Marse Tom ain't got her" (42).

36. In Hopkins's *Contending Forces*, Will Smith calls this the "[i]rony of ironies! *The men who created the mulatto race, who recruit its ranks year after year by the very means which they invoked lynch law to suppress,* bewailing the sorrows of violated womanhood" (271).

37. Cf. Griggs's "Notes to the Third Edition" (298–99). In his "Notes for the Serious" the author legitimizes the use of gruesome detail with the impact of violent acts on black subjectivity: "they have entered into the thoughtlife of the Negroes, and their influence must be taken into account" (293).

38. Griggs could not yet foresee the real scope of Dixon's success. The sales of *The Leopard's Spots*, which turned Doubleday into a significant publishing house, were triggered substantially by Griffith's technically innovative film adaptation, *Birth of a Nation.* Cf. Rogin 190–235.

39. Cf. Sander L. Gilman, esp. 226.

40. Cf. Ickstadt, "*Portraits*" 21–22.

41. Accusing Lily of deceit, for instance, Trenor takes a female position: "Of course I know now what you wanted—it wasn't my beautiful eyes you were after—but I tell you what, Miss Lily, you've got to pay up for making me think so—" (165).

42. In her analysis of the mores of working-class sexuality, Kathy Peiss claims that owing to their limited financial means, New York City working-class "women offered sexual favors of varying degrees, ranging from flirtatious companionship to sexual intercourse, in exchange for men's treats" (159).

43. Lily's decline is highlighted, for instance, through associations with Gerty Farish that Wharton's novel works by way of structure and imagery: chapter 13, for instance, opens with Lily awakening from happy dreams (158); in chapter 14 Gerty Farish awakes "from dreams as happy as Lily's" (169).

44. This applies to constructions of black femininity as well. As Carby convincingly argues, black female reformers' attempts to protect African American migrants from city vices and prostitution tended to reinforce intraracial class divisions and to confirm the working-class status of migrant women ("Policing" 747).

45. Despite its melodramatic pitch the play is considered "a major event in the history of American drama" and "one of the most successful runs to date in American commercial theatre." Two years of performances were followed by a triumphant American road trip and a successful run in London in the fall of 1909 (Halpern 132, 116, 117–18). Cf. also Maurice F. Brown 220–23.

46. "I belong out yonder—," Ghent claims in the final scene, "beyond the Rockies, beyond—the Great Divide!" (164).

47. Moody himself categorized his text as " 'realism' of a rather grim and uncompromising type" (qtd. in Maurice F. Brown 217). According to Halpern, it dramatizes a "true contemporary story" (116).

48. Cf. Jed 9.

49. Cf. Dietze 167.

50. This scene, though, was deleted from *The Great Divide* (Maurice F. Brown 216).

51. Or as Brownmiller puts it, distinguishing Southern practices and Northern perspectives: "As Southern white men continued to round up black men, lynch them or try them in a courtroom and give them the maximum sentence for the holy purpose

of 'protecting their women,' Northern liberals looking at the ghastly pattern through an inverted prism saw the picture of a lying white woman crying rape-rape-rape" (258).

52. In fact, as Susan Jeffords suggests in a different context, the othering of rape simultaneously masks intraracial rape. In her analysis of *Opposing Force*—a 1986 movie screened on ABC about a mock Air Force prisoner-of-war camp—Jeffords argues that the othering of rape (in the context of war) and rape of women in the army (as part of the military "training") work hand in hand. Similar observations have been made with regard to the sexual violence imposed during the war in former Yugoslavia.

53. On the issue, cf. Awkward, "Representing Rape." Reading Tyson's conviction in the light of a history of disempowerment of black masculinity, rapper Queen Latifah and filmmaker Spike Lee, among many others, consider the Tyson trial the "rape of Mike Tyson" (105). Owing to the need, among blacks, to have inspiring black male heroes in circulation, Awkward writes, many hold that Desiree Washington should not even have reported the incident and should instead "endure her pain in order to serve the greater good of the race" (110). Tyson himself, by contrast, entertains a rather limited conception of rape. "I'm not guilty of this crime," he claimed; "there were no black eyes, no broken ribs. When I'm in the ring, I break their ribs; I break their jaws. To me that's hurting somebody" (qtd. in Awkward 106).

54. Paglia elaborates on this very order in her theoretical exposition to *Sexual Personae*, "Sex and Violence, or Nature and Art," as well as in her various essays on rape.

CHAPTER THREE
RAPE AND THE ARTIFICE OF REPRESENTATION: FOUR MODERNIST MODES

1. For a more detailed account of this reading of *Gatsby*, see Michaels, "Souls," and Sielke, "(Post-)Modernist or Misfits?"

2. Cf., for instance, Herring, *Djuna* 268–71.

3. The following account of the novel's narrative line is indebted to Stevenson's essays.

4. In chapter 8 Wendell carries on with six women of different ages; in chapter 10 he preaches the gospel of polygamy and bestiality, in Chaucerian style, and his sexual partners include animals. In chapter 39 he tells us that "[n]o man . . . can judge this world an [*sic*] he had risen from one bed only, for according to that bed will he arise, and a one-bed judge never made a lenient judge . . . polygamy is the only bed a man rolls out of, conditioned to meet the world, and in fettle for the midwife or the gravedigger" (167).

5. Wendell, who has a particular liking for Oscar Wilde (166), displays "a body like a girl's" (17), "mothers" his children (100–101), and announces that he "sport[s] a changing countenance. I am all things to all men, and all women's man" (164).

6. For a further discussion of mimicry as an interim strategy in the formation of female subjectivity, see Sielke, *Fashioning the Female Subject* 91–165.

7. Cf. Stevenson, "Ryder."

8. Cf. Fiedler, "Pop" 88.

9. For both Tanner and Roberts the frame of reference for *Sanctuary* is real sexual violence. Tanner's book *Intimate Violence*, the author confesses, "grew out of my own fears and frustration as a woman who felt . . . vulnerable to the threat of a violence that I could neither understand nor control." She considers her study of reading "a move

toward empowering myself and other readers with the ability to resist the pull of viola-tion" (ix). Her analyses of rape and torture thus focus on how novels construct their "own terms of readership." Ideal readers are what she calls "oppositional readers" who resist the text's (violent) politics and aesthetics (114). Cf. Tanner, *Intimate Violence* 1–16. Roberts goes so far as to associate Temple's assault "by the true politics of the South, ownership written on her flesh," with "the slogans and initials written on the body" of the victim of a 1987 gang rape on the campus of Florida State University in Tallahassee (26). To my mind, such alignments amount to misreading rape.

10. This focus on the gaze, of course, also translates cinematic technique into literary discourse, underlining the modernist preoccupation with the visual in general and the moving picture specifically. On the subject of Faulkner and film, see, for instance, Har-rington and Abadie.

11. Following the paradigm of rape and lynching, some critics privilege the figure of castration. "Faulkner's novel," writes Pettey, for instance, "works through series after series of symbolic castrations: Temple's rape, Narcissa's domination and frequent emas-culations of Horace, Temple's verbal and physical rapes against Popeye, Red's murder, the sacrificial death of Lee Godwin, and Popeye's almost suicidal death" (76).

12. According to Arnold and Trouard, the figure of Popeye was inspired by a Mem-phis criminal named Neale Karens (or Kerens) Pumphrey, nicknamed Popeye, who was said to be impotent, though he had relations with women and was accused of raping one with a bizarre object; born in 1904, he committed suicide in 1931. Faulkner's protagonist also evokes Popeye the sailor, introduced by Elzie Segar's comic strip *Thim-ble Theatre* in January 1929.

13. My excursus into psychic defense mechanisms is indebted to Mönth, "Einige bedeutende psychische Abwehrmechanismen," *Schrei nach Innen* 200–202.

14. Arnold and Trouard note that the expression "kissing your elbow" means that if you could actually do it, you could change your sex.

15. A similar movement occurs as Popeye tries to overpower Temple once again at Miss Reba's: as he lifts her bedclothes, uncovering her body, "[s]he lay motionless, her palms lifted, her flesh beneath the envelope of her loins cringing rearward in furious disintegration like frightened people in a crowd" (159).

16. Benbow, for instance, leaves his wife "[b]ecause she ate shrimp," which he had to get from the train station every Friday (17); Miss Reba's house is full of "discreet whispers of flesh stale and oft-assailed and impregnable" (144).

17. Temple and Popeye are connected in part by their clothes and hats worn aslant (Seed 84), as well as by their "doll-likeness." Popeye has "doll-like hands" (5); Ruby calls Temple a "doll-faced slut" (59). Artificial appearance thus underlines the con-structedness of both Southern womanhood and racialized rapist here. At the same time, Temple conceives of Popeye as black other ("Does that black man think he can tell me what to do?" [42]), as childlike and emasculated (" 'You're not even a man! ... You could not fool me but once, could you?"), with arms "frail, no larger than a child's, dead and hard and light as a stick" (231), a kind of matchstick man.

18. While "shrimp" is used as a derogatory term for femininity in *Sanctuary*, it is also a slang expression for a small and weak person (Arnold and Trouard 25).

19. This dynamic finds its repercussions in the real, e.g., in Eldridge Cleaver's "poli-tics" of rape as "an insurrectionary act" (14).

20. Bigger's modest command of language is foregrounded in situations of interracial contact and when he makes attempts at writing. Cf. Tanner, "Uncovering" 137 and 134–35; see also Barbara Johnson, "The Re(a)d and the Black."

21. Max repeats the narrator's interpretations of Bigger's crimes, conclusions borrowed from the narrative, "to which," as Tanner perceptively points out, "he as a character had no access" ("Uncovering" 144).

22. In *Beloved* Morrison likewise dramatizes the subjection of black men by enforced fellatio.

23. Cf. JanMohamed 101, 102, 108.

24. This discussion took place at the Literaturhaus in Berlin on May 7, 1993.

25. *The Street* was the first novel by a black woman writer that sold over one million copies (McKay vii).

26. For a review of the criticism, see Holladay 14.

27. Issues of miscegenation and interracial rape are central to Petry's second novel, *The Narrows* (1953). In many ways a more "free-floating" and imaginative book, *The Narrows* focuses on the affair between an unemployed young black man and a "stinkingly rich" white heiress, thus taking its clue from Wright's *Native Son*, yet also draws intensely upon Faulkner. Unlike Bigger, Link Williams is an educated, rhetorically skilled person integrated into what indeed qualifies as a black community; Camilo Sheffield, unlike Mary Dalton, is a married woman of independent spirits who persistently pursues Link and unsettles a New England community by crying rape after he calls it quits—which he does because he feels sexually and emotionally exploited, appropriated as a "black stud." Plotted by her family, the murder of Link provides the forbidden affair with the "appropriate" closure. Teasing out both a white woman's sexual desire at the racial border and the social and rhetorical framework in which such desire develops and withers, Petry illuminates what has been easily dismissed as the "ploy" of rape: representations of (interracial) female sexuality.

28. This emphasis on the cinematic and in particular Hitchcock's *Psycho*—Ellis's protagonist Patrick Bateman even makes reference to the famous shower-curtain scene (108)—attests to the post-modernist mode of Ellis's novel, which has predominantly been read as a realist text. Cf. also my discussion of Ellis in the afterword.

29. In Petry's novels movies function as distractions from the real and as a medium that foregrounds the rift between racially different realities. Lutie sends her son Bub to the movies, for instance, when he needs to be taken care of or provided with a particular treat. She herself visits the theater to "take her mind away from these fears that kept closing in on her," even though, preoccupied with a "technicolor world of bright lights and vast beautiful rooms"—the world of Park and Fifth Avenues that was not her own (412)—she finds that the pictures hardly ever "make sense" to her. Likewise in Petry's second novel, *The Narrows*, white Camilo Williams suggests on her third date with her black lover, Link, that they drive to New York to go to the cinema. Link, however, wonders "how [Camilo] could identify herself so completely with the action that took place in a movie. When he was eight, a movie could carry him"—as it carries Lutie's son Bub in *The Street*—"straight into another world but he'd seen a hell of a lot of different worlds since then, and he'd had far more at stake in all of them than he'd ever have in anything they cooked up in Hollywood" (141–42). Petry's novels thus acknowledge how the dream machine has cooked up paradigmatic representations.

30. My summary of *Blackmail* is indebted to Modleski, "Rape" 304–5.

31. This in fact corresponds to studies that compare the sociocultural context of African American and white American women's rape. "African American women," Gail Elizabeth Wyatt writes, "may seem more vulnerable to crime because they do not anticipate that they will be protected by traditional authorities and institutions. There is no historical basis for women of color to grow up with that assumption" (88).

32. At the same time, Petry's novel subtly likens Lutie to the figures she others, thus foregrounding how they serve to construct her own sense of self. While she despises Hedges, like Hedges she employs sexual denial as an "armor of self-sufficient strength" (Holladay 50). Like Min, Lutie is a domestic servant, and while they never interact, Min senses that Lutie's presence motivates Jones's change. Accordingly, in Jones's mind, the two women consistently bounce off each other, collaborating with Hedges as castrating forces. And as Lutie's sexual alienation feeds into her masculinization, Jones's oversexualization effects his feminization.

33. For a discussion of this essay, see Sielke, *Fashioning the Female Subject* 98.

34. Finding that a white man has literally "grabbed off what belonged to him," Smith, ready to kill his lover, Jubilee, repeatedly slams her against the wall, just as Hitchcock's movie portrays the shadows of Alice and Crewe fighting. And just like Alice, Jubilee "fool[s]" Smith, ducks and suddenly slashes a knife across his face. Rehabilitating Jubilee despite her sexual guilt, this scene, like *Blackmail*, ends not in manslaughter but in man's laughter: having wrested the knife away from Jubilee, Smith

> threw it on the floor and laughed.
> "You ain't worth cutting, baby," he said. "You ain't worth going to jail for. You ain't worth nothing." He laughed again. (270)

35. Likewise, Nell Painter insists that, in addition, historians of slavery have tended to deny black people's inner lives and psychic damages (131).

CHAPTER FOUR
VOICING SEXUAL VIOLENCE, REPOLITICIZING RAPE:
POST-MODERNIST NARRATIVES OF SEXUALITY AND POWER

1. Owing to its rough diction and detailed descriptions of violence and (homo)sexual acts, the novel was challenged by public prosecution and censored as obscene in November 1967. This decision was repealed in July 1968.

2. See also the sections "Janey Becomes a Woman" in Acker's *Blood and Guts in High School* (1978) and "Rape by the Father" in *Empire of the Senseless* 3–18, as well as "Rape by Dad" and "B's Dream about Being Raped" in *My Mother: Demonology*, 167–70.

3. After all, two black women—Rosa Parks and Lucy Autherine—became central figures in Alabama history as they challenged Jim Crow legislation and claimed their rights to physical as well as intellectual mobility. On November 30, 1955, Parks refused to give up her bus seat to a white passenger; on February 3, 1956, Autherine presented herself to register at the segregated University of Alabama. Similarly, as Higginbotham argues in her work on racial constructions of citizenship, it was African American women who challenged Jim Crow codes and legislation pertaining to transportation on trains and steamboats, for instance, thus pleading for their rights of mobility. (I

allude here to Higginbotham's presentation at the colloquium of the W.E.B. Du Bois Institute for Afro-American Research at Harvard University, November 5, 1997.)

4. Cf. Showalter, "Rethinking the Seventies."

5. I am not suggesting that these texts are unproblematic in their representation of female sexuality; especially when viewed from late-twentieth-century American perspectives, Wharton's celebration of an incestuous relationship and the overdetermination, in Chopin's text, of fulfilled female sexuality by religious imagery of sacrifice and ritual bespeak the ambivalences that characterize the issue. In fact, Chopin's and Wharton's texts highlight that even where women are imagined, by women, as sexually desired *and* desiring, the traditional opposition of male activity and female passivity remains intact when it comes to the sexual act.

6. On the issue, see Sielke, "Drawing the Line."

7. Himes himself published a two-volume autobiography, *The Quality of Hurt* (1972) and *The Life of Absurdity* (1973), was of middle-class background, spent a seven-year term in jail, and, like Wright and Baldwin, went to Paris in 1953. Cf. Skinner 25–27.

8. On the issue, cf. Sielke, "The Discourse of Liberation."

9. For illuminating discussions of the function and force of rape in *Beloved*, see Henderson and Barnett.

10. For "key examples of the accusations raised against Alice Walker and her book," see Hernton, *Sexual Mountain* 31. Tony Brown went so far as to read *The Color Purple* as the " 'most savage treatment of Black men since *Birth of a Nation*' " (qtd. in Hernton, *Sexual Mountain* 34).

11. Cf. Matt. 19:24: "It is easier for a camel to go through the eye of a needle than for a rich man to enter the kingdom of God!" See also Mark 10:25, Luke 18:25.

12. In his work on African American Muslims, Allan Austin stresses the number of educated Africans among the African American black population and takes issue with the dominant sense of a common African American experience—the passage from bondage to freedom—deployed by the slave narrative and echoed throughout an African American literature that adopts the conventions of black autobiography.

13. Hernton in fact subtitles his chapter on Walker "*The Color Purple* as Slave Narrative" (*Sexual Mountain* 1) and argues that Walker, "utiliz[ing] the slave narrative to reveal the enslavement that black men level against black women," makes "a radical leap forward" in the development of the tradition (6). Capitalizing on "black-on-black oppression," the novel, according to the critic, presents gender relations in terms of the hierarchies of masters and slaves.

14. Walker herself discusses issues of censorship and voice in her essay "Finding Celie's Voice."

15. On these issues, cf. Sielke. " 'Celebrating AIDS.' "

16. The same can be said for critical prose such as Audre Lorde's essay "The Uses of the Erotic: The Erotic as Power," *Sister Outsider* 53–59.

17. Whitman's poem "A Woman Waits for Me" comes to mind here; cf. Sielke "Gewalt gegen Frauen" 204–6.

18. Or Ellison's work, for that matter: in *Invisible Man* (1952), Jim Trueblood dreams of raping his daughter.

19. These are the words Hill used during the presentation of her book at the Boston Public Library, October 3, 1997.

20. Peter Lehman discusses rape-revenge as a prominent topos of 1970s and 1980s B movie cult classics such as *I Spit on Your Grave* (1978) and *Alley Cat* (1982). Produced predominantly by men for men, these movies place women in positions generally reserved for men (106), "make male characters victims and specularize their punishment for the pleasure of the male viewers" (107), and tend to eroticize female violence against male bodies. Here, rape-revenge is frequently triggered by gang rapes, often involving men "strongly coded as lower class" (108), thus, like Sam Peckinpah's *Straw Dogs*, "point[ing] to male homoerotic bonding" (107). Films such as *Thelma and Louise* (1991), by contrast, show women avenging themselves against their attackers without overtly eroticizing their actions.

21. Rape law reforms, instigated by the passage of new rape statutes in Michigan in 1974, addressed both the definition of the crime and court procedures. The Michigan law, upon which other states modeled their reform bills, included the following changes. It displaced the distinction between "simple" rape (penetration) and attempted rape by "a ladder of offenses, each of which is described as criminal sexual conduct" (Temkin 28; cf. also Tong 92 f.). New charges were applicable to a husband who sexually assaulted his wife when she was living apart from him and either party had filed for divorce or legal separation (Temkin 28). In court, the prosecution no longer had to establish the victim's resistance (Temkin 28; see also Tong 96 f.). Strict rules were instituted governing the use of the victim's prior sexual history as evidence (Tong 106 ff.). Only her sexual history with the defendant himself or regarding the origin of semen, pregnancy, or disease could be introduced (Temkin 28). The changes in subsequent reforms and other jurisdictions included making rape laws (as opposed to just sodomy laws) applicable to male victims as well (Tong 91, Bessmer 370), reform of rules requiring corroboration (Tong 104), and laws governing cautionary instructions given to juries (Tong 105 f.). In some jurisdictions, reforms assimilated rape laws to laws prohibiting assault (Tong 112 f.) and reduced the penalties for rape (Tong 114 f.). Cf. also D'Emilio and Freedman 314.

22. On the subject, see Jeffreys, who argues that the much heralded sexual freedom has in fact prolonged women's oppression.

23. My reference here is to the landmark text *Our Bodies, Our Selves: A Book by and for Women*, first published in 1971 by the Boston Women's Health Book Collective.

24. Accordingly, the 1970s controversies around the phenomenon of female rape fantasies have to be seen in the context of the contemporaneous feminist critique of the "Freudian mystique" (Donovan 105) and its notion of female masochism. Freud identified sadism and mastery with masculinity and masochism and submission with femininity because he located the fundamental gender difference in (male) activity versus (female) passivity (92). His beliefs were reinforced by Helen Deutsch's *The Psychology of Women* (1944), whose author takes masochism to be a key to female character and assigns fantasies about rape (and prostitution) a pivotal place in women's psyche (Haskell, "Rape Fantasy" 86, 94, and Shanor 81–82). Deutsch's claim that female libido and pain are interdependent has been refuted by Kinsey's studies on female sexuality as well as by Karen Horney. Horney did not doubt that women fantasize rape, but argued that such fantasies are a product of traditional female acculturation rather than a symptom of some essential aspect of femininity and female desire. Along with Horney, Wilhelm Reich furthermore assumed that rape fantasies function as a means to diminish women's guilt feelings about their sexual desires and practices (Shanor 83). Evi-

dently, such views not only reflect traditional assumptions about female sexuality; they also attest to the interdependent cultural construction of (female) sexuality and sexual violence.

25. For more examples, cf. 191, 198, 203, 255, 265, 275, 278, 280.

26. Cf. Shanor 90 ff.

27. *New York Times*, Sept. 7, 1974, 27.

28. For a more intricate discussion of Irigaray's sense of mimicry, see Sielke, *Fashioning the Female Subject* 95–96.

29. Meanwhile law interprets both "non-consensual active or passive anal penetration with male offender(s)" and "vaginal penetration with female offender(s)" as rape (Mullen 13).

30. On the issue, cf. Michael Warner.

31. Williams's article was occasioned by the release of a new print of *Deliverance* featured by *Warner's Elite Collection*.

32. Cf. section 5 of "Song of Myself."

33. Hooks has retained that position in her more recent work; see, for instance, her discussion of gangsta rap in *Outlaw Culture* 115–23.

34. Cf. Stoltenberg, "Other Men," in *Refusing* 187–98. Robert Bly, by contrast—whose best-selling *Iron John* (1990) represents the other pole of male writers' engagement with feminist views of masculinity, and who is out to redeem the "wild man"—tries to painstakingly distinguish healthy masculinity from "the destructive, macho personality type," to separate the "Wild Man" from "the savage man" (26).

35. On the issue, see Lowers, for instance.

AFTERWORD
CHALLENGING READINGS OF RAPE

1. For Tanner, *American Psycho* "is a forbidden book not because it invites us into forbidden territories but because, once there, it coopts our essential properties as readers, conspiring to appropriate even our right to resist" (*Intimate Violence* 112).

2. My own understanding of *American Psycho* is indebted to the insightful unpublished essays of Ammon and May.

3. Cf., in particular, MacKinnon's argument in *Only Words*.

4. Cf. Ferguson, "Pornography" 682.

5. Accordingly, it is not, as Tanner suggests, contradictory that Ellis, on the one hand, presents his novel as "a cultural analysis of '80s capitalism that uses violence *only as a metaphor*" while, on the other, tracing his depictions of rape and torture to testimonies of serial killers and public records of their violent acts (*Intimate Violence* 113). Such records are themselves refigurations of violence.

6. May perceptively depicts the various uses Ellis makes of the cinema. Most obvious is the synchronicity between the protagonist's daily routine and the TV timetable: Bateman's day begins with Patty Winters and winds down with David Letterman. Replete with stage directions pertaining to camera movement, cuts, and superimposition (4), the novel reads like a screenplay at times. Details are frequently registered from a distance, as if by way of camera movement. Repeatedly, the novels' scenes, including those of Bateman's bloody excesses, are illuminated by halogen lamps. Accordingly, the fictional space lacks depth; characters are flat. Action occurs mostly in private spaces such

as apartments, offices, restaurants, and bars. In public spaces, by contrast, Bateman appears to run amok and finds himself in good company: in addition to Ted Bundy and Ed Gein we meet with Norman Bates from Hitchcock's *Psycho*, which itself is the first of a whole series of movies dealing with serial killers. The novel mentions Tobe Hooper's *Texas Chain Saw Masssacre* (1974) and Brian De Palma's *Body Double*, which Bateman takes home from the video store more than thirty-seven times (Ellis 112). Preoccupied with porn movies such as *Inside Lydia's Ass* (97) and masturbation, he frequently misses appointments and dates.

7. I thank Susanne Rohr for this insight.

8. In conversation, MacKinnon insisted that Dworkin's *Mercy* (1990) would not please the porno-bum, while *American Psycho* would.

9. See, for instance, the *Spiegel* interview with Ellis and Michel Houellebecq, "Überall Bilder von perfektem Sex."

10. Cf. Robert von Rimscha, "Küssen mit sechs," *Tagesspiegel*, October 6, 1996, 25.

11. Cf. Sielke " 'Celebrating AIDS.' "

12. For a more comprehensive analysis of Walker's and Charles's work, see Sielke, " 'Images That Injure.' "

13. I allude here to Julien's talk on Tracy Muffet and Walker as well as his own early cinematic work, presented at the colloquium of the W.E.B. Du Bois Institute for Afro-American Research, Harvard University, March 11, 1998.

14. *Harvard Gazette*, March 19, 1998, 17.

15. The exhibition, entitled *Change the Joke and Slip the Yoke*, March 1998, was accompanied by a symposium on "the use of black stereotypes in contemporary visual practice." Among the speakers were Michael Ray Charles, Henry Louis Gates, Thelma Golden, Isaac Julien, and Carrie Mae Weems.

16. I thank Mary Ebbott for drawing my attention to this campaign, sending one of its tokens my way, and inspiring my conclusion.

17. In the spring of 1995 the rape hotline at Harvard University made students aware of the dangers lurking on the streets surrounding Harvard Square and of the hotline's own services with a flyer that read: "I am angry I cannot walk alone at night."

Works Cited and Consulted

PRIMARY TEXTS

Acker, Kathy. *Blood and Guts in High School.* New York: Grove, 1978.

———. *Empire of the Senseless.* New York: Grove, 1988.

———. *In Memoriam to Identity.* New York: Pantheon, 1990.

———. *My Mother: Demonology.* New York: Grove, 1993.

Angelou, Maya. *I Know Why the Caged Bird Sings.* New York: Bantam, 1970.

Atwood, Margaret. "Rape Fantasies." *Dancing Girls and Other Stories.* Toronto: McClelland and Stewart, 1977. 101–10.

Barnes, Djuna. *Ryder.* New York: St. Martin's, 1979.

Brown, William Hill. "The Power of Sympathy." 1789. Ed. William S. Osborne. New Haven: Southern Connecticut College & UP, 1970. 27–129.

Brown, William Wells. "Clotelle: A Tale of the Southern States." 1853. *Violence in the Black Imagination: Essays and Documents.* Ed. Ronald T. Takaki. New York: Oxford UP, 1993. 231–340.

Califia, Pat. *Macho Sluts.* 1988. Boston: Alyson, 1989.

———. "Slipping." *Discontents: New Queer Writers.* Ed. Dennis Cooper. New York: Amethyst Press, 1992.

Carver, Raymond. *What We Talk about When We Talk about Love: Stories.* New York: Knopf, 1981.

Charles, Michael Ray. *Michael Ray Charles: An American Artist's Work.* Houston: The Art Museum of the University of Houston, 1997.

Chopin, Kate. *The Awakening.* 1899. New York: Avon, 1972.

Crane, Stephen. *Maggie: A Girl of the Streets.* 1893. Ed. Thomas A. Gullason. New York: Norton, 1979.

Dickey, James. *Deliverance.* New York: Laurel, 1970.

Dickinson, Emily. *The Poems of Emily Dickinson.* Ed. Thomas H. Johnson. 3 vols. Cambridge: Harvard UP, 1979.

Dixon, Thomas. *The Clansman: An Historical Romance of the Ku Klux Klan.* 1905. Lexington: UP of Kentucky, 1970.

———. *The Leopard's Spots: A Romance of the White Man's Burden, 1865–1900.* New York: Doubleday, 1902.

Douglass, Frederick. "The Heroic Slave." 1853. *Violence in the Black Imagination: Essays and Documents.* Ed. Ronald T. Takaki. New York: Oxford UP, 1993. 37–77.

———. *Narrative of the Life of Frederick Douglass, an American Slave. Written by Himself.* 1845. Harmondsworth: Penguin, 1986.

Dreiser, Theodore. "Nigger Jeff." *Free and Other Stories.* New York: Boni and Liveright, 1918. 76–111.

Dworkin, Andrea. *Mercy.* 1990. New York: Four Walls Eight Windows, 1991.

Eliot, T. S. *Collected Poems, 1909–1962.* New York: Harcourt, 1963.

Ellis, Bret Easton. *American Psycho.* New York: Vintage, 1991.

Ellison, Ralph. *Invisible Man.* 1952. New York: Vintage, 1972.

Faulkner, William. "Dry September." *Collected Stories of William Faulkner.* New York: Random, 1946. 169–83.

——. *Light in August.* 1932. New York: Vintage, 1990.

——. *Sanctuary.* 1931. New York: Vintage, 1985.

——. *Sanctuary: The Original Text.* New York: Random, 1981.

Fitzgerald, Scott F. *The Great Gatsby.* 1925. Harmondsworth: Penguin, 1979.

Foster, Hannah. "The Coquette." 1797. Ed. William S. Osborne. New Haven: Southern Connecticut College & UP, 1970. 131–272.

Gates, Henry Louis, Jr., ed. *The Classic Slave Narratives.* New York: Penguin, 1987.

Gilman, Charlotte Perkins. *Herland.* 1915. New York: Pantheon, 1978.

Gould, Lois. *A Sea Change.* 1976. New York: Avon, 1977.

Griggs, Sutton E. *The Hindered Hand: or, The Reign of the Repressionist.* 1905. New York: AMS Press, 1969.

Harper, Frances E. W. *A Brighter Coming Day: A Frances Ellen Watkins Harper Reader.* Ed. Frances Smith Foster. New York: Feminist, 1990.

——*Iola Leroy or Shadows Uplifted.* New York: Oxford UP, 1988.

Himes, Chester. 1963. *A Case of Rape.* Washington, D.C.: Howard UP, 1984.

——. *The Collected Stories of Chester Himes.* New York: Thunder Mouth, 1990.

Hopkins, Pauline E. *Contending Forces: A Romance Illustrative of Negro Life North and South.* 1900. New York: Oxford UP, 1991.

Hurston, Zora Neale. *Their Eyes Were Watching God.* 1937. New York: Harper, 1990.

Jacobs, Harriet A. *Incidents in the Life of a Slave Girl.* 1861. Ed. Jean Fagan Yellin. Cambridge: Harvard UP, 1987.

James, Henry. *The Wings of the Dove.* 1902. New York: Signet, 1964.

Jones, Gayl. *Corregidora.* 1975. Boston: Beacon, 1986.

Jong, Erica. *Fear of Flying.* 1973. New York: Signet, 1988.

Keckley, Elizabeth. *Behind the Scenes. Or, Thirty Years as a Slave, and Four Years in the White House.* New York: Oxford UP, 1988.

Larsen, Nella. *Quicksand* and *Passing.* Ed. Deborah E. McDowell. New Brunswick: Rutgers UP, 1986.

Lee, Harper. *To Kill a Mockingbird.* 1960. London: Heinemann, 1971.

Masters, Edgar Lee. *Spoon River Anthology.* 1914. New York: Collier, 1962.

Mattison, Hiram. *Louisa Picquet, the Octoroon: A Tale of Southern Slave Life.* New York, 1861.

McKay, Claude. *Selected Poems.* New York: Bookman, 1953.

Michaels, George. *Older.* Virgin, 1996.

Mitchell, Margaret. *Gone with the Wind.* 1936. New York: Avon, 1973.

Moody, William Vaughn. 1906. *A Sabine Woman.* Republished as *The Great Divide.* New York: Macmillan, 1909.

Morrison, Toni. *Beloved.* 1987. New York: Plume, 1988.

——. *The Bluest Eye.* 1970. New York: Simon, 1972.

Naylor, Gloria. *The Women of Brewster Place.* 1982. Harmondsworth: Penguin, 1983.

Norris Frank. *McTeague.* 1899. New York: Signet, 1964.

Oates, Joyce Carol. *Where Are You Going, Where Have You Been? Selected Early Stories.* Princeton: Ontario Review, 1993.

——. *Zombie.* New York: Plume, 1995.

Page, Thomas Nelson. 1898. *Red Rock: A Chronical of Reconstruction.* Albany: N. C. U. P., 1991.

Petry, Ann. *The Narrows.* 1953. Boston: Beacon, 1988.

———. *The Street.* 1946. Boston: Houghton, 1974.

Rechy, John. *City of Night.* 1963. New York: Triangle, 1984.

Reed, Ishmael. *Reckless Eyeballing.* 1986. New York: Atheneum, 1988.

Rich, Adrienne. *Diving into the Wreck: Poems 1971–1972.* New York: Norton, 1973.

———. *The Dream of a Common Language: Poems 1974–1977.* New York: Norton, 1978.

———. *Snapshots of a Daughter-in-Law: Poems 1954–62.* New York: Norton, 1963.

Richardson, Samuel. *Clarissa.* 1747–48. Boston: Houghton Mifflin, 1962.

———. *Pamela.* 1740. New York: Norton, 1958.

Rowson, Susanna. *Charlotte Temple* and *Lucy Temple.* Ed. Ann Douglas. New York: Penguin, 1991.

Selby, Hubert. *Last Exit to Brooklyn.* 1957. London: Calder and Boyars, 1975.

Sinclair, Upton. *The Jungle.* 1906. New York: Vanguard, 1927.

———. *The Lost First Edition of Upton Sinclair's "The Jungle."* Ed. Gene DeGruson. Memphis: Peachtree, 1988.

Stein, Gertrude. *Selected Writings of Gertrude Stein.* Ed. Carl Van Vechten. New York: Vintage, 1972.

Tate, Allen. *The Fathers.* 1938. Chicago: Swallow, 1970.

Toomer, Jean. *Cane.* 1923. New York: Liveright, 1975.

Walker, Alice. *The Color Purple.* San Diego: Harcourt, 1982.

———. *You Can't Keep a Good Woman Down.* 1971. San Diego: Harcourt, 1981.

Walker, Kara. *Kara Walker.* Chicago: The Renaissance Society at the University of Chicago, 1997.

Wharton, Edith. *The House of Mirth.* 1905. Harmondsworth: Penguin, 1979.

Whitman, Walt. *Leaves of Grass.* Ed. Harold W. Blodgett and Sculley Bradley. New York: Norton, 1965.

Wideman, John Edgar. *The Lynchers.* 1973. New York: Holt, 1986.

Wright, Richard. *Native Son.* 1940. New York: Harper, 1987.

SECONDARY SOURCES

Ackley, Katherine A., ed. *Women and Violence in Literature.* New York: Garland, 1990.

Adisa, Opal Palmer. "Undeclared War: African-American Women Writers Explicating Rape." *Women's Studies International Forum* 15.3 (June 1992): 363–74.

American Slavery as It Is: Testimony of a Thousand Witnesses. New York: American Anti-Slavery Society, 1939.

Ammon, Markus. "Bret Easton Ellis' *American Psycho*: Gegen die Macht des Diskurses?" Unpublished essay, 1994.

Andolsen, Barbara Hilkert. *"Daughters of Jefferson, Daughters of Bootblacks": Racism and American Feminism.* Macon: Mercer UP, 1986.

Andrews, William L. "The Changing Moral Discourse of Nineteenth-Century African American Women's Autobiography: Harriet Jacobs and Elizabeth Keckley." *De/Colonizing the Subject: The Politics of Gender in Women's Autobiography.* Ed. Sidonie Smith and Julia Watson. Minneapolis: U of Minnesota P, 1992. 225–41.

Andrews, William L. "The Representation of Slavery and the Rise of Afro-American Realism 1865–1920." *Slavery and the Literary Imagination*. Ed. Deborah E. McDowell and Arnold Rampersad. Baltimore: Johns Hopkins UP, 1989. 62–80.

———. *To Tell a Free Story*. Urbana: U of Illinois P, 1986.

Armstrong, Nancy. "The American Origin of the English Novel." *American Literary History* 4.3 (1992): 386–410.

———. *Desire and Domestic Fiction: A Political History of the Novel*. New York: Oxford UP, 1987.

Armstrong, Nancy, and Leonard Tennenhouse, eds. *The Ideology of Conduct: Essays on Literature and the History of Sexuality*. New York: Methuen, 1987.

———. *The Violence of Representation: Literature and the History of Violence*. London: Routledge, 1989.

Arnold, Edwin T., and Dawn Trouard. *Reading Faulkner: Sanctuary*. Jackson: UP of Mississippi, 1996.

Arnold, Marybeth Hamilton. " 'The Life of a Citizen in the Hands of a Woman': Sexual Assault in New York City, 1790 to 1820." *Passion and Power: Sexuality in History*. Ed. Kathy Peiss and Christina Simmons. Philadelphia: Temple UP, 1989. 35–56.

Austin, Allan D. *African Muslims in Antebellum America: A Sourcebook*. New York: Garland, 1984.

Awkward, Michael. "A Black Man's Place in Black Feminist Criticism." *Negotiating Difference: Race, Gender, and the Politics of Positionality*. Chicago: U of Chicago P, 1995. 43–57.

———. *Negotiating Difference: Race, Gender, and the Politics of Positionality*. Chicago: U of Chicago P, 1995.

———. "Representing Rape: On Spike, Iron Mike, and the 'Desire Dynamic.' " *Negotiating Difference: Race, Gender, and the Politics of Positionality*. Chicago: U of Chicago P, 1995. 95–135.

Baker, Houston A. "Modernism and the Harlem Renaissance." *American Quarterly* 39.1 (1987): 84–97.

———. "On Knowing Our Place." *Richard Wright: Perspectives Past and Present*. Ed. Henry Louis Gates, Jr., and Kwame A. Appiah. New York: Amistad, 1993. 200–225.

Bal, Mieke. *Death and Dissymmetry: The Politics of Coherence in the Book of Judges*. Chicago: U of Chicago P, 1988.

———. "The Rape of Narrative and the Narrative of Rape: Speech Acts and Body Languages in Judges." *Literature and the Body: Essays on Populations and Persons*. Ed. Elaine Scarry. Baltimore: Johns Hopkins UP, 1988. 1–32.

———. "Reading with the Other Art." *Theory between the Disciplines: Authority/Vision/Politics*. Ed. Martin Kreiswirth and Mark A. Cheetham. Ann Arbor: U of Michigan P, 1990. 135–51.

Barnett, Pamela E. "Figurations of Rape and the Supernatural in *Beloved*." *PMLA* 112.3 (May 1997): 418–27.

Baron, Larry, and Murray A. Straus. *Four Theories of Rape in American Society: A State-Level Analysis*. New Haven: Yale UP, 1989.

Baudrillard, Jean. *Seduction*. New York: St. Martin's, 1990.

Baym, Nina. *Novels, Readers, and Reviewers: Responses to Fiction in Antebellum America*. Ithaca: Cornell UP, 1984.

———. *Women's Fiction: A Guide to Novels by and about Women in America 1820–1870.* Ithaca: Cornell UP, 1992.

Bederman, Gail. *Manhood and Civilization: A Cultural History of Gender and Race in the United States, 1880–1917.* Chicago: U of Chicago P, 1995.

Beneke, Timothy. *Men on Rape.* New York: St. Martin's P, 1982.

Benjamin, Jessica. "Master and Slave." *Powers of Desire: The Politics of Sexuality.* Ed. Ann Snitow, Christine Stansell, and Sharon Thompson. New York: Monthly Review, 1983. 280–99.

Benjamin, Walter. *Illuminations.* Ed. Hannah Ahrendt. New York: Schocken, 1969.

Berlant, Lauren. "The Queen of America Goes to Washington City: Harriet Jacobs, Frances Harper, Anita Hill." *American Literature* 65.3 (Sept. 1993): 549–74.

———. "Race, Gender, and Nation in *The Color Purple.*" *Critical Inquiry* 14 (June 1983): 831–59.

Bernstein, Susan David. *Confessional Subjects: Revelations of Gender and Power in Victorian Literature and Culture.* Chapel Hill: U of North Carolina P, 1997.

Bessmer, Sue. *The Laws of Rape.* New York: Praeger, 1984.

Bhimji, Zarina, et al., eds. *No Place (Like Home).* Minneapolis: Walker Art Center, 1997.

Bluestein, Gene. "Faulkner and Miscegenation." *Arizona Quarterly* 43.2 (1987): 151–62.

Bly, Robert. *Iron John: A Book about Man.* New York: Vintage, 1992.

Boesenberg, Eva. "Censoring the Body: Rape and Voice in Alice Walker's *The Color Purple.*" *Democracy and the Arts in the United States.* Ed. Alfred Hornung, Reinhard R. Doerries, and Gerhard Hoffmann. Munich: Fink, 1996. 301–9.

Bogle, Donald. *Toms, Coons, Mulattoes, Mammies, and Bucks: An Interpretive History of Blacks in American Films.* New York: Viking, 1973.

Bonilla, Margaret D. "Cultural Assault: What Feminists Are Doing to Rape Ought to Be a Crime." *Policy Review* 66 (Sept. 1993): 22–29.

Boone, Joseph A. "Male Independence and the American Quest Genre: Hidden Sexual Politics in the All-Male Worlds of Melville, Twain and London." *Feminisms: An Anthology of Literary Theory and Criticism.* Ed. Robyn R. Warhol. New Brunswick: Rutgers UP, 1991. 961–97.

Bordo, Susan. "Reading the Male Body." *The Male Body: Features, Destiny, Exposures.* Ed. Laurence Goldstein. Ann Arbor: U of Michigan P. 265–306.

Boyd, Jennifer. *Frank Norris: Spatial Form and Narrative Time.* New York: Lang, 1993.

Boyd, Melba Joyce. *Discarded Legacy: Politics and Poetics in the Life of Frances E. W. Harper, 1825–1911.* Detroit: Wayne State UP, 1994.

Brandt, Stefan. *Männerblicke: Zur Konstruktion von "Männlichkeit" in der Literatur und Kultur der amerikanischen Jahrhundertwende.* Stuttgart: Metzler, 1997.

Brauerholz, Elizabeth, and Mary A. Kowalewski. *Sexual Coercion: A Sourcebook on Its Nature, Causes, and Prevention.* Lexington: Lexington Books, 1991.

Braxton, Joanne M. *Black Women Writing Autobiography: A Tradition within a Tradition.* Philadelphia: Temple UP, 1989.

Brodie, James Michael. "GWU Rape Hoax." *Black Issues on Higher Education* 7.22 (Jan. 3, 1991): 29.

Bronfen, Elisabeth. "Weiblichkeit und Repräsentation—aus der Perspektive von Ästhetik, Semiotik und Psychoanalyse." *Genus: Zur Geschlechterdifferenz in den Kultur-*

wissenschaften. Ed. Hadumod Bußmann and Renate Hof. Stuttgart: Kröner, 1995. 408–46.

Brooks, Peter. *Body Work: Objects of Desire in Modern Narrative.* Cambridge: Harvard UP, 1993.

Brown, Maurice F. *Estranging Dawn: The Life and Works of William Vaughn Moody.* Carbondale: Southern Illinois UP, 1973.

Brownmiller, Susan. *Against Our Will: Men, Women, and Rape.* New York: Simon, 1975.

Buchwald, Emilie, Pamela R. Fletcher, and Martha Roth. *Transforming a Rape Culture.* Minneapolis: Milkweed Editions, 1993.

Butler, Judith. *Gender Trouble: Feminism and the Subversion of Identity.* New York: Routledge, 1990.

Butler, Judith, and Joan L. Scott, eds. *Feminists Theorize the Political.* New York: Routledge, 1992.

Butler, Robert James. "The Function of Violence in Richard Wright's *Native Son.*" *Black American Literature Forum* 20.1–2 (Mar. 1986): 9–25.

Butler-Evans, Elliott. *Race, Gender, and Desire: Narrative Strategies in the Fiction of Toni Cade Bambara, Toni Morrison, and Alice Walker.* Philadelphia: Temple UP, 1989.

Carby, Hazel. " 'It Jus Be's Dat Way Sometime': The Sexual Politics of Women's Blues." *Unequal Sisters: A Multicultural Reader in U.S. Women's History.* Ed. Ellen Carol Du-Bois and Vicki L. Ruiz. New York: Routledge, 1990. 238–49.

———. " 'On the Threshold of Women's Era': Lynching, Empire, and Sexuality in Black Feminist Theory." *Critical Inquiry* 12.1 (1985): 262–77.

———. "Policing the Black Woman's Body in an Urban Context." *Critical Inquiry* 18.4 (1992): 738–55.

———. *Reconstructing Womanhood: The Emergence of the Afro-American Woman Novelist.* New York: Oxford UP, 1987.

Carter, Dan T. *Scottsboro: A Tragedy of the American South.* London: Oxford UP, 1969.

Cash, W. J. *The Mind of the South.* 1941. New York: Vintage, 1991.

Cherniavsky, Eva. "Charlotte Temple's Remains." *Discovering Difference: Contemporary Essays in American Culture.* Ed. Christoph K. Lohmann. Bloomington: Indiana UP, 1993. 35–47.

Child, Lydia Maria Francis. *An Appeal in Favor of That Class of Americans Called Africans.* New York: John S. Taylor, 1836.

Christian, Barbara. *Black Feminist Criticism: Perspectives on Black Women Writers.* New York: Pergamon, 1985.

———. "But What Do We Think We're Doing Anyway: The State of Black Feminist Criticism(s) or My Version of a Little Bit of History." *Changing Our Own Words.* Ed. Cheryl A. Wall. New Brunswick: Rutgers UP, 1989. 58–74.

Clark, Anna. *Women's Silence, Men's Violence: Sexual Assault in England 1770–1845.* London: Pandora, 1987.

Clark, VéVé A., Ruth-Ellen B. Joeres, and Madelon Sprengnether, eds. *Revising the Word and the World: Essays in Feminist Literary Criticism.* Chicago: U of Chicago P, 1993.

Cleaver, Eldridge. *Soul on Ice.* New York: Delta, 1968.

Clinton, Catherine. *The Plantation Mistress: Woman's World in the Old South.* New York: Pantheon, 1982.

Collins, Winfield Hazlitt. *The Truth about Lynching and the Negro in the South: In Which the Author Pleads That the South Be Made Safe for the White Race.* New York: Neale, 1918.

Connell, Noreen, and Cassandra Wilson, eds. *Rape: The First Sourcebook for Women.* New York: New American Library, 1974.

Cooper, Anna J. *A Voice from the South, by a Black Woman of the South.* New York: Negro UP, 1969.

Crichton, Sarah. "Sexual Correctness: Has It Gone Too Far?" *Newsweek* 122 (1995): 52–58.

Cutler, James Elbert. *Lynching: An Investigation into the History of Lynching in the U.S.* 1905. New York: Negro UP, 1969.

Dalton, Anne B. " 'This is Obscene': Female Voyeurism, Sexual Abuse, and Maternal Power in *The Dove.*" *Review of Contemporary Fiction* 13.3 (Sept. 1993): 117–39.

Davidson, Cathy N. *Revolution and the Word: The Rise of the Novel in America.* New York: Oxford UP, 1986.

Davis, Angela. "The Dialectics of Rape." *Ms.*, June 1975, 74.

———. "Rape, Racism, and the Myth of the Black Rapist." *Women, Race and Class.* New York: Random, 1983. 172–201.

Davis, Cynthia J. "Speaking the Body's Pain: Harriet Wilson's Our Nig." *African American Review* 27.3 (Sept. 1993): 391–404.

Dawson, Hugh J. "McTeague as Ethnic Stereotype." *American Literary Realism* 20.1 (1987): 34–44.

Degler, Carl H. "What Ought to Be and What Was: Women's Sexuality in the Nineteenth Century." *American Historical Review* 79.5 (1974): 1467–90.

Delacorte, Frederique, and Felice Newman, eds. *Fight Back: Feminist Resistance to Male Violence.* Minneapolis: Cleis, 1981.

D'Emilio, John, and Estelle B. Freedman. *Intimate Matters: A History of Sexuality in America.* New York: Harper, 1988.

Denfield, Rene. *The New Victorians: A Young Woman's Challenge to the Old Order.* New York: Warner, 1995.

DeSalvo, Louise A. " 'To Make Her Mutton at Sixteen': Rape, Incest, and Child Abuse in *The Antiphon.*" *Silence and Power: A Reevaluation of Djuna Barnes.* Ed. Mary Lynn Broe. Carbondale: Southern Illinois UP, 1991. 300–315.

Didion, Joan. "Sentimental Journeys." *After Henry.* New York: Simon, 1992. 253–319.

Diedrich, Maria. " 'My Love is Black as Yours is Fair': Premarital Love and Sexuality in the Antebellum Slave Narrative." *Phylon* 47.3 (Sept. 1986): 238–47.

Dietze, Gabriele. *Hardboiled Woman: Geschlechterkrieg im amerikanischen Kriminalroman.* Hamburg: Europäische Verlagsanstalt, 1997.

di Leonardo, Micaela. "White Lies, Black Myths: Rape, Race, and the Black 'Underclass.' " *Voice*, Sept. 22, 1992, 29–36.

Donovan, Josephine. *Feminist Theory: The Intellectual Traditions of American Feminism.* New York: Ungar, 1987.

Douglas, Ann. Introduction. *Charlotte Temple* and *Lucy Temple.* By Susanna Rowson. New York: Penguin, 1991. VII–XLVI.

Douglass, Frederick. "Why Is the Negro Lynched?" *The Life and Writings of Frederick Douglass.* Ed. Philip S. Foner. New York: International Publishers, 1975. 4:491–523.

Dripps, Donald A. "Beyond Rape: An Essay on the Difference between the Presence of Force and the Absence of Consent." *Columbia Law Review* 92.7 (Nov. 1992): 1780–1809.

———. "More on Distinguishing Sex, Sexual Expropriation, and Sexual Assault: A Reply to Professor West." *Columbia Law Review* 93.6 (1993): 1460–72.

duCille, Ann. *The Coupling Convention: Sex, Text, and Tradition in Black Women's Fiction.* New York: Oxford UP, 1993.

Duffey, Eliza. *What Women Should Know: A Woman's Book about Women.* 1873. New York: Arno, 1974.

Dworkin, Andrea. *Intercourse.* New York: Free Press, 1987.

Eagleton, Terry. *Literary Theory: An Introduction.* Minneapolis: U of Minnesota P, 1983.

Ehrenreich, Barbara. *For Her Own Good: 150 Years of the Experts' Advice to Women.* New York: Anchor, 1979.

Eisenstein, Hester. *Contemporary Feminist Thought.* London: Allen and Unwin, 1984.

Ervin, Hazel Arnett. *Ann Petry: A Bio-Bibliography.* New York: G. K. Hall, 1993.

Estrich, Susan. *Real Rape.* Cambridge: Harvard UP, 1987.

Faludi, Susan. *Backlash: The Undeclared War against Women.* London: Chatto, 1992.

———. "Whose Hype?" *Newsweek* 122 (1925): 61.

Fanon, Frantz. *Black Skin, White Masks.* New York: Grove, 1967.

Ferguson, Frances. "Pornography: The Theory." *Critical Inquiry* 21.1 (1995): 670–95.

———. "Rape and the Rise of the Novel." *Representations* 20 (Sept. 1987): 88–112.

Fiedler, Leslie. *Love and Death in the American Novel.* 1966. New York: Anchor, 1992.

———. "Pop Goes the Faulkner: In Quest of *Sanctuary.*" *Faulkner and Popular Culture: Faulkner and Yoknapatawpha, 1988.* Ed. Doreen Fowler and Ann J. Abadie. Jackson: UP of Mississippi, 1990. 75–92.

Fineman, Joel. "Shakespeare's Will: The Temporality of Rape." *Representations* 20 (Sept. 1987): 25–76.

Fitzpatrick, Tara. "The Figure of Captivity: The Cultural Work of the Puritan Captivity Narrative." *American Literary History* 3.1 (1991): 1–26.

Fluck, Winfried. *Inszenierte Wirklichkeit: Der amerikanische Realismus 1865–1900.* Munich: Fink, 1992.

———. *Das kulturelle Imaginäre: Eine Funktionsgeschichte des amerikanischen Romans 1790–1900.* Frankfurt: Suhrkamp, 1997.

———. "The Masculinization of American Realism." *Amerikastudien/American Studies* 36.1 (1991): 71–76.

Foner, Eric. *Politics and Ideology in the Age of Civil War.* Oxford: Oxford UP, 1980.

———. *Reconstruction: America's Unfinished Revolution, 1863–1877.* New York: Harper, 1988.

Forrester, John. "Rape, Seduction, and Psychoanalysis." *Rape.* Ed. Sylvana Tomaselli and Roy Porter. Oxford: Basil Blackwell, 1986. 57–83.

Foster, Frances Smith. Introduction. *Iola Leroy, or Shadows Uplifted.* By Frances E. W. Harper. New York: Oxford UP, 1988. xxii–xxxix.

Foucault, Michel. *The History of Sexuality. Volume 1: An Introduction.* New York: Vintage, 1980.

Fout, John C., and Maura Shaw Tantillo, eds. *American Sexual Politics: Sex, Gender, and Race since the Civil War.* Chicago: U of Chicago P, 1993.

France, Alan W. "Misogyny and Appropriation in Wright's *Native Son.*" *Modern Fiction Studies* 34.3 (Aug. 1988): 413–23.

Franchot, Jenny. "The Punishment of Esther." *Frederick Douglass: New Literary and Historical Essays.* Ed. Eric J. Sundquist. New York: Cambridge UP, 1990. 141–65.

Fredrickson, George M. *The Black Image in the White Mind.* New York: Harper, 1971.

Freedman, Estelle B. " 'Uncontrolled Desires': The Response to the Sexual Psychopath, 1920–1960." *Passion and Power: Sexuality and History.* Ed. Kathy Peiss and Christina Simmons. Philadelphia: Temple UP, 1989. 199–225.

Freud, Sigmund. *Introductory Lectures on Psychoanalysis.* Ed. James Strachey. New York: Norton, 1977.

Friedman, Lawrence Jacob. *The White Savage: Racial Fantasies in the Postbellum South.* Englewood Cliffs: Prentice-Hall, 1970.

Froula, Christine. "The Daughter's Seduction: Sexual Violence and Literary History." *Signs* 11.4 (1986): 621–44.

Gaitskill, Mary. "On Not Being a Victim." *Debating Sexual Correctness: Pornography, Sexual Harassment, Date Rape, and the Politics of Sexual Equality.* Ed. Adele M. Stan. New York: Delta, 1995. 259–72.

Gates, Henry Louis, Jr. *The Signifying Monkey: A Theory of African American Literary Criticism.* New York: Oxford UP, 1988.

————. "The Trope of a New Negro and the Reconstruction of the Image of the Black." *Representations* 24 (1988): 129–55.

————, ed. *Reading Black, Reading Feminist: A Critical Anthology.* New York: Meridian, 1990.

Gehrke, Claudia. "Mal fünf Minuten ohne Normen." *Die Tageszeitung,* Mar. 8, 1994, 16–17.

Geneva Convention of August 12, 1949 for the Protection of War Victims. Washington, D.C.: U.S. Government Printing Office, 1950.

Genovese, Eugene D. *Roll, Jordan, Roll: The World the Slaves Made.* New York: Vintage, 1976.

Gibbs, Nancy. "When Is It Rape?" *Time* 137 (June 3, 1991): 48–54.

Giddings, Paula. *When and Where I Enter: The Impact of Black Women on Race and Sex in America.* New York: Morrow, 1984.

Gillespie, Marcia Ann. "In the Matter of Rape." *Essence* 22.9 (Jan. 1992): 60–61+.

Gillis, Christina Marsden. " 'Where Are You Going, Where Have You Been?': Seduction, Space, and a Fictional Mode." *Studies in Short Fiction* 18.1 (Dec. 1981): 65–70.

Gilman, Sander L. "Black Bodies, White Bodies: Toward an Iconography of Female Sexuality in Late Nineteenth-Century Art, Medicine, and Literature." *Critical Inquiry* 12.1 (1985): 204–42.

Golden, Thelma, ed. *Black Male: Representations of Masculinity in Contemporary American Art.* New York: Whitney Museum of Contemporary Art, 1994.

Goldstein, Lawrence, ed. *The Female Body: Figures, Styles, Speculations.* Ann Arbor: U of Michigan P, 1991.

Goodell, William. *The American Slave Code.* 1858. New York: Arno, 1969.

Goodman, Ellen. "In Defense of Adolescent Girls (Jailbait)." *Boston Globe,* Feb. 19, 1995, 87.

Goodman, James. *Stories of Scottsboro.* New York: Vintage, 1994.

Gordon, Linda. "Family Violence, Feminism, and Social Control." *Unequal Sisters: A Multicultural Reader in U.S. Women's History.* Ed. Ellen Carol DuBois and Vicki L. Ruiz. New York: Routledge, 1990. 141–56.

Govan, Sandra Y. "Forbidden Fruits and Unholy Lusts: Illicit Sex in Black American Literature." Ed. Diane Raymond. Bowling Green: Bowling Green State U Popular P, 1990. 68–80.

Griffin, Susan. *Rape: The Politics of Consciousness.* New York: Harper, 1986.

———. "Rape, the All-American Crime." *Ramparts* 10.3 (1971): 26–56.

Guillaumin, Colette. "Race and Nature: The System of Marks, the Idea of a Natural Group and Social Relationships." *Feminist Issues* 8.2 (Fall 1988): 25–43.

Gunning, Sandra. *Race, Rape, and Lynching: The Red Record of American Literature, 1890–1912.* New York: Oxford UP, 1996.

Hall, Jacqueline Dowd. "'The Mind That Burns in Each Body': Women, Rape, and Racial Violence." *Powers of Desire: The Politics of Sexuality.* Ed. Ann Snitow, Christine Stansell, and Sharon Thompson. New York: Monthly Review, 1983. 328–45.

———. *Revolt against Chivalry: Jessie Daniel Ames and the Women's Campaign against Lynching.* New York: Columbia UP, 1979.

Halpern, Martin. *William Vaughn Moody.* New York: Twayne, 1964.

Hansen, Debra Gold. *Strained Sisterhood.* Amherst: U of Massachusetts P, 1993.

Hansen, Klaus P. "The Sentimental Novel and Its Feminist Critique." *Early American Literature* 26.1 (1991): 39–54.

Harley, Sharon. "For the Good of Family and Race: Gender, Work and Domestic Roles in the Black Community, 1880–1930." *Black Women in America: Social Science Perspectives.* Ed. Micheline R. Malson. Chicago: U of Chicago P, 1988. 159–72.

Harrington, Evans, and Ann J. Abadie, eds. *Faulkner, Modernism, and Film: Faulkner and Yoknapatawpha.* Jackson: U of Mississippi P, 1979.

Harris, Trudier. *Exorcising Blackness: Historical and Literary Lynching and Burning Rituals.* Bloomington: Indiana UP, 1984.

———. "Native Sons and Foreign Daughters." *New Essays on Native Son.* Ed. Kenneth Kinnamon. Cambridge: Cambridge UP, 1990. 63–84.

Hartman, Saidiya. "Seduction and the Ruses of Power." *Callaloo* 19.2 (1996): 537–60.

Hartsock, Nancy. "Gender and Sexuality: Masculinity, Violence, and Domination." *Humanities in Society* 7.1–2 (1984): 19–46.

Haskell, Molly. *From Reverence to Rape: The Treatment of Women in the Movies.* New York: Holt, 1974.

———. "The 2000-Year-Old Misunderstanding: Rape Fantasy." *Ms.,* Nov. 1976, 84–86, 92–98.

Hazen, Helen. *Endless Rapture: Rape, Romance, and the Female Imagination.* New York: Scribner, 1983.

Heller, Arno. *Gewaltphantasien: Untersuchungen zu einem Phänomen des amerikanischen Gegenwartromans.* Tübingen: Narr, 1990.

Henderson, Mae G. "Toni Morrison's *Beloved*: Remembering the Body as Historical Text." *Discourses of Sexuality: From Aristotle to AIDS.* Ed. Domna C. Stanton. Ann Arbor: U of Michigan P, 1992. 312–42.

Hernton, Calvin. "Postscript." *A Case of Rape.* Chester Himes. Washington, D.C.: Howard UP, 1984. 107–40.

———. *The Sexual Mountain and Black Women Writers: Adventures in Sex, Literature, and Real Life.* New York: Doubleday, 1987.

Herring, Phillip F. "Djuna Barnes and the Narrative of Violation." *Modes of Narrative: Approaches to American, Canadian and British Fiction.* Ed. Reingard M. Nischik and Barbara Korte. Würzburg: Könighausen and Neumann, 1990. 100–109.

———. *Djuna: The Life and Work of Djuna Barnes.* New York: Viking, 1995.

Higginbotham, Evelyn Brooks. "African-American Women's History and the Metalanguage of Race." *Revising the Word and the World.* Ed. VéVé A. Clark, Ruth-Ellen B. Joeres, and Madelon Sprengnether. Chicago: U of Chicago P, 1993. 91–114.

Higgins, Lynn, and Brenda Silver, eds. *Rape and Representation.* New York: Columbia UP, 1991.

Hill, Anita. *Speaking Truth to Power.* New York: Doubleday, 1997.

Hinck, Edward A. "*The Lily,* 1849–1856: From Temperance to Woman's Rights." *A Voice of Their Own: The Woman Suffrage Press, 1840–1910.* Ed. Martha M. Solomon. Tuscaloosa: U of Alabama P, 1991. 30–47.

Hine, Darlene Clark. "Rape and the Inner Lives of Black Women in the Middle West: Preliminary Thoughts on the Culture of Dissemblance." *Unequal Sisters: A Multicultural Reader in U.S. Women's History.* Ed. Ellen Carol DuBois and Vicki L. Ruiz. New York: Routledge, 1990. 292–97.

Hoch, Paul. *White Hero, Black Beast: Racism, Sexism and the Mask of Masculinity.* London: Pluto, 1979.

Hodes, Martha. "The Sexualization of Reconstruction Politics: White Women and Black Men in the South after the Civil War." *American Sexual Politics: Sex, Gender, and Race since the Civil War.* Ed. John C. Fout and Maura Shaw Tantillo. Chicago: U of Chicago P, 1993. 59–74.

Hoffman, Frederick L. *Race Traits and Tendencies of the American Negro.* New York: Macmillan for the American Economic Association, 1896.

Holladay, Hilary. *Ann Petry.* New York: Twayne, 1996.

Hooks, Bell. *Ain't I a Woman: Black Women and Feminism.* Boston: South End, 1981.

———. *Feminist Theory from Margin to Center.* Boston: South End, 1984.

———. *Outlaw Culture: Resisting Representations.* New York: Routledge, 1994.

———. "Violence in Intimate Relationships: A Feminist Perspective." *Talking Back: Thinking Feminist, Thinking Black.* Boston: South End Press, 1984. 84–91.

Hull, Gloria T., Patricia Bell Scott, and Barbara Smith, eds. *All the Women Are White, All the Blacks Are Men, But Some of Us Are Brave.* Old Westbury: Feminist Press, 1982.

Huyssen, Andreas. *After the Great Divide: Modernism, Mass Culture, Postmodernism.* Bloomington: Indiana UP, 1986.

Ickstadt, Heinz. "Die amerikanische Moderne." *Amerikanische Literaturgeschichte.* Ed. Hubert Zapf. Stuttgart: Metzler, 1997. 218–81.

———. *Der amerikanische Roman im 20. Jahrhundert: Transformation des Mimetischen.* Darmstadt: Wissenschaftliche Buchgesellschaft, 1998.

———. "Liberated Women, Reconstructed Men: Symptoms of Cultural Crisis at the Turn of the Century." *Engendering Manhood.* Ed. Ulfried Reichardt and Sabine Sielke. *Amerikastudien/American Studies* 43.4 (1998): 593–98.

Ickstadt, Heinz. "*Portraits of Ladies*: von Henry James bis Edith Wharton." *Gender Matters: Geschlechterforschung und Amerikastudien*. Berliner Beiträge zur Amerikanistik 6. Ed. Sabine Sielke. Berlin: John F. Kennedy-Institut, 1997. 17–31.

Inscoe, John C. "*The Clansman* on Stage and Screen: North Carolina Reacts." *North Carolina Historical Review* 64.2 (Apr. 1987): 139–61.

Irigaray, Luce. *This Sex Which Is Not One*. Ithaca: Cornell UP, 1985.

Irving, John. "Pornography and the New Puritans." *New York Times Book Review*, Mar. 29, 1992, 1, 24–25.

Jackson, Margaret. "Eroticizing Women's Oppression: Havelock Ellis and the Construction of the 'Natural.' " *The Real Facts of Life: Feminism and the Politics of Sexuality, 1850–1940*. London: Taylor and Francis, 1994. 106–28.

———. "Sexology and the Social Construction of Male Sexuality." *The Sexuality Papers: Male Sexuality and the Social Control of Women*. Ed. L. Coveney, M. Jackson, S. Jeffreys, et al. London: Hutchinson, 1984. 45–68.

———. "Sexology and the Universalization of Male Sexuality (from Ellis to Kinsey, and Masters and Johnson)." *The Sexuality Papers: Male Sexuality and the Social Control of Women*. Ed. L. Coveney, M. Jackson, S. Jeffreys, et al. London: Hutchinson, 1984. 69–84.

Jameson, Fredric. *The Political Unconscious: Narrative as a Socially Symbolic Act*. Ithaca: Cornell UP, 1982.

———. "Postmodernism and Consumer Society." *The Anti-Aesthetic: Essays on Postmodern Culture*. Ed. Hal Foster. Port Townsend: Bay, 1983. 111–25.

JanMohamed, Abdul R. "Sexuality on/of the Racial Border: Foucault, Wright, and the Articulation of 'Racialized Sexuality.' " *Discourses of Sexuality: From Aristotle to AIDS*. Ed. Domna C. Stanton. Ann Arbor: U of Michigan P, 1992. 94–116.

Jed, Stephanie H. *Chaste Thinking: The Rape of Lucretia and the Birth of Humanism*. Bloomington: Indiana UP, 1989.

Jeffords, Susan. "Performative Masculinities, or, 'After a Few Times You Won't Be Afraid of Rape at All.' " *Discourse* 13.2 (1991): 102–18.

Jeffreys, Sheila. *Anticlimax: A Feminist Perspective on the Sexual Revolution*. New York: New York UP, 1990.

Joas, Hans, and Wolfgang Knöbl, eds. *Gewalt in den USA*. Frankfurt: Fischer, 1994.

Johnson, Barbara. "Lesbian Spectacles: Reading *Sula, Passing, Thelma and Louise*, and *The Accused*." *Media Spectacles*. Ed. Marjorie Garber, Jann Matlock, and Rebecca L. Walkowitz. New York: Routledge, 1993. 160–66.

———. "The Re(a)d and the Black." *Richard Wright: Perspectives Past and Present*. Ed. Henry Louis Gates, Jr., and Kwame A. Appiah. New York: Amistad, 1993. 149–55.

———. *A World of Difference*. Baltimore: Johns Hopkins UP, 1987.

Johnson, Claudia Durst. "The Secret Court of Men's Hearts: Code and Law in Harper Lee's *To Kill A Mockingbird*." *Studies in American Fiction* 19.2 (1991): 129–39.

———. *To Kill a Mockingbird: Threatening Boundaries*. New York: Twayne, 1994.

Jordan, Winthrop D. *White over Black*. Chapel Hill: U of North Carolina P, 1968.

Kannenstine, Louis F. *The Art of Djuna Barnes*. New York: New York UP, 1977.

Kappeler, Susanne. *The Pornography of Representation*. Minneapolis: U of Minnesota P, 1986.

Kelly, Liz. *Surviving Sexual Violence*. Cambridge: Polity, 1988.

Kinney, James. *Amalgamation! Race, Sex, and Rhetoric in the Nineteenth-Century American Novel.* Westport: Greenwood, 1985.

Kolodny, Annette. *The Lay of the Land: Metaphor as Experience and History in American Life and Letters.* Chapel Hill: U of North Carolina P, 1975.

Kreyling, Michael. "*The Fathers*: A Postsouthern Narrative Reading." *Southern Literature and Literary Theory.* Ed. Jefferson Humphries. Athens: U of Georgia P, 1990. 186–205.

Kubitschek, Missy Dehn. "Subjugated Knowledge: Toward a Feminist Exploration of Rape in Afro-American Fiction." *Black Feminist Criticism and Critical Theory.* Ed. Joe Weixlmann and Houston A. Baker. Greenwood: Penkevill, 1988. 43–56.

Laqueur, Thomas. *Making Sex: Body and Gender from the Greeks to Freud.* Cambridge: Harvard UP, 1990.

Lauretis, Teresa de. "The Violence of Rhetoric: Considerations on Representation and Gender." *The Violence of Representation: Literature and the History of Violence.* Ed. Nancy Armstrong and Leonard Tennenhouse. London: Routledge, 1989. 239–58.

Leavy, Walter. "Sex in Black America: Reality and Myth." *Ebony* 148.10 (Aug. 1993): 126–30.

LeBeau, James. "Is Interracial Rape Different?" *Sociology and Social Research* 73.1 (1988): 43–46.

Leder, Laura. *Take Back the Night: Women on Pornography.* New York: Bantam. 1982.

Lehman, Peter. " 'Don't Blame This on a Girl': Female Rape-Revenge Films." *Screening the Male: Exploring Masculinities in Hollywood Cinema.* Ed. Steven Cohan and Ina Rae Hark. New York: Routledge, 1993. 103–17.

Lerner, Gerda. *Black Women in White America.* New York: Pantheon, 1972.

Levenson, J. C. "*The Red Badge of Courage* and *McTeague*: Passage to Modernity." *The Cambridge Companion to American Realism and Naturalism: Howells to London.* Ed. Donald Pizer. Cambridge: Cambridge UP, 1995. 154–77.

Lewis, James R. "Images of Captive Rape in the Nineteenth Century." *Journal of American Culture* 15.2 (June 1992): 69–77.

Lewis, Jan. "The Republican Wife: Virtue and Seduction in the Early Republic." *William and Mary Quarterly* 44 (1987): 689–721.

Lindemann, Barbara S. " 'To Ravish and Carnally Know': Rape in Eighteenth Century Massachusetts." *Signs* 10.1 (1984): 63–82.

Lloyd, David. "Race under Representation." *Culture/Contexture: Explorations in Anthropology and Literary Studies.* Ed. E. Valentine Daniel and Jeffrey M. Peck. Berkeley: U of California P, 1996. 249–72.

Lorde, Audre. *A Burst of Light: Essays.* Ithaca: Firebrand Books, 1988.

———. *Sister Outsider: Essays and Speeches.* Trumansburg: Crossing Press, 1989.

Lowers, Jane. "Rape: When the Assailant Is One of Our Own." *Deneuve*, Sept. 1995, 36, 38.

MacKinnon, Catharine. *Feminism Unmodified: Discourse on Life and Law.* Cambridge: Harvard UP, 1987.

———. *Only Words.* Cambridge: Harvard UP, 1993.

———. "Reflections on Sex Equality under Law." *American Feminist Thought at Century's End: A Reader.* Ed. Linda F. Kauffman. Cambridge: Blackwell, 1993. 367–424.

———. *Sexual Harassment of Working Women: A Case of Sexual Discrimination.* New Haven: Yale UP, 1979.

MacKinnon, Catharine. *Toward a Feminist Theory of the State*. Cambridge: Harvard UP, 1989.

Mann, Susan A. "Slavery, Sharecropping, and Sexual Inequality." *Signs* 14 (1988): 774–98.

Marcus, Sharon. "Fighting Bodies, Fighting Words: A Theory and Politics of Rape Prevention." *Feminists Theorize the Political*. Ed. Judith Butler and Joan Scott. New York: Routledge, 1992.

Martin, Biddy. "Feminism, Criticism and Foucault." *Knowing Women: Feminism and Knowledge*. Ed. Helen Crowley and Susan Himmelweit. Cambridge: Polity, 1992. 275–86.

Martin, Wendy. "Seduced and Abandoned in the New World: The Image of Woman in American Fiction." *Women in Sexist Society: Studies in Power and Powerlessness*. New York: Basic Books, 1971. 329–46.

Matalin, Mary. "Stop Whining!" *Newsweek* 122 (1993): 62.

Matlock, Jann. "Scandals of Naming: The Blue Blob, Identity, and Gender in the William Kennedy Smith Case." *Media Spectacles*. Ed. Marjorie Garber, Jann Matlock, and Rebecca L. Walkowitz. New York: Routledge, 1993. 137–59.

Matthews, John T. "The Elliptical Nature of *Sanctuary*." *Novel* 17.3 (1984): 246–65.

May, Tanja. "Der Tod der Bilder: Filmische Aspekte in Bret Easton Ellis' Roman *American Psycho*." Unpublished essay, 1994.

Mayer, Jane, and Jill Abramson. "Sinned Against—but Who?" *Boston Sunday Globe*, Nov. 6, 1994, 83.

McDowell, Deborah E. "Reading Family Matters." *Changing Our Own Words*. Ed. Cheryl A. Wall. New Brunswick: Rutgers UP, 1989. 75–97.

McKay, Nellie Y. Introduction. *The Narrows*. By Ann Petry. Boston: Beacon, 1988. vii–xx.

Meritt, Russell. "D. W. Griffith's *Birth of a Nation*: Going After Little Sister." *Close Viewings: An Anthology of New Film Criticism*. Ed. Peter Lehman. Tallahassee: Florida State UP, 1990. 215–37.

Michaels, Walter Benn. *The Gold Standard and the Logic of Naturalism: American Literature at the Turn of the Century*. Berkeley: U of California P, 1987.

———. "Race into Culture: A Critical Genealogy of Cultural Identity." *Critical Inquiry* 18.4 (June 1992): 655–85.

———. "The Souls of White Folk." *Literature and the Body: Essays on Populations and Persons*. Ed. Elaine Scarry. Baltimore: Johns Hopkins UP, 1988. 185–209.

Miller, Jane. *Seductions: Studies in Reading and Culture*. Cambridge: Harvard UP, 1990.

Modleski, Tania. "The Disappearing Act: Harlequin Romances." *Gender, Language, and Myth: Essays and Popular Narrative*. Ed. Glenwood Irons. Toronto: U of Toronto P, 1992. 20–45.

———. "Rape Versus Mans/Laughter: Hitchcock's *Blackmail* and Feminist Interpretation." *PMLA* 102.3 (1987): 304–15.

Mönth, Gabriele. *Schrei nach Innen: Vergewaltigung und das Leben danach*. Vienna: Picus, 1994.

Morgan, Robin. "Theory and Practice: Pornography and Rape." *Take Back the Night: Women on Pornography*. Ed. Laura Lederer. New York: Morrow, 1980. 134–40.

———. "What Do Our Masochist Fantasies Really Mean." *Ms.*, June 1977, 66–68, 99–100.

Morrison, Toni. *Playing in the Dark: Whiteness and the Literary Imagination.* New York: Random, 1992.

Moses, Wilson J. "Literary Garveyism: The Novels of Reverend Sutton E. Griggs." *Phylon* 40.3 (Sept. 1979): 203–16.

Mullen, Richie. *Male Rape: Breaking the Silence on the Last Taboo.* London: GMP, 1990.

Murray, Douglas. "Classical Myth in Richardson's *Clarissa:* Ovid Revisited." *Eighteenth-Century Fiction* 3.2 (Jan. 1991): 113–24.

Naylor, Gloria. "Love and Sex in the Afro-American Novel." *Yale Review* 78.1 (Autumn 1989): 19–31.

Neale, Steve. "Masculinity as Spectacle." *Screening the Male: Exploring Masculinities in Hollywood Cinema.* Ed. Steven Cohan and Ina Rae Hark. New York: Routledge, 1993. 9–20.

Newman, Jenny, ed. *The Faber Book of Seductions.* London: Faber, 1988.

———. Introduction. *The Faber Book of Seductions.* Ed. Jenny Newman. London: Faber, 1988. iv–xxix.

Norment, Lynn. "What's behind the Dramatic Rise in Rapes?" *Ebony* 46.11 (Sept. 1991): 92–98.

Norris, Frank. *The Responsibilities of the Novelist and Other Literary Essays.* New York: Haskell, 1969.

Nowatzki, Robert. "Race, Rape, Lynching, and Manhood Suffrage: Constructions of White and Black Masculinity in Turn-of-the-Century White Supremacist Literature." *Journal of Men's Studies* 3.2 (Nov. 1994): 161–70.

O'Brien, Kenneth. "Race, Romance, and the Southern Literary Tradition." *Recasting Gone with the Wind in American Culture.* Ed. Darden-Asbury Pyron. Miami: UPs of Florida, 1983. 153–66.

Ostertag, Isa. " 'I Got Them All': (De-)Constructing Masculinity through Violence in Peckinpah's *Straw Dogs.*" *Engendering Manhood.* Ed. Ulfried Reichardt and Sabine Sielke. *Amerikastudien/American Studies* 43.4 (1998): 657–70.

Paglia, Camille. *Sex, Art, and American Culture.* New York: Vintage, 1992.

———. *Sexual Personae: Art and Decadence from Nefertiti to Emily Dickinson.* New York: Vintage, 1991.

———. *Vamps and Tramps: New Essays.* New York: Vintage, 1994.

Painter, Nell Irvin. "Soul Murder and Slavery: Toward a Fully Loaded Cost Accounting." *Women's History as United States History.* Ed. Linda Kerber, Alice Kessler-Harris, and Kathryn Kish Sklar. Chapel Hill: U of North Carolina P, 1995. 125–46.

Pally, Marcia. *Sense and Censorship: The Vanity of Bonfires.* New York: Americans for Constitutional Freedom and Freedom to Read Foundation, 1991.

Park, Katharine. "Kimberly Bergalis, AIDS, and the Plague Metaphor." *Media Spectacles.* Ed. Marjorie Garber, Jann Matlock, and Rebecca L. Walkowitz. New York: Routledge, 1993. 232–53.

Parrot, Andrea, and Laurie Bechhofer, eds. *Acquaintance Rape: The Hidden Crime.* New York: Wiley, 1991.

Patterson, Orlando. "Race, Gender, and Liberal Fallacies." *Black Scholar* 22.1–2 (Dec. 1991): 77–80.

Patton, Gwen. "Black People and the Victorian Ethos." *The Black Woman: An Anthology.* Ed. Toni Cade. New York: Signet, 1970. 143–48.

Peiss, Kathy. " 'Charity Girls' and City Pleasures: Historical Notes on Working-Class Sexuality, 1880–1920." *Unequal Sisters: A Multicultural Reader in U.S. Women's History.* Ed. Ellen Carol DuBois and Vicki L. Ruiz. New York: Routledge, 1990. 157–66.

Petry, Ann. "The Novel as Social Criticism." *The Writer's Book.* Ed. Helen Hull. New York: Barnes and Noble, 1950. 32–39.

Pettey, Homer B. "Reading and Raping in *Sanctuary.*" *Faulkner Journal* 3.1 (1987): 71–84.

Pizer, Donald. "Theodore Dreiser's 'Nigger Jeff': The Development of an Aesthetic." *American Literature* 41 (1968): 331–41.

———. *The Theory and Practice of American Literary Naturalism.* Carbondale: Southern Illinois UP, 1993.

———, ed. *The Cambridge Companion to American Realism and Naturalism.* Cambridge: Cambridge UP, 1995.

Pollitt, Katha. "Not Just Bad Sex." *Debating Sexual Correctness: Pornography, Sexual Harassment, Date Rape, and the Politics of Sexual Equality.* Ed. Adele M. Stan. New York: Delta, 1995. 162–71.

Ponsot, Marie. "A Reader's Ryder." *Silence and Power: A Reevaluation of Djuna Barnes.* Ed. Mary Lynn Broe. Carbondale: Southern Illinois UP, 1991. 94–135.

Porter, Roy. "Rape—Does It Have a Historical Meaning?" *Rape.* Ed. Sylvana Tomaselli and Roy Porter. Oxford: Blackwell, 1988. 216–36.

Radway, Janice A. *Reading the Romance: Women, Patriarchy, and Popular Literature.* Chapel Hill: U of North Carolina P, 1991.

Rich, Adrienne. "Compulsory Heterosexuality and Lesbian Existence." *Blood, Bread, and Poetry: Selected Prose 1979–1985.* New York: Norton, 1986. 23–75.

Roberts, Diane. "Ravished Belles: Stories of Rape and Resistance in *Flags in the Dust* and *Sanctuary.*" *Faulkner Journal* 4.1–2 (1988): 21–35.

Rogin, Michael Paul. *Ronald Reagan, the Movies, and Other Episodes in Political Demonology.* Berkeley: U of California P, 1987.

Roiphe, Katie. "Making the Incest Scene." *Harper's,* Nov. 1995, 65–71.

———. *The Morning After: Sex, Fear, and Feminism.* Boston: Little, Brown, and Company, 1993.

Rooney, Ellen. "Criticism and the Subject of Sexual Violence." *MLN* 98.5 (1983): 1269–78.

Rosenblatt, Roger. "Snuff This Book! Will Bret Easton Ellis Get Away with Murder?" *New York Times Book Review,* Dec. 16, 1990, 3+.

Ross, Andrew. "The Gangsta and the Diva." *Black Male: Representations of Masculinity in Contemporary American Art.* Ed. Thelma Golden. New York: Whitney Museum of Contemporary Art, 1994. 159–66.

Rotundo, E. Anthony. *American Manhood: Transformations in Masculinity from the Revolution to the Modern Era.* New York: Basic, 1993.

Rubin, Gayle. "Thinking Sex: Notes for a Radical Theory of the Politics of Sexuality." *Pleasure and Danger: Exploring Female Sexuality.* Ed. Carole S. Vance. London: Pandora, 1989. 267–319.

Ruddick, Lisa. *Reading Gertrude Stein: Body, Gnosis, Text.* Ithaca: Cornell UP, 1991.

Russell, Diana. *The Politics of Rape: The Victim's Perspective.* New York: Stein and Day, 1974.

Saillant, John. "The Black Body Erotic and the Republican Body Politic, 1790—1820." *Journal of the History of Sexuality* 5.3 (1995): 403–28.

Sanchez-Eppler, Karen. *Touching Liberty: Abolition, Feminism, and the Politics of the Body.* Berkeley: U of California P, 1993.

Sanday, Peggy Reeves. *Fraternity Gang Rape: Sex, Brotherhood, and Privilege on Campus.* New York: New York UP, 1990.

Sawicki, Jana. *Disciplining Foucault: Feminism, Power, and the Body.* New York: Routledge, 1991.

Scarry, Elaine. *The Body in Pain: The Making and Unmaking of the World.* New York: Oxford UP, 1985.

Schramer, James, and Timothy Sweet. "Violence and Body Politic in Seventeenth-Century New England." *Arizona Quarterly* 48.2 (June 1992): 1–32.

Schuckmann, Patrick. "Masculinity, the Male Spectator and the Homoerotic Gaze." Engendering Manhood. *Amerikastudien/American Studies* 43.4: 671–80.

Schwarzman, Allan. "After Four Years, the Message Is Murder." *New York Times*, May 8, 1994, H34+.

Schwenk, Katrin. "Lynching and Rape: Border Cases in African-American History and Fiction." *The Black Columbiad: Defining Moments in African-American Literature and Culture.* Ed. Werner Sollors and Maria Diedrich. Cambridge: Harvard UP, 1994. 312–24.

Scott, Bonnie Kime. "Barnes Being 'Beast Familiar': Representation on the Margins of Modernism." *Review of Contemporary Fiction* 13.3 (1993): 41–52.

Scott, James B. *Djuna Barnes.* Boston: Twayne, 1976.

Sedgwick, Eve Kosofsky. *Between Men: English Literature and Male Homosocial Desire.* New York: Columbia UP, 1985.

———. *Epistemology of the Closet.* Berkeley: U of California P, 1990.

Seed, David. "The Evidence of Things Seen and Unseen: William Faulkner's *Sanctuary.*" *American Horror Fiction: From Brockden Brown to Stephen King.* Ed. Brian Doherty. New York: Macmillan, 1990. 73–91.

Sekora, John, and Darwin T. Turner, eds. *The Art of Slave Narrative: Original Essays in Criticism and Theory.* Macomb: Western Illinois UP, 1982.

Shanor, Karen. *Verschwiegene Träume: Die sexuellen Phantasien der Frau.* Berlin: Ullstein, 1986.

Showalter, Elaine. "Rethinking the Seventies: Women Writers and Violence." *Women and Violence in Literature.* Ed. Katherine A. Ackley. New York: Garland, 1990. 237–54.

———. *Sexual Anarchy: Gender and Culture at the Fin du Siècle.* New York: Viking, 1990.

Sielke, Sabine. " 'Celebrating AIDS': Quilts, Confessions, and Questions of National Identity." *Ceremonies and Spectacles: Performing American Culture.* Ed. Teresa Alves, Teresa Cid, and Heinz Ickstadt. Amsterdam: VU UP, 2000. 281–93.

———"The Discourse of Liberation, the Deployment of Silence, and the 'Liberation' of Discourse." Black Liberation in the Americas. *Forecaast* 6. Münster: LIT-Verlag, 2001. 241–57.

———. "Drawing the Line between Art and Pornography: Censorship and the Representation of the Sexual Body." *Democracy and the Arts in the United States.* Ed. Alfred

Hornung, Reinhard R. Doerries, and Gerhard Hoffmann. Munich: Fink, 1996. 287–98.

———. *Fashioning the Female Subject: The Intertexual Networking of Dickinson, Moore, and Rich.* Ann Arbor: U of Michigan P, 1997.

———. "Gewalt gegen Frauen oder: *Reading Rape.*" *Gewalt in den USA.* Ed. Hans Joas and Wolfgang Knöbl. Frankfurt: Fischer, 1994. 191–221.

———. " 'I HAVE THE BLOOD JELLY': Sexual Violence and the Media." *Blurred Boundaries: Critical Essays on American Studies.* Ed. Klaus Schmidt and David Sawyer. Frankfurt: Lang, 1995. 221–47.

———. " 'Images That Injure': Stereotype schwarzer Körperlichkeit und die Visualisierung der Bilder im Kopf. Kara Walkers Scherenschnitte und Michael Ray Charles' Poster Art." *Sprachformen des Körpers in Kunst und Wissenschaft.* Tübingen: Francke, 2000. 63–74.

———. "(Post-)Modernists or Misfits? Nonsynchronism, Subjectivity, and the Paradigms of Literary History." *Making America: The Cultural Work of Literature.* Ed. Susanne Rohr, Ernst-Peter Schneck, and Sabine Sielke. Heidelberg: Winter, 2000. 215–33.

———. "Seduced and Enslaved: Sexual Violence in Antebellum American Literature and Contemporary Feminist Discourse." The Historical and Political Turn in Literary Studies. Ed. Winfried Fluck. *REAL* 11 (1995): 299–324.

Sielke, Sabine, and Anne Hofmann. "Serienmörder und andere Killer: Die Endzeitfiktionen von Bret Easton Ellis und Michel Houellebecq." *Anglo-romanische Kulturkontakte: von Humanismus bis Postkolonialismus.* Ed. Andrew James Johnston and Ulrike Schneider. Berlin: Dahlem UP, forthcoming 2002.

Sielke, Sabine, and Ulfried Reichardt, eds. Engendering Manhood. *Amerikastudien/ American Studies* 43.4 (1998).

Singer, Linda. *Erotic Welfare: Sexual Theory and Politics in an Age of Epidemic.* Ed. Judith Butler and Maureen MacGrogan. New York: Routledge, 1993.

Skinner, Robert E. "Collecting Chester Himes." *Firsts: Collecting Modern First Editions* 4.5 (1994): 24–31.

Slotkin, Richard. *Regeneration through Violence: The Mythology of the American Frontier, 1600–1860.* Middletown: Wesleyan UP, 1973.

Smith, Sidonie, and Julia Watson, eds. *De/colonizing the Subject: The Politics of Gender in Women's Autobiography.* Minneapolis: U of Minnesota P, 1992.

Smith, Valerie. *Self-Discovery and Authority in Afro-American Narrative.* Cambridge: Harvard UP, 1987.

———. "Split Affinities: The Case of Interracial Rape." *Conflicts in Feminism.* Ed. Marianne Hirsch and Evelyn Fox Keller. New York: Routledge, 1990. 271–87.

Smith-Rosenberg, Caroll. *Disorderly Conduct: Visions of Gender in Victorian America.* New York: Knopf, 1985.

Snitow, Ann, Christine Stansell, and Sharon Thompson, eds. *Powers of Desire: The Politics of Sexuality.* New York: Monthly Review, 1983.

Sollors, Werner. *Beyond Ethnicity: Consent and Descent in American Culture.* New York: Oxford UP, 1986.

———. " 'Never Was Born': The Mulatto, an American Tragedy?" *Massachusetts Review* 27.2 (Summer 1986): 293–316.

Sollors, Werner, and Maria Diedrich, eds. *The Black Columbiad: Defining Moments in African-American Literature and Culture.* Cambridge: Harvard UP, 1994.

Somerville, Siobhan. "Scientific Racism and the Emergence of the Homosexual Body." *Journal of the History of Sexuality* 5.2 (1994): 243–66.

Sommers, Christina Hoff. *Who Stole Feminism? How Women Have Betrayed Women.* New York: Simon & Schuster, 1994.

Spillers, Hortense. " 'All the Things You Could Be by Now, If Sigmund Freud's Wife Was Your Mother': Psychoanalysis and Race." *Boundary 2* 23.3 (1996): 75–141.

———. "Mama's Baby, Papa's Maybe: An American Grammar Book." *Within the Circle: African American Literary Criticism from the Harlem Renaissance to the Present.* Ed. Angelyn Mitchell. Durham: Duke UP, 1994. 454–81.

Stanton, Domna C. *Discourses of Sexuality: From Aristotle to AIDS.* Ann Arbor: Michigan UP, 1993.

Staples, Robert. "Black Male Genocide: A Final Solution to the Race Problem in America." *Black Scholar,* June 1987, 2–11.

———. "The Myth of the Black Macho: A Response to Angry Black Feminists." *Black Scholar,* Apr. 1979, 24–33.

Stevenson, Sheryl. "Ryder as Contraception: Barnes vs. the Reproduction of Mothering." *Review of Contemporary Fiction* 13.3 (1993): 97–106.

———. "Writing the Grotesque Body: Djuna Barnes' Carnival Parody." *Silence and Power: A Revaluation of Djuna Barnes.* Ed. Mary Lynn Broe. Carbondale: Southern Illinois UP, 1991. 81–91.

Stoddard, Lothrop. *The Rising Tide of Color against White World Supremacy.* New York: Scribner, 1920.

Stoltenberg, John. *Refusing to Be a Man: Essays on Sex and Justice.* Portland: Breitenbush, 1989.

Storey, John. *An Introductory Guide to Cultural Theory and Popular Culture.* Athens: U of Georgia P, 1993.

Strossen, Nadine. *Defending Pornography: Free Speech, Sex, and the Fight for Women's Rights.* New York: Scribner, 1995.

Suleiman, Susan Rubin. "Rewriting the Body: The Politics and Poetics of Female Eroticism." *The Female Body in Western Culture: Contemporary Perspectives.* Ed. Susan Rubin Suleiman. Cambridge: Harvard UP, 1985. 7–29.

———, ed. *The Female Body in Western Culture: Contemporary Perspectives.* Cambridge: Harvard UP, 1985.

Sundquist, Eric J. *To Wake the Nation: Race in the Making of American Literature.* Cambridge: Harvard UP, 1993.

Sword, Helen. "Leda and the Modernists." *PMLA* 107.2 (1992): 305–18.

Takaki, Ronald T. *Violence in the Black Imagination: Essays and Documents.* New York: Oxford UP, 1993.

Tanner, Laura E. *Intimate Violence: Reading Rape and Torture in Twentieth-Century Fiction.* Bloomington: Indiana UP, 1994.

———. "Uncovering the Magical Disguise of Language: The Narrative Presence in Richard Wright's *Native Son.*" *Richard Wright: Perspectives Past and Present.* Ed. Henry Louis Gates, Jr., and Kwame A. Appiah. New York: Amistad, 1993. 132–48.

Tate, Allen. "Faulkner's 'Sanctuary' and the Southern Myth." *Virginia Quarterly Review* 44 (1968): 418–27.

Tate, Claudia. "Allegories of Black Female Desire; or, Rereading Nineteenth-Century Sentimental Narratives of Black Female Authority." *Changing Our Own Words.* Ed. Cheryl A. Wall. New Brunswick: Rutgers UP, 1989. 98–126.

Taubin, Amy. "Under His Thumb." *Debating Sexual Correctness: Pornography, Sexual Harassment, Date Rape, and the Politics of Sexual Equality.* Ed. Adele M. Stan. New York: Delta, 1995. 172–74.

Tavernier-Courbin, Jacqueline. "*The Call of the Wild* and *The Jungle*: Jack London's and Upton Sinclair's Animal and Human Jungles." *The Cambridge Companion to American Realism and Naturalism: Howells to London.* Ed. Donald Pizer. Cambridge: Cambridge UP, 1995. 236–62.

Taves, Ann. "Spiritual Purity and Sexual Shame: Religious Themes in the Writings of Harriet Jacobs." *Church History* 56.1 (1987): 59–72.

Temkin, Jennifer. "Women, Rape, and Law Reform." *Rape.* Ed. Sylvana Tomaselli and Roy Porter. Oxford: Basil Blackwell, 1986. 16–40.

Terrell, Mary Church. *The Progress of Colored Women.* Washington, D.C.: Smith Brothers, 1898.

Terry, Don. "A Week of Rapes: The Jogger and 28 Not in the News." *New York Times,* May 29, 1989, 25, 28–29.

Thomas, Brook. *The New Historicism and Other Old-Fashioned Topics.* Princeton: Princeton UP, 1991.

Thompson, Mildred I. *Ida B. Wells-Barnett: An Exploratory Study of an American Black Woman, 1893–1930.* Brooklyn: Carlson, 1990.

Tolnay, Stewart E., and E. M. Beck. *A Festival of Violence: An Analysis of Southern Lynchings, 1882–1930.* Urbana: U of Illinois P, 1995.

Tomaselli, Sylvana, and Roy Porter, eds. *Rape.* Oxford: Basil Blackwell, 1986.

Tong, Rosemarie. *Women, Sex, and the Law.* Totowa: Rowman and Allanheld, 1984.

Turner, Renée D. "Date Rape." *Ebony* 46.2 (1990): 104–7.

Twain, Mark. "The United States of Lyncherdom." *The Norton Anthology of American Literature.* Vol. 2. Ed. Ronald Gottesman et al. New York: Norton, 1979. 276–83.

"Überall Bilder von perfektem Sex." Interview with Bret Easton Ellis and Michel Houellebecq. *Der Spiegel,* Oct., 25, 1999.

Vermillion, Mary. "Reembodying the Self: Representations of Rape in *Incidents in the Life of a Slave Girl* and *I Know Why the Caged Bird Sings.*" *Biography* 15.3 (June 1992): 243–60.

Vicinus, Martha. "Sexuality and Power: A Review of Current Work in the History of Sexuality." *Feminist Studies* 8 (1982): 133–56.

von Rimscha, Robert. "Küssen mit sechs." *Tagesspiegel,* Oct. 6, 1996, 25.

Walby, Sylvia. "Sexuality." *Theorizing Patriarchy.* Oxford: Blackwell, 1990. 109–27.

———. "Violence." *Theorizing Patriarchy.* Oxford: Blackwell, 1990. 128–45.

Walker, Alice. "Finding Celie's Voice." *Ms.,* Dec. 1985, 71–72+.

Walker, Kara. "(Like Home)." Interview with Liz Armstrong. *No Place (Like Home).* Ed. Zarina Bhimji et al. Minneapolis: Walker Art Center, 1997. 102–13.

Walkowitz, Judith R. "Jack the Ripper and the Myth of Male Violence." *Feminist Studies* 8.3 (Sept. 1982): 542–74.

Wallace, Michele. *Black Macho and the Myth of the Superwoman.* New York: Warner, 1978.

———. *Invisibility Blues: From Pop to Theory.* London: Verso, 1990.

Walters, Ronald F. "The Erotic South: Civilization and Sexuality in American Abolitionism." *American Quarterly* 25 (1973): 177–201.

Warhol, Robyn R., ed. *Feminisms: An Anthology of Literary Theory and Criticism.* New Brunswick: Rutgers UP, 1991.

Warner, Michael. "New English Sodom." *American Literature* 64.1 (1992): 19–47.

Warner, Warren Beatty. "Reading Rape: Marxist Feminist Figurations of the Literal." *Diacritics* 13.3 (1983): 12–32.

Warshaw, Robin. *I Never Called It Rape.* New York: Harper, 1988.

Weir, Sybil. "*The Narrows*: A Black New England Novel." *Studies in American Fiction* 15.1 (1987): 81–93.

Weixlmann, Joe, and Houston A. Baker, eds. *Black Feminist Criticism and Critical Theory.* Greenwood: Penkevill, 1988.

Weld, Theodore ed. *American Slavery As It Is: Testimony of a Thousand Witnesses.* New York: American Anti-Slavery Society, 1839.

Wells, Ida B. *Crusade for Justice: The Autobiography of Ida B. Wells.* Ed. Alfreda M. Duster. Chicago: U of Chicago P, 1970.

West, Cornel. *Race Matters.* Boston: Beacon, 1993.

West, Paul. "Afterword: 'The Havoc of This Nicety.' " *Ryder.* By Djuna Barnes. Elmwood Park: Dalkey Archive, 1979. 243–50.

"What Is Pornography?" *ARTnews* 88.8 (1989): 138+.

White, Deborah Gray. "Female Slaves: Sex Roles and Status in the Antebellum Plantation South." *Unequal Sisters: A Multicultural Reader in U.S. Women's History.* Ed. Ellen Carol DuBois and Vicki L. Ruiz. New York: Routledge, 1990. 22–33.

Wiegman, Robyn. *American Anatomies: Theorizing Race and Gender.* Durham: Duke UP, 1995.

———. "The Anatomy of Lynching." *Journal of the History of Sexuality* 3.3 (1993): 445–67.

———. "Feminism, 'The Boyz,' and Other Matters regarding the Male." *Screening the Male: Exploring Masculinities in Hollywood Cinema.* Ed. Steven Cohan and Ina Rae Hark. New York: Routledge, 1993. 173–93.

Williams, Daniel. "The Gratification of That Corrupt and Lawless Passion: Character Types and Themes in Early New England Rape Narratives." *A Mixed Race: Ethnicity in Early America.* Ed. Frank Shuffleton. New York: Oxford UP, 1993. 194–221.

Williams, Linda. *Hard Core: Power, Pleasure, and the "Frenzy of the Visible."* Berkeley: U of California P, 1989.

Williams, Linda Ruth. "Blood Brothers." *Sight and Sound* 9 (Sept. 1994): 16–19.

Willis, Ellen. "Porn Free: MacKinnon's Neo-conservatism and the Politics of Speech." *Transition* 63 (1994): 4–23.

Wilson, Elizabeth. " 'Not in this House': Incest, Denial, and Doubt in the White Middle Class Family." *Yale Journal of Criticism* 8 (1995): 35–53.

Winter, Kari J. *Subjects of Slavery, Agents of Change: Women and Power in Gothic Novels and Slave Narratives, 1790–1865.* Athens: U of Georgia P, 1992.

Wyatt, Gail Elizabeth. "The Sociocultural Context of African American and White American Women's Rape." *Journal of Social Issues* 48.1 (1992): 77–91.

Yarborough, Richard. "Race, Violence, and Manhood: The Masculine Ideal in Frederick Douglass's 'The Heroic Slave.' " *Frederick Douglass: New Literary and Historical Essays*. Ed. Eric J. Sundquist. New York: Cambridge UP, 1990. 166–88.

Yellin, Jean Fagan. *Women and Sisters: The Anti-Slavery Feminists in American Culture.* New Haven: Yale UP, 1989.

———. "Written by Herself: Harriet Jacobs' Slave Narrative." *American Literature* 53.3 (1981): 479–86.

Young, Elizabeth. "The Beast in the Jungle, the Figure in the Carpet." *Shopping in Space: Essays on America's Blank Generation Fiction.* Ed. Elizabeth Young and Graham Caveney. New York: Atlantic Monthly, 1992. 85–122.

Index

abolitionism, 16, 22, 24, 34, 36, 40, 139, 195nn.35 and 39
abortion, 63, 193n.16
The Accused, 139
Acker, Kathy, 140, 141, 141–42, 170–71, 192n.14, 206n.2
adultery, 22, 24–25, 35, 195n.35, 197n.3
Althusser, Louis, 3, 6
Angelou, Maya, 77, 142, 151, 152, 153–155, 184
anger, 121, 136, 152, 159, 160, 210n.17
Armstrong, Nancy, 5, 192–93n.9
Arnold, Edwin T., 89, 96, 204nn.12 and 18
Arnold, Marybeth Hamilton, 19, 194nn.20 and 21
Atwood, Margaret, 178, 183
Austin, Allan, 207n.12
Autherine, Lucy, 206n.3
autobiography, 27, 144, 151, 158, 193n.9, 207n.12; and Angelou, 153, 155; and Himes, 147, 207n.7. *See also* slave narrative
Awkward, Michael, 16, 203n.53

Baker, Houston, 116
Bal, Mieke, 4, 5, 18–19, 39, 68, 142
Baldwin, James, 103, 142, 207n.7
Barnes, Djuna, 9, 76, 77–86, 117, 141, 164, 170, 173, 170–71, 180
Bataille, Georges, 175, 177, 181
Baym, Nina, 195n.31
Beck, E. M., 198n.7
Beneke, Timothy, 177
Benjamin, Walter, 87–88
Bible, 78, 82, 114, 153, 153–54, 175, 207n.11
blackness, construction of, 33, 53, 77, 103, 158, 179, 185; and Griggs, 57, 59; and Petry, 124, and Wright, 105, 111
Bloch, Ernst, 7, 191n.12
Bly, Robert, 209n.34
body, 8, 15–16, 76, 87–88, 181–82, 193n.16, 204n.9; and Angelou, 153–54; and Barnes, 79, 81, 85, 86, 203n.5; black, 16, 150, 195n.40; black, enslaved, 16, 26, 26–27; and Dickey, 173, 175, 176, 177; and Dixon, 39, 42; and Faulkner, 89, 91, 92, 93, 94, 96, 97, 100, 204n.5; female, 8, 12, 16, 30, 31, 32,

34, 39, 160, 166; female, black, 9, 77, 158, 166; —, enslaved, 15, 16; and Griggs, 57; and Harper, 201n.34; and Hopkins, 199n.12; and Jacobs, 23; and Jong, 167, 170; male, 8, 21, 30, 31, 32, 144, 164–65, 196–97n.2; male, absence of, 18, 25; —, black, 8, 33, 36, 37; and Moody, 72; and Norris, 43, 45, 47; and Petry, *The Street*, 121, 122, 123, 125, 126, 127, 128, 131–32, 136; and Rowson, 18, 26; and Selby, 140; and Sinclair, 61, 62, 64; and Walker 156; and Wharton, 65, 66, 67; and Wright, 107, 107–8, 108–9, 110, 112, 114
Boesenberg, Eva, 155, 156
Bogle, Daniel, 196n.1
Boorman, John, 172
Bordo, Susan, 164–65
Bourdieu, Pierre, 23
Brandt, Stefan, 197n.5, 200n.24
Braxton, Joanne M., 155
Brooks, Peter, 16
Brown, Maurice F., 69
Brown, William Hill, 20
Brown, William Wells, 194n.28, 195n.37
Brownmiller, Susan, 13, 165, 177, 192n.1, 202–3n.51
Bundy, Ted, 210n.6
Butler, Robert, 103
Butler-Evans, Elliott, 143, 150
Butterfield, Stephen, 193n.9

Califia, Pat, 21, 142
capitalism, 59–61, 62, 63–64, 65, 178, 180, 209n.5
captivity, 97, 164; tale of, 17, 38, 68, 102, 161, 192–93n.9
Carby, Hazel, 198n.7, 199n.12, 200n.26
Carver, Raymond, 134, 140, 141, 191n.4
Cash, W. J., 1–2
castration, 30, 36, 37, 158, 160, 206n.32; and Dickey, 173, 176, 177; and Dixon, 49; Gillespie on, 16, 30; and Griggs, 57; and lynching, 44, 57, 106; and Norris, 47; and Petry, 124, 206n.32; and Wright, 109
The Catcher in the Rye, 166
censorship, 11, 179; and Ellis, 180; and feminist criticism, 13; and representations of